Professional LAMP

Professional LAMP

Linux®, Apache, MySQL®, and PHP5 Web Development

Jason Gerner
Elizabeth Naramore
Morgan L. Owens
Matt Warden

Wiley Publishing, Inc.

Professional LAMP: Linux®, Apache, MySQL®, and PHP5 Web Development

Published by
Wiley Publishing, Inc.
10475 Crosspoint Boulevard
Indianapolis, IN 46256
www.wiley.com

ISBN-13: 978-0-7645-9723-7
ISBN-10: 0-7645-9723-X

Printed in the United States of America

Manufactured in the United States of America

10 9 8 7 6 5 4 3 2 1

1MA/RW/RR/QV/IN

Library of Congress Cataloging-in-Publication Data
Professional LAMP : Linux, Apache, MySQL, and PHP Web development / Jason Gerner ... [et al.].
    p. cm.
  ISBN-13: 978-0-7645-9723-7 (paper/website)
  ISBN-10: 0-7645-9723-X (paper/website)
  1. Web site development. 2. Open source software. I. Title: Linux, Apache, MySQL, and PHP Web development. II. Gerner, Jason, 1978–
  TK5105.888.P677 2006
  005.2'762—dc22

                              2005026487

For general information on our other products and services please contact our Customer Care Department within the United States at (800) 762-2974, outside the United States at (317) 572-3993 or fax (317) 572-4002.

About the Authors

Jason Gerner currently spends his days working as a web developer in Cincinnati and burns free time complaining about lack of support for web standards and abusing XML. He can often be found lurking in the PHPBuilder.com discussion forums, where he is a moderator.

Elizabeth Naramore earned her B.S. in Organizational Behavior from Miami University (Ohio) and has been developing websites since 1997. Her main focus has been on PHP/MySQL, e-commerce, and freelance writing and teaching. Her writing can be seen in PHPBuilder.com and International PHP Magazine. She is a proud member of OINK-PUG (Ohio, Indiana, Northern Kentucky PHP Users Group) and she lives in Cincinnati, Ohio with her husband and two small children.

After graduating from the University of Auckland with a mathematics degree no one was interested in, **Morgan L. Owens** knocked around the IT industry, becoming a backend web developer and programmer for web-based applications for both intranet and Internet environments. He still lives in Auckland but suggests that for the right career he might—might—consider moving.

Matt Warden has been developing web-based applications for over six years. His work has primarily focused on designing and implementing LAMP applications for other businesses to use internally to increase productivity. Recently, Matt has been using AJAX to offer a web-based alternative to productivity gains typically only available with native desktop solutions. Currently, Matt is a lead developer at Signal US Communications in Cincinnati, Ohio.

Credits

Executive Editor
Carol Long

Senior Acquisitions Editor
Debra Williams Cauley

Development Editor
Brian MacDonald

Contributors
William Barnett
Wm. Christopher Mastin

Technical Editors
Jason Gerner
Elizabeth Naramore

Production Editor
Kenyon Brown

Copy Editor
Kathryn Duggan

Editorial Manager
Mary Beth Wakefield

Production Manager
Tim Tate

Vice President and Executive Group Publisher
Richard Swadley

Vice President and Executive Publisher
Joseph B. Wikert

Project Coordinator
Kristie Rees

Graphics and Production Specialists
Carrie Foster
Lauren Goddard
Denny Hager
Barbara Moore
Alicia B. South

Quality Control Technicians
Amanda Briggs
John Greenough
Jessica Kramer
Joe Niesen

Media Development Specialists
Angie Denny
Kate Jenkins
Steve Kudirka
Kit Malone
Travis Silvers

Media Development Coordinator
Laura Atkinson

Proofreading and Indexing
TECHBOOKS Production Services

Acknowledgments

Thanks to my lovely wife for putting up with me for the past few years, and being so supportive. I'd also like to thank my co-authors for their great work and the time they spent working on this project. Also, thanks to the folks at Wiley for giving us a chance, and big thanks to Brian for his huge help and having faith in us.—*Jason Gerner*

I'd like to thank my parents, who always made me feel cool, even though I am and always will be a geek. I'd also like to thank my husband and kids for taking care of me when I'm stressed out, and for being my comic relief. Thanks also to Jason and Brian for bringing our book in for a landing.—*Elizabeth Naramore*

I would like to thank Scott and the rest of the crew from HIT Studios not least for introducing me to this "PHP" thingy; my fellow authors for inviting me on this gig even after they saw my writing; Karl Gustafson of the University of Colorado for a piece of advice years ago, though he no doubt has no idea what I'm talking about; and my friends and family who really are a life support system—especially my grandmother Doris Madeline Rachael Shipton (1918–2005).—*Morgan L. Owens*

Special thanks go to Sam Foster, who worked with me via email when we were initially trying to determine best practices with XMLHTTP and XMLHttpRequest object use, during a time when there was very little documentation on the subject. His ideas inspired many aspects of the design of the RemoteConnection object.—*Matt Warden*

Contents

Contents

Contents

Contents

Introduction

So what's all the hubbub surrounding LAMP? What is this "LAMP" and how do I get one? These questions will be answered within the pages of this book. In this case, LAMP stands for Linux, Apache, MySQL, and PHP, and has proven to be one of the fastest growing ways to develop enterprise-level web applications. All these packages are open source, so you are basically free to use them as you wish; the only limit is your own imagination. In addition, with Open Source technologies you not only have the best minds in the industry working together to provide great packages, you also have the immense support of the rest of the open source community if you come across any troubles. After reading this book, you will have an expanded knowledge of LAMP and can put it to work for you as you develop your dynamic websites. Because this is currently the only advanced level LAMP book available, and a part of Wrox's Professional Series, you can be assured that the information contained within its pages will help make you a better coder and a step ahead of the rest.

It should be noted that although the term "LAMP" can also include Perl and Python in its broader definition, we have chosen to focus on PHP in this book.

The goal of this book is to take the beginning to intermediate level web developer one step further, equipping him or her with a more advanced-level knowledge of each of these modules. We give you the tools in this book to allow you to think "out of the box" and find new solutions to old problems.

Whom Is This Book For?

This book is for web developers with some experience who want to take their websites to the next level. If you're interested in using Open Source tools to run a dynamic, exciting web site, you'll find what you need here. We assume that anyone reading this book has some basic experience in the following areas:

- ❏   Web server technology
- ❏   OO coding
- ❏   Database structure, set up, and interaction (retrieving, modifying, and adding data)
- ❏   Setting up users and permissions
- ❏   Installing new software
- ❏   Using the command line

While it is helpful if you have a current LAMP setup that you are familiar with, it is not necessary. As long as you are familiar with installing new software, you can easily install Apache, MySQL, and PHP together. There are also software packages that complete the installation of the three modules for you in one shot, such as XAMPP (available at `http://www.apachefriends.org/en/xampp.html`).

After reading this book, you will be able to conquer any LAMP obstacle with confidence, have some great new ideas for future applications you might wish to write, or rework some of your old code with new efficiency and power.

What's Covered in the Book

A variety of topics are covered in this book:

- ❑   A guide to what's new in PHP 5.0
- ❑   In-depth discussion of OOP in PHP
- ❑   Code efficiency, benchmarking, and improving results
- ❑   Configuring PHP for optimal performance
- ❑   Advanced MySQL queries
- ❑   Apache tips and tricks
- ❑   Site security, locally and remotely
- ❑   Using advanced PHP extensions
- ❑   Common PEAR packages
- ❑   Ajax and PHP
- ❑   Obscure PHP commands
- ❑   CMSs compared and explained
- ❑   Blogging packages
- ❑   A guide for transitioning from other programming languages
- ❑   Caching engines

What You Need to Use This Book

This book is designed to be used with Linux machines, although much of the information in this book can be applied to Windows users as well. You will need PHP, MySQL, and Apache to do the exercises in this book. All three are Open Source programs, so you can download and use them free of charge. You will also need a text editor to enter your code. Finally, you'll need a web browser, such as Internet Explorer, Netscape Navigator, Firefox, Safari, or Opera, to view your web pages.

As any programmer knows, software is constantly being improved and debugged, and while we used the latest and greatest versions of our modules at the time of publishing, chances are those versions won't be around for long. It is important for you to visit the source websites for PHP, Apache, and MySQL to get the most updated versions and recent release notes. When developing websites using applications, we recommend that you always use the most recent stable release. Using software versions that have not been fully tested can be dangerous to your application and leave bugs in your code. The same is true for the new learner—you should be learning on a stable release of the application, not on a beta version.

The most recent stable versions that were in effect at the time of this book's writing were:

❑ **PHP:** Version 5.0.4 (available at `http://www.php.net`)

❑ **Apache:** Version 2.0.54 (available at `http://www.apache.org`)

❑ **MySQL:** Version 4.1.12 (available at `http://www.mysql.com`)

Future editions of this book will address changes and improvements in these programs as they become available.

Conventions

To help you get the most from the text and keep track of what's happening, we've used a number of conventions throughout the book.

> **Boxes like this one hold important, not-to-be forgotten information that is directly relevant to the surrounding text.**

Tips, hints, tricks, and asides to the current discussion are offset and placed in italics like this.

As for styles in the text:

❑ We *highlight* important words when we introduce them.

❑ We present URLs like so: `http://www.mysite.com`

❑ We show code within the text like so: `persistence.properties`

❑ We present code in two different ways:

```
In code examples we highlight new and important code with a gray background.
```

```
The gray highlighting is not used for code that's less important in the present
context, or has been shown before.
```

Source Code

As you work through the examples in this book, you may choose either to type in all the code manually or to use the source code files that accompany the book. All of the source code used in this book is available for download at `http://www.wrox.com`. Once at the site, simply locate the book's title (either by using the Search box or by using one of the title lists) and click the Download Code link on the book's detail page to obtain all the source code for the book.

Because many books have similar titles, you may find it easiest to search by ISBN. This book's ISBN is 0-7645-9723-X.

Once you download the code, just decompress it with your favorite compression tool. Alternately, you can go to the main Wrox code download page at `http://www.wrox.com/dynamic/books/download.aspx` to see the code available for this book and all other Wrox books.

Errata

We make every effort to ensure that there are no errors in the text or in the code. However, no one is perfect, and mistakes do occur. If you find an error in one of our books, like a spelling mistake or faulty piece of code, we would be very grateful for your feedback. By sending in errata you may save another reader hours of frustration and at the same time you will be helping us provide even higher quality information.

To find the errata page for this book, go to http://www.wrox.com and locate the title using the Search box or one of the title lists. Then, on the book details page, click the Book Errata link. On this page you can view all errata that has been submitted for this book and posted by Wrox editors. A complete book list including links to each book's errata is also available at www.wrox.com/misc-pages/booklist.shtml.

If you don't spot "your" error on the Book Errata page, go to www.wrox.com/contact/techsupport .shtml and complete the form there to send us the error you have found. We'll check the information and, if appropriate, post a message to the book's errata page and fix the problem in subsequent editions of the book.

p2p.wrox.com

For author and peer discussion, join the P2P forums at p2p.wrox.com. The forums are a web-based system for you to post messages relating to Wrox books and related technologies and interact with other readers and technology users. The forums offer a subscription feature to email you topics of interest of your choosing when new posts are made to the forums. Wrox authors, editors, other industry experts, and your fellow readers are present on these forums.

At http://p2p.wrox.com you will find a number of different forums that will help you not only as you read this book, but also as you develop your own applications. To join the forums, just follow these steps:

1. Go to p2p.wrox.com and click the Register link.
2. Read the terms of use and click Agree.
3. Complete the required information to join as well as any optional information you wish to provide and click Submit.
4. You will receive an email with information describing how to verify your account and complete the joining process.

   You can read messages in the forums without joining P2P but in order to post your own messages, you must join.

Once you join, you can post new messages and respond to messages other users post. You can read messages at any time on the web. If you would like to have new messages from a particular forum emailed to you, click the Subscribe to This Forum icon by the forum name in the forum listing.

For more information about how to use the Wrox P2P, be sure to read the P2P FAQs for answers to questions about how the forum software works as well as many common questions specific to P2P and Wrox books. To read the FAQs, click the FAQ link on any P2P page.

Professional LAMP

What's New in PHP5?

So what's the big deal about PHP5? If you're experienced with PHP4, you probably know about object-oriented programming and the way this was handled with PHP4. If you're unfamiliar with PHP, but you're familiar with other programming languages, you'll probably find PHP5's implementation of object-oriented principles familiar. Luckily, things have become a lot easier with the release of PHP5. However, there are other improvements and changes, such as more configuration options in php.ini and a host of new array-related and other functions, besides just "better object-oriented programming" handling. This chapter outlines these changes for you.

Object-Oriented Changes

The changes that follow relate to the OOP model and associated features and related topics. The majority of these changes are covered in greater detail in Chapter 2, but are also briefly outlined here for your quick reference.

Passing Objects

One big impact of OOP changes in PHP5 is the way that variables are passed as parameters to functions. In PHP4, by default, variables were passed by value instead of by reference, unless denoted otherwise with the syntax `&$varname`. In PHP5, the default is to assign a value by reference.

Exceptions

In a nutshell, exceptions are the procedures that happen when something goes wrong. Instead of your program completely halting when it reaches an unexpected error, you can now exert a little more control over what the program should do when it reaches said error. You are probably familiar with the `set_error_handler()` function available in PHP4. If you aren't, the purpose of this function is to define a user function for error handling. However, it had many limitations in its implementation. For example, it would not work if the error was type E_ERROR, E_PARSE,

E_CORE_ERROR, E_CORE_WARNING, E_COMPILE_ERROR, E_COMPILE_WARNING, and most of E_STRICT. Also, if the error occurred before the set_error_handler() function script, the function would never be called. With PHP5 comes a new framework for handling exceptions.

Try/Catch/Throw

If you have previous programming experience with languages like C++ or Java, you have undoubtedly heard the terms "try," "catch," and "throw." An exception is "thrown" when an error occurs. Code that could possibly cause an error is put in a try/catch block where it attempts to run (under try), and if an exception is thrown, it is "caught" and a user-defined action should be taken (under catch). The syntax for the try/catch/throw block is as follows:

```php
<?php

try
{
   $error_message = 'Hello, I am an error.';
   throw new Exception($error_message);
}
catch (Exception $e)
{
   echo 'Exception caught: ',  $e->getMessage(), "\n";
}

?>
```

Built-In Exception Class

The class Exception that you just saw is also an improvement for PHP5, and it is built-in by default. With PHP5, you can now obtain information about exceptions that have been thrown and use that data to react appropriately. The built-in exception class, which processes and stores that data, looks like this:

```php
<?php

class Exception
{
    protected $message = 'Exception Thrown';
    protected $code = 0;
    protected $file;
    protected $line;

    function __construct($message = null, $code = 0);

    final function getMessage();
    final function getCode();
    final function getFile();
    final function getLine();
    final function getTrace();
    final function getTraceAsString();

    function __toString();
}

?>
```

Take a closer look at the `Exception` class:

Member or Method Name	What It Represents
`$message`	The exception message; default can be set to whatever you like
`$code`	The user-defined code
`$file`	The filename where the error occurred
`$line`	The line number where the error occurred
`getMessage()`	Returns `$message`
`getCode()`	Returns `$code`
`getFile()`	Returns `$file`
`getLine()`	Returns `$line`
`getTrace()`	Returns an array that contains the information from a `debug_backtrace()` function
`getTraceasString()`	Returns the same result as the `getTrace()` function, but in a formatted string
`toString()`	A PHP5 magic method that allows the object to be formatted to a string when used in conjunction with `print` or `echo`

In the previous `try/catch/throw` example, we used the `getMessage()` function in the built-in exception class to return and display what the error message was.

Extending the Built-In Exception Class

Obviously the built-in exception class is the most generic form of the class, and while it is very useful in a lot of situations, sometimes you may want to be more specific in the ways that your exceptions are handled. For instance, when sending email, you do not receive a PHP error if the recipient's email address is null. Unless you are monitoring your `sendmail` logs, you probably wouldn't know that your email hadn't been sent. This would be helpful information to have, so you can easily extend the built-in class with the `extends` keyword, as follows:

```php
<?php

class emailException extends Exception
{
  function __construct($message)
  {
    echo "There was an error sending your email: <br \>";
    echo $message;
  }
}

function sendEmail($to, $subject, $message)
{
  if ($to == NULL)
```

```
    {
        throw new emailException ("Recipient email address is NULL");
    }

    mail($to, $subject, $message);
}

try
{
  sendEmail("", "Exception Testing",
              "We are testing the exception handling in PHP5");
}
catch (emailException $e)
{
  echo " in file <strong>" . $e->getFile() . "</strong>";
  echo " on line <strong>" . $e->getLine() . "</strong>";
}

?>
```

This results in the following:

```
There was an error sending your email:
Recipient email address is NULL in file /usersites/email_exception.php on line 11
```

You were able to access the filename and line information that was stored in the built-in exception class, but you were also able to add a more detailed error message for debugging purposes.

The set_exception_handler() Function

By default, any exception that isn't caught is going to produce a fatal error and halt execution of your script. PHP5 gives you a chance to clean up any uncaught exceptions with the set_exception_handler() function. The class name, error message, and a backtrace are passed to the set_exception_handler function, but you can also access the built-in exception class information. The function is used as follows:

```
<?php

function lastResort ($e)
{
  echo "Previously uncaught exception being caught from " . get_class($e);
  echo " in file: " . $e->getFile() . " on line " . $e->getLine();
}

set_exception_handler("lastResort");

throw new Exception();

?>
```

Your result will be something like this:

```
Previously uncaught exception being caught from Exception in file:
/usersites/set_exception_handler.php on line 9
```

Note that you must use quotation marks around your function name within the `set_exception_handler()` function; otherwise you will get a notice that you are attempting to use an undefined constant.

Interfaces

Interfaces have been added to PHP5, allowing you to bind classes to more than one place. They consist of empty functions (which will be defined in implementing classes) and any constants you want to apply to the implementing classes. All implementing classes of an interface must provide an implementation of each method defined in the interface, thereby ensuring that future users of your code know what methods to expect.

Interfaces are discussed in greater detail in Chapter 2.

Iterators

Through the Standard Public Library (SPL) you have access to a whole new set of classes and interfaces that allow you to manipulate and utilize iterators. The SPL is an extension that is compiled and available by default in PHP, and it is basically a library of interfaces and classes for you to use. The next section discusses the `Iterator` class itself. You will note that many of the functions are similar to the array functions.

Main Iterator Interface

The `Iterator` class is a built-in interface that allows you to loop through anything that can be looped with a `foreach()` statement—for example, a directory of files, a result from a query, or an array of data. It comes with certain inherent functions:

❑   `Iterator::current()`: Returns the current element.

❑   `Iterator::key()`: Returns the current element's key.

❑   `Iterator::next()`: Moves the pointer to the next element.

❑   `Iterator::valid()`: Verifies if there is an element present after calling next() or `rewind()`.

By pre-defining the generic Iterator functionality, these can all help you use iteration to make your code more powerful and more efficient. The most important thing about the Iterator interface is that it is one of the building blocks for the other Iterator classes.

Other Iterator Classes

The following sections give a brief description of some of the major classes that inherit from the `Iterator` class. More detailed information about any of the following classes, and a more comprehensive list can be found at the online SPL documentation:
`http://www.php.net/~helly/php/ext/spl/main.html`.

DirectoryIterator

As the name suggests, `DirectoryIterator` is an Iterator class that implements `Iterator` and allows you to work with a directory of files. Within this class lies a powerful set of functions that can glean information about each file such as times and dates of modification, file size, file type, owner of the file, full path of the file, and what permissions are associated with the file (just to name a few).

RecursiveIterator

The `RecursiveIterator` class assists with recursive iteration, or the act of functions being automatically called over and over again until a certain criterion is reached. Functions that come with this class help you determine if there are child iterators, and what those children might be.

ArrayIterator

With the `ArrayIterator` built-in class, you can modify array values and keys while iterating over an object. It allows you to manipulate arrays with each iteration. Functions such as `append()`, `copy()`, and `seek()` enable the coder to work with arrays above and beyond the usual set of array functions.

Iterators are continually being improved upon and enhanced, and you can expect to see some big changes with PHP 5.1.

Constructors and Destructors

In PHP4, you could call a method immediately in a class by naming it the same as the class name. In PHP5, there is a new "magic method" name for this purpose, called __construct(). By including this method in your class, it will be called automatically when the object is created.

Likewise, the object will be destroyed when the magic method __destruct() is included in your class. This method destroys the object when called. The __destruct() method will also be called if there are no more references to your object, or if you reach the end of your PHP script.

Chapter 2 includes a more in-depth discussion of constructors and destructors.

Access Modifiers

You can now control the level of visibility of your class members and methods with three keywords new to PHP5: `public`, `private`, and `protected`. Methods and members are denoted as public, private, or protected.

The following is a brief summary of the `private`, `protected`, and `public` keywords (you can read more about these properties in Chapter 2):

❏ `Public`: These members and methods are available to the entire script. They can be referenced from within the object or outside of the object.

❏ `Protected`: Members or methods that are identified as protected are available only from within the object or an inheriting class.

❏ `Private`: Private methods and members are available only from within the object itself and are not available to any inheriting class.

The final Keyword

The `final` keyword can be used with a class or a method within a class. When used with a class, this keyword blocks any other class from inheriting it. When used with a method, it keeps any inheriting class from overriding the method, effectively ensuring their permanency, and protecting them from other programmers or even yourself.

The static Keyword

Declaring a member or method as static binds it to the class under which it resides, and not to any one object or instance of the class. Static members and methods can be accessed throughout the script.

There are some important things to note about the use of the static keyword. First, instead of accessing the variable from within the class with the $this->varName syntax, you should use self::$varName. In the previous example, you accessed the self::$count member from a different function, but because static members are available to anything inside the class, you still used the self:: syntax. Second, when accessing a static member from outside the class, you should use the syntax className::$varName. Likewise when accessing a static method from anywhere inside the class, you should use self::methodName(), and when accessing it from outside the class, you should use className::methodName().

The use of the static keyword is discussed in greater detail in Chapter 2.

The abstract Keyword

The abstract keyword is used when you have a high-level class that you know will need to be inherited by more specific, lower-level classes. For example, you can use the abstract class and method as follows:

```php
<?php

abstract class getToday {
    public $today = getdate();

    abstract function showCalendar();
}

class monthlyCalendar extends getToday {

    function showCalendar() {
    //show this month's calendar
    }
}

class dailyCalendar extends getToday {

    function showCalendar () {
    //show today's daily calendar
    }
}

class yearlyCalendar extends getToday {

    function showCalendar () {
    //show the calendar for this year
    }

}

?>
```

This abstract class basically says "create a calendar, but then you must specify what type in the child class." As you can see, the showCalendar() function is intentionally left blank and abstract in the first class because that class should be extended and the proper calendar shown based on the inherited class that was called. The getToday() class was incomplete, and was a perfect candidate for abstraction. Abstract methods, like those in the interface, are effectively blank and require further implementation in child classes.

Some rules when using the abstract class include:

- ❑ If you have an abstract method, the entire class must be defined as abstract as well.
- ❑ You cannot instantiate an abstract class.
- ❑ You can define a class as being abstract without having any abstract methods contained in it.
- ❑ The inheriting classes that are implementing abstract methods must have the same (or weaker) visibility than their parents.

In Chapter 2, we discuss abstraction in greater detail.

Built-In Method Overloading Functions

Unlike PHP4, where you had to use the overload() function to force an overload check, PHP5 natively allows you to overload any method or member reference that is not what is expected, thus effectively giving you control over what happens next. The new magic methods __get(), __set(), and __call() are used in overloading, as follows:

```php
<?php

class overLoad {

    function __get($property) {
     //check to see if the property exists within the class
     //and if not, do something we want it to
     //such as show an error. Otherwise return
     //a value.

    }

    function __set($property, $value) {
     //check to see if the property exists within the class
     //and if it does, set it to the value being passed
     //otherwise do something we want it to, such
     //as show an error.

    }

    function __call($method, $array_of_arguments) {
     //check to see if method exists within the class
     //and if not, do something such as defer it to
     //another class containing the method or
     //print an error statement.
```

```
        }

    }
    ?>
```

Chapter 2 discusses overloading in greater detail.

New Functions

Here is a comprehensive list of all the new functions in PHP5, with the exception of those requiring extensions:

❑ array_combine(): Combines two arrays into one and uses one array for values, the other for keys.

❑ array_diff_uassoc(): Determines the differences between two or more arrays with additional key comparison, determined by the named function.

❑ array_udiff(): Determines the differences between two or more arrays by using a named function for data comparison.

❑ array_udiff_assoc(): Determines the differences between two or more arrays with additional key comparison and by using a named function for data comparison.

❑ array_udiff_uassoc(): Determines the differences between two or more arrays with additional key comparison using a named function and by using a named function for data comparison.

❑ array_uintersect(): Determines the intersection between two or more arrays by using a named function for data comparison.

❑ array_uintersect_assoc(): Determines the intersection between two or more arrays with additional key comparison and by using a named function for data comparison.

❑ array_uintersect_uassoc(): Determines the intersection between two or more arrays with additional key comparison using a named function and by using a named function for data comparison.

❑ array_walk_recursive(): Applies a named function recursively to each element of an array.

❑ convert_uudecode(): Decodes a uuencoded string.

❑ convert_uuencode(): Uuencodes a string.

❑ curl_copy_handle(): Copies a cURL handle along with all of its preferences.

❑ date_sunrise(): Returns the time of sunrise based on given latitude, longitude, zenith, and GMT offset.

❑ date_sunset(): Returns the time of sunset based on given latitude, longitude, zenith, and GMT offset.

❑ dba_key_split(): Splits an index in a string representation into an array representation.

❑ dbase_get_header_info(): Returns the column structure information for a dBase database.

❑ `dbx_fetch_row()`: Fetches rows from a query-result, but will fail if `DBX_RESULT_UNBUFFERED` is not set in the query.

❑ `fbsql_set_password()`: Changes a named user's password.

❑ `file_put_contents()`: Equivalent to opening a file, writing to a file, and closing the file.

❑ `ftp_alloc()`: Sends the `ALLO` command to an FTP server, which sets aside space for an uploaded file.

❑ `get_declared_interfaces()`: Returns any declared interface in the script.

❑ `get_headers()`: Returns the headers sent by the server in response to a HTTP request.

❑ `headers_list()`: Returns a list of response headers sent (or ready to send).

❑ `http_build_query()`: Builds a URL-encoded query string from the given array.

❑ `ibase_affected_rows()`: Returns the number of rows that were affected by the previous query (Interbase).

❑ `ibase_backup()`: Initiates a backup task in the service manager and returns immediately (Interbase).

❑ `ibase_commit_ret()`: Commits a transaction, and then returns without closing it (Interbase).

❑ `ibase_db_info()`: Returns information about a database (Interbase).

❑ `ibase_drop_db()`: Drops a database (Interbase).

❑ `ibase_errcode()`: Returns an error code (Interbase).

❑ `ibase_free_event_handler()`: Frees a registered event handler (Interbase).

❑ `ibase_gen_id()`: Increments a generator and returns the incremented value (Interbase).

❑ `ibase_maintain_db()`: Executes a maintenance command on the database server (Interbase).

❑ `ibase_name_result()`: Gives a name to a result set (Interbase).

❑ `ibase_num_params()`: Returns the number of parameters in a named query (Interbase).

❑ `ibase_param_info()`: Returns parameter information from a named query (Interbase).

❑ `ibase_restore()`: Initiates a restore task in the service manager and returns immediately (Interbase).

❑ `ibase_rollback_ret()`: Rolls back a transaction without closing it (Interbase).

❑ `ibase_server_info()`: Returns information about a database (Interbase).

❑ `ibase_service_attach()`: Connects to the service manager (Interbase).

❑ `ibase_service_detach()`: Disconnects from the service manager (Interbase).

❑ `ibase_set_event_handler()`: Registers a user-defined function to be called after certain events (Interbase).

❑ `ibase_wait_event()`: Waits for an event to be posted by the database (Interbase).

❑ `iconv_mime_decode()`: Decodes a MIME header field.

❑ `iconv_mime_decode_headers()`: Decodes more than one MIME header field simultaneously.

- ❑ `iconv_mime_encode()`: Creates a MIME header field.
- ❑ `iconv_strlen()`: Returns the character count of a string.
- ❑ `iconv_strpos()`: Finds the position of the first occurrence of a named character within a string.
- ❑ `iconv_strrpos()`: Finds the position of the last occurrence of a named character within the specified range of a string.
- ❑ `iconv_substr()`: Returns a portion of a string.
- ❑ `idate()`: Formats a local time/date as an integer.
- ❑ `imagefilter()`: Applies a named filter to an image.
- ❑ `image_type_to_extension()`: Returns an image file's extension.
- ❑ `imap_getacl()`: Returns the ACL for a given mailbox.
- ❑ `ldap_sasl_bind()`: Binds a resource to the LDAP directory using SASL.
- ❑ `mb_list_encodings()`: Returns an array of all supported encodings.
- ❑ `pcntl_getpriority()`: Returns the priority of a pid.
- ❑ `pcntl_wait()`: Pauses the current process until a child process has exited and returns the child process's id.
- ❑ `pg_version()`: Returns the client, protocol, and server version in an array.
- ❑ `php_strip_whitespace()`: Removes comments, whitespace, and newlines from source code and returns the result.
- ❑ `proc_nice()`: Alters the priority of the current process by a given increment.
- ❑ `pspell_config_data_dir()`: Sets the location of language data files.
- ❑ `pspell_config_dict_dir()`: Sets the location of the main word list.
- ❑ `setrawcookie()`: Equivalent to `setcookie()` without a URL encode of the value.
- ❑ `snmp_read_mib()`: Reads and parses a MIB file into the active MIB tree.
- ❑ `sqlite_fetch_column_types()`: Returns applicable column types from a given table.
- ❑ `str_split()`: Splits a string into an array of characters.
- ❑ `stream_copy_to_stream()`: Copies data between streams and returns the amount of data copied.
- ❑ `stream_get_line()`: Similar to `fgets()` but allows named delimiter.
- ❑ `stream_socket_accept()`: Accepts a connection on a socket created from a previous use of the `stream_socket_server()` function.
- ❑ `stream_socket_client()`: Opens a stream to an Internet or Unix domain destination.
- ❑ `stream_socket_get_name()`: Returns the name of the socket connection.
- ❑ `stream_socket_recvfrom()`: Receives data from a socket up to a specified length.
- ❑ `stream_socket_sendto()`: Sends data to a specified socket, whether it is connected or not.
- ❑ `stream_socket_server()`: Creates a stream on the specified server.

- ❑ strpbrk(): Searches a string for any of a list of given characters, and returns the remainder of the string from the first instance of success.

- ❑ substr_compare(): Compares two strings with named offset and optional case sensitivity.

- ❑ time_nanosleep(): Delays execution of the script for a number of seconds and nanoseconds.

More information about these functions can be found at the source, http://www.php.net.

Other Changes to PHP5

Besides the laundry list of OOP changes and the multitude of new functions available, there are also other improvements that have been made in the release of PHP5.

Configuration Changes

In PHP5 there are numerous changes to the php.ini configuration file. These are discussed in greater detail in Chapter 5, but here is a list for your reference:

- ❑ mail.force_extra_parameters
- ❑ register_long_arrays
- ❑ session.hash_function
- ❑ session.hash_bits_per_character
- ❑ zend.ze1_compatibility_mode

With these new directives, you can exert a little more control over your PHP environment, which gives you a little more freedom in coding.

MySQLi

MySQL, as you well know, fits well with PHP in delivering database-driven dynamic websites. Thus, it is the release of the MySQLi (MySQL improved) extension that makes life easier for everyone.

Configuration Settings

There are several new MySQLi configuration settings available in php.ini. Here's a brief description:

- ❑ mysqli.max_links: Sets the maximum number of MySQL connections per process.
- ❑ mysqli.default_port: Sets the default TCP/IP port to connect to the MySQL server.
- ❑ mysqli.default_socket: Sets the default socket name for connecting to the MySQL server.
- ❑ mysqli.default_host: Sets the default hostname for connecting to the MySQL server.
- ❑ mysqli.default_user: Sets the default username for connecting to the MySQL server.
- ❑ mysqli.default_pw: Sets the default password for connecting to the MySQL server.

Built-in Classes and Properties

With the mysqli extension comes a new set of built-in classes and properties that you can access in your PHP scripts. These new methods can also be used as functions if your script is procedural in nature as opposed to being object-oriented. To call the functions procedurally, simply use the syntax mysqli_ before the method name. For example, to create a new connection using OOP, you would type the following:

```php
<?php

$connect = new mysqli("server", "user", "pass", "dbname");

//call methods through the mysqli class

$connect->close();

?>
```

To accomplish the same thing using traditional procedural programming, you would type the following:

```php
<?php

$connect = mysqli_connect("server", "user", "pass", "dbname");

//call functions using mysqli_ preface

mysqli_close($connect);

?>
```

The following sections describe the type of functions inherent in PHP5.

class mysqli

This class addresses a basic MySQL connection. The constructor of this class creates a new PHP/MySQL connection, and thus a new mysqli object. You would use this class to manipulate or retrieve information about the current connection, or perform basic query functions.

The methods available to this class are:

❑ autocommit: Toggles whether or not transactions are automatically committed to the database.

❑ change_user: Switches to another user.

❑ character_set_name: Returns the default character set.

❑ close: Closes a database connection.

❑ commit: Commits a transaction to the database.

❑ connect: Opens a new connection to MySQL database server (also the mysqli constructor).

❑ debug: Uses the Fred Fish debugging library to debug.

❑ dump_debug_info: Uses the Fred Fish debugging library to dump debugging information.

❑ get_client_info: Retrieves information about the client.

❑ `get_host_info`: Retrieves information about the connection.

❑ `get_server_info`: Retrieves information about the MySQL server.

❑ `get_server_version`: Retrieves the current MySQL server version.

❑ `info`: Returns information about the most recently executed query.

❑ `init`: Initializes an object prior to calling the `real_connect` function.

❑ `kill`: Kills a MySQL thread.

❑ `more_results`: Looks for results from previously called `multi_query`.

❑ `multi_query`: Executes one or more queries.

❑ `next_result`: Returns the next result from previously called `multi_query`.

❑ `options`: Changes or sets connection options for `real_connect` object.

❑ `ping`: Pings a server connection or reconnects if there is no connection.

❑ `prepare`: Prepares a single SQL query statement for execution.

❑ `query`: Executes a query.

❑ `real_connect`: Connects to the MySQL database server and allows for additional options or parameters to be set.

❑ `real_escape_string`: Returns an escaped string for valid use in an SQL statement.

❑ `rollback`: Rolls back the current transaction.

❑ `select_db`: Selects the named database as active.

❑ `set_charset`: Sets the character set to be used.

❑ `ssl_set`: Sets SSL parameters, enabling a secure connection.

❑ `stat`: Returns information about the system status.

❑ `stmt_init`: Initializes a statement for use with `mysqli_stmt_prepare`.

❑ `store_result`: Transfers a resultset from last query.

❑ `thread_safe`: Returns whether thread safety is given or not.

❑ `use_result`: Transfers an unbuffered resultset from last query.

The properties available to this class are as follows:

❑ `affected_rows`: Gets the number of affected rows in a previous MySQL operation.

❑ `client_info`: Returns the MySQL client version as a string.

❑ `client_version`: Returns the MySQL client version as an integer.

❑ `errno`: Returns the error code for the most recent function call.

❑ `error`: Returns the error string for the most recent function call.

❑ `field_count`: Returns the number of columns for the most recent query.

❏   `host_info`: Returns a string representing the type of connection used.

❏   `info`: Retrieves information about the most recently executed query.

❏   `insert_id`: Returns the auto generated id used in the last query.

❏   `protocol_version`: Returns the version of the MySQL protocol used.

❏   `sqlstate`: Returns a string containing the SQLSTATE error code for the last error.

❏   `thread_id`: Returns the thread ID for the current connection.

❏   `warning_count`: Returns the number of warnings generated during execution of the previous SQL statement.

mysqli_stmt

This class addresses a prepared statement, or an SQL statement that is temporarily stored by the MySQL server until it is needed. An example of a prepared statement is `"SELECT * FROM customer WHERE lastname = ?"`. Then, when you are ready to execute the statement, all you need to do is plug in the value for `lastname`. Note that when you are using these methods as functions in procedural programming, you would use a `mysqli_stmt_` preface to the method name (`mysqli_stmt_close`).

The methods available to this class are as follows:

❏   `bind_param`: Binds variables to a prepared statement.

❏   `bind_result`: Binds variables to a prepared statement for result storage.

❏   `close`: Closes a prepared statement.

❏   `data_seek`: Seeks to an arbitrary row in a statement resultset.

❏   `execute`: Executes a prepared statement.

❏   `fetch`: Fetches the result from a prepared statement into bound variables.

❏   `free_result`: Frees stored result memory for the given statement handle.

❏   `prepare`: Prepares a SQL query.

❏   `reset`: Resets a prepared statement.

❏   `result_metadata`: Retrieves a resultset from a prepared statement for metadata information.

❏   `send_long_data`: Sends data in chunks.

❏   `store_result`: Buffers a complete resultset from a prepared statement.

The properties available to this class are as follows:

❏   `affected_rows`: Returns affected rows from last statement execution.

❏   `errno`: Returns an error code for the last statement function.

❏   `errno`: Returns an error message for the last statement function.

❏   `param_count`: Returns the number of parameters for a given prepared statement.

❏   `sqlstate`: Returns a string containing the SQLSTATE error code for the last statement function.

mysqli_result

This class represents the resultset obtained from a query against the database. You use this class to manipulate and display query results.

The methods available to this class are:

- ❑   `close`: Closes the resultset (named `mysqli_free_result` in procedural programming).
- ❑   `data_seek`: Moves internal result pointer.
- ❑   `fetch_field`: Retrieves column information from a resultset.
- ❑   `fetch_fields`: Retrieves information for all columns from a resulset.
- ❑   `fetch_field_direct`: Retrieves column information for specified column.
- ❑   `fetch_array`: Retrieves a result row as an associative array, a numeric array, or both.
- ❑   `fetch_assoc`: Retrieves a result row as an associative array.
- ❑   `fetch_object`: Retrieves a result row as an object.
- ❑   `fetch_row`: Retrieves a result row as an enumerated array.
- ❑   `field_seek`: Moves result pointer to a specified field offset.

The properties available to this class are as follows:

- ❑   `current_field`: Returns the offset of the current field pointer.
- ❑   `field_count`: Returns the number of fields in the resultset.
- ❑   `lengths`: Returns an array of column lengths.
- ❑   `num_rows`: Returns the number of rows in the resultset.

As you can see, the new mysqli class can assist you in writing more efficient code, and give you additional flexibility and control over the MySQL functions available in PHP 4.

XML Support

PHP5 saw an improvement over PHP4's XML libraries. There are several new XML extensions that have been written using libxml2 for improved standardization and maintenance:

- ❑   **DOM:** This new set of functions replaces the DOMXML functions from PHP4. They have been reworked to comply with DOM Level 2 Standards put forth by the W3C.
- ❑   **XSL:** Formerly known as the XSLT extension, this extension assists in transforming one XML file to another, using the W3C's XSL stylesheet as the standard.
- ❑   **SimpleXML:** This set of functions allows you to extract data from an XML file simply and easily. You can then manipulate, display, and compare attributes and elements using the common array `iterator foreach()`.

❑   **SOAP:** The SOAP extension allows you to write SOAP servers and clients, and requires the GNOME XML Library (libxml) to be installed.

Chapter 8 discusses the XML extensions in greater detail.

Tidy Extension

PHP5 now supports the Tidy library, which is available at `http://tidy.sourceforge.net/`. It assists the coder in cleaning up and perfecting HTML code. This extension is available in the PECL library at `http://pecl.php.net/package/tidy`. For a complete list of the Tidy functions and classes available, you can access the PHP manual at `http://us2.php.net/tidy`.

SQLite

Although SQLite was introduced with later versions of PHP4, it has been improved upon for PHP5. SQLite is akin to a mini SQL server. Numerous classes and methods have been built in to PHP5, and it comes bundled with the installation of PHP5. For more information about SQLite, visit the source website: `http://sqlite.org`.

Summary

While the reworking of the OOP model in PHP5 is undoubtedly the biggest and best improvement over PHP4, there are many other areas that have been improved upon to make the PHP coder's life a little easier.

One of the best aspects of PHP is that it is always changing and growing through incremental improvement, as any Open Source language should. The small improvements that make up PHP5 will help you work better with MySQL, help streamline your code, and give you improved access to the strength of XML. The biggest and best improvement, though, is the inclusion of the OOP model. Using OOP instead of procedural programming will literally change the way you think about code. In the next chapter, you'll find out how to get the most out of this new model in PHP.

2

PHP5 OOP

When you begin a new project, one of the first things you have to consider is the structure of your code. Whether you're coding something as simple as an online contact form, or as complex as a full-featured content management system, how you organize your code is going to influence the performance and maintainability of the end product.

When you use a language like PHP, there are two main routes you can go: procedural programming and object-oriented programming—OOP for short. Each strategy has its own benefits and limitations.

Procedural Programming versus OOP

Procedural programming often emphasizes writing code that is as concise as possible and coding directly for the end result. In other words, most procedural programming uses targeted groups of functions that immediately address the problem at hand—usually nothing more, and nothing less. In most situations, this gets you extremely efficient and high-performance applications. One of the downsides to this approach is a lack of maintainability. If the project grows large enough, the developer or developers could end up having to maintain a large number of individual functions, and in some cases, the logic of different functions can become confusingly similar.

Object-oriented programming (OOP), on the other hand, emphasizes abstract relationships and a hierarchy of related functionality. Similar functionality can all share a common core, making maintenance much easier. Code reuse is increased as well, as you can easily adapt the abstracted base functionality for new tasks. OOP also can aid in large-scale program design, helping encapsulate and categorize the different sets of functionality required by each part of the system. Such organization and modularity can come at a price, however. If your object-oriented system is poorly designed, it can actually be harder to maintain than any of the alternatives. Often, the extreme modularity and "code-heaviness" of object-oriented designs can suffer from poor performance.

Once you get past the problems caused by poor object-oriented design, you will find that creating a system using a custom set of PHP objects, or even a full-blown API, can yield benefits that most every developer will appreciate. With that, you can now begin to take a look at how PHP5 implements object-oriented programming.

Basic Class Definitions

The basic unit of code in object-oriented PHP is the *class*. Simply put, a class is a way to encapsulate related functionality and data in one entity. This encapsulation can be used to hide internal operations from external code, and helps simplify the external interaction with the data. A class is a formal description of a grouping of code, a programmatic recipe if you will. A class by itself, like a recipe, is merely a cluster of instructions, and not something that can directly be used — you don't eat the actual recipe, do you? To use classes, you will create an instance of the class, called an *object* — similar to using the recipe to prepare a dish you can actually eat. Classes define the properties and actions of a group of code, and objects are individual instances of that set of commands.

An easy way to understand classes is to relate class code to physical objects. Many times, classes would represent these real-world objects. You might have a class named `Car` that has a property called `occupants`, which might keep track of the number of people in the car. It might even contain a method called `brake()`, which would perform its similarly-named task. Like many real world items, classes have a combination of attributes that describe the individual object, called *properties* in OOP, and a set of actions that they can perform, which are called *methods* in the object-oriented world.

Defining the Class

Defining a class in PHP5 is a relatively straightforward process — very similar to defining a function, albeit with a different keyword:

```
class Circle
{
    // Class code goes here
}
```

This code defines a simple class by using the `class` keyword, followed by the name of the class, and a set of curly braces.

In standard PHP5 classes, there are two main parts to a class definition — properties and methods. Properties represent the data held in the object, while the methods perform actions with that data.

Properties

When creating your classes in PHP5, properties are where you will store the various bits of data the object will represent.

To define a property in PHP5 is as simple as the following:

```
visibility $property_name;
```

In this definition, `visibility` represents the code visibility of the property, which is one of three values: `public`, `private`, or `protected`. The meaning of these three keywords is discussed later in this chapter.

The second part of the property definition, `property_name` is simply the name that you want the property to have.

For example, say you wanted to create a class named `Circle`. You might want to have a public property to hold the radius, like so:

```
class Circle
{
    public $radius;
}
```

Optionally, you can specify an initial value for the property in its definition. Suppose you wanted to have the initial radius of your `Circle` set to 10; you might do the following:

```
class Circle
{
    public $radius = 10;
}
```

Then, each time a `Circle` object is created, it will start out with an initial radius of 10.

Methods

You've created properties to hold your data inside objects, now you need to create a way to act on that data. To perform these actions, you'll create functions inside the class, called *methods*.

Defining a method in PHP5 is very similar to creating a standard function elsewhere in your code:

```
visibility function function_name (parameters)
{
    // method implementation here
}
```

Similar to the property definition, method definitions require a visibility component. Aside from the visibility prefix, methods are defined identically to standard PHP functions — simply use the function keyword, followed by the name of the function, then the optional parameter list inside parentheses.

Using the `Circle` example again, you'll add a method to calculate the area of the circle:

```
class Circle
{
    public $radius;

    public function calcArea($radius)
    {
        return pi() * pow($radius, 2);
    }
}
```

You've simply created a method named `calcArea()` that takes a parameter `$radius`, and returns the area of a circle with the given radius.

Now that you've created these properties and methods, you're going to need a way to actually use your properties and methods. Enter *instantiation*.

Using Classes: Instances

In order to access the properties and use the methods of a class, you first need to instantiate, or create an instance, of the class. When a class is instantiated, it returns an individual *object* of that class type that you can use. In PHP5, object instances are created using the new keyword, like so:

```php
$c = new Circle();
```

Once an object is created, the individual properties and methods are accessed by using an "arrow" operator (a hyphen immediately followed by a greater-than sign), as shown in the following code:

```php
<?php

class Circle
{
  public $radius;

  public function calcArea($radius)
  {
    return pi() * pow($radius, 2);
  }
}

// Create a new instance of Circle
$c = new Circle();

// Change a property
$c->radius = 5;

// Use a method
echo 'The area of the circle is ' . $c->calcArea(5);

?>
```

If you run the code, you will see something similar to:

```
The area of the circle is 78.539816339745
```

Looking at the code, you'll see that you start out by defining the class Circle. Then, you added the code that instantiates the object:

```php
// Create a new instance of Circle
$c = new Circle();
```

Finally, you changed the $radius property to a value of 5, and calculated the area of a circle given a radius of 5:

```php
// Change a property
$c->radius = 5;

// Use a method
echo 'The area of the circle is ' . $c->calcArea($c->radius);
```

Looking carefully at the previous bit of code, you may have noticed something a bit awkward in the way you used the radius property. You've explicitly set the radius property, but then you reuse that property as an explicit value for the parameter of the calcArea method. Since the object knows about the radius property internally, there's no reason it needs to be explicitly provided to the calcArea() method. To remove the requirement to provide a radius parameter and use the object's own internal radius property, you're going to need a method to access it. PHP provides us with a reference named $this to achieve such a goal. Using the specially named variable $this is just like referencing an instantiated object, but $this references the object in which it is contained.

Change the Circle class, as shown here:

```php
<?php

class Circle
{
    public $radius;

    public function calcArea()
    {
        return pi() * pow($this->radius,  2);
    }
}

// Create a new instance of Circle
$c = new Circle();

// Change a property
$c->radius = 5;

// Use a method
echo 'The area of the circle is ' . $c->calcArea();

?>
```

Running the code will produce exactly the same results as the previous example — the only changes occur in the way you use the calcArea() method. Since you are referencing the Circle object's radius property inside the method, you no longer need the parameter in the function definition, and in the method call.

Visibility

One of the new features of the PHP5 OOP model is the ability to specify a level of visibility for all class properties and methods. Using these new visibility keywords, you can hide certain parts of your class from external code, and expose other functionality that you want accessible to all. PHP5 provides three visibility levels to use in classes: public, private, and protected.

A visibility of public means that a property or method is available to all other code that wishes to access it. If no visibility is specified for a method, it defaults to public visibility.

Specifying a class member as private makes the property or method visible only within the class definition to which it belongs. All other methods in the same class can access the private member, but anything outside that specific class cannot.

Finally, the `protected` keyword specifies that the property or method is available only within the defining class, and any other classes that extend or inherit from the defining class. Extending and inheriting classes are discussed later in the chapter.

> *When reusing PHP4 classes under PHP5, it is important to keep in mind that properties defined with the* var *keyword, such as* var $propertyname, *will be treated as public, and an E_STRICT warning is issued.*

Specifying the visibility for a class member is as easy as putting the appropriate prefix in front of the property or method declaration. In the `Circle` class that you defined earlier, all class members were defined as public. Now you're going to change some of the old class members to private, and add some new methods.

```php
<?php

class Circle
{
    private $center = array('x' => 0, 'y' => 0);
    private $radius = 1;

    public function setRadius($radius)
    {
        $this->radius = $radius;
    }
    public function setCenter($x, $y)
    {
        $this->center['x'] = $x;
        $this->center['y'] = $y;
    }
    public function calcArea()
    {
        return pi() * pow($this->radius, 2);
    }
}
```

Instead of leaving the properties as public, you changed them to private and created functions to set their values. In simple situations such as this, it is probably overkill to do so, but if you were to expand the application, the set functions could be used to do complex calculations on data before setting the internal values. Such a separation can also add a layer of protection to the private members by validating the externally provided values before allowing the internal data to change.

You can use your modified class with the following code:

```php
$c = new Circle();
$c->setCenter(0,0);
$c->setRadius(10);

echo "The area of the circle is " . $c->calcArea() . "\n";

// Attempt to access a private property
echo "The private value of radius is " . $c->radius;

?>
```

If you run this code, you would see something like the following:

```
The area of the circle is 314.15926535898
Fatal error: Cannot access private property Circle::$radius in /www/plamp/ch02/02-
002.php on line 31
```

As you can see, it is not much different than your previous use of Circle, but because of the public/private specifications, you must now use methods to access the $center and $radius properties, instead of accessing the properties directly. Notice what happens when you try to directly access a private member at the end—a fatal error occurs.

Constructors and Destructors

In some situations when dealing with classes, you might want to have a way to automatically perform actions when the object is created. You might want to initialize object parameters or automatically call a class method. Perhaps you want the object to check the local environment to see that necessary resources are available or maybe even set up initial connections. For such situations, PHP provides *constructors*.

A constructor is nothing more than a specially named method that is automatically called when an object is instantiated. In PHP5, to implement a constructor, all you need to do is implement a method named __construct. For example:

```php
<?php

class Circle
{
  public function __construct()
  {
    // Perform actions when object is created
    echo "A circle object is being created.\n";
  }
}

$c = new Circle();

?>
```

When you execute this code, you see the following:

```
A circle object is being created.
```

As expected, the code defined inside the constructor method executed automatically when the object was instantiated.

You can still use PHP4-style constructors (methods with the same name as the class) with PHP5, but the new-style __construct method is preferred.

Like standard methods and functions, constructors can also process arguments. To pass arguments to a constructor, you include them inside the parentheses when an object is created, like this:

```php
<?php

class Circle
{
  public $radius;

  public function __construct($r)
  {
    // Perform actions when object is created
    echo "A circle object is being created.\n";

    $this->radius = $r;
  }
}

$c = new Circle(10);

?>
```

In this example, you've simply provided a radius parameter when creating the object — 10 in this case — which is automatically interpreted by the constructor, which in turn sets the radius of the circle when instantiated.

Now that you have a way to perform actions when an object is created, you'll look at a way to perform additional actions when an object is destroyed. PHP5 now includes a special method that is called when an object is destroyed, referred to as, logically enough, a destructor. An object's destructor is called when all references to an object are removed, or it is manually destroyed in your code. Destructors are often used for various clean-up tasks, such as closing database connections and releasing file handles. To create a destructor, add a method to your class, and call it __destruct:

```php
<?php

class Circle
{
  public function __construct()
  {
    // Perform actions when object is created
    echo "A circle object is being created.\n";
  }

  public function __destruct()
  {
    // Perform actions when object is destroyed
    echo "A circle object is being destroyed.\n";
  }
}

$c = new Circle();

// Destroy the circle object
unset($c);

?>
```

Running this code gives you:

```
A circle object is being created.
A circle object is being destroyed.
```

Notice how you see the message placed inside the destructor, without having to do anything. This is because PHP automatically cleans up all references to objects when a script finishes executing, which automatically calls the destructors for objects.

One last thing to keep in mind is that unlike constructors, which can have parameters, destructors can have no parameters.

Static Keyword

Sometimes when using object-oriented programming, you might need to access a method of a class, but without the need to create a full-blown object. To fill that need, PHP5 has provided the `static` keyword. New to PHP5, the `static` keyword allows class properties and methods to be available without instantiating the class. To make a class member static, just add the `static` keyword between the visibility and property or method definition, like so:

```php
<?php

class Circle
{
  public static function calcArea($r)
  {
    return pi() * pow($r, 2);
  }
}
```

To use the newly created static property, you simply use the class name, followed by two colons, then the property name or method call:

```php
$r = 5;
echo "Given a radius of " . $r .
    ", a circle has the area " . Circle::calcArea($r);

?>
```

Running this code in your browser would produce results similar to the following:

```
Given a radius of 5, a circle has the area 78.539816339745
```

There are, however, some limitations to using static methods. Static methods cannot change or access object variables or methods using `$this->`; they can directly access only other static properties and methods in the class.

In order to access other static variables within the same class, you can use the `self` keyword, in conjunction with a double-colon. Using `self::` is similar to `$this->`, but it is for static members only. If you wanted to modify the `Circle` class to use static methods and properties, you might do something similar to the following:

```php
<?php

class Circle
{
  private static $radius;

  public static function setRadius($r)
  {
    self::$radius = $r;
  }

  public static function getRadius()
  {
    return self::$radius;
  }
}

Circle::setRadius(5);
echo "Our statically accessed circle has a radius of " .
    Circle::getRadius() . ".\n";

?>
```

A quick run through the PHP5 engine would produce the following:

```
Our statically accessed circle has a radius of 5.
```

Class Constants

Along with the improved object model in PHP5, the notion of class constants was introduced to PHP. Class constants are similar to regular PHP constants, but are available only within the definition of a class. Like standard PHP constants, their value can be set only once to a scalar value—a simple number or string—and any attempts to set a constant to the result of a function will result in an error.

When using class constants, keep in mind that they behave like static members in the way they are accessed—to access a class constant, you must use the double-colon (::) syntax. To define a class constant, use the const keyword before the constant name, as shown in the following code:

```php
<?php

class Circle
{
  const pi = 3.14159265359;

  public function getPi()
  {
    return self::pi;
  }
}

echo "The value of Pi in our Circle class is " . Circle::pi . "\n";

$c = new Circle();
```

```
echo "To recap, the value of Pi in our Circle class is " . $c->getPi()

?>
```

Running this code would produce the following:

```
The value of Pi in our Circle class is 3.14159265359
To recap, the value of Pi in our Circle class is 3.14159265359
```

In this example, you created the class constant `pi`, which holds the value of, shockingly enough, the mathematical constant Pi. You then used a `self::` reference in the `getPi` method to return the value of the class constant. It is important to notice the lack of a dollar sign in front of the name `pi` when you access `self::pi`. Class constants do not use the dollar sign prefix, where a standard class variable would.

You are creating a Pi constant simply as an example. PHP already has a built-in `pi()` *function that returns the value of Pi.*

Assignment versus Cloning

As you may already know by now, in standard PHP, there are two ways to assign data to a variable: assignment by value, and assignment by reference. The first, assignment by value, is most commonly used when setting simple values for variables, or copying other variables:

```
$a = 5;
$b = $a;
```

Here you are using assignment by value. When the value of $a is changed, $b remains unchanged; when you assigned $b = $a, you simply created a copy of the value of $a, and assigned that value to $b.

Assignment by reference is a bit different, however. Take the following example:

```
$a = 5;
$b =& $a;
```

In this example, you are assigning by reference, using the `=&` operator. When the value of $a is changed in this situation, $b would change as well — since $b was assigned, by reference, the value of $a, both variables point to the same location in memory, and when that value in memory is changed, both variables change as well.

In PHP5, all objects are assigned by reference, by default. This behavior is unlike PHP4, which assigned by value, unless the reference operator (`=&`) was used. In PHP5, if you want to make a copy of an object, instead of using a reference, you must use the `clone` statement, as follows:

```php
<?php

class Circle
{
    public $radius = 10;
}

// Create the original object and set its parameters
```

```
$original = new Circle();

// Create a cloned and assigned (by reference) object
$cloned = clone $original;
$assigned = $original;

// Now, change the original radius value:
$original->radius = 5;

// Show the state of all three objects
echo "\nOriginal:\n";
print_r($original);

echo "\nAssigned:\n";
print_r($assigned);

echo "\nCloned:\n";
print_r($cloned);

?>
```

This code will produce the following output:

```
Original:
Circle Object
(
    [radius] => 5
)

Assigned:
Circle Object
(
    [radius] => 5
)

Cloned:
Circle Object
(
    [radius] => 10
)
```

As you can see, $assigned references the $original object, but because you cloned $cloned, therefore making a detached copy of $original, its value doesn't change when you modify $original.

Inheritance and Interfaces

One of the benefits to using OOP with PHP5 is that it allows you to break down your code into logical chunks, in order to facilitate reuse. These chunks, when carefully written, can be reused again and again, in many different projects, leaving the programmer free to write code that is specific to the problem he or she is trying to solve.

In OOP, there are a couple of ways in which a group of methods and properties can be specified for use in multiple classes. The first, *inheritance*, allows you to define a base set of properties and methods that belong to a base class, and can be used as a building block for more specific classes. The second, *interfaces*, allow you prescribe a list of methods that a class must implement.

Inheritance

Suppose you are creating a code library, one for manipulation of different geometric shapes. The `Circle` class that you've been using throughout the chapter could be part of that very library. In creating different classes for different shapes—square, circle, triangle, and so on—you may find that you're duplicating methods that are similar or identical among all shapes. This would be a good opportunity to use inheritance.

The extends Keyword

Assume that all of the geometric shape classes are going to be drawn on a grid. Therefore, they will all need some sort of origin point (x,y). You could include an origin property in each of the different classes, or using the `extends` keyword, you could use inheritance to define the property in one shared location. To do this, you'll create a class named `Shape`, which will serve as a parent of all geometric classes that you might create. Each specific geometric shape class—be it a Circle, Square, Ellipse, or Star—all have a base set of functionality that `Shape` provides. An easy way to think of this parent-child relationship, is with the phrase "is a." In this example, `Circle` *is a* `Shape`, just like a `Square` *is a* `Shape`, and a `Triangle` *is a* `Shape`.

To use your parent class `Shape`, you could do something similar to the following:

```php
<?php

class Shape
{
    public $origin = array('x'=>0, 'y'=>0);
}

class Circle extends Shape
{
    public $radius;
}


$c = new Circle();
print_r($c->origin);

?>
```

Running this code would produce the following:

```
Array
(
    [x] => 0
    [y] => 0
)
```

As you can see, you created a base class named Shape that defines a generic origin property. By using the extends keyword in the class definition for Circle, all properties and methods of Shape become part of the Circle object. Because Circle is a subclass of Shape, you can get the value of $origin, which is not defined explicitly in Circle — it's inherited from Shape.

When extending base classes, it is possible to redefine the properties and methods that exist in the parent (base) class. For example:

```php
<?php

class Shape
{
    public $origin = array('x'=>0, 'y'=>0);
}

class Circle extends Shape
{
    public $origin = 'New origin';
}


$c = new Circle();
print_r($c);

?>
```

This code would output the following:

```
Circle Object
(
    [origin] => New origin
)
```

By redefining the base property $origin in the subclass, the new definition hides the parent's values. Methods would behave the same way — redefining them in the subclass overrides the functionality of the parent method or methods. Take for example, the following code:

```php
<?php

class Shape
{
    public $origin = array('x'=>0, 'y'=>0);
    public function getOrigin()
    {
        return $this->origin;
    }
}

class Circle extends Shape
{
    public function getOrigin()
    {
```

```
        return array('x'=>1, 'y'=>1);
    }
}


$c = new Circle();
print_r($c->getOrigin());

?>
```

In this example, the getOrigin() method defined in the Shape parent class is redefined in the Circle subclass. When calling getOrigin() on the instantiated Circle object, it returns 1,1 as the origin, and does not call the getOrigin() method in the base class Shape. A redefined method masks any same-named method in the parent class or classes.

The final Keyword

In some situations, you want to prohibit a subclass from redefining a member that exists in a base class. You can prevent properties and methods from being redefined by using the final keyword:

```
<?php

class Shape
{
    final public $origin = array('x'=>0, 'y'=>0);
}

class Circle extends Shape
{
    public $origin = 'This is invalid.';
}

$c = new Circle();

?>
```

If you attempt to run this code, a fatal error will occur:

```
Fatal error: Cannot declare property Shape::$origin final, the final modifier is
allowed only for methods in /www/plamp/ch02/02-008.php on line 5
```

Since you used the final keyword in the base class's definition for $origin, when you tried to redefine it in the Circle subclass, it resulted in a fatal error.

Note that in the case of properties, the final keyword does not prohibit the changing of their values — only their redefinition.

Using parent:: References

In some situations you may want to reference the original property or method from the base class, after you've redefined it in a subclass. To achieve this, you can use the parent keyword in conjunction with the :: (double colon) you saw in the previous section on static members. For example:

```php
<?php

class Shape
{
   public function draw()
   {
      echo "Shape::draw() has been called.\n";
   }
}

class Circle extends Shape
{
   public function draw()
   {
      echo "Circle::draw() has been called.\n";
      parent::draw();
   }
}


$c = new Circle();
$c->draw();

?>
```

This would show the following when run:

```
Circle::draw() has been called.
Shape::draw() has been called.
```

In this example, you've defined a subclass `Circle` that extends from the base class, `Shape`. Since you created a new `draw()` method in the subclass, you use `parent::draw()` to call the same-named function in the parent class. Calling a parent method in this way is a common practice when overriding a base method in a subclass, and is quite frequently used in constructors to call the parent constructor — the base class's constructor is not automatically called otherwise.

Abstract Classes

You may find during programming or design that you have classes like `Shape` that need to be created to give subclasses identical properties or methods, but never need to be instantiated on their own. The `Shape` class you used earlier would be a perfect candidate for becoming an abstract class — you'll never want to create a `Shape` object directly, but it's necessary for provided functionality to more concrete subclasses of geometric objects. For this type of scenario, there is the `abstract` keyword.

When a class is defined as `abstract`, other classes can extend it, but it cannot itself be instantiated. For example:

```php
<?php

abstract class Shape
{
   public $origin = array('x'=>0, 'y'=>0);
```

```
}

class Circle extends Shape
{
    // Circle implementation
}


$c = new Circle();
print_r($c->origin);

$s = new Shape();
print_r($s->origin);

?>
```

Run this code and you should see something similar to the following:

```
Array
(
    [x] => 0
    [y] => 0
)

Fatal error: Cannot instantiate abstract class Shape in /www/plamp/ch02/02-010.php
on line 17
```

As you can see by running this example, the `Circle` class inherited from `Shape` as expected, but when you tried to instantiate `Shape` by itself, a fatal error occurred.

Now that you've had a quick look at inheritance in PHP, take a look at another way to prescribe object behavior: interfaces.

Interfaces

Another new object-oriented feature in PHP5 is the ability to create and use *interfaces*. Interfaces, in a nutshell, are a way to specify what methods a class must explicitly implement. This is useful when dealing with many interconnected objects that rely on the specific methods of one another.

By using interfaces, you can specify a specific set of methods for different interchangeable classes to share. That way, if you ever need to replace functionality contained within a class in your program, all you have to do is make sure the replacement class implements the same interface, or group of functions, that the original exposed.

For example, you might have a business class that contains the method `calculateInterest()`. At some point you might want to have multiple ways to calculate the interest, so you create different classes for each algorithm you wish to use. Assuming all the classes implement a consistent interface — one that defines `calculateInterest()` — each of the classes should now be interchangeable in the program.

In PHP5, an interface is defined using the `interface` keyword, and implemented using the `implements` keyword, like the following:

```
interface TwoDimensionalOperations
{
  public calculateArea();
}

class Circle implements TwoDimensionalOperations
{
  public calculateArea();
  {
    // Implementation of calculateArea, specific to this Circle class
  }
}
```

By creating the interface `TwoDimensionalOperations`, you can then create classes for different shapes — Circle, Square, Triangle, Pentagon, etc. — all implementing the interface. This way, you can be assured that by implementing `TwoDimensionalOperations`, all of your shape classes will have a `calculateArea` method.

When using interfaces, it is important to keep a couple of things in mind. First, if a class implements an interface but does not define the methods from that interface, a fatal error will occur. Second, all methods defined in an interface must have public visibility.

With PHP5, a class can both extend a base class and implement an interface at the same time:

```
class Circle extends Shape implements TwoDimensionalOperations
{
  // Circle implementation
}
```

In another neat trick, an interface can use the `extends` keyword to inherit from other interfaces:

```
interface GeometricOperations
{
  public getOrigin();
}

interface TwoDimensionalOperations extends GeometricOperations
{
  public calculateArea();
}

class Circle extends Shape implements TwoDimensionalOperations
{
  // Implement the required methods
  public getOrigin()
  {
    // Circle->getOrigin() implementation
  }
  public calculateArea()
```

```
    {
       // Circle->calculateArea() implementation
    }
 }
```

In this small example, you could have easily created a method inside the base Shape class and simply extended it to the subclass Circle. Such an approach, while possible, is limiting, due to the fact that classes in PHP can extend only one base class.

PHP5 classes can, however, implement multiple interfaces, separated by commas:

```
interface GeometricOperations
{
  public getOrigin();
}

interface TwoDimensionalOperations
{
  public calculateArea();
}

class Circle implements TwoDimensionalOperations, GeometricOperations
{
  // Implement the required methods
  public getOrigin()
  {
    // Circle->getOrigin() implementation
  }
  public calculateArea()
  {
    // Circle->calculateArea() implementation
  }
}
```

Using both inheritance and multiple interfaces, in conjunction with inherited interfaces, you can build some seriously complex and powerful applications using simple building blocks.

Magic Methods

To help make things easier when using object-oriented programming, PHP5 has provided a handful of so-called "magic methods." These magic methods are specially named methods for all classes, which are called automatically in certain scenarios.

You've already seen two magic methods in this chapter so far, __construct and __destruct. They are called when an object is instantiated or destroyed, correspondingly. PHP5 includes a handful of magic methods that you can implement to provide special functionality for your classes. The three magic methods— __call, __get, and __set—all allow you to access methods and properties of an object that haven't been explicitly defined. A sixth, __toString(), defines what happens when an object is directly used as a string.

__call

The magic method __call allows you to provide actions or return values when undefined methods are called on an object. The __call magic method can be used to simulate method overloading, or even to provide smooth error handling when an undefined method is called on an object. __call takes two arguments: the name of the method and an array of the arguments passed to the undefined method. For example:

```php
<?php

class Circle
{
  public function __call($m, $a)
  {
    echo "The method " . $m . " was called.\n" .
        "The arguments were as follows:\n";
    print_r($a);
  }
}


$c = new Circle();
$c->undefinedmethod(1, 'a', 2, 'b');

?>
```

When you run this code, you would see something similar to the following:

```
The method undefinedmethod was called.
The arguments were as follows:
Array
(
    [0] => 1
    [1] => a
    [2] => 2
    [3] => b
)
```

Here you've defined a __call function to handle the call to the undefinedmethod method. As expected, it took the comma-delimited list of arguments and turned them into an array, which were captured in the $a parameter.

__get and __set

The magic methods __get and __set allow you to specify custom functions to store and retrieve data in properties that aren't already defined in the class.

__get takes one argument, the name of the property, while __set requires two: the name of the property and the new value.

```php
<?php

class Circle
{
  public function __get($p)
  {
    return $this->$p;
  }

  public function __set($p, $v)
  {
    $this->$p = $v;
  }
}



$c = new Circle();
$c->nonexistent = 5;
echo "The value of our nonexistent property: " . $c->nonexistent;

?>
```

When you execute the preceding code, PHP recognizes immediately that no property named "nonexistent" exists in the class. Since the named property doesn't exists, the __set() method is called, which then assigns the value to the newly-created property of the class, allowing you to see the following:

```
The value of our nonexistent property: 5
```

In this example, you created the magic methods __get and __set to handle any undefined property accesses, and proceeded to use an undefined property named nonexistent.

__sleep

When you use PHP classes to store data that must persist across pages or long periods of time, you can store the object using your favorite method of persistence (files, database, session variables, or cookies), but the objects must first be prepared.

When you're readying object data to be stored, use the serialize() function. The serialize() function takes any complex data structure and converts it into a string that can be stored using your method of choice. Conversely, to retrieve your persisted data, use the unserialize() function. The unserialize() function takes your serialized string and converts it back to whatever complex structure it used to be.

To give the developer more flexibility when dealing with the serialization of objects, the __sleep and __wakeup magic methods are provided.

The __sleep magic method, if defined in the class, is automatically called immediately before the object is serialized. This method is extremely useful for closing database connections and cleaning up object resources.

The __sleep method can also return an array containing the names or object values to be serialized, which is useful when dealing with large objects. Only the necessary data will be serialized while other data can be ignored.

__wakeup

The __wakeup magic method does the exact opposite of the __sleep method. When unserialize() is called, __wakeup is automatically called, which is helpful for resetting object values, restoring connections, and other initialization tasks.

Look at this simple example of __sleep and __wakeup in action. This example is going to require two files. The first file, you'll create as page1.php:

```php
<?php
session_start();

class Circle
{
  public $radius;

  public $origin = array('x'=>0, 'y'=>0);

  public function __sleep()
  {
    echo 'zzzzz';

    return array('radius','origin');
  }

  public function __wakeup()
  {
    echo 'good morning!';
  }
}

$c = new Circle();
$c->radius = 5;
$c->origin['x'] = 3;
$c->origin['y'] = 4;

echo 'Preparing to sleep.....';

$_SESSION['c'] = serialize($c);

echo '<br /><a href="page2.php">Wake the object</a>';

?>
```

The second file you'll name page2.php:

```php
<?php
session_start();

class Circle
{
  public $radius;

  public $origin = array('x'=>0, 'y'=>0);
```

```
  public function __sleep()
  {
    echo 'zzzzz';

    return array('radius','origin');
  }

  public function __wakeup()
  {
    echo 'good morning!';
  }
}

echo 'Rise and shine.....';

$c = unserialize($_SESSION['c']);

echo '<br />The contents of our Circle object are:<br />';
echo 'Radius: ' . $c->radius . '<br />';
echo 'Origin: (' . $c->origin['x'] . ',' . $c->origin['y'] . ')';

?>
```

Load the first page, page1.php, into your browser, and you should see something similar to Figure 2.1.

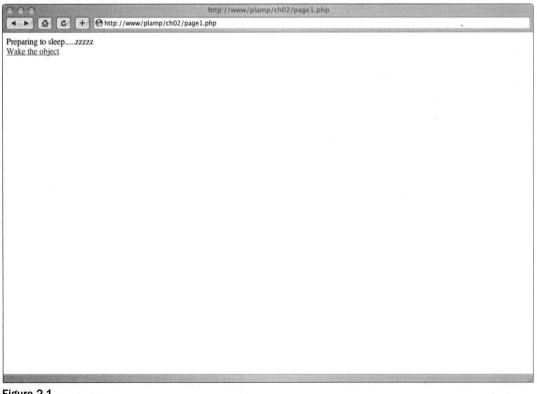

Figure 2.1

Click the link, and you will be directed to page2.php, where you should see something like Figure 2.2.

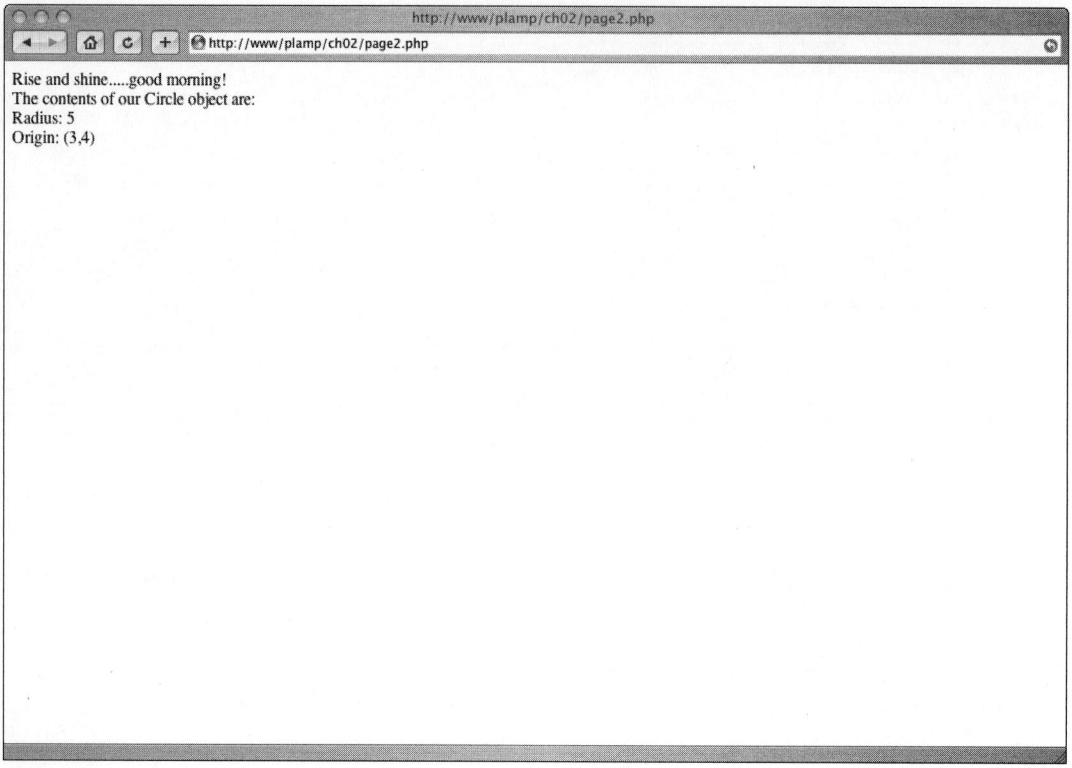

Figure 2.2

In the first file, page1.php, you start your session so you can store the object in a session variable; then you proceed to create the class definition for circle:

```php
<?php
session_start();

class Circle
{
  public $radius;

  public $origin = array('x'=>0, 'y'=>0);

  public function __sleep()
  {
    echo 'zzzzz';

    return array('radius','origin');
  }

  public function __wakeup()
```

```
    {
      echo 'good morning!';
    }
  }
```

Note that you create the functions for both __sleep and __wakeup here. Creating the __wakeup method is not necessary in this case, but if you were to move the class definition to an include file later on, all you'd have to do is cut and paste. Also notice that you return an array of strings in __sleep. These strings match up with property names inside Circle, and tell the serialization functions what parts of the object you want to serialize, and to ignore all others.

You then proceed to instantiate the circle object, change some of its values, serialize it to a session variable, and finally provide a link to go to page2.php:

```
$c = new Circle();
$c->radius = 5;
$c->origin['x'] = 3;
$c->origin['y'] = 4;

echo 'Preparing to sleep.....';

$_SESSION['c'] = serialize($c);

echo '<br /><a href="page2.php">Wake the object</a>';

?>
```

Looking at page2.php, you once again start out with a call to start the session, and an identical class definition as the previous page. When unserializing an object, the class definition for that object *must* be present before the unserialize() function is called, either typed in the file itself, or included via the include or require statements.

Getting into the meat of page2.php, you unserialize the data from the session variable you set in the previous page, and echo some of the newly recreated object's properties to the screen:

```
echo 'Rise and shine.....';

$c = unserialize($_SESSION['c']);

echo '<br />The contents of our Circle object are:<br />';
echo 'Radius: ' . $c->radius . '<br />';
echo 'Origin: (' . $c->origin['x'] . ',' . $c->origin['y'] . ')';

?>
```

__toString

The final magic method that can be built into classes is __toString. As you might guess, __toString returns a custom string value that is automatically used when the object is converted to a string. Take the following example:

```php
<?php

class Circle
{
  public function __toString()
  {
    return "Automatic string value for Circle";
  }
}

$c = new Circle();
echo "The value of \$c is: ";
echo $c;

?>
```

This code would produce the following when executed:

```
The value of $c is: Automatic string value for Circle
```

In this example, you added the __toString() magic method, and used it to provide a value when the object was echoed to the screen. Note that you didn't simply concatenate the object on to the end of the string in the previous echo statement, or include it inside the double-quoted string.

What exactly would happen if you simply included the object with another string in a single echo statement? Look at the following code (the changes are highlighted):

```php
<?php

class Circle
{
  public function __toString()
  {
    return "Automatic string value for Circle";
  }
}

$c = new Circle();
echo "The value of \$c is: " . $c;

?>
```

When you run this code, you see the following:

```
The value of $c is: Object id #1
```

That's definitely not what you expected! Instead of returning the value from the __toString() method, it instead returned an object id for $c — exactly the same as you would see had you not defined toString(). The __toString() magic method is only called when used directly with echo or print — if any other strings or casts are present, the object id will be returned instead.

Summary

As you can see, PHP5 brings to the table a much-improved object model to use in your projects. Whether you decide to stick with procedural programming, dabbling seldom with OOP, head down the full-on OOP route, or find a path somewhere in between, hopefully with some of the things you've seen in this chapter, you can go on and start to build your own systems using PHP5's new OOP.

From here, you're going to move away from OOP, and into some of the darker corners of the PHP language. You probably already know how powerful arrays are in PHP, but you may not know just how many functions PHP has to let you harness that power. Once you have that down, we'll introduce you to the concept of streams, which will let you work with both network resources and local files using a common set of functions.

3

More Obscure PHP

One of the more prominent features of PHP is its vast collection of built-in functions, even before you start adding in optional extensions. This is arguably a failing because it makes the job of deciding which function to use in a given situation that much more difficult. Many of the functions are so similar in behavior that it's sometimes hard to see why they exist as distinct functions. `split()` or `preg_split()`? `str_replace()` or `strtr()`? `ksort()`, `asort()`, `rsort()`, `natsort()`, `usort()` or `uksort()`? `strftime()` or `date()`? This book doesn't go into the lack of conventions regarding the naming of functions or the order of arguments, or the way in which several functions are merely aliases of others.

One cause of PHP's overlapping set of functions is its early existence as a mere wrapper over Perl's and later C's own libraries. Users familiar with those languages' function libraries would find their PHP equivalents going by the same names with the same calling conventions, overlaid with PHP's memory management and type handling. Extensions exacerbated this — with different DBMSs exposing different APIs, PHP introduced different sets of functions for each DBMS it supported. When two extensions boasted functions for two similar things, PHP provided both.

As PHP became implemented more expansively on a wider variety of platforms and built into a wider variety of environments, platform-independent implementations of functions began to be introduced. Hence the existence of both `rand()` (which uses whatever pseudorandom number generator was supplied by the C compiler PHP was built on) and `mt_rand()` (which has identical behavior across all platforms). At the same time, PHP developers have been committed to backward-compatibility; even as new mechanisms are introduced, they do their best to retain the old ones in case there are people relying on them.

So PHP's function list burgeoned, bulging out like a loaf of bread rising in a tin that's too small for it. At last count, the PHP manual had 3,630 function entries, distributed among 129 chapters, of which 855 are listed in the 30 chapters that the manual describes as "core" or are bundled and require an explicit configuration switch to disable. Those figures are already out of date.

The practical upshot of this is that many PHP programmers are like English speakers — they use only a small subset of the language. There are parts of the language they may just not have any use for. But hidden among PHP's esoterica are some functions that don't get the attention they deserve. These are functions that have been present in PHP since version 4.3.2 at the latest—many have been around since the early days of PHP 4. Despite this, they are often overlooked, even when they are ideal for the task at hand. Some of them seem to be used only in tutorials about them. They are by no means the only obscure features of the language. Rather, they represent some of the more powerful core functionality of the PHP environment and are areas which are the site of active development in recent versions.

This chapter seeks to redress some of this injustice.

Array Functions and Callbacks

Array functions allow you to access and manipulate the contents of arrays without having to extract them first. Most, if not all, of the operations you may wish to carry out on "every element of an array" can be carried out using these functions, without requiring the additional infrastructure of a `for` or `foreach` loop. Also, many array manipulation tasks require the entire array to be taken into consideration. Sorting is the obvious example here: you can't move the smallest element to the start of the array without looking at all of the array's elements in order to locate the smallest element. Anyone who has tried to write a reasonably efficient sorting algorithm will know that the task is not trivial.

Because there is no way PHP's developers could predict everything you want to do with your array, most of the array functions, as well as the array or arrays in question, take an additional argument known as a callback, which names another function that, depending on what the array function does, would be used to manipulate array elements, or compare them to each other or against some criterion you specify. In this way, PHP needs to provide only implementations of the more abstract aspects of array manipulation, such as mapping and traversing, leaving you free to provide the concrete details of your choice.

Callbacks can be so useful for abstracting functionality, in fact, that a selection of functions are provided to allow their use in almost any situation. It's entirely conceivable (if quixotic) to implement your very own architecture for OOP, with an object's "methods" represented as an array of callbacks.

Using Callbacks

Consider the following script:

```
$input_file = file('generic.txt');
foreach($input_file as $k=>$line)
{
    $input_file[$k] = rtrim($line);
}
```

You're loading in a text file as an array of single lines. PHP doesn't throw away the linebreak characters at the end, so now that they have served their purpose, you want to drop them yourself. Writing an entire loop and using two extra variables within it seems long-winded. For a start, you have to keep in mind that `$line` is copied, so `$line=rtrim($line);` won't work, meaning that you have to refer back to the original by array and key. Either that, or remember to declare `$line` by reference by writing `foreach($input_file as &$line)`. Mistakes in either will mean that the final array won't have its lines trimmed.

Now consider this:

```
$input_file = array_map('rtrim', file('generic.txt'));
```

This line of code achieves the same effect. `file()` returns an array containing the lines of `generic.txt`; `array_map()` applies the function `rtrim()` to each element of that array, and returns the resulting "trimmed" array.

There are several functions that abstract the most common reasons for iterating over an array, reducing the need for writing loops and other flow-control statements. While writing one-liners solely for the sake of it can lead to hard-to-read code, cutting down the number of "moving parts" in a program can help reduce the incidence of error.

When you have an array in which you have a task to perform on each element in turn, `array_map()` and `array_walk()` deserve consideration. There are other functions that employ so-called callback functions in a similar fashion to save you having to call a function on every element of an array yourself.

Callbacks take one of two forms. The first, and most common, is that it is simply a string containing the name of a function. In the previous line of code, it is the `'rtrim'`.

> *It does have to be a function, which is why the PHP manual makes the point of stating that* echo, *empty,* include, array, *and so on are not functions. Passing* 'include' *as your callback will fail. The reason these are excluded is because they are given special attention during parsing and have their own internal structures.*

The second kind of callback is used to specify class and object methods. Both are represented by two-element arrays, where the second element is the name of the method, stored as a string. If the first element is an object, then the callback refers to that object's method: `array($object, 'method')` refers to `$object->method()`. If on the other hand the first element is a string or string variable, then the callback refers to a static method of the named class: `array('thing_factory', 'create_new')` refers to the static `thing_factory::create_new()` method.

```php
// Using an object's method as a callback in array_map().
// Each element of $untidy_array is passed in turn to $parser->tidy(),
// and the returned values are stored in $tidied_array
$tidied_array = array_map(array($parser, 'tidy'), $untidy_array);

// Using a static class method as a callback in array_map().
// Each element of $untidy_array is passed in turn to Parser::tidy(),
// and the returned values are stored in $tidied_array
$tidied_array = array_map(array('Parser', 'tidy'), $untidy_array);
class Parser
{
// An example method that trims trailing whitespace and
// shell-style comments starting with '#' from a single
// line of text.
static function strip_comments($element)
{
    $element = preg_replace('/#[^#]*$/', '', $element);
    $element = rtrim($element);
    return $element;
}
}
```

```
    }

    $shell_script = file('foo.sh');
    $tidied_script = array_map(array('Parser', 'strip_comments'), $shell_script);
```

Within classes and objects, the magic `self` and `$this` work within callbacks, and will work just as you would expect: `array($this, 'method')` and `array('self', 'method')` will respectively be interpreted as referring to `$this->method()` and `self::method()`. The usual limitations regarding things like static functions not being allowed to use `$this` apply. For example:

```
    // An object is able to use its own methods in array callbacks,
    // both on arguments passed to it and on its own properties.
    $tidied_code = array_map(array($this, 'tidy'), $this->code_array);

    // Class methods are also accessible as callbacks within the class.
```

If you want to check that a given `$variable`'s contents does in fact specify a callable function or method at any point, the Boolean function `is_callable($variable)` will state this.

array_map()

You have just seen one of the simplest applications of `array_map()`, but it can go much further.

Most significantly, it can operate on several arrays concurrently. Imagine you have two arrays — `$arr1` and `$arr2` — and you want to construct an array consisting of `func($arr1[0],$arr2[0])`, `func($arr1[1],$arr2[1])`, ... `func($arr1[n], $arr2[n])`. The code for doing this as a loop would be something like the following:

```
    $new_array = array();
    for($i=0, $limit=max(count($arr1), count($arr2)); $i<$limit; $i++)
    {
        $arg1 = isset($arr1[$i]) ? $arr1[$i] : null;
        $arg2 = isset($arr2[$i]) ? $arr2[$i] : null;
        $new_array[$i] = func($arg1, $arg2);
    }
```

Note the testing required to make sure that the loop doesn't run out of arguments for `func()` when the arrays are different lengths.

Now compare it with the equivalent code that results from a use of `array_map()`:

```
    $new_array = array_map('func', $arr1, $arr2);
```

If *that* doesn't work you're entitled to log a report with bugs.php.net. And when you come back six months later to look at your code, which will it take longer to reacquaint yourself with?

Another trick that `array_map()` can play comes from the fact that it is able to take `null` as its callback. Its behavior in this situation can be described as "take a bunch of arrays of things and return an array of bunches of things." The 0thelements of each array are combined into a single array that becomes the 0th element of the result array; the first elements of each array are combined into a single array that becomes the first element of the result array; and so on. In other words, if you picture its array arguments as being the columns of a matrix, `array_map(null, ...)` returns the transposed matrix. It is effectively what you would have expected from `array_map('array', $arr1, $arr2)` if you'd been allowed to use `'array'` as a callback.

This trick isn't limited to combining only two arrays at a time either. If the callback function requires *n* arguments, then `array_map()` requires *n* arrays to be passed to it. So if you have a function that takes six arguments, and an array of sextets, each of which you want to run the function on, and collect all the results in a new array, `array_map()` will be suitable.

> *Strictly speaking, there are two calls to* `array_map()`. *The first uses a null callback to take the original* `array[0..n][0..5]` *and return the transpose* `array[0..5][0..n]`, *the second to use the call-back function on successive elements of* `array[0]`, `array[1]`, `...` `array[5]`.

`array_map()` has two glaring limitations. First, every argument after the callback must be an array. If you want to use a single variable in a whole array's worth of operations (such as clamping all the values of an array to a certain maximum), then you have to do one of the following:

❑   Declare the variable in global scope and use the global inside the callback function (not the most attractive option)

❑   Use `array_fill()` to make an array of duplicates (useful only if you don't mind the operations being carried out on separate copies of the variable, or if the variable is a passed-by-reference object or resource)

❑   Fall back to using a loop after all

❑   Use a different function: specifically, `array_walk()`

❑   Use an option that can be considered when writing OOP: make the callback a method and the variable a property of the object

The other glaring limitation is that you need to know in advance just how many arrays are to be mapped together, and list them all explicitly in the function call. You could work around this by wrapping corresponding elements of the input arrays into a single element of one consolidated array and passing the elements of that array to the callback function. But this requires rewriting the callback function or, when that's not possible, writing a wrapper function to unpack the consolidated element and passing the contents to the real callback. And you'll realize that when you do that you're back where you started. Fortunately PHP supplies a solution to this, too, in the form of `call_user_func_array()`, covered later in this chapter.

array_walk()

Imagine that you're using the GD Lib graphics drawing extension to draw up a chart, and you have a lot of data points to indicate with circles of varying sizes and colors. The positions and radii have already been scaled to image coordinates, and the colors have already been allocated and are identified by the image palette indexes (as returned by `imagecolorallocate()`). You are supplied an array of the data points, each element containing the x-coordinate, the y-coordinate, the radius, and the color, respectively. For example:

```
$data_points = array(
    array(10,10,5, $palette['black']),
    array(10,20,5, $palette['black']),
    array(20,13,5, $palette['darkolivegreen']),
    ...
);
```

Checking the PHP manual, the appropriate function would appear to be `imageellipse()`. The only difference between your data and its arguments is that it expects a width and height, while the supplied data contains only a radius. But that's a trivial difference. First, define a function:

```
function imagedatapoint($image, $datapoint)
{
    $width = $height = $datapoint[2]*2;
    imageellipse($image, $datapoint[0], $datapoint[1], $width, $height,
                $datapoint[3]);
}
```

Then call it.

```
foreach($datapoints as $datapoint)
{
    imagedatapoint($image, $datapoint);
}
```

That's actually quite straightforward. `imagedatapoint()` would of course have been more readable had each data point been an associative array or an object; something that identified its components by name. One question you could ask is, why have the loop outside the function? Indeed, you will be more likely to be plotting multiple data points on a chart instead of just one. Here's an example:

```
function imagedatapoints($image, $datapoints)
{
    foreach($datapoints as $datapoint)
    {
    $width = $height = $datapoint[2]*2;
        imageellipse($image, $datapoint[0], $datapoint[1], $width, $height,
                    $datapoint[3]);
    }
}
imagedatapoints($image, $datapoint);
```

But how might `array_walk()` do it? First, it uses a callback function. This is effectively the body of the previous loop.

```
function imagedatapoint($datapoint, $key, $image)
{
    $width = $height = $datapoint[2]*2;
    imageellipse($image, $datapoint[0], $datapoint[1], $width, $height,
                $datapoint[3]);
}
```

Then it makes the following call:

```
array_walk('imagedatapoint', $datapoints, $image);
```

Unlike `array_map()`, `array_walk()` works on a reference to the original array. So if the callback function takes its array element argument by reference, the element's value can be modified by the function and the change will be reflected back in the array passed to `array_walk()`.

array_filter() and preg_grep()

The operation of `array_filter()` is easily inferred from its name: given an array, it returns those elements of the array that satisfy a given condition, that condition being supplied in terms of a callback to a Boolean-valued function (think of the WHERE clause in an SQL query). A chain of `array_filter()` calls can be much easier to comprehend than a single loop that runs through an array, filled with all sorts of tests and branches that have the aim of deciding whether or not a given element is to be retained, and building a new array of the successful elements. However, a similar limitation to that of `array_map()` applies, in that beyond the input array and callback, it takes no additional arguments.

```php
function is_a_square_number($n)
{
    // Fail values unsuitable for sqrt().
    if(!is_numeric($n))
        return false;
    if($n<0)
        return false;
    $square_root = sqrt($n);
    return ($square_root == intval($square_root));
}

$numbers = array(-1,0,1,2,3,4,5,6,7,8,9,10,11,12,13,14,15,16,17,18,19,20,'!');
$squares = array_filter($numbers, 'is_a_square_number');
// $squares now contains the array (0,1,4,9,16);
```

Since filtering strings that contain certain patterns is such a common subclass of array filtering tasks, and since regular expressions are so often useful in describing such patterns, PHP offers a function specifically for the task. `preg_grep()` is as the name suggests one of the PCRE functions and similar in behavior to the grep program. It doesn't use a callback function (it uses a regular expression instead), but it makes a nice segue between `array_filter()` and the function of the next section. Here's an example of a `preg.grep()` statement:

```php
// This use of preg_grep takes a listing of the current directory, and retains only
// those file names that end with four digits followed by "".jpg" or ".jpeg".
$images = preg_grep('/\d{4}\.jpe?g$/', scandir('.'));
```

For a function to filter directory listings according to simpler criteria using a shell-like syntax, see the `glob()` function.

preg_replace_callback()

The syntax used by `preg_replace()` includes the `/e` modifier switch. When you use this modifier, the given replacement text is treated as PHP code and evaluated to determine what the actual replacement text should be. But it can easily get troublesome trying to squeeze in all the necessary code. So `preg_replace_callback()` was implemented so that instead of having to write the replacement code directly into the function call, you need only supply a callback. This can be used to greatly simplify complicated regular expressions. Since the callback function can contain any amount of string-processing and pattern-recognition code, the regular expression used in `preg_replace_callback()` need only be complicated enough to guarantee that every desired match is found, even if some unwanted ones get through. Further testing can be done in the callback; if further tests fail, then the callback need only return the match unchanged. (Be warned however, that if an unwanted match happens to overlap a subsequent desired match, the latter will be missed. `preg_replace_callback()` isn't aware of whether later tests "succeed" or not.)

Matching email addresses for wrapping in `"mailto:"` links, for example, can result in some frightening regular expressions if you want to be thorough. It is far easier to approach it in stages. You could start by simply trying to locate the @ character with non-white-space on either side, as follows:

```
preg_replace_callback('/\S+@\S+/', $text, 'wrap_emails');
```

And leave the hard work of verifying that the matched string really is an email to the callback:

```
function wrap_emails($possible_match)
{
    $possible_email = $possible_match[0]; // The callback will be passed an array
    if(is_rfc822_compliant($possible_email)) // A hypothetical function that
                                            // does all the boring stuff
        return '<a href="mailto:'.$possible_email.'">'.$possible_email.'</a>';
    else
        return $possible_email; // Not an email, return the substring unchanged.
}
```

A second example of its using `preg_replace_callback()` is with templating systems. With `preg_replace_callback()` merely identifying slots in the template, the callback function it passes the matches to would then examine the slots in finer detail — a task made easier by the fact that they have already been isolated from the rest of the template by a function that is also keeping track of where in the template they came from. Here's an example:

```
function include_templates($template_name)
{
    if(is_string($template_file))
        $template_file = $template_name;
    else
        $template_file = $template_name[1].'.tpl';    $template =
file_get_contents($template_file);
    return preg_replace_callback('\{include:\s*([^\s}]+)\}', 'include_templates',
                                 $template);
}
```

This recursive function assumes that your template files all have the extension `'.tpl'`, and that the syntax you use in your templates for including `foo.tpl` is `{include: foo}`. Needless to say, if `foo.tpl` itself contains includes, you want those included as well.

If the function is passed a string, then the string is interpreted as the name of a template file. If it's passed an array (for reasons that will become apparent shortly), then the desired filename is the second element of the array, with `.tpl` appended. The contents of the named file are then read into `$template`. (There is virtually no error checking going on here.)

The call to `preg_replace_callback()` searches through `$template` for strings matching the `{include: foo}` syntax. Arrays containing the matching strings (where the 0th element contains the entire matching string and the 1st element contains the first parenthesized substring), are then passed one by one to `include_templates()`, which extracts the name of the template file from the array, and after calling `preg_replace_callback()`, returns the content of the template file — with all of the `{include: foo}` parts replaced by the contents of the corresponding template files.

There is no `preg_match_callback()` or `preg_match_all_callback()`, unfortunately. But since the callback function can do anything, it can also store the matches that have been passed to it somewhere (a global variable, perhaps, or preferably a class or object property). Then it can simply return the 0th element of its argument, causing `preg_replace_callback()` to replace any matched substring with itself, unchanged. An address-harvesting object may therefore include a method that works like this:

```
function collect_email($possible_match)
{
    $possible_email = $possible_match[0];
    if(self::is_rfc822_compliant($possible_email))
        $this->emails = $possible_email;
    return $possible_email; // Return the match unchanged
}
```

Whether the preceding method stores an email address or not, it returns it unchanged. `preg_replace_callback()` would therefore replace the matched substring with itself, leaving the original text intact.

call_user_func_array() and call_user_func()

Recall the *two* glaring limitations discussed at the end of the `array_map()` section. The first was addressed by `array_walk()`. The second is that you need to know in advance just how many arrays are being mapped together, and list them all explicitly in the function call. Sometimes you might not know this until run time. In one of my programs, I had a numeric matrix (which varied in size), stored as an array of rows (each row itself an array), and I required a transpose (so that I'd end up with an array of columns). I could have written a doubly nested loop, one to iterate over the rows, and the other to iterate within each row, something like this:

```
$transposed_matrix = array();
for($row=0, $row_count=count($matrix); $row<$row_count; $row++)
{
    for($column=0, $column_count=count($matrix[$row]), $column<$column_count;
        $column++)
    {
        $transposed_matrix[$column][$row] = $matrix[$row][$column];
    }
}
```

Even while writing out that example code, I had to pause a couple of times to make sure my rows and columns were the right way around, but the desired effect could be achieved by writing the following code:

```
$temp = $matrix;
array_push(null, $temp);
$transposed_matrix = call_user_func_array('array_map', $temp);
unset($temp);
```

`call_user_func_array()` is another function that takes a callback. Its second argument is an array that lists all of the arguments to be passed to the callback function (it's the same array you'd get if you called `func_get_args()` from within the callback function). For the sake of example, say that `$matrix` was `((1,2), (3,4))` and follow what happens:

```
$matrix = array(array(1, 2), array(3, 4));
$temp = $matrix;
array_push(null, $temp);
$transposed_matrix = call_user_func_array('array_map', $temp);
```

The first argument to array_map() is the name of the callback function, so make the first argument of $temp that callback (in this case, a null callback). This is why I needed the temp variable; array_push() modifies the original array rather than returning a copy. I could have lived dangerously by using $transposed_matrix itself instead of $temp, and saved myself the variable and the final unset(). Dangerous, because it would have reduced the readability of the code slightly (creating the variable as one thing (the list arguments to array_map()), and two lines later using it for something quite different (the result of the array_map() call).

```
$temp = array(null, array(1,2), array(3,4));
$transposed_matrix = call_user_func_array('array_map', $temp);
```

Here's the result of carrying out call_user_func_array() by hand.

```
$transposed_matrix = array_map(null, array(1,2), array(3,4));
```

So one way to look at the operation of call_user_func('foo', array(arguments)) is to look on it as taking an array and replacing array(arguments) with foo(arguments).

To complete the example, evaluate the array_map() call:

```
$transposed_matrix = array(array(1,3), array(2,4));
```

The practical upshot of call_user_func_array() is that you can store all of the arguments to a function in a single array, without needing to know how many arguments there are (consider that several PHP functions accept variable numbers of arguments, and so can yours), nor needing to take each of the elements out of the array and inserting them into the function call by hand.

The reason for the slightly long-winded name is that there is also a call_user_func() function. Instead of taking a callback and its arguments as an array, it takes the callback and its arguments *explicitly*. Just as you can think of PHP as converting call_user_func_array('foo', array(arguments)) to foo(arguments), call_user_func('foo', arguments) converts to foo(arguments) without using the intermediate array.

It may sound as though it's effectively the same as putting 'foo' into a variable $func, and then writing $func(...). And for ordinary functions, it is. But for object methods it's another story. Try it:

```
<?php
class foo
{

public function bar($a, $b)
{
    echo "I'm here! $a! $b! And all that!";
}

}
```

```
$t = new foo;
$x = array($t, 'bar');
$x('1066', '42');
?>
```

The result is a fatal error: PHP demands that the function name be a string. Instead of the variable function, it's necessary to write the following:

```
call_user_func($x, '1066', '42');
```

And then you get the desired result:

```
I'm here! 1066! 42! And all that!
```

create_function()

There is just one more hurdle to overcome. So far *all* of the callbacks mentioned have been pre-existing functions that were written into the original code. Sometimes, though, that just isn't good enough. Sometimes the exact form a function may take isn't known until the moment it is needed for a callback, or perhaps it's simply a matter of not wanting to have a whole function sitting around for a single specific task that is going to be performed only *once*. If only there was some way of defining a function at runtime; or explicitly, instead of via a callback's name.

Well, there already is: build up a string containing the text of the function, wrap it in `"function whatever(...){...}"`, and call `eval()` on that. But problems can occur. You have to remember that since a function can be declared only once, that string can be evaluated only once; you have to remember to give each such function a unique name—`whatever0()`, `whatever1()`, and so forth—so if this act of creation might be carried out more than once, a counter of some sort (possibly a static variable) is required somewhere in the function, method, or class that contains the evaluation. And of course if you do this in more than one place in your code, you need to ensure that the function names generated at different places don't collide. One elegant way of doing this would be to have a single "function-creating function" with a single static variable to prevent namespace collisions, and pass *it* the text of the function, letting it work out an appropriate name, evaluate the resulting definition, and return the generated name for the callback. You would actually want to pass it *two* strings—one for the body of the function and one for the list of arguments—and it would go `eval("function whatever$n($arguments){$body}");`. There is the possibility that there is *already* a function named `whatever1()`, so when your function goes to create a new function name, it would have to check that it's not already defined. Then there is the possibility that *it* might create a function named `whatever1()`, unaware that further on through the program *you* will attempt to create a function named `whatever1()`. The only prevention for that is to enforce coding standards stating that you are not allowed to declare functions with names of a certain form.

But don't bother. Such a function already exists, and it works exactly as just described, with an extra subtlety that prevents any chance of namespace collision with your own functions. PHP's `create_function()` creates an *anonymous function*, which simply means that it doesn't appear in the list generated by `get_defined_functions()`. It does, however, *have* a name (even anonymous people have names—you just don't know them). First of all, there is the name it has while it is being parsed and compiled: in its own mind (that is, the value of the magic `__FUNCTION__` constant), it thinks of itself as `__lambda_func`. (The term "lambda function" is synonymous with "anonymous function," and comes from a 1936 model of computation called the Lambda Calculus via LISP.) Once it has been created, there is the name it is known by to the rest of the program, which is what is actually returned by `create_function()` as a string fresh and ready for use as a callback. The first string returned from `create_function()` is " lambda_1"; the second is " lambda_2", and so on. Okay, so what happens if *you* define a function named `lambda_1()` and then use `create_function()`? Does one overwrite the other, is there an error, or does the anonymous function get called `lambda_2()` instead? If these options appeared in a multiple-choice test, you could dismiss the first as being in violation of PHP's own rules regarding function immutability, leaving you with choices B or C. The correct answer, however, is D, none of the above.

```php
<?php
function lambda_1($a)
{
    return $a;
}
$anonymous_function = create_function('$a', 'return strrev($a);');
echo "The anonymous function has been named $anonymous_function.\n";
$use_this = 'lambda_1';
echo $use_this('generic string'), "\n";
$use_this = $anonymous_function;
echo $use_this('generic string'),"\n";
?>
```

Running this gives you the following:

```
The anonymous function has been named  lambda_1.
generic string
gnirts cireneg
```

So how did PHP know which one to use if they have the same name? The simple fact is they don't. If you peer closely at the typography of the code sample's output and previous paragraph, the name of the anonymous function appears to start with a space. In fact it's not a space but a null character `0x00`. That is sneaky: it's impossible to declare a function with a name of this form or to *call* a function with such a name, since in both cases the NUL in the source code is ignored by PHP's lexer as being whitespace. However, knowing this does make it possible to construct the names of anonymous functions as string literals by hand (using code like `chr(0) . 'lambda_n'`, or an editor that will let you insert NULs directly). This may be of little benefit, however, since once you've discarded the original strings or you've lost track of which variable contains the name of which anonymous function it's up to you to work out whether you want the third or fifth or 750th such function. If you were creating a distinct anonymous function for every element in an array, you could easily end up with hundreds of the things, even if they are functionally identical. (PHP makes no attempt to compare one anonymous function with another to see if they contain identical code, any more than it attempts to do so with ordinary functions; and besides, if you're creating functions in a loop, there are most likely parts that vary from iteration to iteration – otherwise, why do it in a loop?) If you can keep track of such things — for example, say you know somehow that your 750 functions will all be numbered from 10 to 759 — then you don't need to keep an array of 750 strings to store all the names, it can be recreated by writing the following code:

```php
function recreate_function($lambda)
{
return chr(0).'lambda_'.$lambda;
}
$lambda_functions = array_map('recreate_function', range(10,759));
```

Final Observations on the Array Functions

In terms of the number of functions listed, the array functions form one of the largest sections in the manual's function listing; only just behind the filesystem functions and not far behind string handling. Even with the amount of abstraction that callbacks allow, why are there so many? And how can using them contribute to code quality?

So Many Array Functions

Throughout PHP3 and PHP4, there have been noticeable gaps in the list of array functions. There was a function with which you could sort an array using your own definition of "less than, greater than, or equal to," but there wasn't a single array function that let you remove all the elements of one array that were "the same as" the elements in another, using your definition of "the same." Over successive versions of PHP, these gaps are being identified, and new functions implemented to fill them.

A principle factor harks back to the overlapping functionality mentioned at the start of the chapter. Having two functions with very similar behavior leads to the differences in how they are highlighted. There is a function to sort an array and a function to sort an array using a callback. There is a function to sort by key, and a function to sort by key using a callback. The natural question to ask is whether the same differences have meaning for the other array functions.

If you imagine all the possible functions as being single points in some vast space, the existing functions provide a set of reference points from which the space can be charted. Having sort() and usort() suggests the idea of moving toward providing callbacks; from these, ksort() and uksort() suggest you can move independently in the direction of "by *key* rather than by *value*." Now that those directions have been pointed out, having array_diff() is inevitably going to suggest array_diff() with callback, "array_diff() by key," and of course array_diff() by key with callback. PHP5 has implemented many of these new functions, such as array_udiff(), and many others are in CVS versions, if not already in stable releases.

"Orthogonal" means at right angles to; in other words, as far from parallel as you can get. With PHP's early functions having so many that are so similar to each other that they "point in nearly parallel directions in function space," using them will suggest other functions that are nearly parallel (e.g., array_uintersect_assoc() and array_uintersect_uassoc()), leading to regions of function space where PHP's functions are clustered thickly. The array functions form such a dense cluster. You will certainly find that you don't *need* to be intimate with all of PHP's array functions to use them effectively, and that consistent application of simple combinations of a few functions that are as much unalike as possible will net you all the functionality you require. That is orthogonality. *Which* few functions are up to you.

Array Function after Array Function

When using a series of array functions to manipulate the contents of an array there is a distinct difference in the order manipulations are carried out, when compared to carrying out the manipulations directly on array elements within a loop. This can have an impact on considerations such as the memory requirements of your program.

Consider this short example:

```
$array = array_map('do_something_fancy', $array);
```

This is equivalent to:

```
foreach($array as &$value)
{
    $value = do_something_fancy($value);
}
```

In the former case, there is a brief moment after the `array_map()` has been evaluated when there are *two entire* arrays. Following the assignment, of course, the previous version of the `$array` is discarded and memory retrieved, but that doesn't happen until the assignment has been completed, and the number of references to the original has decreased to zero. If the array is large, the extra space required can be significant, with large chunks of memory being allocated and then a short time later *other* large chunks of memory being *de*allocated. Naturally, if the output array is going into a different variable than the input array, the deallocation doesn't happen, and the one-off economy-sized allocation carried out by the array function's implementation may well be more efficient than the piecemeal element-by-element activity that occurs in `$new_array[] = do_something_fancy($value);`. Clearly, `array_filter()`, `array_udiff()`, and other functions that can output arrays shorter than their inputs ought to be applied prior to those that can't when possible, as it gives those later functions less work to do.

If there are a series of `array_*`-type functions that return arrays, each using the results of the previous, this bulk to-and-fro can become quite tedious for both PHP's memory management and the operating system. It can be obviated to some extent (but only *some* extent) by writing something like this:

```
array_walk(
    array_map(
        'do_something_fancy',
        array_filter(
            array_map('nothing_fancy', $array),
        'purge')),
    'traverse', 'sideways');
```

Instead of this:

```
$array = array_map('nothing_fancy', $array);
$array = array_filter($array, 'purge');
$array = array_map('do_something_fancy', $array);
array_walk($array, 'traverse', 'sideways');
```

But no one is going to believe you if you say that the former is easier to read. If nothing else, the functions appear in the reverse order that they are applied. Admittedly, it does not help appearances that there does not appear to be any consistency in the order in which arguments are passed to the functions. The best you can say about it is that it helps suppress errors at runtime — if you accidentally mistype `array_map` instead of `array_filter`, PHP would complain at runtime that the "first argument, `'Array'`, should have been NULL or a valid callback."

glob()

A task you may often find yourself doing is reading through a directory for files with names matching a certain pattern — all the text files, for example, or image files. This can be simpler than storing the files in the filesystem, maintaining a list of those files elsewhere, and then having to keep the two synchronized.

And it's possible that other types of files are in the same directory. This is such a common task that any shell interface provides "globbing" — you can list `*.png`, delete `temp_*`, and so forth. Prior to PHP 4.3, the typical method of achieving the same effect would have used `readdir()` and, based on the examples of that function's use given in the manual, ended up with something that looks like this:

```
$filelist = array();
if ($handle = opendir('directory'))
{
    while (false !== ($file = readdir($handle)))
    {
        if(substr($file, -4)=='.txt')
        {
            $filelist[] = $file;
        }
    }
    closedir($handle);
}
```

PHP 5 introduces `scandir()`, which encapsulates the whole `opendir()`/`readdir()`/`loop()`/`closedir()` business, leaving the job of filtering the filenames until afterwards, which in this example could be handled by `preg_grep()` like this:

```
$filelist = preg_grep('/\.txt$/', scandir('directory'));
```

But since PHP 4.3, even this is unnecessarily complicated. By using the same shell-like globbing syntax, where `?` represents "any single character" and `*` represents "any string," you can use the same syntax that you use in the shell to do the same filtering of file names. `$filelist = glob('*.txt', 'directory');`

The `glob()` function has a few optional flags that can be bitwise-ORed together to adjust the behavior of the function. For example, if the directory in question had a mix of JPEG and PNG files (along with a miscellaneous scattering of other types, and of course the inevitable `.` and `..` directories), the `GLOB_BRACE` flag can be set, and the alternative glob patterns for identifying those files by their extensions passed to `glob()` as a comma-separated list in braces:

```
$filelist = glob('*..jpg,*.jpeg,*.png}', 'directory', GLOB_BRACE);
```

PHP Streams

Starting with PHP4.3, PHP's URL wrappers (the things that allow you to use URLs in places where filenames are usually expected) has been extended to become the basic mechanism of file interaction in general. One of the consequences of this is that you can now use URLs in almost any context where a local file path would be appropriate. (Some specialized aspects, such as configuration settings, are exempt from this: you can't have a URL in your `include` path, for example.) This includes file access functions used by third-party extensions, with PHP now treating local file accesses as requests via `file://` URLs.

The other consequence is that it became feasible in PHP5 to expose an interface for constructing custom *stream wrappers* to the PHP developer in the so-called *streams interface*.

Programmers who are familiar with Java or C++ will already be familiar with the streams concept; the kioslaves that appear in the K Desktop Environment are another example. In PHP, a stream is an object that behaves like a file — you may be able to read bytes from it, write bytes to it, go to a particular byte position within it, ask how many bytes there are, and so on. Note the use of "may be" — just as some files are read-only and some are write-only, streams too might be read-only or write-only, while some generate their data on the fly so that there is no clearly-defined analog of "file offset" or "file size" or even "end of file." The idea is that users of a stream need have no idea just how the data they work with is stored or handled; they just read and write. The most significant limitation, compared with, say, Java, is that PHP streams are all *byte* streams. To stream something else — objects in particular — you need serialization to convert it into something that will go through a stream. This is PHP's loose typing having an effect once again: since every stream is a byte stream, any stream can be used anywhere (whether it makes sense or not).

Creating and Using Streams

Building a stream wrapper is simply a matter of adding certain methods to the stream object, and using `stream_wrapper_register()` to identify it as a wrapper.

`stream_wrapper_register()` is called with two arguments. The first is the *protocol*, which is simply a name that indicates the wrapper to be used when a stream is to be opened — what is known in URLs as the *scheme*. It's the bit in the URL before the `//`, that is, the `http` of HTTP URLs, the `ftp` of FTP URLs, and the `file` of file URLs. For example, if you implement a stream and register it with a protocol of `foonly`, you will then be able to go `fopen("foonly://...", "r")` to enable reading from a foonly stream. The default protocol used by `fopen()` and the other filesystem functions is `file`, which is why you hardly ever see `file:///path/file.ext`, because `/path/file.ext` has the same effect.

The second argument is a string containing the name of the class that implements your wrapper.

Naturally, the full list of wrapper methods are given in the manual. The principal ones are as follows:

❑ `stream_open()`: This function contains startup code for a new stream — initializing variables, opening streams of its own, and so forth. You call this function with four arguments. The first two are the same path and mode values as the corresponding `fopen()` call. (For third-party extensions, the appropriate options will be worked out and provided.) The third argument could contain up to two flags: `STREAM_USE_PATH` indicates that you should search PHP's `include` path if necessary to find the specified file, and `STREAM_REPORT_ERRORS` indicates whether it is the stream's responsibility to trigger any errors if the stream cannot be opened or something else goes wrong, or whether such things are going to be handled higher up (in which case your stream should not report any errors). `STREAM_USE_PATH` is only relevant if you actually *are* looking for something in the local filesystem, whether it is the file requested, or an auxiliary file that your stream uses. If your stream is read-only, it should return `FALSE` (and possibly trigger a warning) if the requested mode is for writing (`w`, `r+`, `a`, `a+`), and similarly for write-only streams.

The PHP manual mentions "`fopen_with_path()`", but as of 5.0.3 this function doesn't exist. The `include_path` *configuration setting is of course available via* `ini_get()`.

❑ `stream_read()`: If the stream cannot be read, this should return `FALSE`. Otherwise it should return at most the number of bytes requested. As the wrapper's author, it is your responsibility to ensure that any relevant state, including any file pointers, is maintained between successive calls to this method. You *are* allowed to return fewer bytes than requested (although an empty string may be interpreted as indicating the end of the stream).

❑   `stream_write()`: Again, this function should be called only if the stream is actually writable. It is the stream object's responsibility to keep track of what it is doing from one write to the next. You need not write *all* the bytes you are passed; you may truncate the data if necessary. In any case, this method should return the number of bytes that *were* written (including 0 if none could be written at all). This number should be in terms of the bytes that it receives. A stream that carries out base64 encoding would write four bytes for every three it receives. If asked to write "abc" it would write "YWJj," yet return 3. This return value is for the benefit of the caller, after all, which by definition isn't supposed to be intimate with the operation of the "callee." If you do write fewer bytes than requested, it is the caller's responsibility to decide whether or not to try again, but your stream may need to retain some data in any case. The base64 encoder is an example of this: having been passed "ab" it would be able to write "YW," but the last two bits of the "b" have to be retained while the stream waits for the next input byte or a `stream_close()`. This encoder should return a 1 and expect the "b" to be passed again in the next `stream_write()` call. The alternative mechanism is that the encoder doesn't output anything unless it has at least three bytes to encode, and then it only encodes (and outputs) multiples of three input bytes at a time. For this to work, the stream would need to *claim* to write all the bytes that have been passed in even if it *hasn't* actually done so, and hope that no-one finds out about its subterfuge. Otherwise the caller might get upset that it returned 0 when passed "ab" and try again, and again, with the encoder waiting for a third byte that it never gets to see.

❑   `stream_eof()`: A readable stream could be asked at any time whether or not the end of the stream's data has been reached (especially after `stream_read()` returned an empty string for some reason). So this is simply a Boolean function that returns "true" if the end of the stream has been reached.

❑   `stream_close()`: It is the stream object's responsibility to tidy up anything that needs tidying up, close any streams of its own, and so on. Returning to the base64 encoder, there is a better-than-even possibility that the stream will be left with one or two bytes that now will never get to be part of a triple. So it's safe to finally encode these and write them out, padding with the requisite number of = signs.

Those are the basics of opening and closing a stream, and reading and writing. A stream wrapper has other methods that should be implemented if they are appropriate to the protocol and cover such tasks as random access, directory control, and so forth.

When a stream is opened, `stream_open()` is called with the *complete* path as its first argument, including the protocol. This is principally so that you can use `parse_url()` to break the path into its components, and therefore it is a good idea to design your stream name format to use the conventional URL syntax where appropriate (`scheme://username:password@host:port/path?query#fragment`). Incidentally, it also means that the same stream class can handle more than one protocol, but this is better handled by subclassing.

Two Examples of Streams

To fix the ideas of the previous section, here are two simple stream classes. The first maintains a log file that records the activity of files accessed through it, while the second is for selecting portions of a geographic aerial photograph collection.

File Access Logger

Consider the following code:

```php
<?php
class logged_stream
{
    private $stream;
    private $log_stream;
    private $bytes_read=0, $bytes_written=0;
    private $user;

function stream_open($path, $mode, $options, &$opened_path)
{
    static $modes = array(
        'r'=>'reading',
        'r+'=>'reading and writing',
        'w'=>'writing',
        'w+'=>'writing and reading',
        'a'=>'appending',
        'a+'=>'appending and reading',
        'x'=>'creation and writing',
        'x+'=>'creation, writing and reading');
    $path = substr($path, 9);
    $this->user = substr($path, 0, strpos($path, '@'));
    $path = substr($path, strpos($path, '@')+1);
    $this->stream = fopen($path, $mode, $options&STREAM_USE_PATH);
    $this->log_stream = fopen($path.'.log', 'a');
    if(!$this->log_stream)
    {
        if($options|STREAM_REPORT_ERRORS)
        {
            trigger_error('Logged stream: Unable to open log file',
                    E_USER_WARNING);
        }
        return false;
    }
    if(!$this->stream)
    {
        if($options|STREAM_REPORT_ERRORS)
        {
            trigger_error('Logged stream: file '.$path.' could not be opened',
                    E_USER_WARNING);
        }
        return false;
    }
    $binary = strpos($mode, 'b')!==false;
    if($binary)
        $mode = str_replace('b', '', $mode);
    list($micro, $sec) = explode(' ', microtime());
    $date = date('Y-m-d H:i:s').substr($micro, 1);
    fwrite($this->log_stream, 'File opened for '.$modes[$mode].
        ($binary?' in binary mode by ':' by ').$this->user.' at '.$date."\n");
    return true;
}
```

```php
function stream_close()
{
    fclose($this->stream);
    list($micro, $sec) = explode(' ', microtime());
    $date = date('Y-m-d H:i:s').substr($micro, 1);
    fwrite($this->log_stream, 'File closed by '.$this->user.' at '.$date."\n");
    fwrite($this->log_stream, "Total bytes read: ".$this->bytes_read."\n");
    fwrite($this->log_stream, "Total bytes written: ".$this->bytes_written."\n");
    fwrite($this->log_stream, "\n");
    fclose($this->log_stream);
}
function stream_read($count)
{
    ob_start();
    debug_print_backtrace();
    $backtrace = ob_get_clean();
    fwrite($this->log_stream, $backtrace);
    $read = fread($this->stream, $count);
    $this->bytes_read+=strlen($read);
    return $read;
}
function stream_write($data)
{
    $read = fwrite($this->stream, $data);
    $this->bytes_written+=strlen($read);
    return $read;
}
function stream_eof()
{
    return feof($this->stream);
}
function stream_tell()
{
    return ftell($this->stream);
}
function stream_seek($offset, $whence=null)
{
    return fseek($this->stream, $offset, $whence);
}
function stream_flush()
{
    return true;
}
function stream_stat()
{
    return fstat($this->stream);
}
function unlink($path)
{
    $log_stream = fopen($path.'.log', 'a');
    if(!$log_stream)
    {
        trigger_error('Logged stream: Unable to open log file. File not deleted.',
                    E_USER_WARNING);
        return false;
```

```
        }
        $success = unlink($path);
        list($micro, $sec) = explode(' ', microtime());
        $date = date('Y-m-d H:i:s').substr($micro, 1);
        if($success)
            fwrite($log_stream, "File $path deleted at $date\n");
        else
            fwrite($log_stream, "Unable to delete file $path at $date\n");
        fclose($this->log_stream);
        return $success;
    }
    function rename($from_path, $to_path)
    {
        $from_log_stream = fopen($from_path.'.log', 'a');
        $to_log_stream = fopen($to_path.'.log', 'a');
        if(!$from_log_stream || !$to_log_stream)
        {
            trigger_error('Logged stream: Unable to open log file. File not renamed.',
                      E_USER_WARNING);
            return false;
        }
        $success = rename($from_path, $to_path);
        list($micro, $sec) = explode(' ', microtime());
        $date = date('Y-m-d H:i:s').substr($micro, 1);
        if($success)
        {
            fwrite($from_log_stream, "File $from_path renamed to $to_path at $date\n");
            fwrite($to_log_stream, "File $to_path renamed from $from_path at $date\n");
        }
        else
        {
            fwrite($from_log_stream, "Unable to rename $from_path as $to_path at
                $date\n");
            fwrite($to_log_stream, "Unable to rename $from_path as $to_path at
                $date\n");
        }
        fclose($from_log_stream);
        fclose($to_log_stream);
        return $success;
    }

}
?>
```

This wrapper is registered by calling `stream_wrapper_register('logged', 'logged_stream');`.
You use a "logged" stream by calling something like `$fp=fopen('logged://eric@documents/`
`benchmarks.txt');`. What this is intended to say is that user "eric" is going to be working with
documents/benchmarks.txt, and that you are to log the event:

```
        $path = substr($path, 9);
        $this->user = substr($path, 0, strpos($path, '@'));
        $path = substr($path, strpos($path, '@')+1);
```

The stream's activity starts at `stream_open()`. The first three `substr()`s split off the `logged://` part of the URL, and then the username. The remainder is the URL of the resource actually requested:

```
$this->stream = fopen($path, $mode,$options&~STREAM_REPORT_ERRORS);
$this->log_stream = fopen($path.'.log','a');
```

The logging stream opens the resource itself (with the `STREAM_REPORT_ERRORS` flag turned off, because those will be handled by this stream), and also readies a log file for appending. In this example, for simplicity the resource is merely another stream with an identical name as the one requested except for an extra `.log` extension. In a more practical setting, the logging would be done in some other way, since (for one thing) this mechanism would fail for read-only streams, but such an issue can be dealt with by writing a new stream class and registering it under a protocol name of its own. The second `fopen()` call would use this protocol and whatever happens from there on is a problem for the new class.

After that the two streams are checked to see that they're actually open. An error is triggered and `FALSE` returned if either failed.

The last thing the stream does before returning `true` is to write a line to the newly opened logfile saying that the stream was opened, how, by whom, and when.

The bulk of the functionality of this class merely passes the corresponding file operations directly on to the stream it is keeping a log for. `stream_read()` and `stream_write()` have the added task of counting bytes as they pass back and forth, and `rename()` makes a note about the new name of the file (which, if it is opened as a logged stream, will have its own log file..

Finally, `stream_close()` writes the time and the total number of bytes transferred each way, before closing both of its own streams down.

GIS Photographic Database Query

Land Information New Zealand (`http://www.linz.govt.nz/`) maintains a 2.5-meter resolution photographic atlas of the country. These aerial photos have been scaled and oriented so that their vertical and horizontal axes are respectively exactly north-south and east-west, to result in so-called "orthophotos." The photography is available in the form of images 8000×6000 pixels in size, corresponding to an area of ground 3.2×2.4 kilometers in extent. Four such photos suffice to encompass Auckland City. Combined as a single grayscale PNG, an image of the entire city is 115MB in size.

Now imagine an online service in which users provide latitude and longitude for a point within Auckland, together with a radius, and the service responds with the appropriate image. The most straightforward method would be to load the image of the entire city, and copy the relevant portion. But that is infeasible simply due to the size of the image (remember that it is 115MB only while it is still compressed into a PNG file: uncompressed it's about a byte for each of 192 million pixels).

Another approach would be to store the imagery in an uncompressed form (LINZ provides the imagery as uncompressed TIFF files), and write a program that can locate and read the relevant bytes only from one or more files (it's 192 million bytes for one city, but it's quite a lot more for the entire country, making for a lot of raw data that needs storing for ready access), without having to load the whole lot into memory. This is certainly the better option of the two, but it is not something that is well-suited to PHP, mainly due to speed considerations when it comes to assembling the final image from the bytes being read. A custom extension written in C would be more appropriate. Since the current discussion is looking at PHP's stream wrapper interface, such a solution wouldn't be especially edifying.

A third solution is suggested by the second one. Uncompressed, the imagery could be stored in multiple random-access files. But if the files are small enough, it becomes feasible to consider storing them in a compressed form and loading them in their entirety as and when needed. Then it's simply a matter of determining which files are required to satisfy a given request, and tiling them to produce the desired image. That is the approach implemented in the following stream wrapper:

```php
<?php
/*
** The orthophoto stream uses the Orthophoto dataset maintained by
** Land Information New Zealand.The photoset follows the Topographic
** Map 260 series; coordinates used are those of the New Zealand
** Map Grid (NZMG), a system unique to that country.
**
** Aerial photos have a resolution of 2.5m per pixel, with an
** accuracy of ±12.5m.
*/

class orthophoto_stream
{
    // This is the generated PNG data that will be fed
    // back by the stream.
    private $png_data;

    // For the ftell() function / stream_tell() method.
    private $data_length;

function stream_open($path, $mode, $options, &$opened_path)
{
    // This is a read-only stream
    if(preg_match('/[w+a]/', $options)) return false;
    $path = parse_url($path);
    $coordinates = $path['host']; // Silly place to find it, but see
                                  // the note at the end of the section.
    if(strlen($coordinates)!=21) return false;
    if(strspn($coordinates, '0123456789')!=21) return false;
    list($northing, $easting, $radius)=sscanf($coordinates, '%07d%07d%07d');

    $full_image_size = ceil($radius*2*100/250);

    $full_image = imagecreate($full_image_size, $full_image_size);
    $black = imagecolorallocate($full_image, 0, 0, 0);
    // We use black as a background for unmapped regions.
    imagefill($full_image, 0, 0, $black);

    $maximum_northing = $northing+$radius;
    $minimum_northing = $northing-$radius;
    $maximum_easting = $easting+$radius;
    $minimum_easting = $easting-$radius;
    $bottommost_tile_northing = floor($minimum_northing/250)*250;
    $topmost_tile_northing = ceil($maximum_northing/250)*250;
    $leftmost_tile_easting = floor($minimum_easting/250)*250;
    $rightmost_tile_easting = ceil($maximum_easting/250)*250;

    for($tile_northing=$bottommost_tile_northing;
        $tile_northing<=$topmost_tile_northing;
```

```
            $tile_northing+=250)
    for($tile_easting=$leftmost_tile_easting;
        $tile_easting<=$rightmost_tile_easting;
        $tile_easting+=250)
    {
        $full_image_x = 100*($tile_easting-$minimum_easting)/250;
        $full_image_y = 100*($maximum_northing-$tile_northing)/250;
        $tile_name = sprintf('%07d%07d.png', $tile_northing, $tile_easting);
        if(!file_exists('tiles/'.$tile_name)) continue;
        $tile = imagecreatefrompng('tiles/'.$tile_name);
        imagecopy($full_image, $tile, $full_image_x, $full_image_y, 0, 0, 100,
                100);
        imagedestroy($tile);
    }
    ob_start();
    imagepng($full_image);
    imagedestroy($full_image);
    $this->png_data = ob_get_contents();
    ob_end_clean();
    $this->data_length = strlen($this->png_data);
    return true;
}

function stream_close()
{
    $this->png_data = null;
}

function stream_read($bytes)
{
    if(strlen($this->png_data)==0)
        return false;
    $return = substr($this->png_data, 0, $bytes);
    $this->png_data = substr($this->png_data, $bytes);
    return $return;
}

function stream_write(){}

function stream_eof()
{
    return $this->png_data == 0;
}

function stream_tell()
{
    return $this->data_length-strlen($this->png_data);
}

function stream_seek()
{
    return false;
}

function stream_flush()
```

```
{
    return false; // We don't store data, silly.
}

function stream_stat()
{
    return false;
}


}

// We put the stream wrapper registration here, with the wrapper it
// registers, to save the hassle of remembering to register it every
// time we include the file.
//
// This of course assumes that we're never tempted to use the same
// wrapper protocol (nzmg) for different types of stream.
stream_wrapper_register('nzmg', 'orthophoto_stream');
?>
```

As noted by the last line in the code, this class is registered with the "nzmg" protocol. The full format for an nzmg URL as implemented here is nzmg://nnnnnnneeeeeeerrrrrrr, with seven digits specifying each of the northing (a certain number of meters between 6460000 and 6489750 for Auckland), easting (meters between 2650000 and 2689750), and radius (also in meters, although there's little point asking for anything larger than 20000, as that is the diagonal length of the entire 16 × 12 kilometer image).

The reason why position is given in terms of "northing" and "easting" rather than latitude and longitude is because with the Earth being neither a perfect sphere nor even an especially symmetrical spheroid, conversion from one to the other is by no means trivial. The New Zealand Map Grid employed in the present example was empirically determined and the resulting latitude/longitude-northing/easting mapping involves such things as evaluating a six-degree complex polynomial. (The precise specification from the Surveyor-General's Office is available as OSG Technical Report 4.1, and can be obtained from the LINZ website.) It's not relevant to the objective of this example, any more so than the exercise of mapping landmarks and delivery addresses to coordinates. Nor, for that matter, is the question of input data validation, including limiting the radius to something more sensible than 20 kilometers. All such specific tasks should be dealt with before reaching this stage, leaving it as broadly applicable as possible.

The imagery is stored as a collection of PNG files, each 100 × 100 pixels in size, corresponding to 250 × 250 meters in the real world, so there are 19,200 such files in total. Each is named according to the northing and easting of their southwest (bottom left) corner. Northings increase upwards, and eastings increase towards the right. Since northings and eastings are themselves measured in meters (that's what they're for), the tile immediately north of 64700002660000.png will be 64702502660000.png, and the tile immediately east would be 64700002660250.png. The tiles have been positioned so that the northings and eastings they're known by are all multiples of 250. Since this property is shared by the parent image, the dimensions of which are also multiples of 100 pixels, these tiles cover the parent image exactly.

Again, most of the work is done in stream_open(), determining the size of the requested image, which tile contains its lower-left pixel, and how many tiles are required vertically and horizontally. GD Lib is used to create a new image (since the imagery is grayscale, there is no need to use truecolor) of the intended size, and then a pair of nested loops reads appropriate tiles from disk and copies them into the image in progress. The total memory consumed at any one time for the storage of image data is sufficient for the image in progress and a single 100 × 100–pixel tile.

The last act of stream_open() is to convert the assembled GD Lib image into PNG data. This is by the simple expedient of asking GD Lib to output the image as a PNG, and using output buffering to capture the result.

Each call of stream_read() returns another chunk of the PNG data, discarding what has already been returned.

Since this is a read-only stream consisting of on-the-fly generated data, most of the remaining stream-access methods are meaningless. One thing that can be said about the data is how much remains available for reading; allowing stream_tell() to be defined.

Code that uses this class need know nothing about what it's doing to match nzmg:// requests with responses. For all it cares, nzmg://6482089266677120000500 is just another file, one that happens to contain a PNG image of a 1 kilometer–wide snapshot of central Auckland.

But hold on. If it's just PNG data, and it's just a file, then for all intents and purposes it *is* just a PNG file. Precisely. Here is an example of the wrapper being used. With the class in its own orthophoto_stream.php file, it assumes that latitude and longitude have been converted to northing and easting, and that the radius isn't too large or small.

```
include_once('orthophoto_stream.php'); // the class has to be declared before
                                       // it can be used, of course.
function display_orthophoto($northing, $easting, $radius)
{
    $filename = sprintf('nzmg://%07d%07d%07d', $northing, $easting, $radius);

    // All the stream-based stuff happens here.
    $image = imagecreatefrompng($filename);

    // A bit of post-processing to raise this code above triviality.
    // Draw a circle of the specified radius (the image is a square, after
    // all), and place a cross at the centre.
    // We need to find the image's white value
    $white = imagecolorexact($image, 255, 255, 255);
    if($white==-1) // Okay, it's not already there.
        $white = imagecolorallocate($image, 255, 255, 255);
    // The circle is centered on the image, and is just large enough to
    // touch the sides.
    $imagesize = imagesx($image);
    $middle = $imagesize>>1;
    imageellipse($image, $middle, $middle, $imagesize, $imagesize, $white);
    imageline($image, $middle, $middle+5, $middle, $middle-5, $white);
    imageline($image, $middle+5, $middle, $middle-5, $middle, $white);
    imagestring($image, 0, 0, 0,
                'Sourced from Orthophoto R11 Auckland Crown Copyright Reserved.',
                $white);
    imagepng($image);
    imagedestroy($image);
}
```

Needless to say, this example has been constructed as a compromise between real-world and pedagogical use, and there are plenty of directions in which the orthophoto_stream class could be improved.

One is that the supplied 21-digit filename could have an extension attached to indicate the desired image format, rather than remain fixed on PNG generation. Others include a more realistic (or at least flexible) storage mechanism that users control through a more fully-developed URL including hostnames and paths. Consider also the possibility of moving some of the tile-reading work into `stream_read()`, thus cutting down on the amount of image data that needs to be retained at any given time. (Observe, however, that since GD Lib proffers only complete images, you'll be required to write your own code to output image data that is correct, yet incomplete pending future input.)

You would be serving yourself well if you follow the URL system for naming stream resources, as defined in RFC 3986, with guidelines given in RFC 2718. There may in fact already be a naming scheme in use that matches your application. (The official registry is maintained by the Internet Assigned Numbers Authority at `http://www.iana.org/assignments/uri-schemes`.) If there is, use it. Then your application will cooperate with other applications in the future that use the same scheme without needing an extra layer of URL conversion to glue them together. (Actually, the same goes for any data format or communications protocol — if the rest of the world already has an agreed-upon standard for what you want, use it and save yourself the time and effort of creating a new one.)

> Note that all PHP URLs require the use of `://` after the scheme name, regardless of whether or not there is a naming authority (host) involved, as PHP uses that character sequence to distinguish URLs from local file paths. In RFC 3986's terms, PHP only implements the first production of the four given for the "hier-part" component and leaves the "naming-authority" component optional. The RFC-compliant workaround would be to use `:///`, implicitly specifying the local host as the naming authority.

Summary

This has been a brief tour of some of the more underutilized areas of PHP's native function set. By using this functionality your code can be more compact and more reliable without sacrificing legibility. Array functions can often be used in place of sometimes complex loops, reducing the task to a single line of code and a helper function that can be captured and stored in a library for reuse. Function-handling functions allow you to decide at runtime not only which function you wish to use (a switch statement could do that), but also decide which functions are in this list you wish to select from, or even create the function from scratch. Streams allow you to hide the implementation details of how external data is read or written, allowing the rest of your program to be able to treat it as just another file.

There are always new features being added to PHP — new initialization settings to fine-tune its operation, new arguments to existing functions that enhance their utility (even the venerable function `str_replace()` has been given a new argument in PHP5), new functions, and even whole new categories of functions. All this makes learning PHP an ongoing affair in which there is always something you don't know about yet.

Advanced MySQL

One of the key elements of most dynamic websites is the database that feeds it. From a simple news page, to an elaborate publishing system or CMS, the database plays a central role in the management of a site's content. To keep a site running smoothly, it helps to know a few tips and tricks of the database system. In this chapter, you'll learn how to create your databases, manage the various user accounts that will access the system, and combine and optimize your SQL code to perform complex and intricate queries.

The Basics, Revisited

Before tackling the more advanced features, here's a quick review of MySQL usage. Pretend you've just landed a new client, a car dealership. The manager at the dealership wants you to create a website that will help them keep track of their car inventories. No problem, you say, and you sit down and begin planning out their web application.

During your planning, you come up with a simple multi-table database scheme to hold the data for their car lots. For the purposes of these exercises, you've decided to create database tables that resemble Figure 4.1.

What you've created is a very simple database structure that involves four tables. In the New_Vehicles table, you'll be storing data for, obviously enough, new cars. Properties such as mileage, price, color, and description can be specified for each car in stock. The Used_Vehicles table has a nearly identical structure to New_Vehicles, but is designed to hold records for, as you might guess, used cars. The Used_Vehicles table has a couple additional columns provided to indicate whether the vehicle is certified or has a warranty, and a column for mileage. The last two tables, Make and Model, store common make and model designations for the various brands the dealer sells.

Makes	
make_id	int
make_name	varchar(100)

Models	
model_id	int
model_name	varchar(200)
make_id	int

New_Vehicles	
vehicle_id	int
model_id	int
modelyear	int
price	decimal(10,2)
color	varchar(200)
description	text

Used_Vehicles	
vehicle_id	int
model_id	int
modelyear	int
mileage	int
price	decimal(10,2)
color	varchar(200)
certified	tinyint
warranty	tinyint
description	text

Figure 4.1

Creating the Databases

The first thing you're going to need to do is create the database and tables in MySQL. Begin by starting up your MySQL client at the command line, or if you have another program you feel more comfortable with, and can enter MySQL commands directly, feel free to use that.

```
shell$ mysql
```

This will bring up the MySQL monitor, which should look similar to the following (if you're using the command-line client):

```
Welcome to the MySQL monitor.  Commands end with ; or \g.
Your MySQL connection id is 2 to server version: 4.1.11-log

Type 'help;' or '\h' for help. Type '\c' to clear the buffer.

mysql>
```

In many situations, you'll need to use a login name and password to access the MySQL client. To do so, just add –u username –p at the end of the mysql command, and MySQL will prompt you for the password, like so:

```
shell$ mysql -u username -p
```

Using the MySQL command-line client is a great way to become familiar with most of the commands and functionality of MySQL, which often times might be automated in a GUI client.

Enter the following commands to create the database, and call it "VehicleInventory":

```
mysql> CREATE DATABASE VehicleInventory;
```

Now that you've created the database, you need to set it as the active database for the remainder of your queries:

```
mysql> USE VehicleInventory;
```

Next, create the tables for your database. The basic SQL statement to create a table in MySQL is:

```
CREATE TABLE tablename (column_definitions);
```

To create the four vehicle information tables, you can use the following:

```
mysql> CREATE TABLE Makes (make_id int PRIMARY KEY AUTO_INCREMENT, make_name
varchar(100) );
mysql> CREATE TABLE Models (model_id int PRIMARY KEY AUTO_INCREMENT, model_name
varchar(200), make_id int );
mysql> CREATE TABLE New_Vehicles (vehicle_id int PRIMARY KEY AUTO_INCREMENT,
model_id int, modelyear int, price decimal(10,2), color varchar(200), description
text );
mysql> CREATE TABLE Used_Vehicles (vehicle_id int PRIMARY KEY AUTO_INCREMENT,
model_id int, modelyear int, mileage int, price decimal(10,2), color varchar(200),
certified tinyint, warranty tinyint, description text );
```

In a nutshell, you simply use the MySQL CREATE TABLE command, followed by the name of the table, and then list the column names and types in parentheses. You'll also note that an auto-incrementing primary key is added to each table, to help you uniquely identify rows after they are added.

Adding Information

Now that you've got your tables created, you need to add some data to them. For that, you're going to use the INSERT statement. The MySQL INSERT command typically follows this format:

```
INSERT INTO tablename (column_list) VALUES (new_values);
```

Start by adding some initial data to the Makes table:

```
INSERT INTO Makes (make_id, make_name) VALUES (1, 'Ford'), (2, 'Honda'), (3,
'Volkswagen'), (4, 'Toyota'), (5, 'Chevrolet');
```

Here, the basic SQL INSERT syntax is used, but with an added twist. In MySQL, you can specify a comma-delimited set of column values, instead of just one set, to populate multiple rows at once. Normally, you might leave out the make_id column when inserting into the Makes table — the auto-incremented ID would automatically assign them a number. In this case, you specify the ID so the rows you'll soon add to other tables will have valid foreign keys.

Use the following to add data to the rest of the tables (remember you can download this code at www.wrox.com and save yourself some typing if you'd like):

```
INSERT INTO Models (model_id, model_name, make_id) VALUES (1, 'Explorer', 1), (2,
'Accord', 2), (3, 'Golf', 3), (4, 'Tacoma', 4), (5, 'Corvette', 5);
INSERT INTO New_Vehicles (model_id, modelyear, color, description) VALUES
(1, 2005, 'Dark Blue', 'Popular SUV; great for moving people or cargo across town,
or wherever your adventures may take you.'),
(NULL, 2004, 'Graphite Pearl', 'Last of the 2004 stock! Must sell! Loaded, all
options!'),
(4, 2005, 'Radiant Red', 'Come drive this terrific truck! 4WD, extended cab, many
options.'),
(5, 2005, 'Daytona Sunset Orange Metallic', 'The all new C6 Corvette, the next
generation of classic American sportscars. 400HP V8; Very fast!'),
(1, 2005, 'Dark Blue', 'Popular SUV; great for moving people or cargo across town,
or wherever your adventures may take you.');
INSERT INTO Used_Vehicles (model_id, modelyear, color, mileage, certified,
warranty, description) VALUES
(1, 2000, 'White', 64800, 0, 0, 'Good condition; One owner; 4WD, V6'),
(2, 2003, 'Deep Green Pearl', 27300, 0, 1, 'Excellent condition, off-lease vehicle;
Must see!'),
(3, 2004, 'Reflex Silver', 3800, 1, 1, 'R32 Limited edition; Low miles; Understated
and surprisingly functional; Loaded.'),
(4, 1993, 'Red', 152000, 0, 0, 'Runs decent; 4WD; Tinted windows, aftermarket
stereo; Needs a little TLC.');
```

Note that there is a NULL value for the model_id of the second vehicle you added to the New_Vehicles table. You'll find out why later on.

Retrieving Information

You've spent all that time creating your database tables and populating them with data; now it's time to get some of that data back out. For this, you will use the SELECT statement. A simplified form of SELECT looks something like this:

```
SELECT [column_names] FROM [table] WHERE [criteria]
```

If you wanted to retrieve a list of the colors of your used cars, for example, you would use something similar to the following:

```
SELECT color FROM Used_Vehicles;
```

which would return the following:

```
+------------------+
| color            |
+------------------+
| White            |
| Deep Green Pearl |
| Reflex Silver    |
| Red              |
+------------------+
```

Or perhaps, you want a listing of all the mileages for cars older than the 2001 model year:

```
SELECT mileage, modelyear FROM Used_Vehicles WHERE modelyear < 2001;
```

Running this query shows the following:

```
+---------+-----------+
| mileage | modelyear |
+---------+-----------+
|   64800 |      2000 |
|  152000 |      1993 |
+---------+-----------+
```

Simple enough, but what if you spotted an error, and wanted to change an existing record?

Updating Information

To update information you use the UPDATE statement. The generic form of an UPDATE statement looks like this:

```
UPDATE [table] SET [column]=[value] WHERE [criteria]
```

Returning to the vehicle inventory example, say that one day the manager of the car lot was out looking through the inventory, and noticed the mileage was incorrectly recorded for one of the vehicles. To change it to the proper value, you might use the following query:

```
UPDATE Used_Vehicles SET mileage=66000 WHERE vehicle_id=1;
```

In this case, the vehicle ID of 1 corresponds to the automatically incremented ID assigned to the used Ford Explorer you added in a previous INSERT statement.

Removing Information

Sales are starting to increase at the hypothetical car lot, and some recent sales require the removal of some vehicles from your database. In this situation, you will use the DELETE statement:

```
DELETE FROM [table] WHERE [criteria];
```

That used Ford Explorer that had its incorrect mileage fixed in the previous example sold today. To remove if from the Used_Vehicles table, you would simply do the following:

```
DELETE FROM Used_Vehicles WHERE vehicle_id=1;
```

That should cover the basics of MySQL usage, so it's time to move on to more powerful queries.

Querying Multiple Tables

You've got your vehicle inventory set up, and you can use the basics to perform simple queries against one table at a time. But you'd like to see a little more — maybe even a query that links the make and model of each car to its individual record. For this, you'd use *joins*.

In SQL, joins are a way of linking two or more tables on a specified column or columns. In MySQL, there are two types of joins that are most commonly used: inner joins and outer joins.

Inner Joins

Inner joins are a way of taking two tables and combining their rows based on a commonly shared value for each row. When you perform an inner join in a SELECT query, you simply specify the tables to be joined in the FROM clause, and provide a hint on what columns they have in common. A generic abstraction of the MySQL INNER JOIN syntax looks like the following:

```
SELECT [column names] FROM [table1] INNER JOIN [table2] ON [table1.column] =
[table2.column]
```

Using the hypothetical car lot inventory, you want the model of each vehicle to return in the results alongside each vehicle's specific information. To accomplish this, your query would look something like this:

```
SELECT Models.model_name, New_Vehicles.color, New_Vehicles.modelyear FROM Models
INNER JOIN New_Vehicles ON Models.model_id = New_Vehicles.model_id;
```

Running this query against your database yields the following results:

```
+------------+-------------------------------+-----------+
| model_name | color                         | modelyear |
+------------+-------------------------------+-----------+
| Explorer   | Dark Blue                     |      2005 |
| Tacoma     | Radiant Red                   |      2005 |
| Corvette   | Daytona Sunset Orange Metallic |      2005 |
+------------+-------------------------------+-----------+
```

You'll notice the in the SELECT query, each of the columns in the select list is prefixed with the name of the table they belong to. While this is not technically required, it is usually a good idea to help avoid conflicts between identically named columns. What would happen if you had such a conflict and neglected the table prefix? Take a look at this example:

```
SELECT model_id, model_name, color, modelyear FROM Models INNER JOIN New_Vehicles
ON Models.model_id = New_Vehicles.model_id;
```

As you can see the table prefixes have been removed, but the model_id column has also been added to the list (because it exists in both tables). Now try to run that query. You'll get the following error:

```
ERROR 1052 (23000): Column 'model_id' in field list is ambiguous
```

Trying to use a column name that exists in both tables, without using a table prefix, will throw such an error whenever the query is executed.

If you happen to like brevity in your SQL queries, have no fear — there's a simple way you can shorten all of those table prefixes. In the FROM clause, you can specify a table *alias* for each table called, like so:

```
SELECT [column names] FROM [table1] alias1 INNER JOIN [table2] alias2 ON
[alias1.column] = [alias2.column]
```

And because table aliases can be as short as a single letter, you can drastically shorten your inventory query:

```
SELECT m.model_name, n.color, n.modelyear FROM Models m INNER JOIN New_Vehicles n
ON m.model_id = n.model_id;
```

Not short enough for you? Well, there's yet another way to tidy up your joins. MySQL provides you with the USING statement, to substitute for the ON statement to link your tables. Use the USING statement when the two linking columns happen to share the exact same column name. A generalized form of inner join with USING looks like the following:

```
SELECT [column names] FROM [table1] INNER JOIN [table2] USING (column list)
```

Because the New_Vehicles table and Models table both have a model_id column, you can use the USING statement in your join:

```
SELECT m.model_name, n.color, n.modelyear FROM Models m INNER JOIN New_Vehicles n
USING (model_id);
```

In some situations, you will need to join more than two tables together in a query. MySQL can handle this easy enough — all you have to do is chain your joins next to each other in the order you want them evaluated. In the vehicle inventory database, you'll need to use multiple joins to return the make of each vehicle with its record, like so:

```
SELECT ma.make_name, mo.model_name, n.color, n.modelyear FROM Makes ma INNER JOIN
Models mo USING (make_id) INNER JOIN New_Vehicles n USING (model_id);
```

When you run this query, you should see the following:

```
+-----------+------------+-------------------------------+-----------+
| make_name | model_name | color                         | modelyear |
+-----------+------------+-------------------------------+-----------+
| Ford      | Explorer   | Dark Blue                     |      2005 |
| Toyota    | Tacoma     | Radiant Red                   |      2005 |
| Chevrolet | Corvette   | Daytona Sunset Orange Metallic |     2005 |
+-----------+------------+-------------------------------+-----------+
```

As you can see, the Makes table was joined to the Models table based on the make_id, and then the result of that join was joined against the New_Vehicles table, giving you the make, model, and vehicle information all in one query.

Before moving on to the next group of joins, you should know that there is another way to do inner joins. The second way simply specifies multiple tables in a comma-delimited list, and uses the WHERE statement to specify how the tables are linked. A generic form of this type of inner join looks like this:

```
SELECT [column names] FROM table1, table2 WHERE table1.column = table2.column
```

If you were to use this form of inner join on the previous query to pull up a list of new vehicles, makes, and models, it would look something like this:

```
SELECT ma.make_name, mo.model_name, n.color, n.modelyear FROM Makes ma, Models mo,
New_Vehicles n WHERE ma.make_id = mo.make_id AND mo.model_id = n.model_id;
```

Execute this query in your MySQL client, and it returns the following:

```
+-----------+------------+------------------------------------+-----------+
| make_name | model_name | color                              | modelyear |
+-----------+------------+------------------------------------+-----------+
| Ford      | Explorer   | Dark Blue                          |      2005 |
| Toyota    | Tacoma     | Radiant Red                        |      2005 |
| Chevrolet | Corvette   | Daytona Sunset Orange Metallic     |      2005 |
+-----------+------------+------------------------------------+-----------+
```

As you can see, the exact same results were retuned as when you used an explicit inner join. What would have happened if you had left off the items in the WHERE clause? Try out this query:

```
SELECT mo.model_name, n.color, n.modelyear FROM Models mo, New_Vehicles n;
```

Running this query against our vehicle inventory produces the following (note that the Makes table has been excluded):

```
+------------+--------------------------------+-----------+
| model_name | color                          | modelyear |
+------------+--------------------------------+-----------+
| Accord     | Dark Blue                      |      2005 |
| Golf       | Dark Blue                      |      2005 |
| Tacoma     | Dark Blue                      |      2005 |
| Corvette   | Dark Blue                      |      2005 |
| Explorer   | Dark Blue                      |      2005 |
| Accord     | Graphite Pearl                 |      2004 |
| Golf       | Graphite Pearl                 |      2004 |
| Tacoma     | Graphite Pearl                 |      2004 |
| Corvette   | Graphite Pearl                 |      2004 |
| Explorer   | Graphite Pearl                 |      2004 |
| Accord     | Radiant Red                    |      2005 |
| Golf       | Radiant Red                    |      2005 |
| Tacoma     | Radiant Red                    |      2005 |
| Corvette   | Radiant Red                    |      2005 |
| Explorer   | Radiant Red                    |      2005 |
| Accord     | Daytona Sunset Orange Metallic |      2005 |
| Golf       | Daytona Sunset Orange Metallic |      2005 |
| Tacoma     | Daytona Sunset Orange Metallic |      2005 |
| Corvette   | Daytona Sunset Orange Metallic |      2005 |
| Explorer   | Daytona Sunset Orange Metallic |      2005 |
| Accord     | Dark Blue                      |      2005 |
| Golf       | Dark Blue                      |      2005 |
| Tacoma     | Dark Blue                      |      2005 |
| Corvette   | Dark Blue                      |      2005 |
| Explorer   | Dark Blue                      |      2005 |
+------------+--------------------------------+-----------+
```

That's not quite right. What happened in this situation is actually a different kind of join called a *cross join*. A cross join is simply a combination of every matching result in each table. In this case, there were five models in the Models table, so each one of those rows was matched up against *every single row* in the New_Vehicles table. This happened simply because you left off the WHERE statement, which provided the hint to MySQL about how to link records together. As previously noted, you didn't include the Makes table partying this query — if you had, the resulting rows would have been five times as long, as there are five distinct makes in your database.

Outer Joins

While most complex linking can be achieved using inner joins, there are some situations where they are limited. If a database row does not have a value defined for the column being linked, it will be ignored by inner joins. In the vehicle inventory example, every time you queried the table using an inner join to link the Models table, only three rows were returned. The fourth vehicle in the New_Vehicles table was ignored, because its value for model_id was null. What you need is a way to return all rows, whether or not there is a model_id specified, and if a model_id is specified, perform the requested joins. For such a task, MySQL provides *outer joins*.

There are two main types of outer joins in MySQL: left outer joins and right outer joins. They behave identically, the only difference pertaining to which table is allowed to not contain matches. The generic form of an outer join is very similar to inner joins. Take this simplified version of a left outer join:

```
SELECT [column names] FROM table1 LEFT OUTER JOIN table2 USING (column list)
```

The left outer join matches the "right" table (table2) against the "left" table (table1) using a common column name or names, but will still return rows if the "left" table contains a value that doesn't match any in the "right" column. A right outer join behaves the same way, but with the roles of the two tables reversed (non-matching values are allowed in the right table).

In the vehicle inventory example, if you wanted to return a set of rows where all new vehicles were returned, regardless of their model_id, you might use the following:

```
SELECT mo.model_name, n.color, n.modelyear FROM New_Vehicles n LEFT OUTER JOIN
Models mo USING (model_id);
```

Querying the vehicle inventory database with this query produces the following:

```
+------------+-------------------------------+-----------+
| model_name | color                         | modelyear |
+------------+-------------------------------+-----------+
| Explorer   | Dark Blue                     |      2005 |
| NULL       | Graphite Pearl                |      2004 |
| Tacoma     | Radiant Red                   |      2005 |
| Corvette   | Daytona Sunset Orange Metallic |     2005 |
| Explorer   | Dark Blue                     |      2005 |
+------------+-------------------------------+-----------+
```

This is very similar to one of the earlier inner join queries you looked at, but with the addition of the second row — Graphite Pearl, from the 2004 model year. Because there was no match in the Models table, MySQL returns NULL for the values in the row that could not be determined — in this case, model_name.

Outer joins and inner joins do not, however, have to live apart from one another. Both can be combined in a single query, to yield powerful multi-table joins that are lenient on requiring all data to match for all rows. To pull a list of new vehicles' colors, makes, models, and models years, including those that do not have models specified, perform a query similar to this:

```
SELECT ma.make_name, mo.model_name, n.color, n.modelyear FROM New_Vehicles n LEFT
OUTER JOIN Models mo USING (model_id) LEFT OUTER JOIN Makes ma USING (make_id);
```

Running this against the vehicle inventory database returns this:

```
+-----------+------------+-------------------------------+-----------+
| make_name | model_name | color                         | modelyear |
+-----------+------------+-------------------------------+-----------+
| Ford      | Explorer   | Dark Blue                     |      2005 |
| NULL      | NULL       | Graphite Pearl                |      2004 |
| Toyota    | Tacoma     | Radiant Red                   |      2005 |
| Chevrolet | Corvette   | Daytona Sunset Orange Metallic|      2005 |
| Ford      | Explorer   | Dark Blue                     |      2005 |
+-----------+------------+-------------------------------+-----------+
```

Note that in this query, the order in which the tables are joined is important. The resulting table from the first join is used as an internal temporary table when joined against the third table.

Unions

Up until now, the queries you've been performing on the vehicle inventory database have been returning records for only one type of vehicle, either new or used. What if you wanted to get a list of *all* vehicles in the database, regardless of previous ownership status? Initially, you might think it's as easy as adding both tables to the query, but that would result in a cross join — not exactly what you're looking for. For this situation, you'll need to use *unions*.

Unions in MySQL are a way to return multiple tables as a single record, without combining them. Unions are akin to concatenation in PHP — they simply add the additional rows to the tail end of the first table. A generalization of unions in MySQL looks like this:

```
(SELECT [column names] FROM [table1]) UNION (SELECT [column names] FROM [table2])
```

Simply put, unions are performed by gluing two separate SELECT statements together with the word UNION. In the code abstraction, parentheses were placed around each of the SELECT statements. While not required, it's generally a good idea to help visually differentiate the two queries.

Assume you wanted to return a list of all the vehicles in the vehicle inventory, regardless whether they are new or used. Use a query similar to the following:

```
(SELECT color, modelyear, model_id FROM New_Vehicles) UNION (SELECT color,
modelyear, model_id FROM Used_Vehicles);
```

If you run this query in MySQL, you should see the following:

```
+--------------------------------+-----------+----------+
| color                          | modelyear | model_id |
+--------------------------------+-----------+----------+
| Dark Blue                      |      2005 |        1 |
| Graphite Pearl                 |      2004 |     NULL |
| Radiant Red                    |      2005 |        4 |
| Daytona Sunset Orange Metallic |      2005 |        5 |
| Deep Green Pearl               |      2003 |        2 |
| Reflex Silver                  |      2004 |        3 |
| Red                            |      1993 |        4 |
+--------------------------------+-----------+----------+
```

Notice that the query specifies exactly what columns you want to return from each table and the number of columns in the list must match across tables. What would happen if you selected a different number of columns for each table? Take a look at this query, in which you will select all records from each table (the Used_Vehicle table having more columns than the New_Vehicles table):

```
(SELECT * FROM New_Vehicles) UNION (SELECT * FROM Used_Vehicles);
```

Try to run this query against the database, and it will return the following:

```
ERROR 1222 (21000): The used SELECT statements have a different number of columns
```

MySQL quickly returns an error letting you know that your column lists are different lengths. Any combination of columns in the list will be valid, as long as there is the same number of columns in each list. If there are differently named columns in each corresponding location in the column lists, MySQL will use the name of the column from the first list when returning rows. Take a look at the following query:

```
(SELECT color FROM New_Vehicles) UNION (SELECT modelyear FROM Used_Vehicles);
```

When the database is queried, it will show the following:

```
+--------------------------------+
| color                          |
+--------------------------------+
| Dark Blue                      |
| Graphite Pearl                 |
| Radiant Red                    |
| Daytona Sunset Orange Metallic |
| 2003                           |
| 2004                           |
| 1993                           |
+--------------------------------+
```

As expected, MySQL used the color name for the column, from the first column list. This example, however, illustrates one possible future point of confusion. The column type for color in the tables was set as a varchar, but the column type for modelyear is an int. When performing a union of the two tables, MySQL disregards the column type and happily combines the tables. This might not necessarily be a problem in most situations, but if you're enforcing referential integrity outside of MySQL (in PHP perhaps), there might be conflicts if the external code is expecting a specific type of return data, and MySQL sends a mixed result such as this.

A simple list of the colors and model years of all the vehicles is nice, but the owner of the car lot expects a little more from you. In addition to returning the colors and model years, you need to provide the make and model as well. You go to happily add the necessary joins to your new unioned tables, using a query that might look like this:

```
(SELECT color, modelyear, model_id FROM New_Vehicles) UNION (SELECT color,
modelyear, model_id FROM Used_Vehicles) LEFT OUTER JOIN Models USING (model_id)
LEFT OUTER JOIN Makes USING (make_id);
```

It looks good, you think, until you run it against MySQL and get this:

```
ERROR 1064 (42000): You have an error in your SQL syntax; check the manual that
corresponds to your MySQL server version for the right syntax to use near 'LEFT
OUTER JOIN Models USING (model_id) LEFT OUTER JOIN Makes USING (make_id)' at line 1
```

What happened? The UNION operation itself is not equivalent to a normal resultset from a table, so you can't simply append the requisite joins to look up the extra information. Additionally, you haven't specified the make_name or model_name anywhere to be returned. The solution: you need to add all the joins and extra return columns to each SELECT statement that makes up the UNION.

```
(SELECT ma.make_name, mo.model_name, n.color, n.modelyear FROM New_Vehicles n LEFT
OUTER JOIN Models mo USING (model_id) LEFT OUTER JOIN Makes ma USING (make_id))
UNION (SELECT ma.make_name, mo.model_name, u.color, u.modelyear FROM Used_Vehicles
u LEFT OUTER JOIN Models mo USING (model_id) LEFT OUTER JOIN Makes ma USING
(make_id));
```

Run this sizeable query in MySQL, and you'll see this:

```
+------------+------------+--------------------------------+-----------+
| make_name  | model_name | color                          | modelyear |
+------------+------------+--------------------------------+-----------+
| Ford       | Explorer   | Dark Blue                      |      2005 |
| NULL       | NULL       | Graphite Pearl                 |      2004 |
| Toyota     | Tacoma     | Radiant Red                    |      2005 |
| Chevrolet  | Corvette   | Daytona Sunset Orange Metallic |      2005 |
| Honda      | Accord     | Deep Green Pearl               |      2003 |
| Volkswagen | Golf       | Reflex Silver                  |      2004 |
| Toyota     | Tacoma     | Red                            |      1993 |
+------------+------------+--------------------------------+-----------+
```

What you end up with is a nice concise listing of all the vehicles on the lot, and their make, model, color and model year. You implement this in your inventory application and send it to the dealership for their approval, but you're not done yet. Like many clients, the owner of the dealership is fickle, and has changed his mind once again regarding which fields need to be in the list of vehicles. This time, you need to return all information in the database, for all vehicles. You already know that the New_Vehicles table and Used_Vehicles table have different numbers of columns, so how will a UNION suffice? The answer is quite simple, actually. All you need to do is specify NULL (or any other value you prefer) for any columns that are missing from their corresponding tables, like so:

```
(SELECT ma.make_name, mo.model_name, n.color, n.modelyear, n.price, n.description,
NULL, 1 FROM New_Vehicles n LEFT OUTER JOIN Models mo USING (model_id) LEFT OUTER
JOIN Makes ma USING (make_id)) UNION (SELECT ma.make_name, mo.model_name, u.color,
u.modelyear, u.price, u.description, u.certified, u.warranty FROM Used_Vehicles u
```

```
LEFT OUTER JOIN Models mo USING (model_id) LEFT OUTER JOIN Makes ma USING
(make_id)) \G
```

Run this and you'll see the following:

```
*************************** 1. row ***************************
  make_name: Ford
 model_name: Explorer
      color: Dark Blue
  modelyear: 2005
      price: NULL
description: Popular SUV; great for moving people or cargo across town, or wherever
your adventures may take you.
       NULL: NULL
          1: 1
*************************** 2. row ***************************
  make_name: NULL
 model_name: NULL
      color: Graphite Pearl
  modelyear: 2004
      price: NULL
description: Last of the 2004 stock! Must sell! Loaded, all options!
       NULL: NULL
          1: 1
*************************** 3. row ***************************
  make_name: Toyota
 model_name: Tacoma
      color: Radiant Red
  modelyear: 2005
      price: NULL
description: Come drive this terrific truck! 4WD, extended cab, many options.
       NULL: NULL
          1: 1
*************************** 4. row ***************************
  make_name: Chevrolet
 model_name: Corvette
      color: Daytona Sunset Orange Metallic
  modelyear: 2005
      price: NULL
description: The all new C6 Corvette, the next generation of classic American
sportscars. 400HP V8; Very fast!
       NULL: NULL
          1: 1
*************************** 5. row ***************************
  make_name: Honda
 model_name: Accord
      color: Deep Green Pearl
  modelyear: 2003
      price: NULL
description: Excellent condition, off-lease vehicle; Must see!
       NULL: 0
          1: 1
*************************** 6. row ***************************
  make_name: Volkswagen
 model_name: Golf
```

```
         color: Reflex Silver
     modelyear: 2004
         price: NULL
   description: R32 Limited edition; Low miles; Understated and suprisigly functional;
Loaded.
          NULL: 1
             1: 1
*************************** 7. row ***************************
     make_name: Toyota
    model_name: Tacoma
         color: Red
     modelyear: 1993
         price: NULL
   description: Runs decent; 4WD; Tinted windows, aftermarket stereo; Needs a little
TLC.
          NULL: 0
             1: 0
```

The first thing you'll notice is that it looks a little different than your previous results. This is because of the \G terminator at the end of the query, which causes MySQL to display results vertically (otherwise, the tables would be far too wide for this book). Aside from that, every bit of information is present and accounted for. The NULL value specified for the missing "certified" column in the New_Vehicles table is present, as well as the placeholder value you specified as 1, since all new cars have a warranty. You send the changes back to the client, and they are pleased (for the time being at least).

Full-Text Searching

The owners of the car lot have been impressed so far with your ability to query exactly what they need, give the various listings to help increase the productivity of their sales staff—but they still want more. What they'd like now is a way to search through the car inventories by keyword. Their search needs aren't too complex, but a simple LIKE comparison in a WHERE clause just isn't going to get the job done.

What you need just happens to be built into MySQL—full-text searching. Full-text search, which is enabled by default in MySQL, allows you to perform a natural language search on any text column you specify. You can't just go out and start full-text searching at will in your database, though—you have to do some preparation first.

Enabling Full-Text Searching

Enabling full text searching in MySQL involves simply creating an index on a column or columns for a table. You can do this one of two ways: when the table is created, as part of the CREATE TABLE command, or later on in the life of the table.

Creating a New Table with Full-Text Search Enabled

The first full-text index you're going to create will be part of a brand new table. To specify a full-text index at table-creation time, all you have to do is specify a full-text index and the list of indexed columns at the end of the column specifications:

```
CREATE TABLE tablename (column_specs, FULLTEXT (columns_to_index) )
```

You can specify a single column in the FULLTEXT column list, or multiple columns in a comma-delimited list. It's time to actually create a table with full-text searching in the VehicleInventory database:

```
CREATE TABLE testft (testint int, testvc varchar(50), testtxt text, FULLTEXT
(testvc, testtxt) );
```

You've just created a new table with a full-text index on the testvc and testtxt columns.

Altering an Existing Table to Support Full-Text Search

Modifying an existing table to support full-text searching is a little bit trickier, but not by much. To add full-text search capability for an existing table, you use MySQL's ALTER TABLE command, like so:

```
ALTER TABLE tablename ADD FULLTEXT (columns)
```

Now add a full-text index to the New_Vehicles table:

```
ALTER TABLE New_Vehicles ADD FULLTEXT (description);
```

Once that's done, it's time to put these indexes to good use.

Querying Using Full-Text Search

Searching through a table in MySQL with full-text indexing enabled is a relatively painless process. All you need to do is use the MATCH() function in a WHERE clause, like so:

```
SELECT [columns] FROM [table] WHERE MATCH ([indexed_columns]) AGAINST ('keyword')
```

Inside the parameter list for MATCH, you can specify any number of columns, as long as they are part of a full-text index.

Returning to the vehicle inventory database, it's time to perform a search on the list of new vehicles. To search for the word "options," you can use the following:

```
SELECT vehicle_id, description FROM New_Vehicles WHERE MATCH (description) AGAINST
('options');
```

Which should return the following:

```
+------------+---------------------------------------------------------------+
| vehicle_id | description                                                   |
+------------+---------------------------------------------------------------+
|          2 | Last of the 2004 stock! Must sell! Loaded, all options!       |
|          3 | Come drive this popular truck! 4WD, extended cab, many options. |
+------------+---------------------------------------------------------------+
```

Another neat trick that full-text searching can do is order the items by relevance, and return the relevance as well. To utilize relevance data, you can use the MATCH() ... AGAINST() functions in both the SELECT list and the ORDER BY clause, like so:

```
SELECT MATCH (description) AGAINST('options') AS relevance, description FROM
New_Vehicles WHERE MATCH (description) AGAINST ('options') ORDER BY MATCH
(description) AGAINST('options') \G
```

Which returns the following:

```
*************************** 1. row ***************************
  relevance: 0.38341856002808
description: Last of the 2004 stock! Must sell! Loaded, all options!
*************************** 2. row ***************************
  relevance: 0.38341856002808
description: Come drive this popular truck! 4WD, extended cab, many options.
```

Limitations

When using full-text search, there are a few limitations you must keep in mind. First, MySQL supports
only full-text indexes on MyISAM table types (covered in the next section). Second, in most situations, if
you create a full-text index on more than one column, the list of columns you provide to MATCH() must
be the exact same list you specified when you created the full-text index. Last, MySQL has a default minimum word/token length of four characters. If you try to match a full-text search against a keyword that
has three or fewer letters, no results will be returned.

To change the default minimum full-text word length, make sure the following exists in your MySQL
configuration file (my.cnf):

```
[mysqld]
ft_min_word_len=3
```

You may use any integer for the minimum length (set to 3 in this example).

InnoDB Tables

One of the advantages to using MySQL is that you're not limited to a certain storage engine for your data.
What's a storage engine? MySQL, as a server, provides the user with a consistent interface and querying
language, but is only loosely coupled with the way it actually stores the data on the disk. The different
storage engines in MySQL provide differing ways to store and access the data, from the trusty default
MyISAM, to the sizzling speed of in-memory Heap tables, and all stops in between. One of the most flexible and powerful table types you can use is InnoDB. The InnoDB storage engine, created by Innobase Oy
in Helsinki, Finland, provides MySQL with a safe and efficient way to store and process data, and gives
MySQL some additional functionality not present with MyISAM or most of the other table types.

InnoDB Advantages

Although the default MyISAM table type gives you a mature and speedy way to store simple data structures, it is lacking a handful of the features that many developers want — and InnoDB can provide.
Available by default since MySQL 4.0, InnoDB tables give you the ability to use transactions, row-level
locking, and best of all, foreign key constraints.

Foreign key constraints provide a way to maintain referential integrity across linked tables. In the VehicleInventory database, the New_Vehicles and Used_Vehicles tables contain a column for model_id, to specify the model, and subsequently, the make, for each vehicle. A foreign key constraint could be applied to the model_id column to guarantee that no value could be inserted into that column that didn't exist already in the Models table. In the default MyISAM table type, there is no way for MySQL to automatically enforce such a rule, and in larger databases that could lead to large quantities of invalid values in the tables. InnoDB provides MySQL with a way to enforce such a rule, so data always stays relevant.

Foreign-key-constrained columns allow only values that exist in the referenced table, with one exception, NULL. A value of NULL is permitted in columns that are otherwise controlled by a foreign key.

InnoDB Disadvantages

Unfortunately, the benefits of InnoDB come with a couple of particularly bothersome problems. First, InnoDB tables do not support full-text searching. When you're deciding whether or not to use InnoDB, you must always consider the need for full-text indexing in the future, and whether it is more important than referential integrity on a given table.

Second, the InnoDB storage engine is slightly limited with regards to AUTO_INCREMENT columns. InnoDB tables do not allow you to specify the initial value of the auto-increment sequence when creating a table. Not necessarily a show-stopper, but it's something to keep in mind when designing your database schema.

Using InnoDB

The best way to get to know the InnoDB storage engine is to put it to work. Now you're going to enable the InnoDB engine by both creating a new table from scratch as well as altering an additional table. After that you're going to experiment with the different aspects of foreign keys.

Creating an InnoDB Table from Scratch

Creating a new table using the InnoDB storage engine is barely any different than creating a standard MyISAM table. The only key difference is you must specify the ENGINE at the end of the create table command:

```
CREATE TABLE tablename (column_definitions) ENGINE=InnoDB;
```

Pretty easy, right? Try it out for real in your MySQL database:

```
CREATE TABLE innodbtest (innocol int) ENGINE=InnoDB;
```

If everything goes smoothly, you should see the following:

```
Query OK, 0 rows affected
```

And with that, you've created a simple InnoDB table.

Converting an Existing MyISAM Table

Creating a new InnoDB table from scratch is all fine and dandy, but you've got a handful of tables that you'd love to see use the InnoDB storage engine. What you need is a way to convert those tables from the default MyISAM table type. Luckily, changing the storage engine for a table in MySQL is a simple task — just use the ALTER TABLE command and re-specify the engine for a table. To convert the New_Vehicles table, which is currently using the default table type of MyISAM, you use the following:

```
ALTER TABLE New_Vehicles ENGINE=InnoDB;
```

Run this command against your database, and you will see this:

```
ERROR 1214 (HY000): The used table type doesn't support FULLTEXT indexes
```

Instead of converting your tables as you'd expect, MySQL has given you an error message. As mentioned earlier, InnoDB tables do not currently support full-text indexing in MySQL. If you try to convert a MyISAM table with a defined full-text index to InnoDB, you will get this message. For the purposes of this exercise, you're going to need to delete the full-text index so you can convert the table:

```
ALTER TABLE New_Vehicles DROP INDEX description;
```

And now you should be able to go ahead and convert the table:

```
ALTER TABLE New_Vehicles ENGINE=InnoDB;
```

This time, you query should succeed, and you will see something similar to the following:

```
Query OK, 4 rows affected (0.76 sec)
Records: 4  Duplicates: 0  Warnings: 0
```

Foreign Keys

You wouldn't switch a table from MyISAM to InnoDB without a good reason, and in most cases, foreign keys are as good a reason as any. Once you've set up your InnoDB table, it's only a matter of adding a foreign key to the table to enforce referential integrity. While it sounds simple on the surface, there are a good number of options to consider when creating a foreign key.

The most basic format of the ALTER TABLE command to create a foreign key looks something like this:

```
ALTER TABLE [tablename] ADD CONSTRAINT [key_name] FOREIGN KEY ([indexed_column])
REFERENCES [foreign_table] ((id_column])
```

Starting out, you're telling MySQL what table to change, and what to do (add a foreign key). Using CON-STRAINT [key_name], you can optionally give the key a name, which is often a good idea if you plan on changing the key in the future. The name of the column that requires referential integrity follows in parentheses. After that is the REFERENCES keyword, the name of the foreign table that will be checked against, and the specific column in that foreign table to reference.

To apply this to the vehicle inventory database, add a foreign key named refmdl to the New_Vehicles table, to check the column model_id against the model_id column in the Models table:

```
ALTER TABLE New_Vehicles ADD CONSTRAINT refmdl FOREIGN KEY (model_id) REFERENCES
Models (model_id);
```

Run this command in MySQL and you will see something similar to this:

```
ERROR 1005 (HY000): Can't create table './vehicleinventory/#sql-1951_2.frm' (errno:
150)
```

This time the error message is not as helpful as it could be in tracking down the cause. In this situation, the error was thrown because one of the tables involved in the foreign key does not use the InnoDB engine. You've already converted the New_Vehicles table to InnoDB, but the Models table is still MyISAM. In order for foreign keys to be properly created, both tables involved need to be using the InnoDB engine, so you must change them accordingly:

```
ALTER TABLE Models ENGINE=InnoDB;
```

And then add the foreign key:

```
ALTER TABLE New_Vehicles ADD CONSTRAINT refmdl FOREIGN KEY (model_id) REFERENCES
Models (model_id);
```

Now your foreign key is protecting the model_id column in New_Vehicles from errant data . . . or is it? The easiest way to know for sure is to test it. Try to insert a line into New_Vehicles using a wildly incorrect model_id:

```
INSERT INTO New_Vehicles (model_id) VALUES (12345);
```

When you try to execute this query, it should return the following:

```
ERROR 1216 (23000): Cannot add or update a child row: a foreign key constraint
fails
```

As expected, the foreign key check saw that the value was not in the Models table, and refused to allow the row to be inserted. You've managed to block any new rows with bad data, but what about existing rows that are being altered? Try this query:

```
UPDATE New_Vehicles SET model_id=12345 WHERE vehicle_id=1;
```

As you can see, the foreign key stops errant updates as well:

```
ERROR 1216 (23000): Cannot add or update a child row: a foreign key constraint
fails
```

So the foreign key successfully protects the table from harmful INSERTs and UPDATEs, but what happens when a value is changed in the Models table? Take a look at the following query, where you attempt to change an existing model_id:

```
UPDATE Models SET model_id=123 WHERE model_id=1;
```

When you run this query, you should get the following error:

```
ERROR 1217 (23000): Cannot delete or update a parent row: a foreign key constraint
fails
```

This error simply reflects another of the behaviors associated with a simple InnoDB foreign key: you cannot modify a referenced column if its value is present in the referencing table. What if that behavior is not what you want? As luck would have it, you can specify the update and delete behavior of foreign keys to one of five different options: RESTRICT, CASCADE, SET NULL, NO ACTION, and SET DEFAULT. Here's a quick breakdown of what each behavior means:

❑ RESTRICT is the default behavior. A referenced value cannot be changed or deleted.

❑ CASCADE allows any updates to propagate down to the referencing table. If you updated the model_id in the Models table, it would cascade down to the New_Vehicles table and update any corresponding rows. Note that this can apply to deletes as well (if specified)—deleting a row in a parent table will automatically delete all rows in the child table that referenced that value.

❑ SET NULL changes the value in the child table to NULL when you update the parent value.

❑ NO ACTION simply tells the database to allow the change to the parent table and do nothing to the child table.

❑ SET DEFAULT changes the values in the child table to their DEFAULT values when the parent values are changed or deleted.

Implementing these behaviors is a simple matter of adding the required ON DELETE or ON UPDATE clause to the end of the foreign key definition, like so:

```
ALTER TABLE [tablename] ADD CONSTRAINT [key_name] FOREIGN KEY ([indexed_column])
REFERENCES [foreign_table] ((id_column]) ON UPDATE [update behavior] ON DELETE
[delete behavior]
```

To change an existing key to support different update and delete behaviors, you first have to delete the old key, then recreate the foreign key using the new behaviors. To change the foreign keys on the New_Vehicles table to cascade any updates, and set NULL when a model is deleted, use the following:

```
ALTER TABLE New_Vehicles DROP FOREIGN KEY refmdl;
ALTER TABLE New_Vehicles ADD CONSTRAINT refmdl FOREIGN KEY (model_id) REFERENCES
Models (model_id) ON UPDATE CASCADE ON DELETE SET NULL;
```

Now every time a model_id is changed in the Models table, the new value will be propagated down to all rows in New_Vehicles that used the original value. Have a look for yourself:

```
UPDATE Models SET model_id=123 WHERE model_id=1;
SELECT * FROM New_Vehicles \G
```

The update will succeed, and return something similar to the following:

```
*************************** 1. row ***************************
  vehicle_id: 1
    model_id: 123
       price: NULL
       color: Dark Blue
 description: Popular SUV; great for moving people or cargo across town, or wherever
your adventures may take you.
   modelyear: 2005
```

```
*************************** 2. row ***************************
 vehicle_id: 2
   model_id: NULL
      price: NULL
      color: Graphite Pearl
description: Last of the 2004 stock! Must sell! Loaded, all options!
  modelyear: 2004
*************************** 3. row ***************************
 vehicle_id: 3
   model_id: 4
      price: NULL
      color: Radiant Red
description: Come drive this popular truck! 4WD, extended cab, many options.
  modelyear: 2005
*************************** 4. row ***************************
 vehicle_id: 4
   model_id: 5
      price: NULL
      color: Daytona Sunset Orange Metallic
description: The all new C6 Corvette, the next generation of classic American
sportscars. 400HP V8; Very fast!
  modelyear: 2005
```

Converting Back to MyISAM from InnoDB

You've given InnoDB tables and foreign keys a whirl, but you've decided that you'd much rather have full-text searching instead. Changing back to MyISAM is a relatively painless process. Usually it will involve only two steps: removing any InnoDB-specific features, such as foreign keys, and changing the storage engine type back to MyISAM with ALTER TABLE. To convert the New Vehicles table back to MyISAM, do the following:

```
ALTER TABLE New_Vehicles DROP FOREIGN KEY refmdl;
ALTER TABLE New_Vehicles ENGINE=MyISAM;
```

At this point, the New_Vehicles table is back to using the MyISAM storage engine and you once again have the ability to add and use full-text indexing on that table.

Controlling Access

One of the most important jobs you'll have as a MySQL database administrator is controlling who can access the system and what resources they can access. In most situations, you'll need only a handful of user accounts for each database, and those that you do need to create should only be given the minimal access required to perform their task. Luckily, MySQL provides you with a handful of ways to control who has access to your systems and to what resources exactly.

User Administration

In order to help control the user accounts in your database, MySQL provides a couple of ways to maintain user accounts. Whether it's an account for a co-developer, a tech-savvy client, or a web-based front end to the system, each user needs to have access specifically granted for the resources they require.

One of the first things you need to do when configuring a database for the real world is set up any accounts that might be needed by any users, or the system itself. In order to set up specialized access for a user in your database, you need to know about the different levels for which MySQL can control access. MySQL 4.1 can differentiate four different access levels in regards to permissions: the global level, database level, table level, and column level.

Global-level privileges are the most powerful and apply to all the databases running on an instance of MySQL. Normally such privileges are reserved for administrator accounts, as it is a rare occasion when an application or end user will require access to all aspects of the database server's operation.

Database-level privileges apply just like they sound — at the database level. Database-level access is often used by the administrator of a specific database or application, and has the ability to give the user complete control over one specific database as specified.

Table-level privileges apply on a per-table basis. You can create or remove access for a user on a specific table or set of tables. This level of access control is often used when configuring a database to be accessed directly by an application — the application only needs certain kinds of access on each table, and no more.

Column-level privileges are the finest level of control that MySQL provides. As you might expect, it controls the access to a specific column or columns within a given table.

Using GRANT

Now that you understand the varying scope of the MySQL access system, it's time to look at how to actually control the privileges.

To create and add privileges to user accounts, MySQL gives you the GRANT command. The GRANT command is relatively simple to use, as long as you know what access you're granting, and to whom. The GRANT command has the following generalized syntax:

```
GRANT [privileges] ON [resource] TO [identity]
```

Let's take a second to dissect GRANT. The first part of the command, GRANT [privileges] is where you specify what privileges to allow on the resource (specified later). Some of the more common privileges you can use are shown in the following table.

Privilege	Provides
ALL [PRIVILEGES]	Sets all simple privileges except GRANT OPTION
ALTER	Allows use of ALTER TABLE
CREATE	Allows use of CREATE TABLE
DELETE	Allows use of DELETE
DROP	Allows use of DROP TABLE
INDEX	Allows use of CREATE INDEX and DROP INDEX
INSERT	Allows use of INSERT
SELECT	Allows use of SELECT

Privilege	Provides
UPDATE	Allows use of UPDATE
USAGE	Synonym for "no privileges"; user can log in but no more

The second part of the command ON [resource] is where you specify what database level and item you are making available. To grant access at the global level, you specify *.* as the resource, like so:

```
GRANT [privileges] ON *.* TO [identity]...
```

When you grant access at the database level, you specify the name of the database, followed by .*. For example, if you wanted to grant access to the testdb database, you would use something similar to the following:

```
GRANT [privileges] ON testdb.* TO [identity]...
```

To create permissions for a specific table within a database, you provide the name of the database, followed by the table name (separated by a period). If you were trying to specify access for the testtable table in the testdb database, you might use something like this:

```
GRANT [privileges] ON testdb.testtable TO [identity]...
```

Granting column-level permissions is slightly different than the logical progression down the previous three levels. When giving column-level permissions, you must specify a column list in parentheses after each privilege in the list, such as the following:

```
GRANT SELECT (column1), INSERT (column1) ON testdb.testtable TO [identity]...
```

When you are specifying column-level privileges, you must use the full table-level syntax after ON, or MySQL will return an error.

The last key part of the GRANT command, TO [identity]..., is where you specify who the access permissions will be granted to, and any optional requirements the user must meet to be granted this access. The minimum you must provide to satisfy the TO ... section of GRANT is a username/host combination. In MySQL, each distinct user *must* have at least basic usage permissions set for their username and the localhost. For example:

```
GRANT USAGE ON *.* TO testuser@localhost
```

Here the user 'testuser' has been granted basic usage access globally, which is equivalent to no access at all, but the user is now known to the system. Once a localhost account is created, you can create additional access statements for the same username at any remote host you specify:

```
GRANT SELECT ON testdb.* TO testuser@192.168.1.2
```

It should be noted MySQL will not complain if you try and create a remote access account for a user without a localhost entry first. Your applications, however, probably will — they might not be able to connect remotely, and it's a common source of hair-pulling when first getting used to the MySQL access system.

In most situations, it's important that the user account also require a password to log in. To add a password when creating an account with GRANT, add the phrase IDENTIFIED BY 'password' to the end of the GRANT command, like so:

```
GRANT [privileges] ON [resource] TO [identity] IDENTIFIED BY '[password]';
```

You are not required to pre-encrypt the password before using it as the password in your GRANT command — MySQL will automatically encrypt the password before storing it in the system.

Now that you've seen some generalized examples of how to use GRANT, you can try it on a real database. You're going to be adding three users to the vehicle inventory database. One user will get full access to the whole database. The second will get SELECT, UPDATE, INSERT, and DELETE access to the New_Vehicles table. The third and final user will get SELECT access only to the color column in the New_Vehicles table. First, create the user who has all privileges in the database:

```
GRANT ALL PRIVILEGES ON VehicleInventory.* TO testuser1@localhost IDENTIFIED BY
'testpass1';
```

Next, create the user with limited table-wide permissions:

```
GRANT SELECT, INSERT, UPDATE, DELETE ON VehicleInventory.New_Vehicles TO
testuser2@localhost IDENTIFIED BY 'testpass2';
```

Last, create the third user with the extremely limited access:

```
GRANT SELECT (color) ON VehicleInventory.New_Vehicles TO testuser3@localhost
IDENTIFIED BY 'testpass3';
```

Using REVOKE

You can now create users and privileges using the GRANT command, but you still need a way to take away privileges. To do that, you use REVOKE. The REVOKE command looks almost exactly like the GRANT command:

```
REVOKE [privileges] ON [resource] FROM [identity]
```

Note the only real differences between the REVOKE and GRANT syntax: the use of the word FROM instead of TO, and there's no need to add the IDENTIFIED BY phrase.

For a quick look at REVOKE in action on a live database, try the following query:

```
REVOKE ALL PRIVILEGES ON VehicleInventory.New_Vehicles FROM testuser2@localhost;
```

And in that one quick stroke, you've wiped out any privileges the testuser2 account had.

When revoking privileges, you normally must list the specific tables, databases, and columns that the user has explicit rights for. If you are using MySQL 4.1.2 or later, you can quickly wipe all of a user's privileges at any privilege level with one swift command:

```
REVOKE ALL PRIVILEGES, GRANT OPTION FROM [identity]
```

If you wanted to obliterate `testuser3` from the system, you would send the following:

```
REVOKE ALL PRIVILEGES, GRANT OPTION FROM testuser3@localhost;
```

Alternatives to GRANT and REVOKE

If, for some reason, you don't feel like using the GRANT or REVOKE commands, you can manually create the users and apply the privileges directly to the MySQL access tables.

MySQL stores the different levels of user privileges in four main tables inside the built-in `mysql` database. Each of the four main access tables corresponds to the four different access levels.

At the global level, there is the `user` table, whose structure looks like this:

Field	Type
Host	varchar(60)
User	varchar(16)
Password	varchar(41)
Select_priv	enum('N','Y')
Insert_priv	enum('N','Y')
Update_priv	enum('N','Y')
Delete_priv	enum('N','Y')
Create_priv	enum('N','Y')
Drop_priv	enum('N','Y')
Reload_priv	enum('N','Y')
Shutdown_priv	enum('N','Y')
Process_priv	enum('N','Y')
File_priv	enum('N','Y')
Grant_priv	enum('N','Y')
References_priv	enum('N','Y')
Index_priv	enum('N','Y')
Alter_priv	enum('N','Y')
Show_db_priv	enum('N','Y')
Super_priv	enum('N','Y')
Create_tmp_table_priv	enum('N','Y')
Lock_tables_priv	enum('N','Y')
Execute_priv	enum('N','Y')

Table continued on following page

Field	Type
Repl_slave_priv	enum('N','Y')
Repl_client_priv	enum('N','Y')
ssl_type	enum('','ANY','X509','SPECIFIED')
ssl_cipher	Blob
x509_issuer	Blob
x509_subject	Blob
max_questions	int(11) unsigned
max_updates	int(11) unsigned
max_connections	int(11) unsigned

The user table contains a list of every user in the system, as well as any global privileges that user might have. The key fields related to access privileges are all the columns that have the suffix _priv. Note that all privilege columns have a default value of no.

The db table holds records for any access permissions at the database-level. The structure for db looks like this:

Field	Type
Host	varchar(60)
Db	varchar(64)
User	varchar(16)
Select_priv	enum('N','Y')
Insert_priv	enum('N','Y')
Update_priv	enum('N','Y')
Delete_priv	enum('N','Y')
Create_priv	enum('N','Y')
Drop_priv	enum('N','Y')
Grant_priv	enum('N','Y')
References_priv	enum('N','Y')
Index_priv	enum('N','Y')
Alter_priv	enum('N','Y')
Create_tmp_table_priv	enum('N','Y')
Lock_tables_priv	enum('N','Y')

A user will show up in this table only when they need explicit database-level permissions.

Another table, `tables_priv`, houses the permissions for table-level operations:

Field	Type
Host	char(60)
Db	char(64)
User	char(16)
Table_name	char(64)
Grantor	char(77)
Timestamp	timestamp
Table_priv	set('Select', 'Insert', 'Update', 'Delete', 'Create', 'Drop', 'Grant', 'References', 'Index', 'Alter')
Column_priv	set('Select', 'Insert', 'Update', 'References')

Like the `db` table, a user need appear in this table only when they require table-level permissions.

The final table, `columns_priv`, contains column-level access definitions, and looks like this:

Field	Type
Host	char(60)
Db	char(64)
User	char(16)
Table_name	char(64)
Column_name	char(64)
Timestamp	timestamp
Column_priv	set('Select', 'Insert', 'Update', 'References')

Why do you need to know all the intimate details of each of these tables? If you want to add or remove access permissions without using GRANT or REVOKE, you must use standard INSERT, UPDATE, and DELETE commands against these core tables.

To first create a user in the database, regardless of the access level, they must exist in the `user` table:

```
INSERT INTO mysql.user (Host, User, Password) VALUES ('localhost', 'testuser6',
PASSWORD('testpass6') );
```

Notice that the PASSWORD() function was used here, whereas in the GRANT syntax it is not. The GRANT command automatically encrypts the password with the PASSWORD() function; a manual insert such as this does not, so you must encrypt it yourself.

To add access permissions, you simply insert a row into the appropriate table, specifying Y for each permission column required. To give your newly created user database-level SELECT, UPDATE, INSERT, and DELETE permissions on the VehicleInventory database, use the following:

```
INSERT INTO mysql.db (Host, Db, User, Select_priv, Insert_priv, Update_priv,
Delete_priv) VALUES ('localhost', 'VehicleInventory', 'testuser6', 'Y', 'Y', 'Y',
'Y');
```

If you need to revoke user permissions, you simply perform a DELETE on the required tables. To remove the database-level permissions for testuser6, use this query:

```
DELETE FROM mysql.db WHERE Host='localhost' AND User='testuser6';
```

Removing a user entirely from the database is only a slight bit more complicated. You must first remove all permissions granted to that user, and *then* you can use a DELETE command to remove them from the user table.

In order for MySQL to be aware of the privileges you've just manually changed, you must reload the privilege tables:

```
FLUSH PRIVILEGES;
```

If you don't flush the privileges after making an access change, it won't be reflected in MySQL until the next time it is restarted. This applies to any privilege changes you make manually to any access level — using GRANT or REVOKE does not require you to reload the privilege tables.

Server Restriction

Another way to restrict server access, at a much larger scale, is to actually restrict remote access on the server as a whole. If your database serves only users logged into the machine directly, there is little need to have the server accept remote network connections. To stop MySQL from listening for incoming network connections, make sure the following exists in the [mysqld] section of your MySQL configuration file (typically my.cnf):

```
[mysqld]
skip-networking
```

Adding that statement to the configuration file, and then restarting the MySQL server process, disables any incoming traffic to MySQL. Such a measure is important if your network and server security is important, and when only local accounts need access.

Analyzing the Database

While your time using a database will most likely be spent adding, updating, retrieving, and deleting data, there will be occasions when you need to immediately find out information about the database structure itself. Thankfully, MySQL provides some easy-to-use informational tools, as well as simple ways to analyze and optimize your databases.

When inside the MySQL command shell, you can use several different commands that share the prefix SHOW, to get various bits of information about the current state of the database. The following sections describe some of the more common SHOW commands.

SHOW COLUMNS

The SHOW COLUMNS command returns a listing of all the columns in a table, and their attributes. The general format of SHOW COLUMNS is as follows:

```
SHOW COLUMNS FROM [table] FROM [database]
```

If you want to get a list of all the columns in the New_Vehicle table, you could use the following:

```
SHOW COLUMNS FROM New_Vehicles FROM VehicleInventory;
```

Which returns the following:

```
+-------------+--------------+------+-----+---------+----------------+
| Field       | Type         | Null | Key | Default | Extra          |
+-------------+--------------+------+-----+---------+----------------+
| vehicle_id  | int(11)      |      | PRI | NULL    | auto_increment |
| model_id    | int(11)      | YES  |     | NULL    |                |
| price       | decimal(10,2)| YES  |     | NULL    |                |
| color       | varchar(200) | YES  |     | NULL    |                |
| description | text         | YES  |     | NULL    |                |
| modelyear   | int(11)      | YES  |     | NULL    |                |
+-------------+--------------+------+-----+---------+----------------+
```

In the return output, the Field column contains the name of each column, Type shows the column data type, Null specifies whether or not NULL values are allowed in the column, Key indicates what key or index types each column belongs to, Default shows any specified default column value, and Extra shows any special treatment given to each column. Note that this command is functionally identical to MySQL's DESCRIBE [table] command.

SHOW CREATE TABLE

You might want to learn what command could be used to create a given table. For that, you have the SHOW CREATE TABLE command:

```
SHOW CREATE TABLE [table name]
```

To get the create command that would create your New_Vehicles table, send:

```
SHOW CREATE TABLE New_Vehicles \G
```

Running this command against the VehicleInventory database gives you this:

```
*************************** 1. row ***************************
       Table: New_Vehicles
Create Table: CREATE TABLE `New_Vehicles` (
```

```
    `vehicle_id` int(11) NOT NULL auto_increment,
    `model_id` int(11) default NULL,
    `price` decimal(10,2) default NULL,
    `color` varchar(200) default NULL,
    `description` text,
    `modelyear` int(11) default NULL,
    PRIMARY KEY  (`vehicle_id`)
) ENGINE=MyISAM DEFAULT CHARSET=latin1
```

This whole CREATE TABLE command can then be entered in a fresh database to create an exact copy of the structure of the New_Vehicles table.

SHOW DATABASES

The SHOW DATABASES command does exactly what it looks like — it shows all databases in the system that the currently logged-in account has access to. Simply run the command:

```
SHOW DATABASES;
```

And it will return a list of the databases accessible by the current user:

```
+------------------+
| Database         |
+------------------+
| VehicleInventory |
| mysql            |
+------------------+
```

SHOW GRANTS

The SHOW GRANTS command lists all access privileges given to a specific user account. For example, to see all the access granted to the testuser1 account in the VehicleInventory database, use the following:

```
SHOW GRANTS FOR 'testuser1'@'localhost' \G
```

Which returns this:

```
*************************** 1. row ***************************
Grants for testuser1@localhost: GRANT USAGE ON *.* TO 'testuser1'@'localhost'
IDENTIFIED BY PASSWORD '*E69570F2322D3DC1F956C48199FEB21FF2D7D984'
*************************** 2. row ***************************
Grants for testuser1@localhost: GRANT ALL PRIVILEGES ON `vehicleinventory`.* TO
'testuser1'@'localhost'
*************************** 3. row ***************************
Grants for testuser1@localhost: GRANT SELECT, SELECT (description), INSERT
(description), UPDATE (description) ON `vehicleinventory`.`used_vehicles` TO
'testuser1'@'localhost'
```

Database Maintenance

You've created your Vehicle Inventory database, put it in production, set up searching, and the client is now pleased with the outcome. Time to sit back and relax, right?

Not quite. There's another thing you might want to consider, to help minimize the cost of a catastrophic loss of the production databases. What you need are backups.

Creating Backups

Backups in MySQL are very easy to perform, thanks to a great set of client tools that come with the system. To create your backup, you can use the `mysqldump` utility. The first thing you need to do is exit the MySQL client, if needed, and find yourself at your standard shell prompt:

```
mysql> exit
```

Once you're back at a command prompt, it's a simple matter of invoking the `mysqldump` command-line tool. For most database backups, the following generic format will work:

```
mysqldump --opt databasename > backupfile.sql
```

Here you're calling the `mysqldump` command and telling it to dump the database named `databasename` into a file called `backupfile.sql`. Also present is the `--opt` option, which tells the backup utility to use a set of common options that output a format that can help MySQL restore the file more accurately.

*For more mysqldump options, type **man mysqldump** at your command prompt.*

To back up the vehicle inventory database, use the following:

```
mysqldump --opt VehicleInventory > vi_backup.sql
```

As with the `mysql` command-line client, if you need to supply a username and password, make sure you use -u and -p accordingly before the name of the database.

You now have a full database-creation script in the file `vi_backup.sql`. You can now archive this file as needed, restore it to a different server, burn it to a CD or DVD, or anything else you prefer.

Restoring Databases from Backups

In the event that a server crashes, or gets hacked, or you just want a copy of the production database for testing in a development environment, you're going to have to know how to restore your database backups. In MySQL, it's extremely simple, as you can use the MySQL command-line client, like so:

```
mysql databasename < backupfile.sql
```

So to restore the `VehicleInventory` database, use this:

```
mysql VehicleInventory < vi_backup.sql
```

Note that the name of the destination database for your restoration must be an actual database that already exists in the system. If you want to restore a backup to a new table, just log into the mysql client, create an empty database with the name you want, exit the client, and then restore your backup as desired.

Summary

Hopefully with the information in this chapter, you'll be able to go out and set up intricate database schemas, use complex queries, and maintain the whole system as well. Armed with these basic tools, there should be very few database obstacles you can't overcome. You might find in your role as a developer that you'll spend less time at a command-line interface, and more with tools such as PhpMyAdmin or MySQL AB's own MySQL Administrator GUI tool. The raw commands and queries you've seen in this chapter should be able to apply in any of these tools, as long as they have a way to enter raw commands. Your understanding of the exact SQL that performs your administrative and data-manipulative duties will also help you understand exactly what is going on behind any text fields, radio buttons, and checkboxes of a GUI MySQL application—or in your PHP application itself.

5

PHP Configuration

When you work with LAMP technologies, there are very few things that influence your coding decisions more than how PHP is configured. The backbone of any PHP installation is the configuration file, `php.ini`. The settings found in this file can greatly affect how you code your applications, how well the server performs, and even how secure it is. This chapter tells you what settings to look for and change in order to improve your PHP installation and provides you with a set of scripts to automatically prepare your PHP environment and configuration settings to your liking.

Modifying php.ini

As mentioned previously, the `php.ini` file is your primary tool for configuring your PHP installation. This section covers a number of the configuration directives that you should set, and several that are new with PHP5.

Recommended Configuration Directives

When you configure PHP, there are a number of settings to keep in mind, in order to keep your system secure and performing at top speed:

❑ `register_globals = off`: One of the most common problems with moving older PHP code to a newer system is how PHP handles form data and variables. In older versions of PHP, form fields were automatically converted into global variables that shared the same name with the PHP engine. While some found this convenient, it eventually became a security risk because of naming and usage confusion. Since PHP 4.2.0, the value for `register_globals` was `off` by default. You should keep this set to `off`, and use the `$_GET`, `$_POST`, and `$_COOKIE` superglobals, instead of relying on the automatically created variables.

When you develop your applications, it is especially imperative to keep `register_globals` set to `off`, as you can't always be sure of the settings of any production servers where it might end up.

❑　`display_errors = off`: While not necessary and actually a burden in a development environment, it's a good idea to set `display_errors` to `off` for any PHP applications on a production or public web server. Turning `display_errors` off prohibits PHP from displaying any parse or runtime errors to the user's web browser. Any error the end-user sees can give insight as to the inner workings of the application, which could be helpful information to any malicious individuals who wish to attack your site.

　　In a development or debugging situation, it's perfectly acceptable to leave `display_errors` on, to help with debugging.

❑　`log_errors = on`: This setting, usually used in conjunction with `display_errors`, tells PHP to log all errors normally seen on the screen to a file. You can use that file for later analysis or debugging, or use your own choice of tools to regularly and automatically notify the webmaster.

❑　`error_log = filename` or `error_log = syslog`: The `error_log` directive tells PHP where to send errors when `log_errors` is enabled. You can either specify a filename where PHP will write the errors, or specify `syslog`, and it will send the errors to the system logging daemon.

❑　`error_reporting = E_ALL`: This directive simply tells PHP to report all errors, warnings, and notices it encounters. By default, PHP shows everything except notices. Showing notices is usually a good idea, especially during development, as it can help you track down uninitialized variables and other minor code gaps.

❑　`magic_quotes_gpc = off`: The `magic_quotes_gpc` directive tells PHP whether it should automatically escape input/form data when a script is loaded. While this setting is intended as a time-saver, it can actually cause problems if you decide to switch databases, or use a database that doesn't escape special characters with a backslash. If you think you might one day switch database systems, or you currently use a mixed database environment or even no database at all, it's a good idea to set this to `off`.

❑　`variables_order = "GPCS"`: Setting `variables_order` to `GPCS` tells PHP not to automatically generate the `$_ENV` array that normally holds environment variables — normally set when `variables_order` is set to `EGPCS`. This setting is recommended for performance reasons only, and if you still need to access environment variables, you can use the `getenv()` function.

❑　`allow_call_time_pass_reference = off`: This directive might not affect all code, but it can help you keep your code from becoming obsoleted by a future version of PHP. Setting `allow_call_time_pass_reference` to `off` prevents you from forcing function arguments to be passed by reference. If you try to pass an argument by reference (using the `&` prefix) when it is set `off`, a warning will be generated. While not currently a critical issue for production servers, it's a good setting to use when developing your applications, to ensure they will be compatible with future versions of PHP.

❑　`asp_tags = off`: Although this is normally not an issue on most setups, using ASP-style tags (`<% %>`) instead of the standard PHP tags (`<?php ?>`) can eventually become a problem if you move an application to a server that has a different setting for `asp_tags`. Although it's not a critical requirement, performance issue, or security problem, it's a good idea to keep `asp_tags` set to off during development in order to avoid code compatibility issues later.

❑　`short_open_tag = off`: Like setting `asp_tags` to `off`, setting `short_open_tag` to `off` also helps ensure your applications will work universally across different servers, instead of being broken by a simple configuration difference.

Another benefit to using short_open_tag = off is that you can use <?xml ?> statements, like an XML document prolog, in your scripts. If short_open_tag was set to on and you tried to use <?xml, it would attempt to parse anything within the <? ?> wrappers as PHP, and throw an error.

❑ zlib.output_compression = on: Setting zlib.output_compression to on tells PHP to compress the output data using the zlib library, before sending it to the end user. This has a similar effect as using mod_gzip or mod_deflate in Apache: the output bytes are reduced, thus improving transfer time over the Internet.

New to PHP5

In addition to the greatly improved object model introduced in PHP5, a handful of new configuration settings were added. New to PHP5 are the following:

❑ mail.force_extra_parameters

❑ register_long_arrays

❑ session.hash_function

❑ session.hash_bits_per_character

❑ zend.ze1_compatibility_mode

The following sections describe these new directives.

mail.force_extra_parameters

This new directive allows you to specify specific values to be passed to Sendmail when you use the mail() function. Normally when using the mail() function, you can pass a fifth parameter that sends extra command-line arguments to Sendmail. When this directive is set, any Sendmail command-line arguments specified in the fifth parameter of mail() are automatically overwritten by the value set in mail.force_extra_parameters.

> *Any value set for* mail.force_extra_parameters *is always used when sending mail — even in safe mode, where the fifth argument to* mail() *is disallowed.*

register_long_arrays

Normally when a form is submitted on a website, PHP takes the values in each of the form fields, and places them in two large arrays, depending on the method of the form (GET or POST). If the form is submitted using GET, an array named $HTTP_GET_VARS is populated with the form values, each field having a corresponding named index in the array, in addition to an identical array named $_GET that holds the same values. This duplication is primarily for backward-compatibility — the superglobals $_GET and $_POST were not introduced until PHP 4.1.0, so many older applications still use the older $HTTP_*_VARS arrays.

If your applications do not use the older-style arrays at all, you should set this to off for performance reasons.

session.hash_function

In the past, when PHP created a new session and session ID for a user, you had no control over what algorithm was used to create the session ID. With `session.hash_function`, you have the ability to choose between two hash algorithms used to create the session ID.

Setting this option to `0` tells PHP to use MD5 to hash the session ID (128bits). If you wanted to use SHA-1 (160bits), you would set the value to `1`.

session.hash_bits_per_character

To further configure the session ID, you can use `session.hash_bits_per_character` to specify how many bits are stored in each character of the session ID when converting to a readable value. The options are as follows:

- ❏ 4 : 0-9, a-f
- ❏ 5 : 0-9, a-v
- ❏ 6 : 0-9, a-z, A-Z, "-", and ","

zend.ze1_compatibility_mode

The last new configuration setting, `zend.ze1_compatibility_mode`, simply specifies whether or not you want to enable compatibility with Zend Engine 1 (PHP4).

PHP Configuration during Runtime

Checking and changing the settings of directives in `php.ini` directly is often a quick and easy solution to monitoring and modifying your installation, but many times you can't bring the server down to make a change, or you need to know a setting while a script is running. The techniques in this part of the chapter will help you make modifications while the server is still running.

Obtaining Current Runtime Settings

If you need to know the exact version of PHP installed, PHP provides the `phpversion()` function, which returns a string listing the full installed version. For example:

```php
<?php

echo "The current version of PHP installed is: " . phpversion();

?>
```

This would output something like the following:

```
The current version of PHP installed is: 5.0.4
```

Retrieving Configuration Settings

There might be times when a simple version check isn't enough information, and you require a little more information about the way PHP is configured, but you don't have access to php.ini directly. To look up runtime configuration settings, you have three main choices: ini_get(), get_cfg_var(), and ini_get_all().

The first option, ini_get(), checks a given string against the current runtime configuration. If a setting matches, it returns the value of that setting; if no match is found, an empty string is returned:

```php
<?php

echo "Error reporting: " . ini_get('error_reporting') . "\n" .
    "Register globals: " . ini_get('register_globals') . "\n" .
    "Nonexistant setting: " . ini_get('nonexistant') . "\n";

?>
```

Running this should produce output similar to the following:

```
Error reporting: 2047
Register globals:
Nonexistant setting:
```

Note that the value of error reporting is actually the numerical equivalent to the constant E_ALL in this case. But where's the value for register_globals? When ini_get() returns what php.ini considers Boolean (off or on, 0 or 1, yes or no), it automatically converts them. Any value of "off" or "no" automatically gets converted to "0"; any value of "yes" or "on" automatically becomes "1."

The second option for retrieving configuration settings, get_cfg_var(), behaves almost identically to ini_get(), except that it pulls its values directly from php.ini and not the current runtime environment. Unless you've changed a configuration variable in your code (more on this later), the value should normally match what is returned by ini_get(). Take, for example, the following code:

```php
<?php

echo "Error reporting: " . get_cfg_var('error_reporting') . "\n" .
    "Register globals: " . get_cfg_var('register_globals') . "\n" .
    "Nonexistant setting: " . get_cfg_var('nonexistant') . "\n";

?>
```

Unless a setting was changed in the active script, this code would produce identical output to the following:

```php
<?php

echo "Error reporting: " . ini_get('error_reporting') . "\n" .
    "Register globals: " . ini_get('register_globals') . "\n" .
    "Nonexistant setting: " . ini_get('nonexistant') . "\n";

?>
```

The third way to get configuration information, `ini_get_all()`, acts like `ini_get()` magnified. Instead of specifying a single value to lookup, `ini_get_all()` returns an array containing all the registered configuration options. Its returned values aren't just limited to the current setting either — `ini_get_all()` returns the global value set in `php.ini`, the current local value as it exists at the moment, and the access level required to change the setting.

Look at this simple example:

```php
<?php

print_r(ini_get_all());

?>
```

You execute this code, and you get something similar to the following:

```
Array
(
    [allow_call_time_pass_reference] => Array
        (
            [global_value] =>
            [local_value] =>
            [access] => 6
        )

    [allow_url_fopen] => Array
        (
            [global_value] => 1
            [local_value] => 1
            [access] => 4
        )

    [always_populate_raw_post_data] => Array
        (
            [global_value] => 0
            [local_value] => 0
            [access] => 6
        )

    [arg_separator.input] => Array
        (
            [global_value] => &
            [local_value] => &
            [access] => 6
        )
    ...
```

Note this output has been greatly abbreviated — the actual returned array has over 150 different items. Also note that some of the values are empty strings, like the global and local values for `allow_call_time_pass_reference`. When `ini_get_all()` returns each setting, it uses the same value transformation that `ini_get()` performs, in regards to off/on values.

Extension Information

Now that you can gather information about the runtime settings, it's time to learn how to check extensions and their properties. PHP provides you with three built-in functions to look up information about loaded extensions.

The first, `extension_loaded()`, simply checks to see if a given extension is loaded. All you need to do is provide the name of the extension, and it will return a Boolean indicating whether or not it is available, like so:

```php
<?php

if (extension_loaded('mysql'))
{
  echo "MySQL is available.\n";
}
else
{
  echo "MySQL is NOT available.\n";
}

if (extension_loaded('fakesql'))
{
  echo "Fake SQL is available.\n";
}
else
{
  echo "Fake SQL is NOT available.\n";
}

?>
```

When you run this, you should see the following:

```
MySQL is available.
Fake SQL is NOT available.
```

If you need to know the status of more than one extension at a time, PHP gives you `get_loaded_extensions()`. Like `ini_get_all()`, `get_loaded_extensions()` returns an array of all the extensions loaded. Consider the following code:

```php
<?php

print_r(get_loaded_extensions());

?>
```

This should produce output similar to the following, give or take a few extensions, based on your current setup:

```
Array
(
    [0] => xml
```

```
    [1] => tokenizer
    [2] => standard
    [3] => SQLite
    [4] => SPL
    [5] => sockets
    [6] => SimpleXML
    [7] => session
    [8] => posix
    [9] => pgsql
    [10] => pcre
    [11] => mysqli
    [12] => mysql
    [13] => iconv
    [14] => gd
    [15] => exif
    [16] => dom
    [17] => ctype
    [18] => calendar
    [19] => bz2
    [20] => bcmath
    [21] => zlib
    [22] => openssl
    [23] => libxml
)
```

Once you know an extension is available, you might want to know a little more about that particular module. To get a listing of all the functions that an extension provides, use `get_extension_funcs()`. Like some of the previous informational commands, it returns an array of available values, but in this case, it provides a list of functions for a given extension. For example:

```php
<?php

print_r(get_extension_funcs('simplexml'));

?>
```

Running this code should give a list of all the functions provided by the SimpleXML extension:

```
Array
(
    [0] => simplexml_load_file
    [1] => simplexml_load_string
    [2] => simplexml_import_dom
)
```

Magic Quotes

As mentioned earlier in the chapter, PHP allows a special data handling device called "magic quotes." When magic quotes are enabled, PHP automatically escapes any special characters—single quote, double quote, NULL—by prefixing them with a backslash, to prevent issues when using the strings in a database.

There are actually two places where PHP can automatically escape strings: input data from a web form or request, or automatically from any function that returns any data at all. Each replacement is controlled by its own configuration directive. Automatic escape of input data is controlled by the `magic_quotes_gpc` directive, and the escaping from any function is controlled by the `magic_quotes_runtime` setting.

Because these are both critical operations that can "dirty" your data if neglected, PHP provides two functions to quickly ascertain the current setting for each: `get_magic_quotes_gpc()`, for the input data, and `get_magic_quotes_runtime()` for the function handler. Both functions require no arguments, and return 1 if the setting is enabled, or 0 if disabled. Run this code:

```php
<?php

echo "Magic quotes GPC: " . get_magic_quotes_gpc() . "\n" .
    "Magic quotes runtime: " . get_magic_quotes_runtime() . "\n";

?>
```

Depending on your current configuration, you'll see something similar to this:

```
Magic quotes GPC: 0
Magic quotes runtime: 0
```

Changing Configuration Dynamically

You can now check configuration settings and extension properties real-time in your code, but if something's not the way you like it, what are you going to do? With some built-in PHP functions, you can change the way PHP behaves in certain situations.

Quotes That Aren't So Magical

If you're like me, you probably don't like it if `magic_quotes_runtime` is enabled, mangling all the output from every function. While it can be seen as a convenience, it usually just gets in the way, and forces you to use `stripslashes()` or `addslashes()` all over the place. To change it, you can use `set_magic_quotes_runtime()`. An argument of "1" turns on the automatic replacement; a value of "0" turns it off:

```php
<?php

// Turn on magic_quotes_runtime
set_magic_quotes_runtime(1);

// Turn off magic_quotes_runtime
set_magic_quotes_runtime(0);

?>
```

Unfortunately, the same cannot be said for `magic_quotes_gpc` — you cannot change its value at runtime (more on this later).

Removing the Time Limit

If you find yourself in a situation where a script is running a bit longer than PHP will allow, you have two choices: optimize your code so it's faster, and tell PHP to be a bit more patient. Perhaps you've already optimized your code as much as you can, and the default 30-second timeout is still too quick.

It's time to make PHP wait a little longer before timing-out. To do this, you use `set_time_limit()`, and simply specify the number of seconds your script is allowed to run:

```php
<?php

// Set the timeout at one minute
set_time_limit(60);

?>
```

If you're not able to accurately guess how long of a time frame your script needs, and are *absolutely sure* you have no infinite loops, you can remove the timeout completely by setting the value to zero:

```php
<?php

// Will run forever if you're not careful
set_time_limit(0);

?>
```

When you use `set_time_limit()`, there are two things to keep in mind. First, if your server is running PHP in safe mode, using `set_time_limit()` will have no effect. You must either disable safe mode, or change the global value in `php.ini`. Second, whenever `set_time_limit()` is called, it resets the internal timer to 0. If your script has run for 15 seconds, and you set the timeout to 20 seconds, it won't exit in 5 more seconds — it will reset the counter to 0 and count for a fresh 20 seconds, a total of 35 seconds.

Changing Directives

What if you wanted to just change any random runtime configuration setting? To do this, you can use the function `ini_set()`. To use `ini_set()`, simply pass the name of the setting, and the new value. If the function is successful, it will return the old value; if not, it will return false. Run this code:

```php
<?php

echo "Setting error_reporting to E_STRICT...\n";

$old = ini_set('error_reporting', E_STRICT);

echo "Old value was: " . $old . "\n";

?>
```

You should see the following:

```
Setting error_reporting to E_STRICT...
Old value was: 2047
```

If you decide you don't want your changed values anymore, you can use `ini_restore()` to reinstate the original values from when the script began execution:

```php
<?php

echo "Setting error_reporting to E_STRICT...\n";

$old = ini_set('error_reporting', E_STRICT);

echo "Old value was: " . $old . "\n" .
    "New value is: " . ini_get('error_reporting') . "\n";

ini_restore('error_reporting');

echo "The value is once again: " . ini_get('error_reporting') . "\n";

?>
```

When you run the code this time, it should successfully restore the old values:

```
Old value was: 2047
New value is: 2048
The value is once again: 2047
```

Before you go hog-wild changing settings, you need to realize there are limitations as to what settings you can actually change during the execution of a script. If you remember back when `ini_get_all()` was shown, the array for each configuration directive returned three values:

```
...
    [allow_call_time_pass_reference] => Array
        (
            [global_value] =>
            [local_value] =>
            [access] => 6
        )
...
```

The third value, `access`, indicates where the configuration directive can actually be changed. The number that is provided for access is actually a sum of any of the following values:

Value	Meaning
1	Directive can be set in user scripts.
2	Directive can be set in `php.ini`, `.htaccess`, or `httpd.conf`.
4	Directive can be set in `php.ini` or `httpd.conf`.
7	Entry can be set anywhere.

In the example directive, `allow_call_time_pass_reference`, `access` has a value of 6, meaning the directive can only be changed in `php.ini`, `.htaccess`, or `httpd.conf`. The key thing to keep in mind is if the setting has an access value of 2, 4, or 6, it cannot be changed during the execution of the script. Any attempts to do so will return false automatically.

Automated Version and Feature Checking

Knowing the various ways to evaluate and change settings at runtime is helpful, but it can be a pain trying to ensure a constant environment across systems and applications, in all scripts or pages. One possible solution is to take all of your version and extension checks, put them in their own script, and include or require that script at the top of each of the pages. This method works just fine, but keeping that verification script updated can quickly become a chore. In this next section, you'll take a look at a variation of a simple environment-checking script—one that uses an easily modifiable configuration file, and takes only a few lines of code to call.

This set of scripts consists of three main blocks of code and one simple configuration file. To begin, have look at the configuration file, in this example, called `reqs.xml`:

```xml
<requirements>

    <packages>
        <package name="gd" />
        <package name="mysql" />
        <package name="pgsql" />
    </packages>

    <environment>
        <setting name="register_globals" value="off" />
        <php minversion="5.0.0" />
    </environment>

</requirements>
```

If you've had any experience with XML, you'll recognize this as a simple set of tags grouped to establish the site configuration. Wrapped inside the main enclosing `<requirements>` tags, there are two main sections.

The first section, `<packages></packages>`, holds a listing of any and all extensions that are required for your application. Each extension is specified by using a `<package />` empty tag, with the attribute `name=""` specifying the name of the extension. The name of the extension should match the name returned by `get_loaded_extensions()`, mentioned earlier.

The second section contains definitions that define specific application settings, by default found in `php.ini`, and version requirements for PHP itself. Each `<setting />` tag can correspond to a PHP runtime configuration setting. The `name=""` attribute matches the configuration setting's name, and the `value=""` attribute holds any value that would be used in `php.ini`. The `<php />` tag allows you to specify version requirements for the application—a minimum version is specified in the `minversion=""` attribute, and a maximum version in a corresponding `maxversion=""` attribute (not shown).

In this example of `reqs.xml`, the GD, MySQL, and PostgreSQL extensions are listed as required, the minimum version of PHP allowed is 5.0.0, and the `register_globals` directive must be set to `off`.

Specifying the minimum version of 5.0.0 in this example is technically unnecessary—the class structures that follow will run only on PHP 5.0 and later because of the different object models.

The next file in the configuration checker is `class.ConfigManager.php`, which acts as the central control point for the scripts:

```php
<?php

class ConfigManager
{

    public $configfile = 'reqs.xml';
    public $configtype = 'xml';
    public $errors;

    public function __construct($configfile = null, $configtype = null)
    {
        if ($configfile)
        {
            $this->configfile = $configfile;
        }
        if ($configtype)
        {
            $this->configtype = $configtype;
        }
    }

    public function processConfig()
    {
        switch ($this->configtype)
        {
            case 'xml':
                require_once 'class.XMLConfigProcessor.php';
                $proc = new XMLConfigProcessor($this->configfile);
                $this->errors = $proc->process();
                break;
        }

        echo nl2br($this->errors);
    }
}

?>
```

The first part of this class should be pretty straightforward. It begins by declaring the class `ConfigManager`, and declaring three public properties:

```php
<?php

class ConfigManager
{

    public $configfile = 'reqs.xml';
    public $configtype = 'xml';
    public $errors;
```

The first property, configfile, holds the name of the configuration file you're going to use. The default value for this configuration file is set to reqs.xml, so you don't need to explicitly set this property unless you use a different filename. The configtype property is where the type of configuration is specified. In this case, a default value of xml is provided to indicate your configuration is in XML format. The last property, errors, is simply a placeholder for any error messages encountered during processing later on.

Next follows the constructor method for the class:

```php
public function __construct($configfile = null, $configtype = null)
{
    if ($configfile)
    {
        $this->configfile = $configfile;
    }
    if ($configtype)
    {
        $this->configtype = $configtype;
    }
}
```

While nothing truly amazing happens in this constructor, it does allow provisions for passing a configuration file and type when the object is created, and uses those values to set the corresponding properties.

The final method in ConfigManager is where all the magic happens:

```php
public function processConfig()
{
    switch ($this->configtype)
    {
        case 'xml':
            require_once 'class.XMLConfigProcessor.php';
            $proc = new XMLConfigProcessor($this->configfile);
            $this->errors = $proc->process();
            break;
    }

    echo nl2br($this->errors);
}

}

?>
```

The processConfig() method first determines the type of configuration, and then calls the necessary code and utilizes component objects based on the configuration type. Currently, there is only one type specified in processConfig, one that handles XML configuration files. Any number of additional cases can be added as new configuration processor types are created. If you wanted to store your configuration in a database, you could devise your own database-configuration-processing object, and then add a case to this switch that calls any processing methods in your new class.

Notice the class file for XMLConfigProcessor is included at this point instead of at the beginning of the file, or earlier in the class. This way, the class file is only parsed if and when needed, to help cut down on extraneous processing if a different configuration type is used. To use XMLConfigProcessor, it's a simple matter of instantiating the object, passing the configuration file name to the constructor, and finally calling the method that processes the configuration (covered in more detail later on in the chapter).

The next file in this set is a simple interface to define a group of methods to be supported by any configuration processing classes:

```php
<?php

interface ConfigProcessor
{
    public function checkExtensions();
    public function checkPHP();
    public function checkConfig();
    public function process();
}

?>
```

This one is pretty straightforward — the four methods defined here will prescribe the common functionality for all processing classes for any configuration types. The first three methods — checkExtensions(), checkPHP(), and checkConfig() — are primarily intended as internal methods for the implementing classes, and the last method, process(), is intended to be the main public method to trigger the other three.

The last file in the configuration checking tool is class.XMLConfigProcessor.php, which, as you might guess from the filename, processes the XML configuration file:

```php
<?php

require_once 'interface.ConfigProcessor.php';

class XMLConfigProcessor implements ConfigProcessor
{

    public  $xmlfile;
    private $message = '';
    private $xml;


    public function __construct($xmlfile = null)
    {
        if ($xmlfile)
        {
            $this->xmlfile = $xmlfile;
        }
    }

    public function process()
    {
        // Check for needed libraries
        if (!$this->checkDeps() or
            !$this->checkConfigAccess())
        {
```

```php
            return $this->message;
        }

        $this->xml = simplexml_load_file($this->xmlfile);

        if (!$this->checkPHP() or
            !$this->checkExtensions() or
            !$this->checkConfig())
        {
            return $this->message;
        }
    }

    private function checkConfigAccess()
    {
        $returnValue = false;

        // Check to see if config file exists and is readable
        if (file_exists($this->xmlfile) and
            is_readable($this->xmlfile))
        {
            $returnValue = true;
        }
        else
        {
            $this->message .= "Warning: " .
                            "Could not access config file.\n";
        }

        // Clear cached filesystem lookups
        clearstatcache();

        return $returnValue;
    }

    private function checkDeps()
    {
        $returnValue = true;

        // Check for SimpleXML
        if (!extension_loaded('SimpleXML'))
        {
            $returnValue = false;
            $this->message .= "Warning: " .
                            "SimpleXML extension not available.\n";
        }

        return $returnValue;
    }

    public function checkExtensions()
    {
        $returnValue = true;

        // Check for all listed extensions
```

```php
        $exts = $this->xml->xpath('packages/package');
        foreach ($exts as $ext)
        {
            if (!extension_loaded($ext['name']))
            {
                $returnValue = false;
                $this->message .= "Warning: " .
                                  $ext['name'] .
                                  " extension not available.\n";
            }
        }

        return $returnValue;
    }

    public function checkPHP()
    {
        // Check if PHP requirement is present
        if (count($phpreq = $this->xml->xpath('environment/php')) == 0)
        {
            return true;
        }

        // Flatten element array
        $phpreq = $phpreq[0];

        // Check minimum version
        if ($phpreq['minversion'] and
            version_compare(phpversion(),
                        $phpreq['minversion']) < 0)
        {
            $this->message .= "Warning: " .
                              "PHP version is less than " .
                              $phpreq['minversion'] . ".\n";
            return false;
        }

        // Check maximum version
        if ($phpreq['maxversion'] and
            version_compare(phpversion(),
                        $phpreq['maxversion']) > 0)
        {
            $this->message .= "Warning: " .
                              "PHP version is greater than " .
                              $phpreq['maxversion'] . ".\n";
            return false;
        }

        return true;
    }

    public function checkConfig()
    {
        $returnValue = true;
```

```
                    // Get all config values
                    $cfg = ini_get_all();

                    // Cycle through setting elements
                    $settings = $this->xml->xpath('environment/setting');
                    foreach ($settings as $setting)
                    {
                        $value = $setting['value'];
                        // Convert boolean values to ini_get() values
                        switch (strtolower($value))
                        {
                            case 'off':
                            case '0':
                            case 'false':
                            case 'no':
                                $value = '';
                                break;
                            case 'on':
                            case 'true':
                            case 'yes':
                                $value = '1';
                                break;
                        }

                        // Flatten name
                        $name = (string) $setting['name'];

                        // Check config value, set if needed
                        if (!array_key_exists($name, $cfg) or
                            ($value !=
                              $cfg[$name]['local_value'] and
                              ini_set($name, $setting['value']) === false))
                        {
                            $returnValue = false;
                            $this->message .= "Warning: " .
                                            $name .
                                            " not set to the required value of: "
                                            . $setting['value'] . ".\n";
                        }
                    }

            return $returnValue;
        }
    }
?>
```

The beginning of the class is pretty normal—you include the interface file, start the class, and define some properties. The first property, $xmlfile, is to hold the filename of your XML configuration. The second property, $message, will be used to capture any error messages created when processing the file. The third and last property, $xml, will hold an XML object created by PHP's SimpleXML extension. After the property definitions is a simple constructor that sets the value of xmlfile if a filename is passed during instantiation:

```php
<?php

require_once 'interface.ConfigProcessor.php';

class XMLConfigProcessor implements ConfigProcessor
{

    public  $xmlfile;
    private $message = '';
    private $xml;


    public function __construct($xmlfile = null)
    {
        if ($xmlfile)
        {
            $this->xmlfile = $xmlfile;
        }
    }
```

The `process()` method following the constructor is the main method called from outside the class. It contains calls to all the other component methods in the class that check the individual requirements and parts of the XML configuration file.

In the first section of `process()`, you check to see if the configuration file is accessible, and the PHP installation has everything necessary for this class to function properly:

```php
    public function process()
    {
        // Check for needed libraries
        if (!$this->checkDeps() or
            !$this->checkConfigAccess())
        {
            return $this->message;
        }
```

If either of those checks fail, the method should terminate and return any error messages encountered.

Next, the SimpleXML extension is used to load the contents of the configuration file into an XML object, a `simplexml_element` object to be exact. This `simplexml_object` can be used to easily traverse the XML and pull out tags and attributes as needed:

```php
        $this->xml = simplexml_load_file($this->xmlfile);
```

Finally, `process()` calls the remaining three methods from the `ConfigProcessor` interface, to check the version of PHP, available extensions, and configuration settings:

```php
        if (!$this->checkPHP() or
            !$this->checkExtensions() or
            !$this->checkConfig())
        {
            return $this->message;
        }
    }
```

The next method you encounter is checkConfigAccess(). This method checks to see if the XML configuration file actually exists on the filesystem, and if it does, it checks then to see if it is readable. If the file does not exist or is not readable, an error message is added to the message property. Note that clearstatcache() is called at the end of the method. The results of file_exists() and is_readable() are cached by PHP, so it's a good idea to clear the result cache when you are finished, to prevent erratic results later on:

```php
private function checkConfigAccess()
{
    $returnValue = false;

    // Check to see if config file exists and is readable
    if (file_exists($this->xmlfile) and
        is_readable($this->xmlfile))
    {
        $returnValue = true;
    }
    else
    {
        $this->message .= "Warning: " .
                          "Could not access config file.\n";
    }

    // Clear cached filesystem lookups
    clearstatcache();

    return $returnValue;
}
```

Next up, checkDeps(). As the name implies, this method checks dependencies of the class itself. For XMLConfigProcessor, the only non-standard PHP requirement is availability of the SimpleXML extension. If you decided later to modify this class to use the XML Parser functions or DOM XML extension, for example, you would add the requisite checks to this method.

To check for SimpleXML, you simply use the extension_loaded() function covered earlier in this chapter. If SimpleXML is not available, add another error message to the pile:

```php
private function checkDeps()
{
    $returnValue = true;

    // Check for SimpleXML
    if (!extension_loaded('SimpleXML'))
    {
        $returnValue = false;
        $this->message .= "Warning: " .
                          "SimpleXML extension not available.\n";
    }

    return $returnValue;
}
```

Now it's time to get your hands dirty and sort through a bit of your XML configuration file. In checkExtensions(), the first thing you need to do is gather all the extensions listed in the configuration file. As mentioned before, each package is listed as a <package /> tag inside a set of surrounding <packages></packages> tags. To get a list of all of these packages, you use the xpath() method of SimpleXML:

```
public function checkExtensions()
{
    $returnValue = true;

    // Check for all listed extensions
    $exts = $this->xml->xpath('packages/package');
```

The xpath() method takes a string representing the element's location in the document hierarchy (its Xpath path), and returns an array of simplexml_element objects — each representing an individual <package /> tag, in this case.

Once you have your array of package tags, you just need to cycle through them, checking for each to see if it is available. Since the package name was stored in the name="" attribute of each <package /> tag, you can access the values similar to array keys, using bracket syntax and a string inside. Once again, you're using the extension_loaded() function to check for each package, and adding an error message to the stack if it's unavailable:

```
foreach ($exts as $ext)
{
    if (!extension_loaded($ext['name']))
    {
        $returnValue = false;
        $this->message .= "Warning: " .
                          $ext['name'] .
                          " extension not available.\n";
    }
}

return $returnValue;
}
```

The next method implemented from ConfigProcessor is checkPHP(). This method checks the version of PHP itself to see if the application can run on that version. Starting out the method, you first check to see if a PHP version requirement even exists in the configuration file, by using the xpath() SimpleXML method once again:

```
public function checkPHP()
{
    // Check if PHP requirement is present
    if (count($phpreq = $this->xml->xpath('environment/php')) == 0)
    {
        return true;
    }
```

If a PHP version requirement is found, you then replace the array of `simplexml_elements` returned from `xpath()` with the first (and hopefully only) object in the array:

```
// Flatten element array
$phpreq = $phpreq[0];
```

The PHP version check can have two attributes assigned: one that specifies a minimum version of PHP allowed, and another that specifies a maximum version. For both the minimum and the maximum, you first check to see if the attribute exists, and then use the built-in `version_compare()` function, in conjunction with the `phpversion()` function. The `version_compare()` function takes two methods, each a "PHP-standardized" version number string, such as 5.0.4, or 5.0.5RC1. If the first argument is lower, the function returns –1; if the second argument is lower, it returns +1; if both arguments are equal, it returns 0:

```
// Check minimum version
if ($phpreq['minversion'] and
    version_compare(phpversion(),
                $phpreq['minversion']) < 0)
{
    $this->message .= "Warning: " .
                    "PHP version is less than " .
                    $phpreq['minversion'] . ".\n";
    return false;
}

// Check maximum version
if ($phpreq['maxversion'] and
    version_compare(phpversion(),
                $phpreq['maxversion']) > 0)
{
    $this->message .= "Warning: " .
                    "PHP version is greater than " .
                    $phpreq['maxversion'] . ".\n";
    return false;
}

    return true;
}
```

Now that you've checked the required extensions, and investigated if the version of PHP installed is supported by your application, you need to check the runtime configuration to make sure the environment matches what you coded against. In `checkConfig()`, you start out by gathering all configuration settings into an array, using `ini_get_all()`:

```
public function checkConfig()
{
    $returnValue = true;

    // Get all config values
    $cfg = ini_get_all();
```

Once you've retrieved all the current runtime settings, you'll need to collect a list of all the `<setting />` tag values from the XML configuration file. To do that, you use SimpleXML's `xpath()` function again:

```
// Cycle through setting elements
$settings = $this->xml->xpath('environment/setting');
```

After you get an array of all the `setting` elements, you need to cycle through them, and check the runtime configuration to see if they match. Before you directly compare the two values, you need to convert each value in the XML configuration file to match expected results from `ini_get_all()`. Normally when setting values in `php.ini`, you can use several different values to mean "true" or "false." For true, you can use `on`, `true`, `yes`, or 1; false is represented by `off`, `false`, `no`, or 0. As mentioned earlier, when returning settings using `ini_get()` or `ini_get_all()`, values representing on or true are returned as 1, but values of off or false will be returned as an empty string, "". To make sure the XML configuration values match, regardless of which `php.ini` indication is used, you can use a simple `switch`:

```
foreach ($settings as $setting)
{
    $value = $setting['value'];
    // Convert boolean values to ini_get() values
    switch (strtolower($value))
    {
        case 'off':
        case '0':
        case 'false':
        case 'no':
            $value = '';
            break;
        case 'on':
        case 'true':
        case 'yes':
            $value = '1';
            break;
    }
```

Next, you retrieve the name of the configuration variable. Because accessing the attribute like an array returns a `simplexml_element` object, you need to cast it explicitly as a string to compare it against the string value later on:

```
// Flatten name
$name = (string) $setting['name'];
```

Now that you have both the name and value of the setting called for in the XML configuration file, you can compare it against the runtime setting. First, you check to see if the configuration setting even exists in the runtime configuration array, and then you compare it against the value in the XML file. Taking it one step further, if the setting is present but doesn't match, attempt to change the current runtime configuration variable using `ini_set()`. If the setting doesn't match *and* you cannot change the setting at runtime, an error message will be generated and the function will return false:

```
// Check config value, set if needed
if (!array_key_exists($name, $cfg) or
    ($value !=
    $cfg[$name]['local_value'] and
```

```
                    ini_set($name, $setting['value']) === false))
        {
            $returnValue = false;
            $this->message .= "Warning: " .
                                $name .
                                " not set to the required value of: "
                                . $setting['value'] . ".\n";
        }
    }

    return $returnValue;
    }
}

?>
```

Now that you've got this small hierarchy of classes and configuration files to check the runtime environment, you need to actually call them a script. In the following `test.php` code, you can see how simple it is to call the configuration checker:

```php
<?php

// Check PHP environment
require_once 'class.ConfigManager.php';
$cfg = new ConfigManager('reqs.xml','xml');
$cfg->processConfig();

?>
```

All you have to do is include the main `ConfigManager` class file, create a new `ConfigManager` object, passing the filename and type during instantiation, and call the `processConfig()` method to actually check the settings.

Summary

Hopefully you've now become acquainted with some of the different configuration settings and functions that can breathe life into your applications. Knowing the value of a setting at runtime can often help avoid any hard-to-diagnose bugs, and being able to change the values at runtime can make your applications flexible enough to cope with varying configurations. This knowledge and power, combined with the automatic configuration checked, should help make your applications as thick-skinned as possible when confronted with the unknown troubles that unfamiliar servers can bring.

6

Apache Tricks

This chapter shifts away from talking about PHP for a bit to discuss some features of Apache that you may not be aware of. You already know that Apache is the most popular and powerful web server available, and that PHP is designed to work with Apache, but you may not know that you can expand Apache itself to make your site run more effectively. True to its open-source nature, there are a number of excellent modules available for Apache that expand its functionality and provide useful features for you as a site administrator.

This chapter discusses three of those modules. Mod_rewrite enables you to provide URL substitutions to accommodate site changes, but if you use it properly, you can use it to secure your site and make it friendlier to search engines. Mod_speling helps correct inadvertent spelling mistakes made by visitors to your site. Mod_deflate will enable you to compress your content as you send it to users, saving you money on bandwidth. Mod_auth_mysql lets you beef up your site security by harnessing the power of a user database with Apache's authentication. Mod_ssl allows you to encrypt the data flowing to and from your web server. Finally, mod_dav allows you to use your Apache web server as a distributed file repository.

URL Rewriting

If you gathered all the web developers and server administrators in the world, and had them make a list of the most important modules that can be used with Apache, it's a good bet that mod_rewrite will be on that list—and with good reason.

Mod_rewrite, for the unfamiliar, is an Apache module that provides URL rewriting functionality. While that may sound simple, in reality mod_rewrite is the Swiss Army knife of Apache modules. What can you do with mod_rewrite? Outside of the obvious simple URL-rewriting, mod_rewrite gives you the ability to keep query-string input safe, keep your site search-engine-friendly, make your URLs user-friendly, retain "old" URLs after a restructuring, and stop hot linking. You will find that mod_rewrite can quickly become more than just a simple URL-changing robot.

Enabling mod_rewrite

The first thing you'll need to do, before you bother getting your hands dirty setting up mod_rewrite, is to check and see if it's already installed. At the command line, type:

```
/path/to/httpd -l
```

Use your own path to Apache's httpd, obviously.

If you see `mod_rewrite.c` listed, it has already been compiled into Apache. If not, check to see if it exists as a dynamic module for Apache:

```
ls /path/to/apache/modules/
```

If `mod_rewrite.so` exists in the file listing, then Apache can load it as a module with a little tweak to the httpd.conf file, shown later in this section. If it's not compiled into Apache or available as a shared object, you can use whatever package management system your OS uses to install it, or if you're the more hands-on type, you can recompile Apache yourself to include mod_rewrite.

When enabling functionality in Apache, you typically have two choices: build statically into the Apache binary itself, or compile the module as a loadable shared object. When building the modules statically into Apache, they are available with no extra configuration directives, but the module will always be active and consuming memory whenever Apache is running, even if you don't need it. Building the module as a loadable shared object allows you to keep your Apache binary stripped of any "optional" items you may or may not need, but they must be manually configured in httpd.conf. Either method is perfectly acceptable, but if you're unsure of which to choose, the shared module route is a popular choice because of its flexibility.

To build mod_rewrite statically into Apache when building from source, make sure your configure file includes `--enable-rewrite`, like so:

```
./configure \
--enable-rewrite \
# ...and any other configure settings you use
```

If you chose the dynamic module route, just add `=shared` to the end of the line that enables mod_rewrite:

```
./configure \
--enable-rewrite=shared \
# ...and any other configure settings you use
```

Then, it's a simple matter of making and installing the server to your system. If you built mod_rewrite into Apache statically, you can make sure your reconfiguration worked, by re-running `httpd -l`. If `mod_rewrite.c` shows up, it has been successfully added to the Apache binary.

If, instead, you went with the dynamic module, check first to see if it actually exists in the Apache modules directory, as a file called `mod_rewrite.so`:

```
ls /path/to/apache/modules/
```

Assuming everything went well, and `mod_rewrite.so` exists in the modules directory, you'll need to enable it in httpd.conf, by either uncommenting any existing line or adding a new one that looks like the following:

```
LoadModule rewrite_module modules/mod_rewrite.so
```

Do not use a `LoadModule` line for any module that is built statically into Apache — only dynamic shared objects. Using `LoadModule` for a static module will only generate an error.

After all required changes are made to httpd.conf, restart Apache. Now that you've successfully installed mod_rewrite, you'll need to take a look at the different configuration settings used to take advantage of mod_rewrite.

RewriteRule

Mod_rewrite provides a handful of configuration directives that can provide a wide range of rewriting abilities, from very simple redirects, to complex multi-rule pattern-matching substitutions. At the heart of every rewritten URL is the `RewriteRule` directive.

RewriteRule Usage

Regardless of how complex your rewriting needs may be, you will need at least one `RewriteRule` to perform a transformation. The basic format for the `RewriteRule` directive is as follows:

```
RewriteRule pattern substitution [flag(s)]
```

`RewriteRule` behaves in a manner similar to PHP's `preg_replace` function: it takes a regular expression pattern, matches it against an incoming URL, and then uses a rule you define to provide a substitution for the URL.

When constructing your regular expression pattern to match against, you can use the following tokens:

Pattern	Meaning
^	The carat symbol denotes the beginning of the line or string.
$	A dollar sign denotes the end of the line or string.
.	A period matches any single character.
(a|b)	Using the "pipe" character as a logical "or," the pattern (a|b) matches a or b.
(...)	Parentheses group sections as a sub-match.
[abc]	Listing values inside a pair of brackets matches any value in the list or range given. The pattern [abc] matches the single letter a, b, or c, whereas the pattern [a-z] matches any lowercase letter a through z.
[^abc]	Using the carat at the beginning of a range matches any values *not* listed in the range. The pattern [^abc] matches any character except a, b, or c; the pattern [^a-z] matches everything but lowercase a through z.

Table continued on following page

Pattern	Meaning
a?	A question mark matches the preceding character exactly zero or one times.
a*	The asterisk instructs Apache to match the preceding character zero or more times — no limit.
a+	Using a plus sign matches the preceding character one or more times — no limit.
a{n}	A single numeric value inside curly braces matches the preceding character exactly the specified number of times.
a{n,}	A single numeric value followed by a comma matches the preceding character at least n times, but possibly more.
a{n,m}	Two numeric values in braces specify at least n matches, but no more than m matches.
!(pattern)	Logical "not" is represented by the exclamation point before a pattern. Used to apply a rule when a URL does not match the given pattern.
\char	Backslash acts as an escape character, making it possible for you to match characters that are normally regular expression tokens, such as "\.", "\[", "\(", and so on.
\d	Matches any decimal digit.
\w	Matches any "word" character — typically any letter, digit, or the underscore character.

For example, you might have recently replaced an older section of your website with a newer more up-to-date version, with a different URL. To automatically redirect any URL in the old structure to the index in the new location, you might use something similar to this:

```
RewriteEngine On
RewriteBase /

# Rewrite requests for the old directory to the new index
RewriteRule ^olddirectory/ newdirectory/index.php [R,NC,L]
```

This rule tells Apache to respond to all requests to any file in the olddirectory/ folder with the index.php in the newdirectory folder. The flags at the end specify to redirect to the new URL, ignore case when matching, and to stop processing any other rules that might match the requested URL — these flags are covered later in the chapter.

One of the more common uses for using mod_rewrite is to provide search-engine-friendly — and human-input-friendly — URLs, while still using a standard PHP file with HTTP GET parameters tacked onto the request. To help illustrate this scenario, begin by creating the following PHP file:

```php
<?php
$category = '';
$item = '';
if (isset($_GET['cat']))
{
  $category = $_GET['cat'];
}
if (isset($_GET['item']))
```

```
{
  $item = $_GET['item'];
}
echo "Category: " . $category . "<br />\n" .
     "Item: " . $item . "<br />\n";
?>
```

Save this file as `catalog.php` in the root folder of your website.

Normally, if you wanted to pull up this file and have it recognize a given category or item value, you'd have to supply values in the query string, like this:

```
http://www.domain.com/catalog.php?cat=categoryvalue&item=itemvalue
```

Unfortunately, some search engines will not catalog dynamic pages with URLs like the one above. In addition, the extra syntax to specify each variable can be a burden to anyone entering the URL by hand. To remedy this situation, you can use mod_rewrite. Add the following directives in a .htaccess file in the same directory as your `category.php` file (or in the server's httpd.conf file if needed):

```
RewriteEngine On
# Rewrite /category/item/ to catalog.php
RewriteRule  ^(\w+)/(\w+)/?$  catalog.php?cat=$1&item=$2
```

In order to use mod_rewrite directives in per-directory configuration files (.htaccess), the directive `Options FollowSymLinks` *or* `Option SymLinksIfOwnerMatch` *must be enabled for the directories in httpd.conf.*

Now, because of the magic of mod_rewrite, you can access category and item records using directories in the URL, instead of query strings:

```
http://www.domain.com/categoryvalue/itemvalue/
```

Note that the corresponding directories referenced in the preceding URL don't actually exist — mod_rewrite intercepts the request and translates it into the query string–appended PHP request, which is then parsed through the PHP engine. Another thing to keep in mind: if the preceding directory actually does exist and the `RewriteRule` shown here is active, Apache will still completely ignore the real path and proceed as planned with its URL rewriting.

Taking a look at the lines from your mod_rewrite configuration, you start with a simple declaration:

```
RewriteEngine On
```

In order to use mod_rewrite, you have to inform Apache that you want to enable the module in the given configuration zone — a .htaccess file, or a `<Directory>` section in `http.conf` for example. `RewriteEngine` takes either `On` or `Off` as its value.

The next key line is simply a regular expression used to match an incoming URL, and the new URL to use in its place:

```
# Rewrite /category/item/ to catalog.php
RewriteRule  ^(\w+)/(\w+)/?$  catalog.php?cat=$1&item=$2
```

The pattern looks for a two-level directory request, using the \w pattern to match only valid "word" characters for each directory. Then, it uses the values of each of the two directories as the category and item number for the PHP script. Like PHP's PCRE syntax, you can use $-prefixed backreferences to refer to submatches in the original pattern. *Backreferences* are a simple way to include a sub-match from the previous pattern directly in the substitution string. Looking again at the rule:

```
# Rewrite /category/item/ to catalog.php
RewriteRule  ^(\w+)/(\w+)/?$  catalog.php?cat=$1&item=$2
```

There are exactly two submatches defined in the regular expression matched against the URL: both of the "word"-character groupings, indicating directories. In the substition string, the backreferences $1 and $2 are used to automatically include the value of the first and second sub-matches, correspondingly. Backreferences simply start counting at 1, which corresponds to the first submatch.

What other tricks can you do with a simple RewriteRule? You can actually use it as a rudimentary type-checking layer for your PHP scripts. In some situations, you might be pulling a number from a query string variable, a page number or item number for example. If you want to make absolutely sure it's a number you're using, and not something potentially more evil—like a SQL injection attack—you have two options.

The first and most commonly used method is adding extra code to your PHP scripts to actually check if the $_GET parameter indeed holds a number. For example, you might have the URL:

```
http://www.domain.com/article.php?page=2
```

URLs such as this are often found in paginated content, usually in page-navigation links. Somewhere in the code that loads the specified page of the article, you might see the following:

```php
<?php
if (isset($_GET['page']) and is_numeric($_GET['page']))
{
   $page = $_GET['page'];
}
else
{
   $page = 1;
}

// And so on....
?>
```

The previous code simply checks first for the existence of a specific $_GET value, in this case 'page', and then checks if the value passed is indeed a number—if not, a default value of one is assigned.

Such type-checking is a good idea, and helps shield your PHP scripts from nasty script kiddies who want to break your website. Unfortunately, it can become somewhat tedious requiring your PHP scripts to check whether or not the value was set, and if it was indeed a number.

Using mod_rewrite, you can eliminate the type checking from your PHP code—all you have to do is ensure the pattern matches only numeric values:

```
RewriteEngine On
# Ensure only numeric values for the page
RewriteRule  ^article/([0-9]+)/?  article.php?page=$1
RewriteRule  ^article/[^0-9]+/?  article.php?page=1
```

The first `RewriteRule` checks for any valid URLs in the form of `/article/page/`, and translates the given request into the call to the PHP script. The second `RewriteRule` is set up to catch all malformed URLs calling for an article, but giving an invalid value for the page number. Any such request is automatically assigned the first page in the article.

There are two things to note in the previous set of RewriteRules. First, both rules are processed in order; processing does not stop at the first rule, but continues through all rules given. Second, the redirection to the `article.php` script is handled internally — no HTTP redirect/moved status code is sent to the client at all. In order to alter these default behaviors, you can use a set of flags at the end of each rule.

RewriteRule Flags

In order to control the ways that mod_rewrite handles and processes each `RewriteRule`, you have a set of 15 different flags that you can add following each rule. Flags are contained within brackets, and multiple flags can be provided in a comma-separated list — all within a common set of brackets. For example:

```
# Rewrite /category/item/ to catalog.php
RewriteRule  ^(\w+)/(\w+)/?$  catalog.php?cat=$1&item=$2 [NC,R,L]
```

nocase|NC

Similar to the `i` flag in PHP's PCRE syntax, the `nocase` flag makes the pattern case-insensitive. For example, the following two patterns are identical:

```
RewriteRule  ^([A-za-z])/?  catalog.php?cat=$1
RewriteRule  ^([a-z])/?  catalog.php?cat=$1 [NC]
```

redirect|R[=code]

Normally mod_rewrite uses an internal Apache redirect when rewriting URLs, and this redirection is invisible to the user. If instead you wanted to do a formal redirect, complete with HTTP status code, you can use the `redirect` or `R` flag. By default, the redirect flag sends a HTTP 302 Moved Temporarily code, such as in the following rule:

```
RewriteRule  ^article/(\d+)/?  article.php?page=$1 [R]
```

If you wanted to change the status code to a HTTP 301 Moved Permanently, or any other status code between 300 and 400, you simply add the code to the end of the redirect flag:

```
RewriteRule  ^article/(\d+)/?  article.php?page=$1 [R=301]
```

forbidden|F

Similar to the `redirect` flag, using the `forbidden` flag immediately sends a HTTP 403 Forbidden response to the client. Whenever both a `redirect` flag and `forbidden` flag are present for the same rule, the `forbidden` flag will have priority (the `redirect` will be ignored, 403 sent).

gone|G

Another HTTP status code control flag, `gone`, sends a response of HTTP 410 Gone, to inform the client the page no longer exits. When combined, the `gone` flag has precedence over the `redirect` flag, but not the `forbidden` flag.

last|L

To stop the processing of RewriteRules after a successful match is found, you use the `last` flag. In the previous example dealing with processing article page numbers, the rule processing would still continue to the second rule (but not find a match), even if the first rule was a successful match. To stop the processing after the first rule matched, you could simply use the `last` flag:

```
RewriteEngine On
# Ensure only numeric values for the page
RewriteRule  ^article/([0-9]+)/?  article.php?page=$1 [L]
RewriteRule  ^article/[^0-9]+/?   article.php?page=1  [L]
```

next|N

The `next` flag restarts the rewriting process at the beginning of the rule list. When the rules are re-processed, the URL matched is not the original request from the client, but the internally rewritten URL at the point where the `next` flag was used. For example:

```
RewriteRule  ^article/(\d+)/?  article.php?page=$1
RewriteRule  ^catalog/(\w+)/?  catalog.php?cat=$1   [N]
RewriteRule  ^catalog/(\w+)/(\w+)/? catalog.php?cat=$1&item=$2
```

In this example, if a URL is called that matches the second rule, such as `http://localhost/catalog/stuff/`, rewriting will stop processing at that point and automatically restart at the beginning of the rule set, using the new substituted URL, `catalog.php?cat=stuff`. The substituted URL is then itself filtered through the whole rule set.

Care should be taken when using the `next` flag, as infinite loops are possible.

chain|C

If you wanted to treat a block of rules as a single related unit, similar to the `try...catch` syntax in PHP, you can use the `chain` flag. When using the chain flag, if a rule matches, the processing continues as expected and ignores the `chain` flag. If a rule does not match and a `chain` flag is present, all of the following rules that are chained together will be skipped as a whole block. For example, the following set of rules skips to the last rule if the first one does not match:

```
RewriteRule  ^article/(\d+)/?  article.php?page=$1  [C]
RewriteRule  ^catalog/(\w+)/?  catalog.php?cat=$1   [C]
RewriteRule  ^catalog/(\w+)/(\w+)/? catalog.php?cat=$1&item=$2

# Skip to this rule if any of the above don't match
RewriteRule  ^article/[^\d]/?  error.php
```

skip|S=number

This flag allows you to skip the next number of rules when the current rule matches. While the behavior of the skip flag is similar to the chain flag, it behaves in exactly the opposite manner — skip jumps on a successful match; chain jumps on a failed match.

type|T=mime-type

If you want to override the MIME type sent for a document, you can use the type flag. For example, if you have a bunch of .xhtml files you want to serve up using a proper XHTML MIME type, instead of text/HTML, you could use the following:

```
RewriteRule  ^.+\.xhtml$ - [T=application/xhtml+xml]
```

cookie|CO=name:value:domain[:lifetime[:path]]

The cookie flag, as you might infer, sets a cookie on the client's browser. The three required fields — name, value, and domain — specify the name of the cookie, the value of the cookie, and the domain for which the cookie is set. The optional lifetime parameter represents the life of the cookie, in minutes. The path parameter sets the path of the cookie.

For example, if you wanted to set a cookie named prevvisit to signify a user has visited the home page before (and shouldn't be bothered with splash screens), you could use this:

```
RewriteRule ^index\.php$ - [CO=prevvisit:true:domain.com]
```

env|E=var:value

The env flag allows you to set an environment variable var to the value provided. The value can also contain regular expression backreferences ($N and %N) for more complex variable control. Multiple environment variables can be set in one group of flags — they just need to be comma-separated like the rest of the flag list.

qsappend|QSA

In most situations when you'll use mod_rewrite, anything provided as a query-string to the original URL is dropped when you perform a rewrite. If you want to preserve that information instead of dropping it, you can use the qsappend flag. When using this flag, the rewrite engine simply takes the original query string and appends it to any new query string provided in the rewrite. For example:

```
RewriteRule ^index\.php$ index.php?foo=bar [QSA]
```

This rule would change the index.php file, using the URL index.php?moo=cow, to be index.php?foo=bar&moo=cow.

In the event that a query-string parameter in the original URL shares the same name as a parameter in the RewriteRule, the original value takes precedence.

noescape|NE

When mod_rewrite performs its transformations, it goes to great lengths to make sure special characters in the rewritten URL are escaped before performing any internal or external redirection. For example:

```
RewriteRule ^somedir/? index.php?page=foo\%3b [R]
```

Given this rule, Apache would redirect the /somedir/ directory as requested, and the $_GET value for page will be a "safe" escaped value of foo%3b—mod_rewrite has escaped the \%3b value instead of replacing it with its semicolon substitute. To tell mod_rewrite to avoid any automatic escaping, you use the noescape flag:

```
RewriteRule ^somedir/? index.php?page=foo\%3b [R,NE]
```

Given this rule, the new value of the page query-string parameter will be foo;.

passthrough|PT

Use the passthrough flag when you want to combine mod_rewrite with other Apache modules that provide similar URL-handling functionality, such as mod_alias. For example, if you wanted to rewrite /foo to point to /bar, and then use mod_alias to translate /bar to /baz, you might try the following:

```
RewriteRule ^/foo /bar
Alias /bar /baz
```

Unfortunately, because of the way Apache handles URIs internally, it would not work as written. To make it work, add the passthrough flag:

```
RewriteRule ^/foo /bar [PT]
Alias /bar /baz
```

A general rule of thumb is to use passthrough if you are using more than one URL translating module to process a file.

nosubreq|NS

Use the nosubreq flag to force the rewrite engine to skip a rule if the request is actually an internal sub-request. When using PHP and Apache together, there are seldom situations when this flag is actually needed. There are, however, some CGI scripting instances where this flag comes into play. For more information, see the Apache manual section on RewriteRule: http://httpd.apache.org/docs-2.0/mod/mod_rewrite.html#rewriterule.

proxy|P

The proxy flag tells the rewrite engine to stop processing the rule-set immediately and force the request through the Apache proxy module, mod_proxy.

With all this attention being given to RewriteRule, you might think that it's the main force behind mod_rewrite. In reality, its best role is part of the dynamic duo that is RewriteRule and RewriteCond.

RewriteCond

The `RewriteCond` directive behaves much like PHP's `if ()` statement: it tests a string against a pattern or condition. If the input matches the pattern or string, the `RewriteRule` immediately following the `RewriteCond` directive is processed. The general format for `RewriteCond` is as follows:

```
RewriteCond TestString CondPattern
```

`TestString` is the string you are evaluating, and `CondPattern` is the regular expression or comparison value to check against.

RewriteCond Usage

The most common way that `RewriteCond` is used is to match the input string against a regular expression, similar to `RewriteRule`. However, when you use `RewriteCond`, you have access to a good number of server variables, so your input string can be more complex than a simple filename match. The following tables list the server variables are available to use in `RewriteCond`.

The following are the HTTP Header variables:

HTTP_USER_AGENT	A string listing the browser's identifying information, such as: `Mozilla/4.0 (compatible; MSIE 6.0; Windows NT 5.1; SV1; .NET CLR 1.1.4322)`
HTTP_REFERER	The previous page visited by the user, as reported by their browser
HTTP_COOKIE	Any cookie string that was part of the request
HTTP_FORWARDED	Contains any forward information if the request is handled by a proxy server
HTTP_HOST	The hostname as referenced in the request
HTTP_PROXY_CONNECTION	The contents of the HTTP Proxy-Connection header
HTTP_ACCEPT	Returns the Accept header value; indicates what kind of content the browser can handle, and what types take precedence

The following are the Request variables:

REMOTE_ADDR	The IP address of the user requesting the file.
REMOTE_HOST	The hostname of the user requesting the file.
REMOTE_USER	The username of the person requesting the file, as reported by the browser.
REMOTE_IDENT	Variable set for identification purposes. Can possibly contain the username.
REQUEST_METHOD	The method used in the request, such as GET or POST.

Table continued on following page

SCRIPT_FILENAME	The full local path to the requested file.
PATH_INFO	Any extra path information added to the end if the URL.
QUERY_STRING	Any query string or GET parameters for the request, typically anything that follows the question mark in a GET request with parameters.
AUTH_TYPE	The type of authentication used to authenticate users.

The following are the Server variables:

DOCUMENT_ROOT	The root folder for the website, as specified in the `Document-Root` directive
SERVER_ADMIN	The email address of the server admin, as specified using the `ServerAdmin` directive
SERVER_ADDR	The server's hostname or IP address
SERVER_PORT	The port number of the server as specified in the request
SERVER_PROTOCOL	Name and version of the request protocol, such as `HTTP/1.1`
SERVER_SOFTWARE	The name of the server software (Apache)

The following are the Time variables:

TIME_YEAR	The current year for the request
TIME_MON	The current month for the request
TIME_DAY	The current day for the request
TIME_HOUR	The current hour for the request
TIME_MIN	The current minute for the request
TIME_SEC	The current second for the request
TIME_WDAY	The current day of the week
TIME	The current time

These are various Special variables:

API_VERSION	The version of the Apache module API (not the same as the Apache version number, but closely related); used mainly for module development (internally)
THE_REQUEST	Complete HTTP file request string, including method, file requested, and HTTP version used
REQUEST_URI	The resource requested in the HTTP request

REQUEST_FILENAME	Full local file system path for the item matching the HTTP request
IS_SUBREQ	Whether or not the request being processed is an internal sub-request; the value will be "true" if the request is a subrequest, "false" if not
HTTPS	A value of "on" indicates SSL/TLS is being used, "off" if not

To use any of the variables from that long list, you wrap the variable name in curly braces, and prefix with a percent sign, like so:

```
%{SCRIPT_FILENAME}
```

To see `RewriteCond` in action, first rewrite a `RewriteRule` to make use of `RewriteCond`. The old rule looked like this:

```
# Rewrite /category/ to catalog.php
RewriteRule  ^(\w+)/?$  catalog.php?cat=$1&item=$2
```

To accomplish the same goal using `RewriteCond` in conjunction with `RewriteRule`, use the following:

```
# Rewrite /category/item/ to catalog.php
RewriteCond %{SCRIPT_FILENAME} ^(\w+)/(\w+)/?$
RewriteRule .*  catalog.php?cat=$1&item=$2
```

Notice how the server variable `SCRIPT_FILENAME` was used as the test input string. Combining `RewriteCond` with `RewriteRule` using these server variables, you can come up with some interesting combinations. The following checks to see if the user's browser can accept XHTML MIME types, and if so, changes the MIME type header sent for .html files:

```
RewriteCond %{HTTP_ACCEPT} application/xhtml\+xml
RewriteRule .*\.html$ - [T=application/xhtml+xml]
```

Another helpful feature of `RewriteCond` is the ability to chain multiple lines together. When listing multiple `RewriteCond` statements in a row, they are each treated like a programmatic AND — the `RewriteRule` at the end will only process if *all* the `RewriteCond` matches return true. The previous set of rules could be rewritten using multiple `RewriteCond` statements, like this:

```
RewriteCond %{HTTP_ACCEPT} application/xhtml\+xml
RewriteCond %{SCRIPT_FILENAME} \.html$
RewriteRule .* - [T=application/xhtml+xml]
```

In addition to the standard string-versus-regex comparisons, you can actually make simple comparison and system-check conditionals with `RewriteCond`. To compare your input string against another simple string, you can use the following as your conditional pattern:

```
<CondPattern
>CondPattern
=CondPattern
```

Each of these checks if the input string is less than, greater than, or equal to, the `CondPattern`, respectively. For example, if you wanted to make a certain area of your website forbidden after a given year, you could use the following:

```
RewriteCond %{TIME_YEAR} >2005
RewriteRule .* - [F]
```

Along with these simple comparison operators, you have access to six more conditional checks that evaluate the statuses of files and directories:

Comparison Operator	Meaning
-d (is directory)	Tests if a directory exists that matches the test string
-f (is regular file)	Tests if a regular file exists that matches the test string
-s (is regular file with size)	Tests if a regular file exists that matches the test string, and has a size greater than 0 bytes
-l (is symbolic link)	Tests if a symbolic link exists that matches the test string
-F (is existing file via subrequest)	Tests if a regular file is accessible after considering all of the server's access controls; uses an internal subrequest to perform the check (performance hit)
-U (is existing URL via subrequest)	Tests if a URL is accessible after considering all of the server's access controls; uses an internal subrequest to perform the check (performance hit)

For example, to check to see if an image exists and actually contains some data, you could use the following:

```
RewriteCond %{REQUEST_FILENAME} \.jpg$
RewriteCond %{REQUEST_FILENAME} !-s
RewriteRule .* - [G]
```

The first condition checks to see if a .jpeg file is called, and the second condition actually checks to see if the file either doesn't exist, or is 0 bytes. Notice the use of the exclamation point before the -s conditional pattern. Any conditional pattern used in `RewriteCond` can be prefixed with an exclamation point, thus negating it — identical to the use of the exclamation point in PHP conditionals.

RewriteCond Flags

To help control `RewriteCond` further, a couple of flags are provided, similar to the `RewriteRule` flags.

nocase|NC

Like the same-named flag used with `RewriteRule`, nocase specifies that the regular expression to be evaluated is case-insensitive.

ornext|OR

The default chaining method for multiple `RewriteCond` directives is to use a logical AND. If the `ornext` flag is used, the two connected `RewriteConds` are compared with a logical OR.

While the `RewriteRule` and `RewriteCond` directives deliver a majority of the power in mod_rewrite, there are a handful of other key directives that can help you control your rewriting and solve problems.

RewriteBase

In most situations, your website URLs will not match your physical file system layout. The root of your website is almost never located at the root (/) of the local file system. In normal operation of Apache server, this is not usually a problem; when using `RewriteRule`, it can be very problematic. `RewriteBase` allows you to specify the base or prefix path for a set of URL rewrites.

To fully understand the reasoning for `RewriteBase`, take a look at the following example ruleset used to rewrite a simple set of files:

```
RewriteEngine On

RewriteRule ^foo\.html$ bar.html [R]
```

Suppose your web root is being served out of the /www folder of the local file system (that is, your `DocumentRoot` is set to /www). If you tried to use the preceding rule in a per-directory access file (.htaccess), it would actually result in the request being rewritten incorrectly — instead of your expected http://www.domain.com/bar.html file being returned, you get http://www.domain.com/www/bar.html. Why is this? Here is a simplified version of what is happening internally to Apache:

```
Request: /www/foo.html (local physical path)

Rewriting:
  /www/foo.html -> foo.html (directory prefix stripped)
  foo.html -> bar.html (RewriteRule applied)
  bar.html -> /www/bar.html (directory prefix re-applied)
  /www/bar.html -> http://www.domain.com/www/bar.html
                   (domain prefix applied to URL, sent to browser)
```

To solve this, you simply add a `RewriteBase` statement to your ruleset:

```
RewriteEngine On
RewriteBase /

RewriteRule ^foo\.html$ bar.html [R]
```

RewriteLog

In order to get a first-hand glimpse of what is actually going on with mod_rewrite, try out the `RewriteLog` directive. You can use `RewriteLog` to specify a log file where a running record of the internal rewrite processing will be sent.

To enable a log of the rewrites alongside the other default Apache log files, use the following:

```
RewriteLog "logs/rewrite_log"
```

When specifying the path for the rewrite log, you can use both absolute and relative paths. If a relative path is used, it will be taken relative to the ServerRoot setting in httpd.conf.

Note that the RewriteLog directive is applied on a per-server basis, so it must be placed in either the server config or a virtual host container inside httpd.conf — it is not allowed inside a <Directory> section or .htaccess file.

RewriteLogLevel

To control how verbose the rewrite log records are, you can use the RewriteLogLevel directive. Given a number 0 through 9, with 9 being the most verbose, you can control how much internal processing is recorded. A setting of 0 disables logging altogether, and anything greater than 2 should be used only for debugging — it can slow down Apache on the higher settings.

If you'd like to delve deeper into the workings of mod_rewrite, check out the mod_rewrite section of the Apache online manual:

```
http://httpd.apache.org/docs-2.0/mod/mod_rewrite.html
```

URL Spell Checking

With the power of mod_rewrite at your side, there's very little in the way of malformed or changed URLs that you can't handle, but what about spelling mistakes? Sure, you could come up with a huge list of possible misspellings for each of the files in your website, and write about a thousand RewriteRules, but it's not necessary. To alleviate you from the burden of "simple" spellchecking, Apache comes with the mod_speling module (and yes, it really is spelled with only one "l"). With mod_speling, you can offload the task of handling URL spelling mistakes to Apache, which will automatically do its best to determine what file the user had intended to load.

To use mod_speling, start by first checking to see if it is already available to Apache as a statically built module:

```
/path/to/httpd -l
```

If you don't see mod_speling.c in the list, check the Apache modules directory for mod_speling.so:

```
ls /path/to/apache/modules
```

If you don't find either the static library or the dynamic module, you'll need to build them yourself. As before, you can choose between statically building the module into Apache itself or building it as a dynamic module.

To build the static version, change your configure command to include mod_speling, as follows:

```
./configure \
--enable-speling \
# ...and any other configure settings you use
```

If you prefer to use the dynamic module instead, just add =shared to the mod_speling line:

```
./configure \
--enable-speling=shared \
# ...and any other configure settings you use
```

After the configure script, it's a simple matter of building and installing the new binaries and modules using make and make install. If you chose to use the dynamic module for mod_speling, you'll need to do one extra step. To enable mod_speling as a dynamic module, uncomment or add the following line in your httpd.conf file:

```
LoadModule speling_module modules/mod_speling.so
```

Once the changes have been made, restart Apache. If no errors are shown in the Apache error log, then you've successfully added mod_speling capabilities to your server.

To actually use the spell-checking, add the following directive to the global server config section, your virtual host section, a <Directory> section, or a simple .htaccess file:

```
CheckSpelling on
```

Configuring mod_speling involves only the CheckSpelling directive — a value of "on" enables the spellchecking, and "off" disables any checks, which is the default behavior.

To see mod_speling in action, enable CheckSpelling in a directory of your choosing, and then create the following script in that directory, called info.php:

```
<?php phpinfo(); ?>
```

By now, you should recognize this as the standard PHP information dump output, but instead of loading the file using the correct info.php URL, try loading it using a slightly misspelled name, like ingo.php. With mod_speling enabled, Apache performs a quick HTTP 301 redirect to its best guess at what you intended, instead of serving up a cold plate of 404 Not Found.

Content Compression

What if we were to tell you that with a couple minutes of Apache configuration, you could shave drastic amounts off your monthly bandwidth usage? You might think it's a lie, but in fact it's quite true — all you need is content compression and a couple of configuration directives.

What's content compression? When web pages are downloaded over the Internet, by default the bits and bytes that make up the page markup, images, stylesheets, and other content are in a mostly uncompressed state. The HTML that you write is sent directly as you saved it, whitespace and all. Content compression allows you to transparently compress the page markup and send it across the Internet to the user's browser, where it is silently uncompressed before it is rendered to the screen. Another way to think about it is in relation to sending zipped files via email. You could just as easily send a large document of multi-media file as a plain attachment to an email, but many times you compress the file into a zip or tar.gz archive before sending, to help shorten the time it takes to download the message and attachment.

Using content compression with Apache is very easy. All you need is mod_deflate, which comes with the Apache source code and is easily compiled in as a module when building Apache.

Using mod_deflate

As with the previously discussed modules, the first thing you need to do is check to see if the module is available either statically part of Apache, or as a module:

```
/path/to/httpd -l
ls /path/to/apache/modules/
# ...and any other configure settings you might use
```

If you see mod_deflate.c in the output of the first command, or mod_deflate.so in the output of the second, you already have access to mod_deflate, and can skip the next steps where you rebuild Apache.

If you don't see mod_deflate in either of the command results, you'll need to add it either statically built into the Apache binary, or as a dynamic module. To include mod_deflate statically in Apache when building from source, all you need to do is add the following when you run configure:

```
./configure \
--enable-deflate
```

If you wish to use the dynamic loadable module, just add =shared to the end of the line enabling mod_deflate:

```
./configure \
--enable-deflate=shared \
# ...and any other configure settings you might use
```

Obviously, if you plan on including other directives when running configure, you'll need to add those as well. After configuring the source, do the usual make and (as root) make install.

If you built mod_deflate as a dynamic module, you'll have to enable the module in httpd.conf using LoadModule:

```
LoadModule deflate_module modules/mod_deflate.so
```

Then restart Apache so the changes take effect.

After you build and enable mod_deflate, it's a simple matter of telling Apache to use mod_deflate, and what file types to compress. To do that, you'll need to edit your httpd.conf file, or create or modify an .htaccess file in the directory you want to use compression — the former being the preferred method if available.

To enable compression globally in Apache, add the following to your httpd.conf:

```
AddOutputFilterByType DEFLATE text/*
AddOutputFilterByType DEFLATE application/ms*
AddOutputFilterByType DEFLATE application/vnd*
AddOutputFilterByType DEFLATE application/postscript
```

Then all you need to do is restart Apache, and you'll have content compression up and running.

What exactly do all those configuration directives mean? It's pretty straightforward actually — in Apache 2.*x*, the AddOutputFilterByType directive does exactly what it looks like: it tells Apache to pass the output through a given filter, mod_deflate in this case, before hurling the response to the end-user's browser. The previous example code told Apache to use the DEFLATE filter, mod_deflate, on any text-based files (text/*), any Microsoft documents such as Word or Excel files (application/ms* and application/vnd*), and any postscript files such as Adobe Illustrator or EPS drawings (application/ postscript). Any document type you like can be added to mod_deflate's filtering list by simply using a combination of the document's MIME type and wildcards, similar to the example.

If you want to compress only plain text and HTML files, use the following:

```
AddOutputFilterByType DEFLATE text/plain
AddOutputFilterByType DEFLATE text/html
```

What if you wanted to compress everything that Apache served? Using another Apache directive, SetOutputFilter, you can tell Apache to send every file through mod_deflate:

```
SetOutputFilter DEFLATE
```

However, in most server setups, this is not a very good idea. There are in fact some file types that do not benefit from compression, and some that become corrupted for the end-user when compressed. In most situations, there is no need to compress image formats, as the most commonly used web formats already have some built-in form of compression. Additionally, PDFs are also compressed, and should absolutely never be filtered through mod_deflate, as they will become unreadable in Acrobat Reader.

It should be noted that versions of Netscape Navigator 4.x cannot reliably decompress any file type other than text/html, and specific versions of Netscape Navigator 4.x cannot decompress any file types.

In order to further tweak the compression of your chosen file types, mod_deflate provides the configuration directives described in the following sections.

DeflateCompressionLevel

DeflateCompressionLevel sets the level of compression used to shrink the files, a range from 1 to 9. A compression level of 1 yields the fastest compression, with the least amount of compression (larger files), and a compression level of 9 uses the slowest compression, but the resulting file sizes are much smaller. When deciding which level to use, you must determine which is more important for you — saving processor cycles or saving download time. The default compression level of 6 is usually a good compromise between the two.

DeflateFilterNote

If you wanted your log files to show the compression ratio for each requested file in the access log, use `DeflateFilterNote`. `DeflateFilterNote` takes the name of a log token as its value — the named token given with `DeflateFilterNote` can then be used to customize the output of your logs using Apache's `LogFormat` directive.

DeflateWindowSize

This specifies the zlib compression window size, used in compressing the files. Values range from 1 to 15, with 1 yielding less compression and 15 giving the most compression. The default value for `DeflateWindowSize` is 15.

How Well Does mod_deflate Work?

In order to see the byte-saving abilities of mod_deflate, this example serves a decent-sized HTML page with Apache, both with and without mod_deflate enabled. In this example, the home page is used for the Wrox P2P community forums, found at `http://p2p.wrox.com`. The raw HTML markup — and the HTML only — for this page weighs in at a hefty 47172 bytes. Have a look at the following table to see how it fared being thrown through mod_deflate at three different compression levels:

Compression Level	Bytes Transferred	% of Original	Approx. Download Time (56k)
Raw	47172 bytes	100% original	11.7 seconds
Default (6)	7621 bytes	16.2% original	3.8 seconds
Level 1	9050 bytes	19.2% original	4.1 seconds
Level 9	7581 bytes	16.1% original	3.8 seconds

As you can see, using mod_deflate clearly has an advantage over serving the raw, uncompressed HTML — eliminating up to nearly 84% of the file size sent over the connection. Also notice that using the maximum compression of 9 edged out the default level of 6 by only a marginal amount, so in this situation it would probably be safe to stick with the default compression level of 6 to save the processor a few cycles.

Many websites have a mixture of HTML, media, and associated scripting files, so sites such as photo-blogs or online shopping malls may not reap tremendous file savings on every file they serve, but each byte saved can really add up to some huge bandwidth reduction at month's end. Text-heavy sites such as blogs and news portals would really see the benefits of content compression, as a majority of the bandwidth utilized on those sites is plain text — text that would find its way through mod_deflate.

Enabling Compression for PHP Scripts

What about PHP files you might be wondering? In many situations there is no need to use compression on PHP files, and in some cases it can be detrimental to the output.

If your PHP script outputs an actual image or PDF for example, you wouldn't want Apache to blindly compress the output, just because the file extension happened to be .php.

In some situations, output buffering and compression might already be enabled for all PHP scripts. To determine, check the value of the configuration variable `output_handler`, or look in php.ini for the values of `output_handler` and `zlib.output_compression`.

To enable output compression within PHP, do the following:

1. Install the zlib libraries on your machine if needed.

2. Configure the PHP source code as needed, making sure you include `--with-zlib`, and then compile/install as normal.

3. Modify your php.ini so it includes the following lines:

```
output_buffering = Off
output_handler =
zlib.output_compression = On
```

4. Restart Apache so the new changes take effect.

Using MySQL with Apache

By now, you've created a security zone or two using Apache and basic authentication, and for most situations, that might be all you need. You may find, however, that basic authentication with Apache, while simple, is a little too limited in the amount of control and customization you can incorporate. For many such situations, you can actually use a combination of Apache basic authentication and the power of relational databases via MySQL. For such a purpose, the mod_auth_mysql Apache module exists.

Like standard Apache basic authentication, mod_auth_mysql can control access per-directory, and can be configured inside both .htaccess files and a `<Directory>` section inside httpd.conf. Unlike standard Apache basic authentication, all user credentials are stored in a database, instead of in flat files.

Setting Up the Database

Installing and configuring mod_auth_mysql involves a few steps, the first of which is to create the necessary database structures to hold the user data. Start by loading up your favorite MySQL client, and creating the database. For example:

```
CREATE DATABASE apacheauth;
```

Next, create a user that will be used by Apache to access the credentials:

```
GRANT SELECT ON apacheauth.* TO apache@localhost IDENTIFIED BY 'apachepass';
```

Now that the database user is created, it's time to add a table to hold the login information. For now start out with a simple table that just holds the username and password:

```
USE apacheauth;
CREATE TABLE user_info (
  user_name varchar(50) NOT NULL,
```

```
    user_password varchar(50) NOT NULL,
    PRIMARY KEY (user_info)
);
```

You can name the table and columns however you like. In the preceding example, user_info is used for the table name, and user_name and user_password are used for the login/password combination because these are the default names recognized by mod_auth_mysql.

In later versions of mod_auth_mysql, the default column for password is user_password, *not* user_passwd *as it states in the module documentation.*

Next, create an initial test user account that you'll use later when testing the authentication:

```
INSERT INTO user_info (user_name, user_password)
VALUES ('testuser', SHA1('testpass'));
```

Notice that the SHA1 function is used on the password in the statement, instead of the PASSWORD() *function. With mod_auth_mysql you can use a handful of encryption methods for the password — this example, just happens to use* SHA1.

Installing the Module

Once you have your database table set up, you'll need to actually download the source for mod_auth_mysql, available at http://modauthmysql.sourceforge.net. At the time of this writing, the current version was 2.9.0, so you would download mod_auth_mysql-2.9.0.tar.gz.

After you've downloaded the module source, extract the tarball:

```
tar -xzvf mod_auth_mysql-2.9.0.tar.gz
```

Once the tarball is extracted, change directories to the newly created source folder:

```
cd mod_auth_mysql-2.9.0
```

To build the module from the downloaded source code, you're actually going to use Apache's apxs command directly. Execute the following command, using the path to your apxs binary on your system; the default Apache location of /usr/local/apache2/bin is used here:

```
/usr/local/apache2/bin/apxs -c -lmysqlclient -lm -lz mod_auth_mysql.c
```

If the build is successful, you should see a couple of compilation lines, and no errors. If, instead, you get an error about a missing mysql.h file, and a whole slew of MySQL-related errors, you might need to manually specify the paths to the MySQL libraries and include files. Using the default locations from MySQL, your command might instead look like this:

```
/usr/local/apache2/bin/apxs -c -lmysqlclient -lm -lz \
-L /usr/local/mysql/lib/mysql \
-I /usr/local/mysql/include/mysql \
mod_auth_mysql.c
```

To install the newly compiled module, you'll need to execute the following command as root. As usual, change the path to `apxs` to point to your `apxs` binary:

```
/usr/local/apache2/bin/apxs -i mod_auth_mysql.la
```

The next installation task you need to perform is to add the necessary command to load the module in httpd.conf. To do this, open your httpd.conf file, find a suitable location to add a module definition—usually at the very end of the configuration file, or next to other `LoadModule` statements—and add the following:

```
LoadModule mysql_auth_module modules/mod_auth_mysql.so
```

Finally, restart Apache.

Configuration and Usage

Once you have your database tables ready and modules installed, all that remains is to tell Apache what needs to be protected. Like standard Apache basic authentication, you'll need to add some configuration directives to either a `<Directory>` section in httpd.conf, or create a .htaccess file in the directory you choose to protect.

Telling Apache to validate user credentials against your MySQL database would usually involve the following at a minimum:

```
AuthName "<zone name>"
AuthType Basic
AuthMySQLDB dbname
AuthMySQLUser userid
AuthMySQLPassword password
AuthMySQLEnable On
require valid-user
```

The first two lines and the last line of these directives should already be familiar to you. They simply define the name of the protected area, the type of authentication, and that any valid user found in the checked resource is allowed access. The other lines tell Apache where to find the authentication information. Instead of giving Apache the name of a file that contains the passwords for each valid user, you're supplying database information—database name, username, and password—so that Apache and mod_auth_mysql know where to look. The sixth line, `AuthMySQLEnable On`, simply tells Apache to actually use mod_auth_mysql—it's a way to disable MySQL authentication without having to completely unload or remove the module.

To use the authentication tables you created earlier, you would add the following in your `<Directory>` or .htaccess definitions:

```
AuthName "MySQLAuth"
AuthType Basic
AuthMySQLDB apacheauth
AuthMySQLUser apache
AuthMySQLPassword apachepass
AuthMySQLEnable On
AuthMySQLPwEncryption sha1
require valid-user
```

Here, you're telling Apache and mod_auth_mysql to authenticate users against your apacheauth database. Apache will be logging into the database using the apache account you created earlier, and you're also telling mod_auth_mysql to hash the given password with SHA1, before matching it against the value in the database.

At this point, you should be able to log into your protected area via a web browser, supply the user credentials added to the user_info table (testuser:testpass), and be successfully authenticated in the directory.

While this example is rather simplistic and stripped down, mod_auth_mysql actually provides a boatload of configuration options, so you can customize your authentication for nearly any situation. The following sections describe some of the configuration options.

AuthMySQLEnable On | Off

This enables or disables mod_auth_mysql authentication, without you having to remove or unload the module from Apache directly.

AuthMySQLHost localhost | hostname | ipaddress

This is the hostname or IP address of the MySQL database server. If your environment runs Apache and MySQL on different machines, you'll need to use this. The default value is localhost, so machines running both Apache and MySQL can usually ignore this setting.

AuthMySQLPort port_number

This is the TCP/IP port on which MySQL is listening. The default value for MySQL is port 3306, but can be changed. The default value for this option is also 3306, so the option needs to be specified only if MySQL is listening on a nonstandard port.

AuthMySQLSocket socket_file_path

This is the UNIX socket file used to access MySQL on a UNIX machine. The default value is /tmp/mysql.sock, and like AuthMySQLPort, it needs to be used only in nonstandard installations.

AuthMySQLUser userid

This is the user ID used to access the MySQL database holding the authentication information. Most database systems will not allow users or the Apache process to access the database without a proper userid/password combination, so set this along with AuthMySQLPassword to a non-root user account that has access to the authentication tables. At a minimum, the user will need SELECT access to the authentication tables.

AuthMySQLPassword password

Used in conjunction with AuthMySQLUser, this option specifies the password for the user account accessing the MySQL authentication tables.

AuthMySQLDB dbname

This is the name of the database in MySQL that holds the authentication tables. If no name is specified, the default value of test will be used.

AuthMySQLUserTable table_name

This is the name of table in the database that holds the usernames and passwords. If no table is specified, the default value of `user_info` is used.

AuthMySQLNameField column_name

This is the name of the column in the user table (`AuthMySQLUserTable`) that holds the usernames. When creating the tables in MySQL, ensure that this column has an index or key, ensuring each value is unique. The `=length` of the column is whatever you decide it should be in MySQL. The default value is `user_name`.

AuthMySQLUserCondition

When mod_auth_mysql performs a user lookup, it performs a simple SQL SELECT statement, with any criteria needed to perform a match. The `AuthMySQLUserCondition` field allows you to specify extra parameters to be used in the `WHERE` clause of the SQL statement.

AuthMySQLPasswordField column_name

This is the name of the column in the user table that holds the users' passwords. The length of the column in MySQL should be at least as long as the encrypted password hash. The default value for `AuthMySQLPasswordField` is `user_password`.

AuthMySQLPwEncryption none | crypt | scrambled | md5 | aes | sha1

This is the method of encryption used when encoding the passwords in the database, as follows:

- ❏   `none`: No encryption/plain text
- ❏   `crypt`: UNIX `crypt()` encryption
- ❏   `scrambled`: MySQL PASSWORD() encryption
- ❏   `md5`: MD5 hashing
- ❏   `aes`: Advanced Encryption Standard (AES) encryption
- ❏   `sha1`: Secure Hash Algorith (SHA1)

If no value is specified, the default value of `crypt` is used.

When using AES password encryption, make sure the password field in your MySQL user tables is a BLOB type, not a CHAR, VARCHAR, or BINARY type. Unless the column type is one of the BLOB variations, MySQL will strip any extra encoded characters from the encrypted passwords—and you'll never be able to match the given password to the database values.

AuthMySQLSaltField

This allows you to specify one of three values to use as the "salt value" when encrypting passwords. A value of <> tells mod_auth_mysql to use the password itself as the salt field. A value of <string> uses the value of *string* as the salt field. Any string not surrounded by less-than/greater-than symbols is treated as the name of a database column, the value of which is used as the salt field.

AuthMySQLGroupTable

This is used to set the name of the table containing group information, when Apache is told to check groups instead of individual users (`require group` versus `require valid-user`).

AuthMySQLGroupCondition

Similar to `AuthMySQLUserCondition`, this directive allows you to specify conditional statements to include in the WHERE clause when matching user groups.

AuthMySQLGroupField

This is the name of the field in the database that contains the group names. This field is used when matching groups using Apache's `require group` directive.

AuthMySQLAuthoritative

This tells Apache whether or not to fallback to other modules if MySQL authentication fails.

Apache and SSL

Protecting your web folders with Basic Authentication by using either htpasswd or mod_auth_mysql increases security. Unfortunately, that added layer of security afforded by Basic Authentication can be eliminated by a serious hacker looking to break into your system. The problem: when you use Basic Authentication on a standard server, the username and password are actually transmitted unencrypted from the client to the server. A network-savvy hacker could be monitoring the transmission between your machine and the server, and sniff out the plain-text passwords as they zing by.

The solution: encrypt the communication between the client and the server. In Apache, this can be achieved by using Secure Sockets Layer (SSL). SSL in Apache comes in the form of mod_ssl, an Apache module that SSL-enables a website that Apache controls, allowing any communication to and from Apache to be encrypted using a wide range of encryption schemes.

To enable SSL in Apache, first check to see if SSL is included in your existing Apache binary or as a loadable module:

```
/path/to/httpd -l
ls /path/to/apache/modules/
```

If you don't see `mod_ssl.c` in the first command output or `mod_ssl.so` in the listing of the Apache modules, you'll need to build Apache SSL functionality yourself. To statically enable SSL, add `-enable-ssl` to your Apache `configure` script when building from source:

```
./configure \
--enable-ssl \
# ...and any other configure settings you use
```

If you want to use the dynamic module instead, just add `=shared` at the end of the SSL-enabling line:

```
./configure \
--enable-ssl=shared \
# ...and any other configure settings you use
```

Then, build and install the new Apache binary and modules using `make` and `make install`. If you built Apache as a dynamic module, enable it in httpd.conf by adding the following line in the global configuration section:

```
LoadModule ssl_module modules/mod_ssl.so
```

Now you might be thinking it's time to restart Apache and configure Apache, but you're not quite done setting up your SSL. Before SSL will work, you need to have a server key and server certificate that will be used to encrypt transmitted data, and present the client/browser with an SSL certificate.

In the next few steps, you'll create your own self-signed certificate for use on your web server. If you already have an SSL certificate from a bona fide Certificate Authority (CA) , you should use that if possible. What exactly is the difference, you might wonder? Any self-signed certificate is not considered truly secure, and will trigger a warning in a user's browser, something like "Your browser does not recognize the Certificate Authority that issued the site's certificate." A certificate from a proper CA is recommended if you're doing any sort of ecommerce or secure transaction.

To begin the certificate creation process, start by creating a private key and certificate request:

```
openssl req -new > testcert.csr
```

This shows the following on the screen, including prompts:

```
Generating a 1024 bit RSA private key
....................++++++
..........++++++
writing new private key to 'privkey.pem'
Enter PEM pass phrase:
Verifying - Enter PEM pass phrase:
-----
You are about to be asked to enter information that will be incorporated
into your certificate request.
What you are about to enter is what is called a Distinguished Name or a DN.
There are quite a few fields but you can leave some blank
For some fields there will be a default value,
If you enter '.', the field will be left blank.
-----
Country Name (2 letter code) [AU]:US
State or Province Name (full name) [Some-State]:Ohio
Locality Name (eg, city) []:Cincinnati
Organization Name (eg, company) [Internet Widgits Pty Ltd]:TestSSL
Organizational Unit Name (eg, section) []:SSL Testing Department
Common Name (eg, YOUR name) []:www.example.com
Email Address []:youremail@example.com
```

```
Please enter the following 'extra' attributes
to be sent with your certificate request
A challenge password []:testchallenge
An optional company name []:Test Company
```

Any responses to the prompts in bold should be replaced by your own appropriate values. Also, be sure that the value you entered for Common Name is the real fully qualified domain name for your server, such as www.yourserver.com.

After the command completes and you've answered all prompts, you will have two new files: privkey.pem, which is a private key used to sign the certificate, and testcert.csr, the certificate request. The next step is to remove the passphrase from the key created in the previous step. If you don't remove the passphrase, you must enter it every time Apache is started. While this may seem like extra security, it's really a nuisance, as it prevents Apache from restarting completely if your server suffers a power failure, or you restart Apache frequently.

To remove the passphrase, use the following command:

```
openssl rsa -in privkey.pem -out testcert.key
```

This will then prompt you to enter the same passphrase you used in the very beginning of the previous command:

```
Enter pass phrase for privkey.pem:
writing RSA key
```

The next step is to convert the certificate request into a signed certificate:

```
openssl x509 \
-in testcert.csr \
-out testcert.cert \
-req \
-signkey testcert.key \
-days 3650
```

This will then show:

```
Signature ok
subject=/C=US/ST=Ohio/L=Cincinnati/O=TestSSL/OU=SSL Testing
Department/CN=www.example.com/emailAddress=youremail@example.com
Getting Private key
```

What you've done here is use the openssl command to request a X.509 certificate, using the testcert.scr certificate request as input, and saved the resultant certificate as testcert.cert, which is self-signed using the private key testcert.key and is a valid certificate for 10 years.

Now that you have both your self-signed server certificate and key, you'll need to copy them both to a location that Apache can use:

```
mkdir -p /etc/apache/ssl.crt
mkdir -p /etc/apache/ssl.key
```

```
cp testcert.cert /etc/apache/ssl.crt/testcert.crt
cp testcert.key /etc/apache/ssl.key/testcert.key
```

Then, create a directory that will house your new SSL website:

```
mkdir -p /wwwssl
```

You can use whatever path you like, or even an existing path—just remember or write down what you used, as you'll need it later when you configure Apache.

Finally, create a simple information file to have something to show later when testing the SSL:

```
echo "<?php phpinfo(); ?>" > /wwwssl/index.php
```

Now that your keys are in place and an SSL web root has been created, you need to enable SSL capabilities in httpd.conf. If your current httpd.conf file includes a line that says "Include /etc/apache/ssl.conf" or similar, then any SSL changes you make should be performed in the specified ssl.conf file. Otherwise, you can make the changes directly in the httpd.conf file, or add your own reference to your own ssl.conf file, and make the changes there.

In your SSL configuration file or section, you'll need to have the following items available in the global configuration scope (not in a Virtual Server or Directory configuration section):

```
Listen 443
```

Next, you need to either reuse an existing VirtualHost section to handle port 443 if it exists, or create a new one that contains the following directives:

```
<VirtualHost _default_:443>

  # Server Certificate:
  SSLCertificateFile /etc/apache/ssl.crt/testcert.crt

  # Server Private Key:
  SSLCertificateKeyFile /etc/apache/ssl.crt/testcert.key

  SSLEngine On

  DocumentRoot "/wwwssl" # Use the SSL directory you created earlier
  Servername www.example.com
  ServerAdmin youremail@example.com
</VirtualHost>
```

Then, once the changes are made to your configuration file, restart Apache. If you load your new SSL site in your browser using an https:// URL, like https://www.example.com, you should be notified that the certificate is not valid (because it is self-signed). Click OK, and you should see the output of your phpinfo() function. If nothing appears, or the browser cannot reach the server, check the Apache error logs for any related error messages—chances are it's a simple typo.

To tweak mod_ssl further, and get a complete list of all the configuration directives that you can use with mod_ssl, visit http://httpd.apache.org/docs/2.0/mod/mod_ssl.html.

Apache as a File Repository

One of the cooler things you can do with Apache is use it as a simple online file repository, with WebDAV. WebDAV, which stands for Web-based Distributed Authoring and Versioning, enables Apache to allow users to treat an enabled directory as a remote directory or drive on their own computers. Similar to a Windows share or NFS export, WebDAV allows remote editing and storage access, only using HTTP as the transport layer instead of a specialized TCP protocol or port like SMB and NFS.

To understand how WebDAV works as a shared drive, it's easier to just see it in action, so next, you're going to enable mod_dav, which ships with Apache, and test it out. To start, as with other modules, check to see if mod_dav is already statically compiled into Apache, or existing as a loadable module:

```
/path/to/httpd -l
ls /path/to/apache/modules
```

As you might have guessed, if you don't see mod_dav.c in the httpd -l output, or mod_dav.so in the file list, you'll need to build it yourself with the Apache httpd source code. To add mod_dav statically into the Apache binary, make sure both --enable-dav and --enable-dav-fs exist in the configure command:

```
./configure \
--enable-dav \
--enable-dav-fs \
# ...and any other configure settings you use
```

To build mod_dav as a shared object, just add =shared to the end of both DAV-related lines:

```
./configure \
--enable-dav=shared \
--enable-dav-fs=shared \
# ...and any other configure settings you use
```

Then build and install the new binary and modules using make and make install.

If you decided to use the dynamic modules for mod_dav, you need to enable them in httpd.conf, using the following lines:

```
LoadModule dav_module     modules/mod_dav.so
LoadModule dav_fs_module modules/mod_dav_fs.so
```

To have a place to actually store the WebDAV file repository, you can create a new directory, or use an existing directory of your choosing. You should place your WebDAV folders inside your SSL-enabled web root, or make sure to enable SSL later on, if you plan to use Basic Authentication to limit access to the WebDAV folders. Basic Authentication sends usernames and passwords in the clear, so you want to SSL-enable the protected directories to encrypt the Basic Auth requests. Create the new folders if needed, and create a dummy file to add to the WebDAV folder:

```
mkdir -p /wwwssl/dav
echo "Testing DAV" > /wwwssl/dav/testing.txt
```

When users access your WebDAV folder, you're going to authenticate them against a database or htpasswd file, to prevent anonymous users all over the Internet from filling up your hard drive. First, create a htpasswd file to store the passwords of valid users, and initialize it with the user account for testdav:

```
mkdir -p /davauth
/path/to/htpasswd -c /davauth/dav.htpasswd testdav
```

When prompted for a password, enter a password of your choosing. Next, create a .htaccess file in the /wwwssl/dav folder to enforce basic authentication. The .htaccess file should contain the following:

```
AuthName "DAV Test"
AuthType Basic
AuthUserFile "/davauth/dav.htpasswd"
require valid-user
```

Finally, create a Directory entry in your httpd.conf to enable WebDAV and basic authentication for the given directory:

```
<Directory "/wwwssl/dav">
  AllowOverride AuthConfig
  Dav On
</Directory>
```

Then you can restart Apache, and WebDAV will be enabled for the /dav/ folder of your HTTPS site, accessible at something like https://www.example.com/dav. You can try to load this URL in your web browser, but it will behave no differently than a standard non-DAV web directory. To use the capabilities of your WebDAV URL, you'll need to use software that is WebDAV-enabled.

Editors such as jEdit, NuSphere's PHPEd, and Macromedia Dreamweaver, among others, all support WebDAV at some level. If you don't have any of those editors at your disposal, have no fear — most modern operating systems actually support the mounting of WebDAV shares natively in their file explorer/browser utilities.

To access your WebDAV share using your operating system's file browser, follow the instructions in whichever of the proceeding sections pertains to your OS.

Windows 2000/XP

To set up WebDAV under Windows 2000 or XP, you need to run through the Add Network Place wizard as follows:

1. Go to My Network Places, and double-click Add Network Place, as shown in Figure 6.1.

2. When the Add Network Place Wizard appears, click Next to bring up a list of service providers. Select the Choose Another Network Location option, as shown in Figure 6.2, and then click Next.

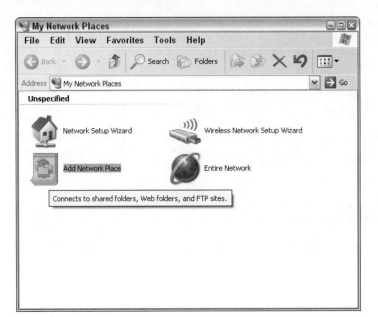

Figure 6.1

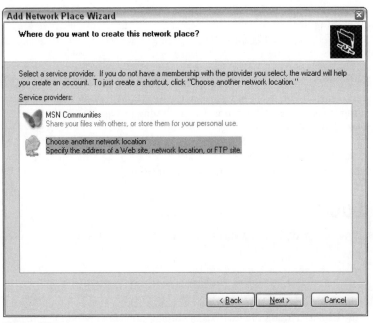

Figure 6.2

3. Enter the URL to your WebDAV directory in the Internet or Network Address field, as shown in Figure 6.3. Then click Next.

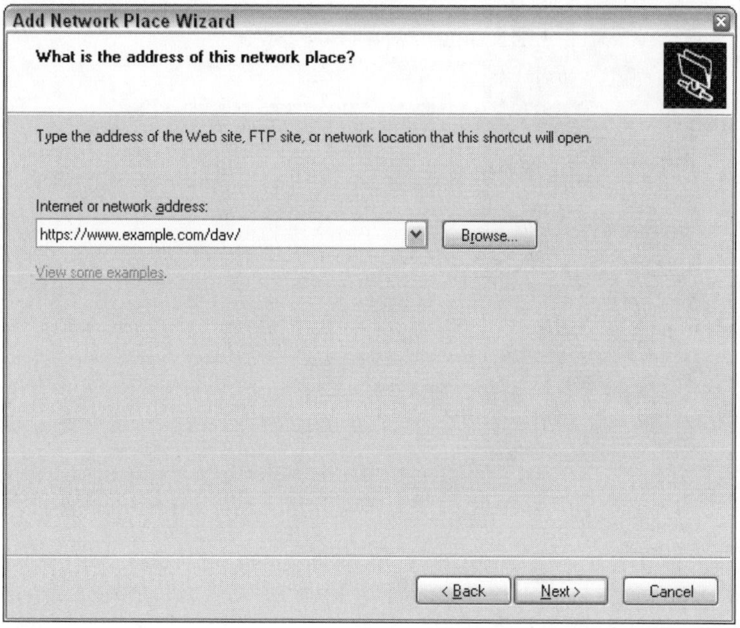

Figure 6.3

4. Click Yes in the SSL Security Alert dialog box. The warning is given because you're using a self-signed certificate — the same warning you saw when trying to access your SSL-enabled website earlier.

5. You will then be prompted to enter a username and password to access the DAV Test realm. Enter the values you used when creating the htpasswd file.

6. You are then prompted to give a name for the network place, to help you easily identify the location later. Enter **My WebDAV** as the name for the network place.

7. Now your WebDAV location should be set up, and you'll see the Completing the Add Network Place Wizard screen. Check the box for Open This Network Place When I Click Finish, as shown in Figure 6.4.

8. You will then be re-prompted to accept the self-signed SSL certificate and enter a username and password. Accept the certificate and enter the credentials you used in step 5.

9. You should then see the contents of the WebDAV share in a standard Windows Explorer window, as shown in Figure 6.5.

10. Use the My WebDAV share as a standard drive or folder — you can add, edit, and delete files on the WebDAV share, just as you would a local folder.

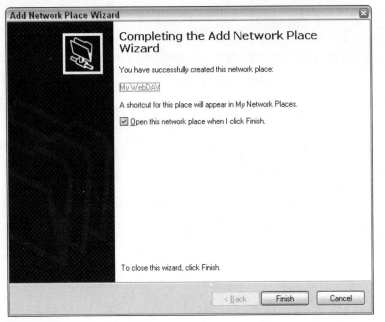

Figure 6.4

Figure 6.5

Mac OS X

To set up WebDAV under Mac OS X, do the following:

1. From the Finder menu, choose Go ⇨ Connect to Server, or simply type Command-K in a Finder window. This will bring up the Connect to Server window as shown in Figure 6.6. Enter the URL for your WebDAV share in the Server Address field, and then click Connect.

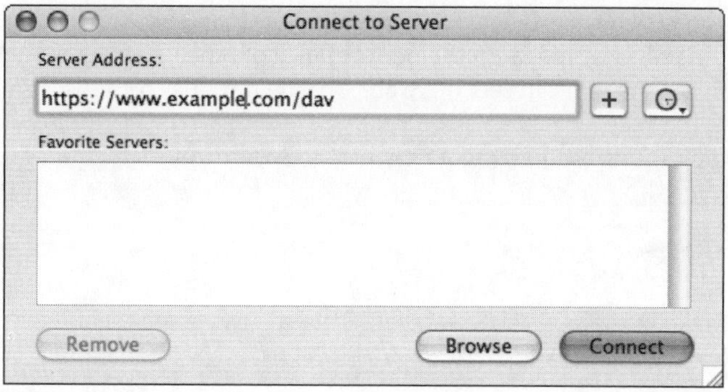

Figure 6.6

2. You are prompted to accept the self-signed SSL certificate. Click Continue.

3. A username and password prompt for the DAV Test realm appears. Enter the username and password you used when creating the htpasswd file earlier.

4. The mapped WebDAV drive should now show up as a regular mounted network volume in the Finder, as in Figure 6.7. You should now be able to use it like any standard local or network volume.

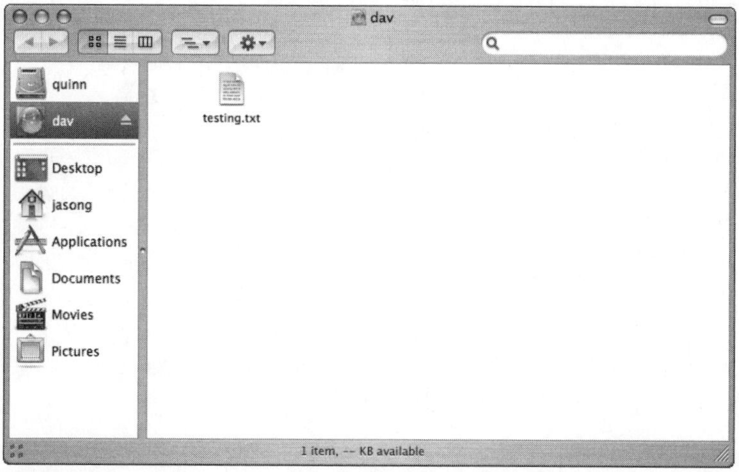

Figure 6.7

Summary

In this chapter, you've seen how adding a few Apache modules can improve the performance of your site considerably. It told you how to streamline URL redirection, fix user typos, compress your content to save bandwidth, create a web-based file share, and secure your site with MySQL and SSL. This extensibility is what makes Apache more than just an ordinary web server.

After you've explored the potential of the modules discussed here, you should investigate others that you can find at httpd.apache.org and sourceforge.net. You'll find modules there that can authenticate users against other databases, speed up the performance of other languages such s Perl, use Apache as a proxy server, and more. As you can see, there are Apache modules for all sorts of purposes.

Although this chapter introduced you to a new way to secure your site, the next chapter tackles the issue of security head-on.

Site Security

Security is one of the foremost concerns of every site administrator — and if it isn't, it should be. Placing your site on the public Internet is an open invitation to intruders of every sort, and you need to be able to handle them, no matter how small or specialized your site may be. Fortunately, PHP can help you protect your site and your users' data. As discussed in the previous chapter, you can use Apache to control authentication, but you can also use PHP's built-in functions to make your own authentication system. After this chapter shows you how to do that, it will take you through some of the more common types of attacks you may encounter, and show you some simple methods to prevent them.

Controlling Access

When you think about securing a website, one of the first things that might come to your mind is a way to restrict access. If the bad guys can't get to the web application, it's safe, right? When you choose a way to protect your sensitive files and scripts, you have a couple of choices, some built-in to Apache, some that are PHP-based, and some that are a mixture of the two.

Apache-Controlled Authentication

The easiest way to lock down a website is to use Basic Authentication, which was covered in Chapter 6. Using a combination of .htaccess and password files, you can quickly restrict access to any given folder of your website. This approach has many advantages.

Primarily, it is extremely easy to implement. Coming standard with the default installation of Apache, simple per-directory Basic Authentication can easily be set up using either .htaccess or `<Directory>` entries.

What is the downside to using the built-in Apache authentication? It can be a hassle to maintain a complex hierarchy of restricted folders and users. If you have a large number of users or groups, and a fair number of protected directories, it can quickly become a nightmare to ensure the proper users are in the proper groups, with access to the proper resources, with current passwords, and so on.

Simple authentication with Apache can also be a problem if you're dealing with multiple load-balanced or mirrored web servers. Because the user credentials are stored on each machine, you can end up in a state of file disparity — some password files might contain a different number of users, with different passwords, or other problems.

As an alternative to simple file-based authentication with Apache, you can also use the mod_auth_mysql Apache module, also covered in Chapter 6. Using mod_auth_mysql centralizes your username/password storage, and also gives you the ability to do complex permission-matching abilities — not a simple user-name-match as with the standard Apache Basic Authentication.

Like simple authentication with Apache, mod_auth_mysql relies on access rights specified in .htaccess files or a `<Directory>` entry in httpd.conf. If you do not have access to change the Apache configuration, and .htaccess files aren't permitted by your host, you'll need to find another method. Enter PHP-based authentication.

PHP-Controlled Authentication

If Apache-controlled authentication is out of the question, you can actually use the power of PHP to emulate standard Basic Authentication. By sending the proper response headers, and checking for the right server variables, you can build your own basic authentication system from scratch, and it'll have just as much power as mod_auth_mysql, if not more.

To show how you can use PHP for basic authentication, you're going to set up a simple database to use as your repository for user credentials. PHP will then check the usernames and passwords against that database; all the end-user will see is the standard Basic Authentication prompt.

Creating the Authentication Database

Start by creating a database in MySQL called `WebAuth`:

```
CREATE DATABASE WebAuth;
USE WebAuth;
```

Next, create a MySQL login for the authentication system, and give it read-only access to the database you just created:

```
GRANT SELECT ON WebAuth.* TO WebAuth@localhost IDENTIFIED BY 'AuthPass';
```

Now, set up the table to hold the usernames and passwords. In this example, the table will store just the username and hashes of the password, but if you wanted, you could easily add extra fields for any other access criteria you want.

```
CREATE TABLE Users (username varchar(50) PRIMARY KEY,
                    passwd_md5 varchar(32) NOT NULL,
                    passwd_sha1 varchar(40) NOT NULL);
```

Notice that instead of simply creating a field to store the user's password as raw text, you're creating fields to store one-way hashes of the user's password. Doing this ensures the password can still be compared to the value entered at the password prompt, but makes it extremely difficult for those who would try to crack the passwords if the database was compromised. If you're familiar with either MD5 or SHA1, you know that they are both one-way hashing algorithms. It is nearly impossible to determine an original password after it has been hashed by either of the two.

MD5 takes an input string and creates a 128-bit "unique" fingerprint, or hash, of the original input. SHA1 behaves in a similar manner, but is slightly more secure, producing a 160-bit "unique" fingerprint.

You may have noticed that the previous discussion didn't speak in the absolute regarding the uniqueness or bullet-proof hashing provided by either of these two solutions. Until recently, MD5 has been considered a reasonable solution for hashing all but the most secure data, and SHA1 was the same. Neither encryption scheme is 100% uncrackable when brute force is used. A password-generating program could run through every combination of every character and every password length until it eventually finds an input string that matches the hash produced by either of the algorithms.

Recent advances in crypto-analysis have proven, however, that MD5 can be defeated quicker by finding an input that produces an identical output hash, even though the input strings did not match — an inherent weakness in MD5. SHA1 as well has come under attacks as of recently, and as processing power increases, the time it takes to brute-force a hash decreases rapidly.

To combat any sort of collision attacks as seen with MD5, you create the Users table to hold both MD5 and SHA1 hashes for the password. Doing this effectively makes any collision attack attempts futile — even if an intruder manages to find an input string that matches the MD5 hash, unless it's the real password, it will not match the SHA1 hash.

To make the database useful to the authentication script, you need to add at least one user:

```
INSERT INTO Users VALUES ('testuser', MD5('testpass'), SHA1('testpass'));
```

Note that the built-in MySQL functions MD5() and SHA1() are used when adding the passwords.

A PHP Basic Authentication Script

Once your database is set up, create the following script, and save it as phpauthbasic.php:

```php
<?php

// Define database constants
define('AUTH_HOST', 'localhost');
define('AUTH_USER', 'WebAuth');
define('AUTH_PASS', 'AuthPass');
define('AUTH_DB',   'WebAuth');


function attempt_auth()
{
  // Send authentication headers
  header('WWW-Authenticate: Basic realm="Protected by PHP"');
  header('HTTP/1.0 401 Unauthorized');
```

```
}

function check_login($username, $password)
{
  $ret = false;

  if ($username && $password)
  {
    // Check if login matches database values
    $conn = mysql_connect(AUTH_HOST, AUTH_USER, AUTH_PASS);

    if (mysql_select_db(AUTH_DB, $conn))
    {
      // Search for matches
      $result =
          mysql_query("SELECT COUNT(username) AS ucount
                       FROM Users
                       WHERE username='" . addslashes($username) . "'
                       AND passwd_md5='" . md5($password) . "'
                       AND passwd_sha1='" . sha1($password) . "'",
                       $conn);

      // Check if a match was found
      if (($row = mysql_fetch_array($result)) && $row['ucount'])
      {
        $ret = true;
        $_SESSION['username'] = $username;
      }
    }

    // Close connection
    mysql_close($conn);
  }

  return $ret;
}

session_start();

// Check if using valid credentials
if (!(isset($_SESSION['username']) ||
      (isset($_SERVER['PHP_AUTH_USER']) &&
       check_login($_SERVER['PHP_AUTH_USER'],
                   $_SERVER['PHP_AUTH_PW']))))
{
  // Show login prompt
  attempt_auth();
  echo 'Authorization Required';
  exit;
}

?>
```

What does all this mean? Take a look at what makes this script tick.

The first thing you are going to do is define some constants for the database connection:

```php
<?php

// Define database constants
define('AUTH_HOST', 'localhost');
define('AUTH_USER', 'WebAuth');
define('AUTH_PASS', 'AuthPass');
define('AUTH_DB',   'WebAuth');
```

Next comes the function definition for `attempt_auth()`. This function simply sends response headers to the browser, telling it to attempt a Basic Authentication login, with the given realm displayed as the security zone in the login prompt:

```php
function attempt_auth()
{
  // Send authentication headers
  header('WWW-Authenticate: Basic realm="Protected by PHP"');
  header('HTTP/1.0 401 Unauthorized');
}
```

After `attempt_auth()` is the function definition for `check_login()`. This is where the passed username and password will actually be checked against values stored in the `WebAuth` database created earlier. The first order of business is to make sure a username and password were passed, and to connect to the database and set `WebAuth` as active:

```php
function check_login($username, $password)
{
  $ret = false;

  if ($username && $password)
  {
    // Check if login matches database values
    $conn = mysql_connect(AUTH_HOST, AUTH_USER, AUTH_PASS);

    if (mysql_select_db(AUTH_DB, $conn))
    {
```

After a database connection is made, you perform the query that checks for a username/password match:

```php
      // Search for matches
      $result =
          mysql_query("SELECT COUNT(username) AS ucount
                      FROM Users
                      WHERE username='" . addslashes($username) . "'
                      AND passwd_md5='" . md5($password) . "'
                      AND passwd_sha1='" . sha1($password) . "'",
                  $conn);
```

To build this query, the username must first be escaped using `addslashes()`, to help avoid any SQL-injection attacks (discussed later). The PHP functions `md5()` and `sha1()` are used here, but if you wanted, you could easily use the MySQL equivalents — they should produce the exact same result:

```
// Search for matches
$result =
    mysql_query("SELECT COUNT(username) AS ucount
                 FROM Users
                 WHERE username='" . addslashes($username) . "'
                 AND passwd_md5=MD5('" . addslashes($password) . "')
                 AND passwd_sha1=SHA1('" . addslashes($password) . "')",
                $conn);
```

You might have noticed that the `addslashes()` function was added as a wrapper for the passwords, where it didn't exist in the previous case where PHP was doing the password hashing. This is again to prevent any SQL injection attacks or even simple errors where a user's password might contain an apostrophe. When hashing the passwords first with PHP, there's no need to escape the result with `addslashes()`, because both the `md5()` and `sha1()` functions produce output consisting solely of hexadecimal values — there's no way an apostrophe or other dangerous character will slip through.

To finish the `check_login()` function, set the return placeholder to `true`, and create a session variable that you'll use later in the script to avoid unnecessary repeat queries:

```
// Check if a match was found
if (($row = mysql_fetch_array($result)) && $row['ucount'])
{
  $ret = true;
  $_SESSION['username'] = $username;
}
}

// Close connection
mysql_close($conn);
}

return $ret;
}
```

On to the actual first-interpreted code in the script, you begin by initializing the session data:

```
session_start();
```

Then you'll first check to see if the session variable from `check_login()` is set. If it is not yet set — meaning the person has not yet authenticated — check for the `PHP_AUTH_USER` server variable and call the `check_login()` function. The server variables `PHP_AUTH_USER` and `PHP_AUTH_PW` both exist when PHP attempts to get login information using Basic Authentication. If they are not set, the user hasn't yet been prompted for the login information. In this case, you want to prompt the user for login information if none has been passed and if the credentials previously passed were not valid. If no valid user information is found, `attempt_auth()` is called, and the user gets another chance to login. If, and only if, the user clicks Cancel on the login prompt, the "Authorization Required" message is displayed:

```
// Check if using valid credentials
if (!(isset($_SESSION['username']) ||
      (isset($_SERVER['PHP_AUTH_USER']) &&
       check_login($_SERVER['PHP_AUTH_USER'],
                   $_SERVER['PHP_AUTH_PW'])))))
{
  // Show login prompt
  attempt_auth();
  echo 'Authorization Required';
  exit;
}

?>
```

To test out the PHP authentication, you could simply attempt to load this script in your browser, but it's much better if you include it in any standard PHP page you've created. You can use the following code to test out this authorization as a simple inclusion:

```
<?php

require_once 'phpauthbasic.php';

echo "Authentication Successful!";

?>
```

When you try to load this script in your browser, use the `testuser`/`testpass` combination, or whatever you originally added to the `Users` table. If the username and password are correct, you should see a nice "Authentication Successful!" message; if you click Cancel, you'll get the dreaded "Authorization Required" message.

Now that you've seen it work, you might think there's no reason not to use this method. But as with many of the choices you'll make when deciding how to write your applications, this method has some drawbacks.

There are two main requirements that must be fulfilled before this authentication method will work. First, `safe_mode` must not be enabled in php.ini. When enabled, `safe_mode` prevents the creation of the `PHP_AUTH_USER` and `PHP_AUTH_PW` server variables. If those variables don't exist, the script will keep redisplaying the login prompt until the user clicked Cancel, regardless if the credentials used were truly valid. A quick way to determine if `safe_mode` is indeed enabled: the uid of the script is added to the end of the realm information in the login prompt.

Second, this method cannot be used in conjunction with Apache's Basic Authentication system. This applies to any Apache-controlled access (.htaccess) at the same level of the script, or at any parent directories. If both authentication systems are enabled, the Apache system takes initial precedence. What will happen is the user can log in initially using the credentials valid with the Apache basic authentication, which is followed by the PHP authentication prompt. At this point, however, PHP has effectively cleared the browser's authentication state with the Apache controls — a result of the HTTP 401 response. Because the browser is no longer authenticated against Apache, it will re-prompt for the Apache-level credentials, and then go back to the PHP credentials, and so on, until the user clicks Cancel or Stop in their browser.

PHP Forms Authentication

If PHP Basic Authentication isn't a viable solution for you, or the look of the browser's login panel isn't your cup of tea, have no fear; you've yet another option. Instead of relying on the standard built-in login window from your browser, you can easily craft your own login form, and you can even use most of the previous PHP authentication code. Enter the following as `phpauthforms.php`. Note that most of it is pulled directly from the phpauthbasic.php file you used earlier:

```php
<?php

// Define database constants
define('AUTH_HOST', 'localhost');
define('AUTH_USER', 'WebAuth');
define('AUTH_PASS', 'AuthPass');
define('AUTH_DB',   'WebAuth');


function check_login($username, $password)
{
  $ret = false;

  if ($username && $password)
  {
    // Check if login matches database values
    $conn = mysql_connect(AUTH_HOST, AUTH_USER, AUTH_PASS);

    if (mysql_select_db(AUTH_DB, $conn))
    {
      // Search for matches
      $result =
          mysql_query("SELECT COUNT(username) AS ucount
                       FROM Users
                       WHERE username='" . addslashes($username) . "'
                       AND passwd_md5='" . md5($password) . "'
                       AND passwd_sha1='" . sha1($password) . "'",
                      $conn);

      // Check if a match was found
      if (($row = mysql_fetch_array($result)) && $row['ucount'])
      {
        $ret = true;
        $_SESSION['username'] = $username;
      }
    }

    // Close connection
    mysql_close($conn);
  }

  return $ret;
}
```

```
session_start();

// Check if using valid credentials
if (!(isset($_SESSION['username']) ||
      check_login($_POST['username'],
                  $_POST['passwd'])))
{

?>
<form method="post" action="testforms.php">
<label for="username">Username:</label>
<input type="text" id="username" name="username" maxlength="50" /><br />
<label for="passwd">Password:</label>
<input type="password" id="passwd" name="passwd" /><br />
<input type="submit" value="Log in" />
</form>
<?php

}

?>
```

What has changed? Not much actually. The key modifications were made at the end of the file:

```
// Check if using valid credentials
if (!(isset($_SESSION['username']) ||
      check_login($_POST['username'],
                  $_POST['passwd'])))
{
```

Instead of checking for the server variables PHP_AUTH_USER and PHP_AUTH_PW, you check the login credentials passed via HTTP POST, named username and passwd. Then, like the basic authentication example, if the login is invalid or not provided, a login prompt is presented to the user. In this case, the attempt_auth() function has been removed, and in the place where it once was called, sits a simple HTML form:

```
?>
<form method="post" action="testforms.php">
<label for="username">Username:</label>
<input type="text" id="username" name="username" maxlength="50" /><br />
<label for="passwd">Password:</label>
<input type="password" id="passwd" name="passwd" /><br />
<input type="submit" value="Log in" />
</form>
<?php

  exit;
}

?>
```

To use this authentication method, you can simply include this script at the top of any page you want to protect. Call this one `testforms.php` (it has to match the target of the form used previously):

```php
<?php

require_once 'phpauthforms.php';

echo "Authentication Successful!";

?>
```

So what are the advantages to this method? Compatibility, for starters. Using simple form-based authentication with PHP works in nearly any situation, regardless if `safe_mode` is enabled, or Apache is using .htaccess authentication of its own. The only real downside to a solution like this is that you must code your own login form, and style it how you want, instead of relying on the browser/OS to do that for you.

Other Access Restrictions

In addition to restricting access by username and password, you can also use PHP to check other user parameters. One common variable to check is the source IP of the user. By referencing the server variable `$_SERVER['REMOTE_ADDR']`, you can make sure than only certain ranges of IPs are allowed to view a resource, or conversely, you can block specific IPs. If you're creating a website for a corporate intranet, you can restrict access to internal IPs (assuming your network uses them). For example, you could decide that only members of the 10.0.1.x network can view a special area of your website. Another example would be BBS sites or web forums. Often times they have the need to ban a specific user by IP, if the person is spamming the boards, for example.

Another server variable worth checking is the `$_SERVER['HTTP_REFERER']` variable. This variable holds the name of the previous page viewed, and can help you eliminate a certain class of web attacks. Suppose you create a simple form that saves data to a database, emails people, or anything that relies on valid user input. You might have even gone to great lengths to perform client-side input validation, and specified maximum lengths on your forms. Unfortunately, anything you might expect as input from a web client can easily be corrupted using an external form. Any site attacker can easily copy your form's HTML markup, and then modify it to suit their needs — whether it be for information-gathering, cross-site scripting, SQL injection, or anything really.

All they need to do is make a copy of the form that can submit improper data to your site, host it on their own machine, but have it post to *your* form, using an absolute URL as the method. This kind of attack can be especially harmful when hidden form variables are used, and when `register_globals` is enabled in php.ini.

By checking the HTTP_REFERER value, you can eliminate a majority of spoofed form attacks, as long as you ensure the input is coming from a page actually on your website.

To see an example of HTTP_REFERER checking and REMOTE_ADDR verification in action, take a look at the following code:

```php
<?php

// Check the referer
if (!preg_match('/http:\/\/(localhost)|' .
```

```
                    '(www\.example\.com)/i',
                    $_SERVER['HTTP_REFERER']))
    {
        echo 'Invalid referer! ' .
             'We don\'t take kindly to spoofed forms in these parts.';
    }

    // Check to see if request came from internal users
    if (!preg_match('/(10\.\d{1,3}\.\d{1,3}\.\d{1,3})|' .
                     '(172\.16\.\d{1,3}\.\d{1,3})|' .
                     '(192\.168\.\d{1,3}\.\d{1,3})/i',
                     $_SERVER['REMOTE_ADDR']))
    {
        echo 'Invalid client address! ' .
             'Who let YOU in here?';
    }
    ?>
```

This code simply checks the referring page first, to make sure it came from localhost or the expected domain (assuming you've changed it to match your own domain), and then checks the user's IP address to make sure it comes from an internal/private IP range.

Another thing PHP can do, to help limit certain kinds of access, is to provide CAPTCHA images for use in registration forms. CAPTCHA, which stands for "Completely Automatic Public Turing Test to Tell Computers and Humans Apart," is a kind of test where typically an image is presented with somewhat mangled text printed in the image. The idea is that humans should be able to figure out what the text actually says, despite its distorted appearance, whereas a computer cannot. Many free email and bulletin board sites use such a technology to keep automated robot scripts from registering and abusing the services with spam or the like.

While currently in an alpha stage of development, the Text_CAPTCHA package in the PHP Pear repository provides an easy interface to implement CAPTCHA functionality. Text_CAPTCHA can be found at http://pear.php.net/package/Text_CAPTCHA.

If you want to try out Text_CAPTCHA, you can simply install it using the pear install command:

```
pear install -f Text_CAPTCHA
```

You need to use the -f flag to force the installation because Text_CAPTCHA is currently not considered stable by the Pear team, so a normal unforced installation will fail. Also note that Text_CAPTCHA is dependant on the Text_Password and Image_Text (also alpha) Pear packages, so you'll need to install those first if you don't have them already.

Once they're all installed, create the following as captchatest.php:

```php
<?php

// Include the Pear class
require_once('Text/CAPTCHA.php');

// Set the options for the generated text;
$opts = array(
```

```
        'font_size' => 25,
        'font_path' => './',
        'font_file' => 'VeraMono.TTF'
);

// Create a CAPTCHA object
$cap = Text_CAPTCHA::factory('Image');

// Initialize the CAPTCHA object with random text
$r = $cap->init(250,100, null, $opts);

// Check if CAPTCHA object is valid
if (PEAR::isError($r))
{
  echo 'CAPTCHA Generation failed.';
  exit;
}

// Generate the PNG CAPTCHA image
$png = $cap->getCAPTCHAAsPNG();

// Show the image in the browser
header('Content-type: image/png');
echo $png;

?>
```

When you run this code in your browser, you should see something like Figure 7.1.

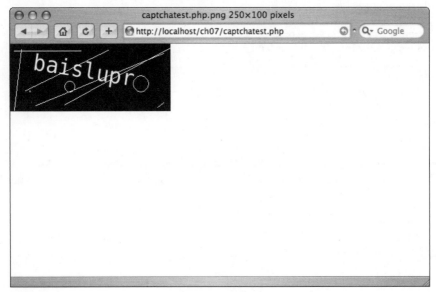

Figure 7.1

How did Text_CAPTCHA know what string you wanted to use? It didn't. When you initialized the CAPTCHA object, you passed in `null` as the test string:

```
// Initialize the CAPTCHA object with random text
$r = $cap->init(250,100, null, $opts);
```

If you wanted to explicitly set the text string that will be rendered by Text_CAPTCHA, just change the input string from `null` to the value you desire:

```
// Initialize the CAPTCHA object with random text
$r = $cap->init(250,100, 'computers be gone!', $opts);
```

Other key things to check in your PHP scripts are local filenames and how they are accessed. Take a look at the following code:

```php
<?php

$contents = file_get_contents('/path/to/content/' . $_POST['file']);

echo $contents;

?>
```

This is the kind of code that can often be found on many home-brewed CMS systems, or some other kind of custom document-retrieval script. Unfortunately, it's a huge security risk. What would happen if an attacker submitted the value `../../../../../etc/passwd` for the `file`? If the server isn't locked down properly — and many aren't — the contents of the system password file will get echoed directly to the screen.

There are a couple easy steps you can take to help prevent this kind of attack. First, if you have control over the Apache web server, make sure it is running as an unprivileged user. Whatever user Apache runs as — apache, nobody, www, it doesn't matter — make sure that user does not have privilege to access any files except bona fide website files.

Second, make sure you're escaping any parent directory access periods in the file paths provided, like so:

```php
<?php

$file = str_replace('..', '', $_POST['file'];
$contents = file_get_contents('/path/to/content/' . $file);

echo $contents;

?>
```

It's also a good idea, if possible, to prefix your escaped filename with its path. That way if an attacker provides an absolute path for the file value, it will still behave relative to the specified folder.

Website Attacks

Whenever you publish a site out in the public Internet, it runs the risk of being attacked. While no application can ever be truly 100% secure, as new exploits and hacking techniques are being discovered daily, there are a couple categories of attacks that you can somewhat easily defend against in your PHP scripts.

Abusing register_globals

If it hasn't been driven into your brain by every article, book, or any bit of documentation that talks about `register_globals`, here it is again: having `register_globals` set to *on* is a disaster waiting to happen.

If you're unfamiliar with `register_globals`, it is a setting in php.ini that controls the auto-population of variables with the same name as form elements or cookies. In the login form you created earlier in the chapter, there was a field called `username`. Normally, with `register_globals` disabled, the only way to access the `username` field from the form after it's posted is to use the `$_POST` or `$_GET` array, depending on the method of the form. When `register_globals` is enabled, the `username` field is accessible again using `$_POST` or `$_GET`, but is also available as `$username`.

Since PHP 4.2.0, the default value for `register_globals` is *off*, but often web hosts will re-enable `register_globals` to provide compatibility with older scripts that assume the existence of, and rely on, `register_globals=on`. Unfortunately, this provides a premium avenue of attack for malicious users. When `register_globals` is enabled, PHP evaluates the environment, form, cookie, and server variables in the order specified in the `variables_order` setting. If the server is using the "recommended" settings file, the GET variables are set first, and then POST is set and any matching GET values are overwritten. Next the cookie values are set, followed by the server variables, overwriting any matching values previously set.

While this behavior seems convenient, it is easily exploitable using a cloned form or spoofed cookie information. For an example of how it might be exploited, take a look at the following PHP code:

```php
<?php

if (user_is_admin())
{
   $access_level = 10;
}

show_menu($access_level);
// ... and so on ...

?>
```

In this hypothetical situation, the script calls a `user_is_admin()` function to determine if the user is an administrator. If so, the `$access_level` variable is set to 10, and presumably a complete administration would be displayed in the script that might follow.

If `register_globals` is enabled, it's a trivial matter of requesting the file and appending your desired access level to the query string, like this:

```
http://www.example.com/file.php?access_level=10
```

Now, if the script is called with that `access_level` added, it doesn't matter if the user is truly an administrator or not — the `$access_level` variable will be set to 10 automatically when the script begins, thanks to `register_globals` and PHP not requiring variable initialization.

Luckily, it's relatively easy to avoid such pitfalls. Make sure you code with `register_globals` disabled, use the proper `$_GET` and `$_POST` superglobals, initialize possibly unsafe variables, and make sure `error_reporting` is set to `E_ALL` when developing and testing the site.

If you cannot disable `register_globals` in php.ini, you can use an .htaccess file to turn it off, if properly enabled in Apache:

```
php_flag register_globals off
```

SQL Injection Attacks

Another dirty-data attack, but with a far higher potential for damage, is the SQL Injection Attack. Used in conjunction with a `register_globals` attack, or just using a normal web form, SQL injection attacks are simply the insertion of malicious SQL statements in the place of what should normally be innocuous data.

SQL injection preys on a lack of input scrubbing and data validation — data that is blindly used in a PHP-built SQL query. Take the following example that would access the WebAuth database you created earlier in the chapter:

```php
<?php

$username = $_POST['username'];

$conn = mysql_connect(AUTH_DB, AUTH_USER, AUTH_PASS);
mysql_select_db(AUTH_DB, $conn);

$sql = "SELECT * FROM Users WHERE username='" . $username . "'";

mysql_close($conn);

?>
```

Looks harmless enough, right? You'd expect it to happily take whatever username was sent from the form and look up all columns related to that specific username. The problem with this code lies in the SQL query. Notice how the `$username` variable is not validated, scrubbed, or prepared in any way before sending it to the database. Under most circumstances, you might not notice anything wrong, and it would rarely if ever throw an error.

However, things turn nasty quickly, when the following value is entered in the username field of the sending form:

```
'; DELETE FROM Users; SELECT 'Own3d' AS username FROM Users WHERE ''='
```

Look carefully at what is going on with this value. It begins by terminating the part of the query before the `$username` variable is appended, deletes all information from the `Users` table, and then performs a query of the attacker's choosing, just to close out the query and match up the final apostrophe.

When the "evil" username value is substituted into the original query, the effective set of commands would look like this:

```
SELECT * FROM Users WHERE username='';
DELETE FROM Users;
SELECT '0wn3d' AS username FROM Users WHERE ''=''
```

When the data sent to the SQL server is not escaped as in this example, any number of bad things can happen. Imagine the damage if the middle command was a DROP DATABASE or GRANT command — not a good situation. This example is a rather simplified case of what can happen during a SQL injection attack, but it should give you a taste of what kind of damage it can do to your data and system integrity.

Like many of the common problems plaguing PHP scripts, SQL injection is somewhat preventable with a little planning and thorough coding practices. If configured with magic_quotes_gpc set to on, PHP has got your back with regards to escaping "dangerous" characters in your form data. When magic_quotes_gpc is enabled, PHP automatically escapes any escape characters, such as apostrophes, before you can even touch them in your script. Unfortunately, this behavior is applied to all GET, POST, and cookie variables, regardless of whether they're going to be used in a SQL statement or not — and most of the time it can be a little annoying.

To make sure your data is escaped only when you need it to be, turn off magic_quotes_gpc in php.ini, and use addslashes() on all data that is being passed to MySQL. The addslashes() function will automatically escape any dangerous characters so your input will not choke MySQL — both on SQL injection attacks, and legitimate data with special characters, such as last names with apostrophes.

As a second line of defense, make sure the user you access the database with in PHP has only the minimum amount of privileges needed to keep the application running. In the previous SQL injection attack, the deletion of all the user records would have actually failed — when the user was set up at the beginning of the chapter, only SELECT rights were granted.

A relative to SQL injection attacks, filesystem execution attacks, should be treated in a similar manner. Any uncleaned input data that becomes part of a call to system() or exec() should be considered suspect, as they can easily be a handful of malicious system commands chained together in a similar way to SQL injection attacks.

Cross-Site Scripting

While SQL injection and register_global abuse deal primarily with the usage of dirty input data, there is another kind of attack that relies on the uncleanliness of the dynamic output instead — cross-site scripting.

Commonly abbreviated XSS, cross-site scripting is the exploiting of unfiltered dynamic output, where the attacker has the ability to add or change the page's generated markup. Most commonly, this means the addition of a small bit of JavaScript to the output of a page, which then does something sinister, such as trick another user into revealing their login credentials or credit card information, or possibly divulging cookie or session information for immediate account compromise.

To better understand the exact flow of the attack, consider the following scenario:

1. The attacker fills out a comment form on a blog or other website. A malicious script is included in the comments.

2. The comments are displayed on the page, with the script intact and active.

3. An innocent user visits the site, and reads the attacker's comments which may or may not contain a clickable link.

4. By either clicking the attacker's link, or merely visiting the page, the user is asked to verify private information, such as a username or password.

5. The user unknowingly submits the private information, believing it was requested by the legitimate site they were visiting.

6. The user's stolen information is instead routed to a different location on the Internet, either to be stored for later analysis or the attacker is notified with the new information.

How can this happen? Cross-site scripting is effective when the "trusted" website does not properly cleanse special characters before sending them as output or markup. In the case of the web, that means the less-than symbol <, greater-than symbol >, ampersand &, single and double quotes, and any UTF-8 character that is present in the dynamic output.

Luckily, PHP gives you an assortment of options to choose from when dealing with cleaning your dynamic output:

❑ `htmlspecialchars()`: Escapes any ampersand, less-than, greater-than, single quote, and double quote, making it a suitable choice for most dynamically generated HTML.

❑ `htmlentities()`: Similar to `htmlspecialchars()`, but `htmlentities()` will escape *any* special character that has an HTML entity equivalent, in addition to the core five covered by `htmlspecialchars()`.

❑ `strip_tags()`: Removes all HTML and PHP tags from a string. You can even provide a list of allowed tags, so you can whitelist "safe" tags, such as formatting, and remove any of the more dangerous tags, such as `<script>`.

❑ `utf8_decode()`: Converts UTF-8 encoded characters to equivalent ISO-8859-1 characters.

Other Considerations

Aside from issues immediately impacting the code you write or how your server is configured, there are a handful of other issues that must be considered during the design, development, and maintenance of your application.

One of the easiest issues to address is that of keeping your system current and updated with all the latest patches. If your operating system has an automated method for updating core system software, it's usually a good idea to take advantage of it. Many recent web server exploits have actually exploited flaws in older versions of the software — virus and worm writers often use vendor-published information about recent server patches to write their own malicious code they know will affect older versions.

Another group that should also not be overlooked when updating the system are the PEAR and PECL packages installed with PHP. Both are easily updated with one simple command: `pear upgrade-all`. The key is remembering to run the command at regular intervals, or better yet, add it as a `cron` job.

When coding your applications, there are a couple of small things you can do to help reduce the likelihood of a `register_globals` exploit or SQL injection attack. First, make sure you initialize all variables before use; that way there's no chance that a form or querystring variable can sneak in. Second, make sure you turn off any error reporting output on the production web servers. By disabling the display of error messages, no sensitive information might leak out when an error occurs, such as a syntax error in your SQL query, or the hostname or IP address of the SQL server.

A few other things that can help maintain the security of your site are not exactly anything you can type or configure. One possible way for a hacker to gain access to your site involves a little social engineering and little or no actual computer intrusion at all. If you are the administrator of a website, responsible for the creation and troubleshooting of user logins, you are in a very serious role that can be exploited without proper safeguards. In many situations, all a hacker needs to do is call the administrator of a website and pretend to be a user that has forgotten his or her password. If the administrator gives out the username or password for the hapless user, the hacker instantly has a legitimate login for the website, without any network sniffing or brute-force attacking required.

Another little thing that goes a long way toward the safety of the site is frequent code/peer review during the development cycle. By having your coworkers or peers examine your code, and vice versa, you can help many obvious security problems be brought to light long before the code actually winds up facing the public.

Last, make sure you keep yourself abreast of the latest security and vulnerability news, by frequenting such security-related sites as Secunia (`http://secunia.com/`), CVE (`http://www.cve.mitre.org/`), and CERT (`http://www.cert.org/`), among others.

Summary

As you can see, there are a fair amount of things to consider when tackling the security of your PHP-driven website. If you keep rigorous data-cleaning practices, making sure all your information is valid going in and out of the system, your site will ward off most any simple attacker that comes at it.

PEAR and PECL

The underlying concept of open source is, of course, using a collaborative effort to accomplish great things. The synergy that exists between the countless contributors and their efforts pushes open source projects through ever-expanding boundaries. However, with this immense and vastly diverse effort come challenges that could potentially hinder the success of the movement. These challenges are organization, coordination, and direction. Without organization, there would be no standards in code writing, or a systematic approach to putting together a package. Without coordination, snippets of code would be dispersed throughout the vast Internet, most likely lost between poorly written HTML pages, never to be seen by human eyes. Without direction, there would be no look to the future, no resource for aspiring contributors to get excited about. In short, there would just be a bunch of techies writing and rewriting the same snippets of code as everybody else, all acting independently in their own little proverbial computing bubbles. Everyone knows that no man is an island, however, and that's where the PEAR and PECL groups come in, to provide desperately needed organization, coordination, and direction, so developers can all be better coders in the long run.

By providing developers with ready-made scripts that accomplish common tasks, such as connecting to a database or interfacing with an XML document, PEAR and PECL packages can save you a lot of coding time and headaches.

While they both accomplish similar tasks, PEAR and PECL do have fundamental differences, which this chapter explains in detail.

What Is PEAR?

PEAR (PHP Extension and Repository) is designed to act as a home for wayward useful classes. As the name suggests, it is a repository of code packages, which may consist of one or more files, and which accomplish common tasks such as creating HTML forms, working with dates and images, or connecting to the database and running queries. Because these are functions that every coder will undoubtedly use from time to time, they make perfect candidates for PEAR packages.

Because there is a strict set of coding standards for developing and releasing a PEAR package, a coder can rest assured that the look and feel of one package will be consistent with the rest. As you become familiar with using them, you will begin to know what to look for and how the code is structured. PEAR packages are also known for their extensive commenting requirements and naming conventions, something that is sorely lacking in many open source programs, leaving you with the daunting task of trying to figure out someone else's logic.

All new packages must go through the PEPr (PEAR Proposal System) before being included in the PEAR distribution list. This four-step process ensures that each package is scrutinized for its accuracy, reliability and relevance. If you would like to learn more about PEPr, you can visit the site `http://pear.php.net/pepr`.

What Is PECL?

PECL (PHP Extension Community Library) is a spin-off of PEAR, and is primarily used to house groups of functions that are no longer bundled with the default installation of PHP. As of PHP 5, these extensions can be downloaded and installed separately from the regular PHP download. It should be noted, however, that some of the extensions currently residing in PECL are now bundled with the default installation (such as SQLite), or were extensions submitted by someone outside the PHP core team, and were never bundled with PHP (such as POP3).

Because most PECL extensions used to be a part of the standard list of PHP functions, the standard dictates that they are written using PHP's coding standards (as opposed to PEAR's). While the general public can still submit packages, the process for submission includes prior approval by the pecl-dev mailing list.

Exploring PEAR

You should be aware before you delve into the world of PEAR that because it is a class-based system, you should be quite familiar with OOP in PHP in order to use the packages properly. If you are a hard-core function-based coder, it would behoove you to hone those OOP skills through a quick tutorial or a brief review of Chapter 2 of this book.

The first thing you need is the PEAR package itself, which enables you to easily install or upgrade new PEAR packages. Thankfully, this manager comes pre-installed with PHP5 (and versions 4.3.0 and up) and will make your life easier when installing, managing, and upgrading the other PEAR packages. The main PEAR package also includes a set of error-handling functions to enable you to easily detect and manage errors encountered by your PEAR package.

The PEAR Manager

The main purpose of the PEAR manager is to assist you in managing and working with your other PEAR packages, as stated previously. With it comes a set of commands that you can run from the command line (which may or may not require root access). This list can be found in its entirety at `http://pear.php.net/manual/en/installation.cli.php`, but the following table highlights the main commands for your reference:

Command	What It Does
bundle [package name]	Download and unpack a PECL extension
download [package name]	Download a package without installing it
download-all	Download every available package
info [package name]	Display information about a package
install [package name]	Download and install a package
list	List installed packages
list-all	List all packages
list-upgrades	List available upgrades for the packages that are already installed
uninstall [package name]	Uninstall and delete a package
upgrade [package name]	Upgrade a package
upgrade-all	Upgrade all installed packages

To use any of the commands, simply preface the command with pear, like this:

```
pear info XML-RPC
```

As you will see, this will give you information about the PEAR package entitled XML-RPC.

There are also PEAR configuration variables over which you can exert control. These primarily relate to directory information and user preferences and more times than not the default value is acceptable. You can visit http://pear.php.net/manual/en/installation.cli.php for the complete list. However, the following table lists a few of the more common ones:

Variable Name	What It Represents	Default Value
bin_dir	Directory that houses executables	/usr/bin
ext_dir	Directory that houses loaded extensions	./
php_dir	Directory that houses PHP installation	/usr/lib/php
preferred_state	The preferred package state that is to be downloaded (stable, beta, alpha, devel, or snapshot)	stable

To see what your current settings are, use the config-show (or config-get for just one variable's value) command, like this:

```
pear config-show
```

This shows a description of each configuration variable, the variable name, and what the current settings are. To change a setting, use the `config-set` command, such as this:

```
pear config-set preferred_state devel
```

The `config-help` command shows you more information about a specific configuration variable.

Installing Packages

Several of the other PEAR packages come pre-installed with PHP 5, and you can find a complete list by running the following command (from root login):

```
pear list
```

This will give you a list of the installed packages, the version that was installed, and the state of the release (stable, beta, and so on). If you would like to install other packages, the following sections briefly outline the installation process for you.

CLI Installation

If you have root access, you can install any new package simply by typing the following command:

```
pear install [package name]
```

This command jumps to the PEAR site, downloads the package you specified (without the brackets of course), and installs it on your machine.

FTP Installation

If you don't have access to the command line, or if your current web host doesn't supply you with the PEAR package that you want, you can also install a package by completing two steps:

1. Download the compressed package directly from the PEAR site, unzip it locally, and upload the files to your Web site (saving them in the var/www/www.yourdomain.com/includes directory). You may also upload the compressed file and extract it while it's on the host server (again, to the var/www/www.yourdomain.com/includes directory).

2. Alter your php.ini file to match the include path you just used.

    ```
    include_path = ".:/www/includes"
    ```

    You may also include a line in each script that will access the package, like this:

    ```
    <?php
    ini_set("include_path", '/var/www/www.yourdomain.com/includes/' . PATH_SEPARATOR .
    ini_get("include_path"));

    //remainder of PHP script here.
    ?>
    ```

Your package is now installed and ready to use.

Using Installed Packages

Once the package has been installed, it is very simple to use and access. Simply include a line at the beginning of your script that includes the necessary files, as follows:

```php
<?php
require_once("HTML/QuickForm.php");

//you are now able to access and reference classes, methods and properties
//contained in the quickform.php file to easily create HTML forms.

?>
```

Quick and Dirty PEAR Packages

As of this writing, there are currently 318 PEAR packages available in a variety of areas, and there are more being added every day. While this book doesn't discuss all of those packages, the following sections explore some of the more common ones, and highlight for you the ones you probably want to make sure you have installed. Also, keep in mind that these sections keep it simple, but also point you in the right direction if you need something a little more robust.

Auth_HTTP

The purpose of this package is to provide an authentication system akin to Apache's .htaccess login box. It is a simple and easy way to password-protect an area of your site. Please note that this package is dependent on the more robust PEAR::Auth, which is also reliant on the PEAR::DB package, thus requiring installation of both before the Auth_HTTP package can run properly.

Simple usage of Auth_HTTP is as follows:

```php
<?php
require_once("Auth/HTTP.php");

$a = new Auth_HTTP("DB", "mysqli://username:password@localhost/databasename");

$a->start();
?>
```

First you include the file `Auth/HTTP.php`, which gives you access to the correct package. Then you instantiate a new Auth_HTTP object using the parameters as described. Because you are actually using the PEAR::DB package to log on to the database, you can alter the type of database you are using and name other options such as sockets, paths, port numbers, and the like. Although this chapter will be briefly discussing this package later, a detailed description of the PEAR::DB package can be found at `http://pear.php.net/manual/en/package.database.db.php`. Next you start the authentication process with the call to the `start()` function, and your page is password-protected.

Granted, this leaves much room for improvement and customization, so you can take it one step further and ask the authentication process to look up users from a table within a database. You can specify login options through the use of the `$authOptions` variable:

```php
<?php

require_once("Auth/HTTP.php");

$AuthOptions = array(
//use the same data source name (database login info) as in previous example
'dsn'=>"mysqli://username:password@localhost/databasename",

//specify the database table that contains user info
'table'=>"users",

//specify the column that holds the username
'usernamecol'=>"username",

//specify the column that holds the passwords
'passwordcol'=>"password",

//specify the encryption type used
'cryptType'=>"md5",

);


$a = new Auth_HTTP("DB", $AuthOptions);

//specify the name of your realm
$a->setRealm('Registered Users Only');

//specify the error message seen by the user if authentication fails
$a->setCancelText('<h2>Access Denied.</h2>');

$a->start();

//check to see if the user is authorized
if($a->getAuth())
{
    //body of authorized text goes here.
    echo "Hi there, authorized user!";

};

?>
```

You can see that this provides a very easy way to authenticate your users. To check for authorization on other pages, simply use the getAuth() function.

There are also other parameters you can specify with the Auth_HTTP package, and the Auth package provides a very robust HTML form-based authentication system. You can read more about these packages at http://pear.php.net/manual/en/package.authentication.auth-http.php and http://pear.php.net/manual/en/package.authentication.auth.php, respectively.

Date

Although PHP provides built-in functions that return date and time information, this PEAR package provides you with easy ways to manipulate that information into commonly used results such as days left in the month, current day of the week, and so on.

There are so many functions available with this package that it would be difficult for us to provide examples for each. However, the following sections describe some of the more commonly used methods of the Date class. Visit `http://pear.php.net/package/Date/docs/latest/Date/Date.html` for a comprehensive list of methods.

Date Class

This class appears in the main date.php file and offers the following methods for your use:

- ❏ `Date`: Constructor method that creates a new date object.
- ❏ `addSeconds`: Adds a specific number of seconds to the date.
- ❏ `addSpan`: Adds a time span to the date.
- ❏ `after`: Determines whether or not one date falls after another.
- ❏ `before`: Determines whether or not one date falls before another.
- ❏ `convertTZ`: Converts the date to another time zone.
- ❏ `equals`: Determines if two dates and/or times are exactly equal.
- ❏ `format`: Formats the date according to user specifications.
- ❏ `getDate`: Returns the date in a specific format.
- ❏ `getDay`: Returns the day of the month of the date object.
- ❏ `getDayName` Returns the day of the week of the date object in string format.
- ❏ `getDayOfWeek`: Returns the day of the week of the date object in integer format.
- ❏ `getDaysInMonth` Returns the number of days in the month of the date object.
- ❏ `getHour`: Returns the hour of the date object.
- ❏ `getMinute`: Returns the minute of the date object.
- ❏ `getMonth`: Returns the month of the date object in integer format.
- ❏ `getMonthName`: Returns the month of the date object in string format.
- ❏ `getNextDay`: Returns the date of the day following the date object.
- ❏ `getNextWeekday`: Returns the date of the weekday following the date object.
- ❏ `getPrevDay`: Returns the date of the day before the date object.
- ❏ `getPrevWeekday`: Returns the date of the weekday before the date object.
- ❏ `getQuarterOfYear`: Returns the quarter of the date object in integer format.

❑ `getSecond`: Returns the seconds of the date object.

❑ `getTime`: Returns the number of seconds since the Unix epoch.

❑ `getWeekOfYear`: Returns the week for the date object in integer format.

❑ `getWeeksInMonth`: Returns the number of weeks in the month of the date object.

❑ `getYear`: Returns the year for the date object.

❑ `inDaylightTime`: Determines whether or not the time/date is in Daylight Savings Time.

❑ `isLeapYear`: Determines if the year of the date object is in a leap year.

❑ `setDate`: Sets the date of the date object.

❑ `setDay`: Sets the day of the date object.

❑ `setHour`: Sets the hour of the date object.

❑ `setMinute`: Sets the minute of the date object.

❑ `setMonth`: Sets the month of the date object.

❑ `setSecond`: Sets the seconds of the date object.

❑ `setTZ`: Sets the time zone for the date object.

❑ `setYear`: Sets the year for the date object.

This is all from the `Date` class. There are two other classes that are used by the date class, but which can also be used directly; these are the `Date_Span` and `Date_TimeZone` classes. They have numerous specific methods within them if you need something more specific than what the `Date` class can offer, such as returning a list of all available time zones, or determining the default time zone of the server.

A Quick Example

The following is a quick example of how easy it is to use the Date package to spit out something like the number of weeks left in the year:

```php
<?php
require_once("date.php");

$currweek = new Date();

$weeksleft = 52 - ($currweek->getWeekofYear());

echo "There are " . $weeksleft . " weeks left in the year.";

?>
```

As you can see, something so simple can really make your life easy when you are trying to complete more complex date calculations or work with time zones.

DB

This is the PEAR package that allows you to easily connect and query your database. There are numerous other database-related packages you can look into. MDB, for example, is similar to DB but provides more portability. DB should work on your standard configuration, but if you're having compatibility issues, there are others you can try. In fact, PEAR dedicates an entire category of packages for dealing with databases which can be found at `http://pear.php.net/packages.php?catpid=7&catname=Database`.

In the next few examples, you are going to need the following information:

- ❑   `MySQL`: Your database type
- ❑   `testdatabase`: Database name
- ❑   `testtable`: Database table
- ❑   `username`: User accessing database
- ❑   `password`: User's password
- ❑   `localhost`: Server name
- ❑   `field1`, `field2`: Fields you will be querying

This will help you "fill in the blanks" when customizing your installation of the package.

Connecting to a Database

In order to connect to the database, you have to pass your new database object the proper Data Source Name (DSN). The syntax is as follows:

```php
<?php
require_once("db.php");

$dsn = "mysql://username:password@localhost/testdatabase";

$db = DB::connect($dsn);
if (PEAR::isError($db)) {
    die($db->getMessage());
}

echo "Connected successfully. Now what?";
?>
```

As you can see, this is all that it takes to connect and, more important, report any errors that may have occurred in the process. Again, feel free to visit the official PEAR documentation for detailed instructions on the various options you can set when connecting to the database, such as the port number or protocol. This documentation is available at `http://pear.php.net/manual/en/package.database.db.intro-connect.php`. Now try querying the imaginary fields from the imaginary tables.

Querying the Database

To query the database, you need to pass along the table name and your desired filter, so you type the following:

```php
<?php
require_once("db.php");
```

```
$dsn = "mysql://username:password@localhost/testdatabase";

$db = DB::connect($dsn);
if (PEAR::isError($db)) {
    die($db->getMessage());
}

//query
$res =& $db->query('SELECT * FROM testtable');

//display number of rows
echo "There were " . $res->numRows() . " rows found.";


//display one column of results, or by row number
while ($row =& $res->fetchRow()) {
  echo $row[0] . "\n";
}

//display more than one field of results
//also switching Associative mode
while ($res->fetchInto($row, DB_FETCHMODE_ASSOC)) {
    echo $row['field1'] . "," . $row['field2'] . "\n";
}

?>
```

This was just a sample of this package. There is so much more you can do with it, such as getting the resultsets from multiple queries, and automatically preparing and executing commonly used SQL statements.

HTML_CSS and HTML_Page

These are the packages that allow you to dynamically create your CSS stylesheets and easily incorporate them into a new HTML page. HTML_Page can also perform other functions for you, but this example focuses on creating a new CSS stylesheet:

```
<?php
require_once("HTML/CSS.php");
require_once("HTML/Page.php");


$css = new HTML_CSS();

//set the styles
  $css->setStyle('body', 'background-color', '#FF00CC');
  $css->setStyle('body', 'color', '#ffffff');
  $css->setStyle('h1', 'text-align', 'center');
  $css->setStyle('h1', 'font', '16pt erdana');
  $css->setStyle('p', 'font', '12pt verdana');

//create a new page
 $p = new HTML_Page();
```

```
$p->setTitle("Testing the CSS");

$p->addStyleDeclaration($css, 'text/css');
$p->addBodyContent("<h1>Wow, this background is really bright</h1>");
$p->addBodyContent("<p>This should wake you up.</p>");

$p->display();
?>
```

Using simple `if` or `switch` statements, you can use something like this to dynamically create a stylesheet based on a person's authorization level, the type of browser or operating system being used, the time or day, or anything else you can think of.

HTML_QuickForm

The purpose of this package is to create HTML forms quickly and easily. It is easy to use, but relatively robust, and allows for quite a bit of customization on your part. Take a look at a quick example:

```
<?php
require_once ("HTML/QuickForm.php");

//create a new form object
$form = new HTML_QuickForm('firstForm');

//add two input fields;  this is completely customizable
$form->addElement('text', 'name', 'Your full name:', array('size' => 50,
'maxlength' => 255));
$form->addElement('text', 'email', 'Your email address:', array('size' => 50,
'maxlength' => 255));

//add a submit button
$form->addElement('submit', null, 'Send');

//add validation rules of our choosing
//using addRule('field_to_be_validated', 'error_message to be displayed',
// 'validation_type',
$form->addRule('name', 'Empty Name Field', 'required', null, 'client');
$form->addRule('email', 'Empty Email Address', 'required', null, 'client');
$form->addRule('email', 'Incorrect Format for Email Address', 'email', null,
'client');

//check to make sure input followed all our rules
//if so, put all form elements into an array for us
//for sake of example, let's print the values
if ($form->validate()) {
    $elements=$form->exportValues();
    print_r ($elements);
    exit;
}

//show the form
$form->display();
?>
```

With this little script, you have created a user form, validated required fields (and an email field as well), and collected the input into a tidy little array for your use. You can set as many rules as you wish to have your script make sure required fields are entered, whether they are of the correct format (numeric, alphabetical, and so on), and as you saw previously, check for things such as a correctly formatted email field. You can also set default values and anything else you can accomplish with forms (such as uploading files and using images for "submit" buttons).

HTML_Table

You can easily output a table of data with this package, either with data obtained from the resultset of a database query or data that's just sitting in an array somewhere waiting for you to emancipate it. Take a quick look at an example that illustrates just how easy this package is to use:

```php
<?php

require_once ("HTML/Table.php");


//set up attributes for our table, using common HTML attributes as
//array keys and their values as array values
$attributes = array("width" => "50%", "border" => "1");

//create a new table object
$table = new HTML_Table($attributes);

//configure table
//AutoGrow is for an unknown number of rows
//AutoFill inserts text for every empty cell
//Because we are pretending not to be sure how big our table will be, we
//will set this option to true.
$table -> setAutoGrow(true);
$table -> setAutoFill("-");


//get some data for our table
$rows = array(
 '0' => array("Number One", "Number Two", "Number Three"),
 '1' => array("Numero Uno", "Numero Dos", "Numero Tres"),
);

//populate the table
for($nr = 0; $nr < count($rows); $nr++) {
 //the header row comes first
 $table -> setHeaderContents( $nr+1, 0, (string)$nr);
 for($i = 0; $i < 3; $i++) {
  if("" != $rows[$nr][$i])
 //the cell contents come next
  $table -> setCellContents( $nr+1, $i+1, $rows[$nr][$i]);
 }
}

//set background for every other row
//skip the first row so we use a value of 1 to start
```

```
$altRow = array("bgcolor"=>"#FFFFCC");
$table -> altRowAttributes(1, null, $altRow);

//set header info for each cell of the table
//based on coordinates. 0,0 is top left cell.
//the third value is the contents to be shown
$table -> setHeaderContents(0, 0, " ");
$table -> setHeaderContents(0, 1, "Field 1");
$table -> setHeaderContents(0, 2, "Field 2");
$table -> setHeaderContents(0, 3, "Field 3");

//set attributes for the header rows and first column
//first row and column = 0.
$hrAttrs = array("bgcolor" => "#FFFF4D");
$table -> setRowAttributes(0, $hrAttrs, true);
$table -> setColAttributes(0, $hrAttrs);

//send it to the browser
echo $table->toHTML();


?>
```

You can imagine how easy it would be to create a table based on user input, or results from a database, and the level of customization you would realize by changing a few variables here and there.

What Else Is There?

Take a gander at the full list of PEAR packages (available at `http://pear.php.net/packages.php`) where you will begin to appreciate the breadth and depth of the PEAR community. There are so many great packages available, this book just doesn't have the space to cover all of them. To give a brief list of the more useful topics available, besides the ones we discussed in this chapter:

❑ Benchmarking

❑ Caching

❑ Configuration

❑ Encryption

❑ Event

❑ File Formats

❑ File System

❑ Gtk Components

❑ HTTP

❑ Images

❑ Internationalization

❑ Logging

- ❏ Mail
- ❏ Math
- ❏ Networking
- ❏ Numbers
- ❏ Payment
- ❏ Streams
- ❏ System
- ❏ Text
- ❏ Tools and Utilities
- ❏ Validate
- ❏ Web Services
- ❏ XML

Exploring PECL

While PECL isn't as extensive as PEAR, it's not to say it is without merit. Documentation and breadth of function of available packages is more limited than with PEAR. Many of the PECL packages are still in beta phase and are experimental; thus using these packages may take some getting used to. However, there are some very helpful, if not specific, packages held within PECL walls, and we'll take a quick look at some of the more popular packages to give you an idea of what they hold. If you would like a more detailed explanation of a PECL package, we have done that with PDFLib in Chapter 10.

Fileinfo

Fileinfo PECL package is one of the top downloads at the PECL site, and it's just downright useful. With this extension, you can glean all sorts of information about a file, such as MIME types. This package can be downloaded at `http://pecl.php.net/Fileinfo`.

Documentation on this package is somewhat limited, as is the case with many of the PECL packages; however, there is a wiki document that briefly touches on this package at the PHP Wiki (`http://www.wiki.cc/php/Fileinfo`).

PDO

At the time of this writing, PDO is still in beta phase and considered to be experimental, but it holds great promise for the future of PHP regarding database interaction. The purpose of this package is to interface with Data Objects and allow you to change database types at the drop of a hat. Instead of having to code using database-specific functions (`mysql_connect` or `pg_connect`, for example), you can create a new PDO object that will take care of that for you. You can then change from MySQL to Postgres (or other numerous other databases) by simply changing a parameter during object instantiation. You can download PDO at `http://pecl.php.net/package/PDO`.

As the implications for PDO grow, so does the documentation. There is documentation on this extension in the PHP manual (`http://us3.php.net/manual/en/ref.pdo.php`) and also at the PHP Wiki mentioned earlier (`http://www.wiki.cc/php/PDO_Basics`).

Xdebug

This is another top PECL download that is available at `http://pecl.php.net/package/Xdebug`. Its function is to assist the PHP developer in debugging a script by providing valuable information on code, activation, execution, and variable values. It also provides for memory allocation and protection from infinite loops, as well as stack and function traces.

Documentation for this package is more extensive than the others; it even has its own Web site at `http://www.xdebug.org`.

Summary

You should now be well-equipped to delve into PEAR and PECL and able to stop writing and rewriting the same code over and over again. Once you are familiar with the PEAR and PECL setup, perhaps you will take some of the code you have written and join the ranks of the prestigious contributors by turning it over to the masses as a new package.

Code Efficiency

The faster you can serve pages, the busier your site can be without users experiencing delays. This chapter covers methods for improving the performance of your sites, and also for identifying which methods are likely to be most effective.

"More pages in less time" is the rationale, but just as there are car enthusiasts who spend every free moment elbow-deep in their car's innards trying to shave another tenth of a second off the quarter mile, there are site developers who want to shave another millisecond off displaying the login page. You can take things too far!

You don't want to waste your time on improvements that no one will notice, so the first section of this chapter will present a couple of cameos that illustrate just how little difference even large improvements can sometimes make, how much difference small improvements can make, and how valuable it is to understand your entire system before messing with it.

Your program runs on PHP, which runs on your web server and communicates with your DBMS, which both run on your operating system, which runs on the physical hardware. Subsequent sections look at all of these for opportunities for improvement and techniques for deciding what needs improving.

Finally, there *will* be a few tiny miscellaneous coding tweaks that might shave a millisecond off the login page, which are presented here because if you know and use them from the beginning, you won't later be tempted to spend time better spent elsewhere going back and introducing them to existing code.

Why Bother?

The first question to ask yourself is "Do I *need* to do anything?" If you haven't started coding yet then the answer is obviously "Yes" — take the time to plan what your program is supposed to do, and try to develop a feel for where its performance might drag. But if you have a site that's up and running that you're tempted to fiddle with to make it go faster, ask yourself if doing so really would be worth the hassle. *Is* it running too slow for your taste? Which part? Will your fiddling make it go faster? By how much? And are you sure you won't break something in the process? By considering some of these questions you can avoid wasting a lot of time and effort on something that produces no benefit, and if you're lucky, discover a trivial change that nets you an enormous performance boost.

A Lot for a Little

In one company I worked for there was a computer used for generating reports. The software was Windows NT4 and Microsoft Access 97 (this was in 2004), the installed memory was 32MB, and printing a report was an exercise in patience. You could go and get a cup of coffee while it repainted the screen. There was talk of upgrading to a new computer because it was "so slow."

The "simple" answer — the one that could be reached without analysis — would have been to replace the existing machine with a new computer, with the latest versions of Windows and Access, followed by setting up the network user accounts and spending a day fighting the fires that seem to inevitably accompany such an upgrade. But an analysis was made, consisting of hitting Ctrl-Alt-Delete and bringing up NT's Task Manager and its process listing to see how much time was being spent on each process while the computer was being used to generate a report. (If you're not familiar with this process in Windows, picture a trimmed-down top(1) using a GUI table widget.)

The most prominent feature of the listing was the entry "System Idle Process." This never got below 85%. In twenty minutes of operation, the processor was actually *doing something* for only three of them; the rest of the time it was waiting for memory to be swapped between RAM and the disk. The computer *could* run more than six times faster than it was, if only it wasn't being held back by the meager 32MB of RAM that it had. 256MB would be more than sufficient to remove the bottleneck; the report would be generated in less time than it takes to walk to the printer; the chips would be a lot cheaper than a new machine and new software licenses; and instead of losing a day to installation, downtime would be on the order of five minutes.

A Little for a Lot

A common idiom in C is to write a<<3 instead of a*8 to multiply a variable by eight. It works, of course, because in binary multiplying by 8 (or 2^3) is equivalent to shifting all the bits of a 3=lg(8) places to the left. Can this be applied to PHP? The short answer is yes. But, just as in C, the saving is a matter of nanoseconds. For example, on my 2.6 GHz P4, the difference was 50ns for PHP5.0.3, and 3.5ns for 4.3.11, with the only significant variation between versions being in the speed of bit shifting. Your results may vary. Incidentally, 8*$a is faster than $a*8.

While eking out such a saving makes sense in an environment where you're carrying out millions of such multiplications on a regular basis (often enough that modern C compilers can recognize a*8 and convert it to a<<3 themselves *anyway*), this is not typical of web-based applications. What's more, in PHP the two "equivalent" operations have *different* behaviors in extreme cases: bit shifting always produces an integer result (which may be 0 or even negative: 1073741824<<1=–2147483648 and –2147483648<<1=0), while multiplication will return a double if such is necessary to contain the result (1073741824*2=2147483648 and 2147483648*2=4294967296). Plus, you have to remember that while multiplication has a higher precedence than addition, bit shifting is *lower*: it's $a+$b*8, but $a+($b<<3).

Is it all worth it? How long would it have taken you to write the operation as a multiplication, and how long as a bit shift? How long to verify that what you wrote is correct? How long to fix any bugs that resulted from things like the different behavior in extreme cases, or forgetting the difference in precedence? What about time spent altering the code (say, to multiply by 9 instead of 8) in the future? (You can't just search for instances of 8; you have to search for instances of 3 as well, and why aren't you using named constants?) How many times will that operation have to be executed to save you the same amount of time you spent making sure that you were using the faster option—a nanosecond here, a nanosecond there? And how long would it be before the operation has been executed that many times?

The point is that *your* time is more valuable than the *computer's*. The only time that is more valuable than yours is that of the visitors to your site. So don't waste your time trying to trim a few nanoseconds off the page's processing time: site visitors won't notice the difference even under exceptionally heavy use.

Comparing the Speed of Strings — A Benchmarking Example

PHP has several ways of combining literal strings and variables, and three methods of quoting strings. The three methods of quoting are to use single quotes, double quotes, and heredoc syntax. Inserting variables into strings can be achieved by using the concatenation operator, variable interpolation in double- and heredoc-quoted strings, and C-style string formatting functions. Every now and then, a curious programmer asks which method is "better." "Better" can be defined in more than one way: Is it faster? Does it make the source code more readable? Is it simpler and less prone to bugs? As far as readability and simplicity go, the debate is fairly evenly split: if one were *clearly* superior to the others, then natural selection would see experienced developers on large-scale applications using the superior method to the exclusion of all others. The fact that no such selection appears to have taken place over the years suggests that the differences are not significant enough to appear in an industry-wide Best Practices document or coding standard.

Whether single-quoted strings are *faster* than double-quoted ones is much more quantifiable. If you're forced to give a yes or no answer, then the safest would be to say "yes," but in reality things are more complicated than that.

Like any question about the real world, it cannot be answered without first obtaining some facts. As an initial experiment you could write the following:

```php
<?php
$variable = 'string';

$start = microtime(true);
for($i=0; $i<1000000; ++$i)
{
    $string = "this string has a $variable embedded into it";
}
$laptime = microtime(true);
for($i=0; $i<1000000; ++$i)
{
    $string = "this string has a ".$variable." inserted into it";
}
$finish = microtime(true);
```

```
echo "Variable interpolation required ",$laptime-$start," seconds for one million
iterations.\n";
echo "Variable concatenation required ",$finish-$laptime," seconds for one million
iterations.\n";
?>
```

The first time I run this script, the times I get for interpolation and concatenation are, respectively, 6.81 and 1.72 seconds. The second time, however, I get times of 6.58 and 1.71 seconds. The variability is due to the fact that the computer I am running on is doing more than simply running the script. It has other demands on its time, and the time it spends on those other demands gets included in how long it takes for this script to complete. When the script was run for the first time, the operating system would have had to organize space in memory for PHP, the script, and its data, with some of that organization occurring while the script was running (most of it would have occurred before the script began executing, however, and so wouldn't appear in the timings). But the second run, immediately afterwards, would be in an environment where there was already a suitable block of free space, and so it started up much faster.

The upshot of this is that you can't trust the results of just one run: there are too many ways for the timings to fluctuate, and many of them are out of your control. What is necessary is to run the script — from start to finish — several times, and take averages of the result. For interpolation, the times over 10 runs ranged from 6.57 to 6.86 seconds with an average of 6.77, and for concatenation, the range was 1.65 to 1.71 with an average of 1.70. You can throw more statistical firepower at the data if you like, but it does seem clear that concatenation is about four times faster than interpolation.

But that isn't the whole story. What if the times depend on how *long* the string is, or how *many* variables are being concatenated or interpolated? Should you not test for variations in *those* as well?

What follows is a command-line PHP program to run tests of this sort. Rather than time *itself* as it concatenates or interpolates variables, it instead writes a *separate* PHP script, and then calls it via the command line, thus not only timing the script itself, but also the time spent starting PHP, loading the script and shutting down. It does this for a range of initial string sizes (64 to 26176 characters, in steps of 512), and number of interpolations/concatenations (0 to 100). It carries out each experiment five times, and writes the average run times to a single log file. If twenty-five thousand separate experiments is too many (it can take somewhere in the vicinity of four hours) then the ranges can be reduced to taste, but testing each size/number combination several times and averaging the result should be kept. As written, it times variable interpolation — uncommenting line 59 and commenting line 58 (i.e., the str_replace() calls) changes it to timing concatenation:

```php
<?php
function generate_test($string)
{
    $code = '<?php
$interpolated="badgers!";

for($i=0; $i<100; ++$i)
    $gstring = "'.$string.'";
?>';
    $temp_file = tempnam('.','_runtest');
    $fp = fopen($temp_file,'wb');
    fwrite($fp, $code);
    fclose($fp);
```

```
        return $temp_file;
}

function run($file)
{
    $average_runtime = 0;
    for($runs=0; $runs<5; ++$runs)
    {
        $start = microtime(true);
        shell_exec("php -f $file"); // If necessary, supply path information here
        $end = microtime(true);
        $average_runtime += $end-$start;
    }
    return $average_runtime/5;
}

$log = fopen('logfile.txt','wb');
for($string_size=1<<6; $string_size<=26176; $string_size+=1<<9)
{
    $generic_string = str_repeat("wibble splunge!\n", $string_size);
    $real_string_size = 16*$string_size;
    $all_positions = range(0,$real_string_size-1);
    for($num_variable_interpolations=0; $num_variable_interpolations<100;
        ++$num_variable_interpolations)
    {
        echo $string_size,"\t",$num_variable_interpolations,"\n";
        $string = $generic_string;
        if($num_variable_interpolations==0)
            $positions = array();
        else
            $positions = array_rand($all_positions,$num_variable_interpolations);
        if(count($positions)==1) $positions = array($positions);
        foreach($positions as $position)
        {
            $string = substr($string,0,$position).'$'.substr($string,$position);
        }
        $string = str_replace('$','{$interpolated}', $string);
//        $string = str_replace('$','".$interpolated."', $string);
        $file = generate_test($string);
        $runtime = run($file);
        unlink($file);
        fwrite($log,
            $string_size."\t".$num_variable_interpolations."\t".$runtime."\n");
    }
}
fclose($log);
?>
```

From the last `frwite()` in the code you can deduce the format of the saved data: one line per experiment, consisting of the size of the string (before variable insertion), the number of variables being inserted, and the number of seconds. You can then read this data into your preferred data analysis or plotting software for exploration.

The resulting plots of time versus length of string and number of variables look very different for concatenation (see Figure 9.1) and interpolation (see Figure 9.2).

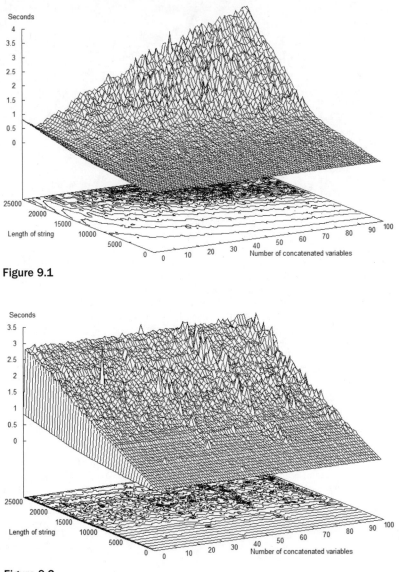

Figure 9.1

Figure 9.2

Probably the first thing you can see in these plots is that when interpolating in double-quoted strings, the number of variables is all but irrelevant. There are hints that processing is especially slow when the number of variables is a multiple of 32. Because changing the number of variables was carried out by the inner loop, the experiments for a *given* number of variables were performed at widely spaced points during the run, ruling out all but suspiciously well-timed transient delays from external sources.

Comparing the two graphs when the number of variables is very small, it's first unusual to see that the speed of concatenation *drops* initially, and second that interpolation *rises* very sharply indeed. Closer inspection reveals that when the number of variables is 0, double-quoted and single-quoted strings are equally fast, with double-quoted strings only slowing down once there are variables to be interpolated. This is because double-quoted strings are scanned for variables while the program is being loaded, during lexical analysis. This is a one-off expense that is even less than you might at first expect: the contents of both single-quoted and double-quoted strings have to be scanned *anyway*, to locate escape sequences and the actual end of the string. The only real difference is that scanning double-quoted strings generates several tokens in sequence when variables are present.

Overall, the shapes of the two charts are distinctive. The difference can be formalized by using "big-O notation," used in program analysis to describe the "size" or "speed" of an algorithm in terms of the size of the problem given. While it can be given a precise technical definition, it's enough to think of $O(f(n))$ as meaning that the graph of the algorithm's behavior is "looking like" the graph of $f(n)$ as n gets larger and larger:

> $O(f(n)) = $ *the set of functions $g(n)$ such that there exist positive constants c and n_0 such that* $0 \leq g(n) \leq cf(n)$ *for all $n \geq n_0$.*

In this case, the graph of double-quoted interpolation doesn't vary with v, the number of variables being interpolated, and only linearly with the l, the length of the string (that is to say, it's twice as slow when the string is twice as long). In big-O notation this would be described as $O(l)$. The graph for single-quoted concatenation is more complex. If you fix the length of the string and look at a single slice of the graph as the number of variables changes (such a slice is shown in Figure 9.1 at the top edge of the graph from the left to the peak), it looks fairly linear in v. Fixing the number of variables and allowing the length of the string to vary (the ridge crest leading from the peak down to the right) curves it in such a way as to suggest a parabola. Overall, these two influences appear to be multiplied, giving a big-O description of $O(l^2 v)$.

In the long run, l increases more slowly than $l^2 v$, and in fact for long strings with many variables, interpolation is *faster* than concatenation. For shorter strings, however, or fewer variables, concatenation still wins out.

Big-O notation only concerns itself with what happens to the program in the long run as the size of the problem gets larger, ignoring features that appear only for small instances of the problem. You'll recall that when there are no variables involved, the two methods are equally quick (since both consist of a single string), but that single-quoted concatenation speeds up slightly before slowing again, while double-quoted interpolation slows sharply as soon as a single variable is introduced, and never recovers. Big-O says that *in the long run*, variable interpolation is faster than concatenation, but you would need to have multi-kilobyte strings with dozens of variables to actually see it happen.

You can see that even in this very simple example, with only two factors to consider, there is the potential for a lot of subtlety when aiming for a definitive answer of what is "best." You could make deeper investigations even in this comparatively trivial example, and with more complicated problems you would probably have to before reaching any conclusions. But here is a good place to end the example, except to note that the slowest time recorded in all of the charted experiments is 3.7 seconds.

Unintuitive Results

Unlike C, which is converted into machine code that really isn't too different from what you actually write (the language has been described as "Assembler with delusions of grandeur"), your PHP program is being run by a virtual machine simulated by the PHP engine. When it comes to performance tuning, this can make for difficulties because it becomes that much harder to predict what will work well and what will not. This will be examined later, but for now you may wish to meditate on the results of the following test code:

```php
<?php
$j=0;
$start_test_1 = microtime(true);
for($i=0; $i<1000000; $i++) $j++;
$end_test_1 = microtime(true);

$j=0;
$start_test_2 = microtime(true);
for($i=0; $i<1000000; $i++) ++$j;
$end_test_2 = microtime(true);

$j=0;
$start_test_3 = microtime(true);
for($i=0; $i<1000000; ++$i) $j++;
$end_test_3 = microtime(true);

$j=0;
$start_test_4 = microtime(true);
for($i=0; $i<1000000; ++$i) ++$j;
$end_test_4 = microtime(true);

$test_1 = $end_test_1 - $start_test_1;
$test_2 = $end_test_2 - $start_test_2;
$test_3 = $end_test_3 - $start_test_3;
$test_4 = $end_test_4 - $start_test_4;

echo "Postincrementing I and J one million times: ",
    $test_1, " seconds.\n";
echo "Postincrementing I and preincrementing J one million times: ",
    $test_2, " seconds.\n";
echo "Preincrementing I and postincrementing J one million times: ",
    $test_3, " seconds.\n";
echo "Preincrementing I and J one million times: ",
    $test_4, " seconds.\n";
?>
```

Benchmarking and Profiling

There are many techniques and utilities for estimating the speed of a program, and they should be used before, during, and after embarking on any mission to speed up your site, so that you don't waste time making changes without any appreciable difference or, worse, slowing your site down. Broadly speaking, they can be divided into two main categories: *benchmarking* is what you do when you conduct experiments to determine the best approach for something before implementing it for real, and *profiling* covers experiments you conduct on the real thing to see just how well it actually performs. Clearly, there is quite a lot of overlap between the two; many of the techniques and the tools are the same (because the tools don't necessarily *care* whether the code you're using them on is natural or synthetic). Tools exist to aid you in these at both OS and PHP levels.

PEAR Benchmark

You've already seen examples of benchmarking in the previous section. They were constructed ad-hoc, but the basic ideas they have in common are common enough to warrant being abstracted into a separate class:

1. Start a timer (noting the current time).

2. Do something.

3. Stop the timer (again noting the current time).

4. Compare the stopping time with the starting time to determine the elapsed duration.

5. Repeat steps 1–4 a lot, accumulating the durations.

6. Have a look at the results.

An obvious enhancement to this would be to label the timers, so that several could be started and stopped independently. Also nice would be if timers could also contain information about the time spent in specific sections of the code they're covering. The PEAR Benchmarking class provides all this functionality. Installation of PEAR and PEAR packages is covered in Chapter 8; so you've already taken care of that, and you're ready to proceed with using it.

To repeat the initial string-building experiment using the Benchmarking class, you could write the following:

```php
<?php
require 'Benchmark/Timer.php';

$variable = 'string';

$timer = new Benchmark_Timer();

$timer->start();
for($i=0; $i<1000000; ++$i)
{
    $string = "this string has a $variable embedded into it";
}
$timer->setMarker('laptime');
for($i=0; $i<1000000; ++$i)
{
    $string = "this string has a ".$variable." inserted into it";
}
$timer->setMarker('finish');

echo "Variable interpolation required ",$timer->timeElapsed('Start','laptime'),"
```

```
      seconds for one million iterations.\n";
      echo "Variable concatenation required ",$timer->timeElapsed('laptime','finish'),"
      seconds for one million iterations.\n";

      $timer->stop();
      $timer->display();
      ?>
```

Benchmark/Iterate subclasses Benchmark/Timer, and provides a `run()` method to which you pass the name of the function you wish to test. Two matters to keep in mind when choosing one over the other. One is that the calling a function itself takes a bit of time. The other is that Benchmark/Iterate retains its timings for each individual experiment. Doing a lot of experiments means a big array, which is why the following code runs only ten thousand experiments instead of a million:

```php
<?php

require 'Benchmark/Iterate.php';

$variable = 'string';

function interpolate($variable)
{
    $string = "this string has a $variable embedded into it";
}

function concatenate($variable)
{
    $string = "this string has a ".$variable." inserted into it";
}

$interpolation_benchmark = new Benchmark_Iterate;
$concatenation_benchmark = new Benchmark_Iterate;

$interpolation_benchmark->run(10000, 'interpolate', 'string');
$concatenation_benchmark->run(10000, 'concatenate', 'string');

$interpolation_result = $interpolation_benchmark->get();
$concatenation_result = $concatenation_benchmark->get();
?>
```

The two result variables are arrays: `$interpolation_result['iterations']` records the number of times the test ran, and `$interpolation_result['mean']` records the average (the Benchmark class uses the bcmath functions if they're available to maintain accuracy when calculating this). Unsetting these two elements leaves you with a numerically-indexed array that contains all of the individual times for each iteration so that you can carry out any other statistical tests you feel are relevant.

top and ab

The NT4/Access report generator anecdote earlier came from the Windows world, and mentioned the use of its Task Manager. The process monitor utility that ships with Unix-type operating systems is named `top`, and is much richer in the amount of information it provides. Meanwhile, the Apache distribution includes the `ab` ApacheBench program, which tests the sharp end of your site: just how fast can you serve stuff? It's often instructive to use the two side by side: ab to see how your performance looks, and top to see how much effort is going into getting that performance.

You run top on the web server itself, of course; ab can be run in the same place, but for fairness's sake it's worth running it from another machine on the local network (running it more remotely than that would introduce additional delays that would hinder your attempts to stress the server). For example, you could open a terminal window on your workstation and ssh to the web server; running ab on your workstation and top on the server with the two terminal windows side-by-side.

Put simply, ab is an http client on speed. A typical invocation has it requesting the same page a thousand times in close succession, thus simulating a thousand users all hitting it nearly at once. It gathers statistics on how long the server took to respond to the requests, and whether any failed to be satisfied. Take a look at this example:

```
ab -n1000 -c10 http://bowman/page2test.php
```

This command tells ab to request page2test.php a total of one thousand times, with up to ten requests running concurrently. So it makes ten requests, and as soon as one of them is satisfied and the response has been received, it starts an eleventh, not letting up until the total has been reached.

After it has made its one thousand requests, it presents a report of the statistics it has gathered. These include the total time for the whole run, the size of the response, how many requests were made and how many failed, how rapidly it had been able to make requests (corresponding to the rate at which requests were satisfied), how quickly the responses themselves were served in bps, and how long the average and slowest response took.

It's less important for benchmarking to adjust the total request parameter -n; this just has to be at least as large as -c, and large enough for the overall statistics to be smoothed out, without any transient behavior at the start of the test throwing off the results. Twiddling the concurrency parameter -c is more informative. Starting with -c1 (the lower you set -c, the lower you can set -n unless you really want to sit and wait that long), you can see if the server is capable of responding to one request at a time. As you increase -c, you increase the number of concurrent requests being made, and you can watch to see if your server is able to handle the increasing load. As an example, versions of IIS that ship with desktop versions of Microsoft Windows are throttled to a maximum 10 concurrent requests. As soon as -c goes above 10, you'll start getting failed requests. Yes, you can use ApacheBenchmark to test other servers; in a way, it's called "Apache" because it's an Apache Group product. With increasing load the transfer rate will drop, the rate at which requests are made will increase, and eventually requests will start failing. If you're feeling sadistic, you could simulate being Slashdotted: hit your server with _n10000 _c1000 and watch it have a hernia.

Meanwhile, over in the other terminal window is the server's view of what is going on. When you run top, the first thing to look at is the load average. The three numbers given are the average number of active processes (that is, either running or waiting to run, as opposed to those that are currently idle) for the past minute, 5 minutes, and 15 minutes, respectively. If you think of the server as a bank, a processor as a teller, and a process as a person, the load averages represent the number of people either being served or standing in line. Obviously, if there aren't enough tellers, there will be a lot of increasingly irritated people. Likewise, too high a load average means that processes are spending too much time queuing for a chance to run. Consequently, the people whose requests initiated those processes are also having to wait for results and they or their browsers may even give up—not a good look for your site.

Ideally, you want the load average to be somewhat lower than the number of processors your server has, keeping some slack available to handle unusually heavy loads. Brief surges are tolerable, but only if they're brief. The 15-minute load shouldn't surge at all; if it does, then it's an indication that when the server is busy it's *too* busy, and a backlog is forming that takes a long time to work through. A spike large enough to significantly influence the 15-minute average could not be dealt with quickly.

Just below the load average in top's display is the activity level for each processor, given as a percentage. This should also stay fairly low, to allow for the Slashdot Effect or attack attempts by the latest worm. If the machine is a dedicated web server, then significant activity from the processor when nothing is being served may suggest that it is doing something it shouldn't be. Check the process listing itself to see which processes are using the processor. You may be able to remove some of them. A site that merely serves static web pages or files would experience very little CPU load at all — a 1980s vintage processor is perfectly capable of transferring data as fast as it can be read from disk — but dynamically generated pages do experience a bottleneck at this point.

On the other hand, the server may be running flat out even with a nearly idle CPU. Recall the Windows report generator anecdote, where simple tasks were taking forever while the processor spent 85 percent of its time twiddling its thumbs, and the determination that the problem lay in the fact there was too little RAM in the machine.

Below top's CPU usage report is a report on the amount of memory available, how much is being used, and how much is still free, both in RAM and in the swap file. You want to rely on the swap file as little as possible, ideally not at all.

Hardware Improvements

So, you've decided that the site is running slowly. You've profiled what's been going on and now you're ready to look at improving matters. The most profound improvements can come with remembering that your server exists in the real world and is subject to physical law. You can't change the laws of physics: you have to accommodate yourself to them.

The first thing to look at is your connection to the outside world. You want a nice big pipe there. If your server is lightly loaded but network traffic is maxed out, then your connection is your bottleneck.

Once that's been dealt with, check the processor. If it's consistently running at the upper limit of its range, then an upgrade could well give you more breathing room. How old is your machine? Two years? You'll probably find that a new box will be more than twice as fast as your current one. Of course, changing the computer is the most fundamental, fraught-with-peril, and almost certainly expensive change you can make. It would be *nice* if you could just bring the new box in, swap the cables from the old machine to the new, perform a hard drive transplant, and fire it up. It never seems to work out that simply though.

If the processor is fairly idle, but memory is tight, then increasing RAM is your next priority. 512MB is easily sufficient for all but the most high-volume sites, or sites with the largest databases, which are usually cached in RAM by MySQL for speed of access.

For sites that principally serve static pages or files, then RAM is more important than processor speed — it's very simple to just move a chunk of data from one part of the machine to another, so being able to quickly work out how to move it is not as important as being able to move a lot of it at once.

Disk access is a comparatively slow process. Consider upgrading to a faster hard drive with greater throughput. If you are close to filling your current drive, then look at getting additional drives instead of moving everything to a bigger one. Even if you *aren't* close to filling your current drive, getting additional drives and distributing content across them may improve access times. The disks' read/write heads will be operating simultaneously, and won't have as far to travel as the heads of a single larger drive. Nor will the disks have to spin as far.

Web Server Improvements

By its very nature, Apache is highly configurable, with many settings that can be tweaked to optimize one aspect or another of its behavior. Some reduce the amount of memory Apache requires, while others have the aim of reducing the amount of work carried out by each process.

When you start Apache, the first thing it does is start up half-a-dozen (the exact figure is, of course, configurable) instances of `httpd`. These are the processes that actually handle HTTP requests. All the server itself does is manage these children, starting new ones and stopping existing ones as needed. Each instance uses up about a megabyte of RAM (it's hard to be more exact, but this is a reasonable heuristic), and sits around waiting for a request. If there are more requests being made than there are instances, then new ones will be started up, and if things go quiet later, then the excess will be shut down. Occasionally an instance of httpd will be shut down even if there is sufficient work available. This allows the operating system to reclaim memory that may have leaked from either the httpd process itself or any of the modules it was using. And of course it is possible for an httpd process to simply crash, in which case that particular request will fail; but another instance will be on standby in case the request is tried again. This is a key reason why Apache operates in this way: it enables the server to keep running even after it has crashed.

The configuration options that control this are found in or can be added to `httpd.conf`:

❑   `MaxClients`: This is the maximum number of httpd processes you're prepared to support at any one time, hence the maximum number of client requests being handled concurrently. Given the 1MB-per-process heuristic, there is little sense in setting this higher than the amount of RAM you have. In fact, you'll run out of RAM long before this. They'll continue to *work*, but they'll be relying on much slower virtual memory to do it, and there'll be an awful lot of tiresome swapping between the disk and RAM.

   You don't want this setting to be too low, either; if there are more requests made than this figure, some will miss out and end up sitting around waiting for one of the others to complete. If the delay is too long, the client will give up and the request will be reported as a failure.

❑   `MaxRequestsPerChild`: Once an instance of httpd has served this many requests, it will be shut down, regardless of current server load, in case unfixed memory leaks exist in the server or installed modules that would cause the instance to fall prey to obesity. Since by definition, the operating system cannot realize that the size increase is unnecessary, Apache must step in arbitrarily to shut a process down. This directive controls how often that happens. Unless you're using an experimental or under-development module that is likely to be buggy, you should be able to set this limit to 100,000 without ill effect. Monitor the RAM consumption of each httpd process with `top`; if they to seem to be growing unchecked, reduce the limit by a factor of 10. Continue to monitor and reduce as necessary. Keep an eye on the behavior of the system as a whole, because if this figure drops too low, then there will be too much time getting wasted in starting and stopping child requests, and it is therefore time for you to try and isolate the module causing the problem.

❑   StartServers and MinSpareServers: StartServers specifies the number of httpd instances that are initialized when you start Apache. A good number for this is the number of concurrent requests your site is typically handling. MinSpareServers would be this number plus a few more. Because there is work involved in starting up a fresh instance, you don't want the server to be doing so when it's already running flat out handling requests, so it pays to keep some slack handy.

When a request comes in for a web page, it is frequently followed by additional requests from the same client for ancillary resources (stylesheets, inline images, and others), and probably subsequent requests for additional pages. It makes sense for the connection between client and server to be maintained in the interim to avoid the waste of opening and closing a connection only to immediately open a new one to the same client a few hundred milliseconds later, and then finding an httpd instance ready to accept the request (which more often than not will turn out to be the very instance that handled the previous connection and is now idle). The modern HTTP 1.1 standard provides this option —known as "Keep_Alive"—and modern versions of Apache respect it by default according (as ever) to settings in Apache's configuration files.

❑   KeepAlive: This is On by default, and you generally wouldn't have much cause to turn it off.

❑   MaxKeepAliveRequests: Once a connection is established between the client and the server, the httpd instance that is handling it will dedicate itself to that client for at most this many requests. This can be set fairly high—around 100. There aren't many page requests that are followed by a hundred ancillary requests, but it can happen that from the first page they load a user, may quickly open half a dozen other pages. Setting this option high won't cause too much trouble since the client typically closes the connection from its end; in cases where it doesn't, the following configuration directive comes into force.

❑   KeepAliveTimeout: If there have been no requests on the current connection from the client for this many seconds, the server assumes the client has gone away for whatever reason without properly closing the connection. The higher the bandwidth between your site and the client, the lower this figure can be. Bandwidth is a bottleneck for people on dialup that reduces the rate at which requests can be made, and so there may be 30–45 seconds between successive requests. A lower bound on this figure would be something like 10–15 seconds.

For the purposes of logging traffic, Apache can use reverse DNS to look up the hostname for the IP the request originates from. It makes it slightly easier to read the logs by eye, but that's about it. Meanwhile, the request is waiting for a response from the DNS server, unable to continue until it has received a response. You'd be better off just storing the IP itself in the logfile, and leaving the lookups to something like Apache's logresolve utility at a time when you actually care.

❑   HostnameLookups. This sets whether to record hostnames (On) or IP addresses (Off) in server logs.

Related to this is whether you use domain names or IPs when allowing or denying connections. Again, using allow from .example.com or deny from .example.com in your .htaccess file means that a reverse DNS has to be carried out to find out what domain name the originating IP belongs to (and then a *forward* DNS lookup to check that the IP really is part of the domain as claimed). Here, too, therefore, allowing or denying specific ranges of IP addresses rather than domain names is more effective. However, remember that half the point of DNS is that specific domain names aren't permanently tied to specific IP addresses, and that the name can be shifted to a different host and a different IP address.

Speaking of .htaccess, when Apache is asked to read a file, it will check for .htaccess in every directory in the file's path on the filesystem (not its path as described by the URL), up to and including the system root. If the path is long, then that's a lot of lookups, so it helps to keep them short. And if (as no doubt you do) you have your entire site stored in a single document tree instead of being scattered all about your system, then there's no point in having Apache search any higher than that tree's root. The access.conf file provides the means for you to inform Apache of this. First, you state that no .htaccess files are allowed to override settings anywhere from the system root directory down, and then you follow that by stating that .htaccess files *can* be honored in your site's document tree:

```
<Directory />
    AllowOverride None
</Directory>
<Directory /www/siteroot>
    AllowOverride All
</Directory>
```

If you are not using .htaccess files at all, say so and Apache won't waste time looking for them:

```
<Directory /www/siteroot>
    AllowOverride None
</Directory>
```

One Apache module that can speed output on its way is mod_gzip. Most browsers these days have a gzip library built in, and can uncompress gzip-compressed data as they receive it. Such browsers will include a statement to this effect in their request headers. In return, Apache with mod_gzip installed will send compressed responses. There is a delay introduced by the compression/decompression steps, but for highly compressible documents (English text compresses by about 30%, HTML by about 60%), the saving in bandwidth is not to be ignored.

Otherwise, remove any and all modules you don't actually use. If, for example, you don't use .htaccess files, then disable mod_access. The same goes for PHP extensions, and any libraries they call on; if you're not going to be using the SimpleXML extension, disable it.

PHP Improvements

Once you've optimized your hardware, your database, and Apache, you can concentrate on tuning your actual code. The best preparation you can do to help yourself at this point is to select and adhere to a consistent coding standard. The less time you spend trying to interpret what you have written, the more time you can spend looking at other tricks to improve its efficiency.

Coding Standards

The visitors to your site have priority. Your job is to put the effort into getting them the information they want as rapidly as possible. On the other hand, your time is more valuable — indeed, more *expensive* — than the computer's.

If you can save yourself five minutes' work at the expense of an extra millisecond of processing time on a page, that is a good investment that would continue to pay off even after the page has been processed three hundred thousand times. You can put those five minutes into something more productive, such as seeing if there is a way to save *twenty* milliseconds when processing the page. It's not just a matter of being able to fill a user's request as fast as possible—considering all the opportunities for delay between your server and their browser, mere speed may not be that much of a factor. (It is if you have an extremely busy site, but if that's so then as you've seen your bottlenecks are probably elsewhere.) It's a matter of if you can get the existing page to run faster, you can start wondering what else the page could do for your site's audience.

But how can you achieve such a transfer of workload? It's not enough to put more and more onto the computer if it doesn't relieve you of any work. A crucial way to save programming time is to write code in such a way that reading it is as hassle-free as possible.

Now, there are few issues more likely to spark heated debate than things like how much to indent by, which bits to indent, where the braces should go, and whether `else`s should be appear on the same line as adjacent braces, like this: `} else {`. Things can get ugly. And if and when you've decided these things, you still have to decide things such as naming conventions for variables, functions, objects, and classes; whether to declare a method as `protected static` or `static protected` (it matters if you ever have to do a search-and-replace); whether you declare `global $foo;`, use "`$GLOBALS['foo']`, or ban the use of global user variables outright; and where to put comments and what to write in them; not to mention more substantive issues such as how your code is divided into files.

> *Avoid "code beautifiers"—programs that take a file of source code and return it reformatted according to some set of standards. At least, don't rely on them. Your code should be beautiful to begin with; otherwise, you're missing the point of having the standards. Use them if you have old code or code from elsewhere with different standards that you wish to make consistent with your own, or to make your code consistent with someone else's standards. But don't work by cheerfully knocking out a mess because you can just use the beautifier on it afterwards to make it pretty.*

PEAR Coding Standards

One way to cut through at least some of the tangle is to adopt an existing style guide. While you could adopt a guide developed for a language with a similar syntax like C, C++, or Java, the fit may not be ideal. For example, it's not necessary for the way you name variables to be distinctly different from the way you name functions; the former are already distinguished by the $. Instead, you could adopt a PHP-specific standard, of which the most widespread is that described in Chapter 4 of the PEAR manual.

Unless you're putting together a repository of code submitted by the public, as is the case for PEAR itself, following PEAR style to the letter may not be appropriate. For example, PEAR style requires that each source file begin with a block of commentary that stating such things as authorship and licensing. For a large in-house application that won't be getting distributed, a distribution license is pointless, nor would it be necessary to list all of the developers on every file. However, the PEAR standard serves as a starting point.

Braces and Indentation

The debate over where braces should go is so long-running and so inconclusive that at least one language (Python) has been deliberately designed to avoid them. Eric S. Raymond, in the Jargon File (version 4.4.7), lists four in the entry on "Indent Style," which are described here along with their names and followed by a couple of others.

K&R style — as in Kernighan and Ritchie, designers of C and authors of the definitive references on the language — is also known as the "One True Brace" style:

```
for($i=0; $i<100; $i++){
    if($foo[$i]==0){
        //...etc.
    }
}
```

In Allman or BSD style, much of the BSD kernel source code was written by Eric Allman, who used this style for the job:

```
for($i=0; $i<100; $i++)
{
    if($foo[$i]==0)
    {
        //...etc.
    }
}
```

Whitesmith's style was named after a commercial C compiler that formatted code in this way:

```
for($i=0; $i<100; $i++)
    {
    if($foo[$i]==0)
        {
        ...etc.
        }
    }
```

GNU style is used (pretty much exclusively) by the Free Software Foundation:

```
for($i=0; $i<100; $i++)
  {
    if($foo[$i]==0)
      {
        ...etc.
      }
  }
```

A more compressed version of Allman style is as follows:

```
for($i=0; $i<100; $i++)
{   if($foo[$i]==0)
    {   ...etc.
    }
}
```

An even more compressed version of Allman style is this:

```
for($i=0; $i<100; $i++)
{   if($foo[$i]==0)
    {   ...etc.
} }
```

All six styles can be varied by choosing whether to use tabs or spaces, or how wide each level of indentation should be. Typically, four or eight spaces (or eight-space-wide tabs) are the most common, and tabs are often frowned upon because different people use tabs of different widths. Any mix of spaces and tabs that looks right with one width tab is unlikely to look right on another, resulting in so-called "tab damage," with lines of code and pieces of lines appearing at all sorts of random-looking indents.

The last style is a hoax: if you're going to align opening and closing parentheses in columns, you should at least make sure you align *matching pairs* of opening and closing parentheses, otherwise the alignment is simply misleading. If saving lines is that important, you might as well use LISP style indentation:

```
for($i=0; $i<100; $i++)
    {if($foo[$i]==0)
        {...etc.}}
```

PEAR specifies K&R-style indentation, with four spaces per indent and no tab characters. The reason for ruling out tab characters is of course due to the effects of tab damage; but knowing the causes of tab damage can go a long way toward preventing it.

Tab damage is caused when you assume that tabs have a certain width. The following piece of code has been written using tabs for indenting, in an editor that has been set to use four spaces per tab:

```
/************************
 * Big Flashy           *
 * Box comment          *
 *                      *
 *   Just Because (TM)  *
 ************************/
for($i=0; $i<100; $i++)
{
    if( ($a==$i || $b==$i)
        &&
        ($c!=$i || $d!=$i))
    {
        echo "Either $a or $b is equal to $i, ";
        echo "and either $c or $d is not.";
    }
}
```

And here is how it would look in an editor that has been configured with eight-space tabs:

```
/************************
 * Big Flashy               *
 * Box comment              *
 *                                      *
 *       Just Because (TM)  *
 ************************/
for($i=0; $i<100; $i++)
{
        if( ($a==$i || $b==$i)
                &&
                ($c!=$i || $d!=$i))
```

```
        {
                   echo "Either $a or $b is equal to $i, ";
                   echo "and either $c or $d is not.";
        }
    }
```

The first thing you can see is that Big Flashy Box comments are generally more trouble than they're worth. They're often the biggest victims of tab damage, which is ironic because they're supposed to be the bits that are specifically for *human* consumption, while the machine doesn't care about niceties of formatting.

If you do want to use tabs for indentation, then the rule of thumb is that they should only be used for *indenting*, and spaces should be used for any additional alignment tasks. In the previous example, the extra tabs used to align the second and third lines of the `if` test with the first line — which worked fine with four-space tabs — have caused them to be pushed too far to the right when they became eight-space tabs. Instead of a third tab, *four spaces* should have been used, *after* the tabs, to match the four characters "`if (`".

Generally, the only tabs in source code should be at the start of lines; they shouldn't follow any other characters. The two exceptions to this would be if a literal tab character really was required, or if you were using the "compressed Allman" style, in which case, a single tab would be used to separate a `{` from the following statement.

You may have noticed that all of the styles described — hoaxes aside — have the closing braces on lines by themselves. The effect this has on code listings is to introduce a visible gap between the end of the statement block and the following code, analogous in some ways to paragraph breaks in English text. You could take the position, therefore, that K&R or compressed Allman is "better" than Allman, in that it doesn't separate the statement block from the construct (`for`, `if`, `switch`, and so on) that introduces it. According to Raymond, the principal claim in defense of K&R is that it is more economical with vertical space, allowing more code to fit on the screen at once. Obviously, though, compressed Allman shares both virtues while still allowing matching braces to be aligned.

Reducing Nesting Levels

If the number of nested braces gets too large, it can become confusing identifying which opening brace a given closing brace is paired with. Most IDEs and some of the better language-sensitive text editors are able to find such pairings without being confused by any braces appearing in comments or string literals, but it is still all too likely that you'll want to locate them by eyeball (as, for example, when you've missed typing one or the other). When reading code you'll often see closing braces followed by tiny comments like "`/* end for */`", or "`/* if($i==0) */,`" in an attempt to assist. However, some judicious use of `break` and `continue` statements can help to reduce the depth of nesting. By doing so, not only do you reduce the tendency of your code to wander off toward the right hand side of the page, but you also reduce the number and size of parenthesized blocks, thus reducing the number of parentheses and drawing each matched pair closer together for quicker eyeball recognition.

For example, the previous samples of indentation style were written so that the body of the `for` loop consists entirely of a single `if` statement — if the `if` statement's test fails, then nothing happens during that iteration of the loop, and processing continues on to the next iteration. When you put it that way, you can see that an equivalent implementation of the loop would be as follows:

```
for($i=0; $i<100; $i++)
{
    if($foo[$i]!=0)
        continue;
    //...etc.
}
```

Note that the test in the `if` statement has been negated, and that the depth to which the remainder of the loop is indented has been reduced by one level of indentation. This can also be used to reduce the complexity of tests. Recalling another example from earlier in the discussion:

```
for($i=0; $i<100; $i++)
{
    if( ($a==$i || $b==$i)
        &&
        ($c!=$i || $d!=$i))
    {
        echo "Either $a or $b is equal to $i, ";
        echo "and either $c or $d is not.";
    }
}
```

You can see immediately that this is another case where there is only a single `if` statement inside the loop, and hence can be written as follows:

```
for($i=0; $i<100; $i++)
{
    if(!(($a==$i || $b==$i) && ($c!=$i || $d!=$i)))
        continue;
    echo "Either $a or $b is equal to $i, ";
    echo "and either $c or $d is not.";
}
```

By employing a little Boolean algebra, the test reduces to this:

```
if(($a!=$i && $b!=$i) || ($c==$i && $d==$i))
```

So if either `$a` and `$b` are both not equal to `$i`, or if both `$c` and `$d` *are*, then the loop will `continue`. But if you test that `$a` and `$b` are both not equal to `$i`, you can know right away if you will be continuing, without having to go on to look at `$c` or `$d`. So the test can be split into two separate statements:

```
for($i=0; $i<100; $i++)
{
    if($a!=$i && $b!=$i)
        continue;
    if($c==$i && $d==$i)
        continue;
    echo "Either $a or $b is equal to $i, ";
    echo "and either $c or $d is not.";
}
```

Because PHP allows `continue` or `break` to take an argument expressing how many levels to continue or break, a simple `continue` or `break` can be employed in situations where in C or Java you would require loops to contain additional variables carrying information about whether loops should be terminated or not from within nested loops, or using goto to jump to a label following the outer loop (except in Java, which doesn't have a goto construct). You can write this:

```
$position = null;
for($i=0; $i<100; $i++)
{
    for($j=0; $j<100; $j++)
    {
        if($array[$i][$j]==$what_we_wanted)
        {
            $position = array($i,$j);
            break 2;
        }
    }
}
if(null==$position) // $what_we_wanted was not found.
```

instead of this:

```
$position = null;
$found_what_we_wanted = false;
for($i=0; $i<100; $i++)
{
    for($j=0; $j<100; $j++)
    {
        if($array[$i][$j]==$what_we_wanted)
        {
            $position = array($i,$j);
            $found_waht_we_wanted = true;
            break;
        }
    }
    if($found_what_we_wanted)
        break;
}
if(null==$position) // $what_we_wanted was not found.
```

As a final observation on continue and break, it is a common practice to write those statements on the same line as the test that governs whether they are executed, especially if those tests are short and simple. Hence, you may want to consider adopting or allowing the practice of writing like this:

```
    if($a!=$i && $b!=$i) continue;
    if($c==$i && $d==$i) continue;
```

An aside on using the equality operator == is the fact that a common typo is to use = when == was intended. You can protect yourself from the bugs that can result from using assignment instead of comparison in certain cases. When comparing a variable to the result of a function or to a literal value, if you write the variable on the right-hand side of the equality operator, accidentally writing = instead of == for the operator itself will result in a parse error: "null=$position" is invalid syntax. These are a lot easier to debug than the sometimes subtle errors resulting from an assignment that should not have been assigned and a comparison that didn't properly compare.

Comments

As well as (or instead of) the authorship and licensing details mandated by PEAR, other things that could go in the top comment include a synopsis of what the code it contained does. If it's a long synopsis, preceding it with a one- or two-line abstract synopsizing the synopsis will help the developer who comes along later and wants to know what the file is for.

PEAR also says you should use Javadoc-style comments, so that they are easily translated into documentation. Opinion is just as divided on this score as on any other style issue. An argument against it is that they make the comments themselves, as they appear in the source code, harder to read because of all the extra formatting they attract. Another opinion, when it is argued that every publicly accessible method should be commented in this way, is that it encourages vapid do-nothing comments that don't actually contribute to either commentary or documentation:

```
/**
 * Gets the number of elements in this Bundle.
 *
 * @return number of elements in this Bundle.
 */
public function Count()
{
    return count($this->elements);
}
```

But the thing that any comments are supposed to do is document the *intent* of the code. If the code itself is well-built, it will do a good job on its own of documenting what it *does*. What it won't document is *why* it was written.

Naming Conventions

Variables and functions with bad names are a rich source of stories that range from comedy to horror. In any application of respectable length, you will need to have some consistent system for inventing names. Here are a few tips.

Generic counter variables for controlling `for` loops should be short and sweet. Unless context provides an obvious choice for the variable, then the convention is to use `$i` first. If you then nest another loop, its variable is `$j`, followed by `$k` and then `$l`. Typically, if you need to nest your loops any deeper, then you may want to reconsider what you are doing and move all but the outermost block of statements into a function. If loops aren't nested, then they can use the same variable, provided they are properly initialized. If you're using a `foreach()` loop to iterate over an array, using a plural name for the array and the corresponding singular for the element will make the relationship between the two variables obvious: `foreach($children as $child)`.

Especially long variable names should be avoided. The longer the variable name, the more opportunity there is for a typo to make a mess. No doubt you do all of your PHP development with error reporting set to (at least) `E_ALL`, so that you get a notice whenever you attempt to use a variable that hasn't been initialized. This will trap instances where you mistype the name of a variable when you use it, but it won't help you if you mistype the name when *assigning* to the variable. In the previous section, the variable name `$found_what_we_wanted` was used, but mistyped in one place. The mistake would not be picked up as it does not involve the use of an uninitialized variable, and only later—when you realize something is wrong and that `$i` always has the value 100—would you discover the mistake.

PHP 5 offers provisions for separating the visible properties and methods of an object from the properties and methods are implemented by the class, by means of the magic __get(), __set(), and __call() methods. Because capitalization matters for variables and properties, you may wish to consider the practice of naming all of your object's properties with lowercase names, declaring them private or protected, and then writing routines to provide access via title-case names:

```
class foo
{
    protected $width, $height;

public function __get($property)
{
    switch($property)
    {
    case 'Width':
        return $this->width;
    case 'Height':
        return $this->height;
    case 'Area':
        return $this->width*$this->height;
    }
}

public function __set($property, $value)
{
    switch($property, $value)
    {
    case 'Width':
        $this->width = $value;
        return;
    }
}

}
```

This also gives you finer control over which properties the object's user may alter or view. Note, for example, that $object->Height can be read from but not assigned to — a distinction that would not be possible if you simply made $object->height public.

If you make a stylistic distinction between real properties and synthetic ones created via __get() and __set(), you should make sure that you provide synthetic access to the real properties, and preferably disallow direct access to those properties. This will allow you to create classes that provide exactly the same properties interface regardless of whether each such class uses the same properties internally or not. A complex number object, for example, may provide $num->Real, $num->Imag, $num->Arg, and $num->Mag; independently of whether it stores the number as a real part plus an imaginary part and providing the argument and magnitude synthetically, or vice versa.

The __get() accessor for a synthetic property may include code so that the previous value retrieved is cached in a private property in case it is asked for again, with the contents of the cache cleared if and when the properties it depends on are altered via __set().

When building function and method names up from several words, use either underscore_separation or TitleCase to show where one word leaves off and the next begins. Opinion is divided over which looks better, but keep in mind the fact that function, method, and class names are all treated in a case-insensitive manner: `Mandate` and `ManDate` will refer to the same entity.

Defined constants created with `define()` or `const` are generally identified by being written in UPPER-CASE. Those created in the global scope with `define()` should be preceded by some distinctive sequence of characters to prevent them from colliding with other constants that may be defined elsewhere (see the PHP manual for many examples of this practice). This isn't necessary for class constants, as their names are already preceded by the name of the class (or `self::` within the class definition).

Since the distinction is already built into PHP's syntax, rules for distinguishing variable/property names from function/method names are unnecessary compared with other languages; but there is no such distinction between classes and functions. You can have a class named `foo` and a function named `foo`, and the only way to tell the difference is that `$v = new foo();` uses the class, and `$v = foo();` uses the function.

> `$v=foo::foo();` *is something else again — to wit, something that won't even compile; constructors can't be called statically, and static functions can't be constructors*

On grammatical grounds, classes, variables, and properties are best described with nouns or noun phrases. Use the same parts of speech you would use in a corresponding verbal description of what the code does. Arrays and other collections should be given names that are plurals (`$children`, `$pages`). Boolean-valued properties should have names starting with "is" or "has" or other means of denoting a predicate (`$isValid`, `$can_be_deleted`). Classes should be named with nouns (`UserFactory`, `NonPlayerCharacter`); abstract classes can be given the prefix `Abstract_` or `Abstract` to prevent accidental attempts to create objects from them (`AbstractCollection`, `Abstract_Document`), while the construct `FooFactory` is a common convention for denoting class that provides static methods returning new objects of class `Foo`. Functions and methods can be named with verbs (`traversePath()`, `anneal()`, `be wonderful()`), allowing adjectives, adverbs, and occasionally nouns for naming constants (`COLOR_GREEN`, `QUICKLY`, `GOLDEN_RATIO`).

Hacking the Grammar

Some rules about coding style can be enforced by turning a violation into a parse error. If you know what you are doing, you can edit the `zend_language_parser.y` and `zend_language_scanner.l` files and rebuild PHP.

If, for example, you want to rule out the possibility of using constructs such as `if():...endif;`, then from the lex file you'd remove the patterns matching `endif`, `endwhile`, `endfor`, `endforeach`, `enddeclare`, and `endswitch` (all of which appear in the `<ST_IN_SCRIPTING>` context); and from the yacc file, the corresponding `T_END*` token declarations, and the production rules:

```
unticked_statement:
    T_IF '(' expr ')' ':' inner_statement_list new_elseif_list new_else_single
T_ENDIF ';'

while_statement:
    ':' inner_statement_list T_ENDWHILE ';'

for_statement:
    ':' inner_statement_list T_ENDFOR ';'

foreach_statement:
    ':' inner_statement_list T_ENDFOREACH ';'
```

```
declare_statement:
    ':' inner_statement_list T_ENDDECLARE ';'

switch_case_list:
    ':' case_list T_ENDSWITCH ';'
    ':' ';' case_list T_ENDSWITCH ';'
```

Also remove the whole of the `new_elseif_list` and `new_else_single` productions. Because `while_statement`, `for_statement`, `foreach_statement`, and `declare_statement` now all reduce to a single rule `statement`, without any associated code, the productions themselves are now redundant. You could replace occurrences of `while_statement` with `statement` (it appears once, in the productions for `unticked_statement`) without ill effect, remove the production for `while_statement`, and gain a slightly smaller and simpler parsing engine in the process.

This will of course break any code written by anyone who uses the now-banned constructs.

Caching

Having a page that is updated on a daily basis, yet is hit several thousand times during each day, means that the same computations are being carried out, producing the same results, several thousand times a day. Carrying them out *once* and holding on to the results for all subsequent requests offers the potential for enormous savings.

Because your PHP application is insulated from the processor by several layers of intermediate software, with instructions filtering down through them to the hardware, and results filtering back up, there are several points where you could potentially short-circuit the process. Between any two such layers there is an interface where you can imagine an assistant who remembers previous requests for information from people and the information provided as a result, and so can supply that information immediately if and when the same requests come in again.

At the PHP level, there are two principal interfaces where caching can be effective. You can either generate static versions of pages and serve those instead of regenerating them every time, you can have the source code of your PHP application stored in a pre-parsed format ready for execution by the Zend engine without need of the additional step of compiling the source code, or you can do both.

Source Pre-Parsing

When a PHP program is run, the source code is loaded, parsed, and compiled into *bytecode* (machine code for an imaginary processor that is simulated by the Zend engine), and then that bytecode is executed. There are several products available that can take that compiled bytecode and save it; a selection of the better ones is given in the following table (in alphabetical order).

afterBURNER*Cache	http://bwcache.bware.it/cache.htm
Alternative PHP Cache	http://pecl.php.net/package/APC
PHP Accelerator	http://www.php-accelerator.co.uk/
Turck MMCache	http://turck-mmcache.sourceforge.net/
Zend Optimizer	http://zend.com/store/products/zend-optimizer.php

For robustness and effectiveness, Zend's own product is obviously going to be hard to beat, but its use requires purchasing the Zend Encoder to generate the bytecode. Note also that APC is distributed as a PECL extension.

When the program is next called for, the bytecode is retrieved and supplied to the Zend engine directly, skipping the parsing and compilation stages. All these products will check the modification dates of the source file and bytecode file to determine if the former has changed since the latter was generated, and re-parse and re-cache if necessary. Some, such as Zend Optimizer, can also (as the name implies) perform optimizations on the bytecode to improve performance, including a number that are impossible to emulate in PHP itself (as the optimizer is operating at a lower level, where a single PHP statement may correspond to several bytecode instructions that may be manipulated independently).

Generally speaking, using a bytecode cache is merely a matter of following its installation instructions, with no changes necessary to your PHP program's source code. So this is often one of the simplest, yet significant, software-level performance boosters that can be achieved.

Note that, especially in the case of an optimizing bytecode cache, the changes wrought in the speed of various scripts will change in a nonlinear fashion: it won't be merely a matter of every script running 20 percent faster or twice as fast. Some will run proportionally faster than others, although the worst that can happen is that certain scripts aren't measurably faster. Consequently, the results of profiling a site without the cache installed have no bearing on the site's profile afterwards.

Output Pre-Generation

In contrast to bytecode caches, saving generated output for redisplay later *does* involve changes to the way your site operates. The first thing a given page needs to do is determine whether or not it needs to run, or if instead it can use a cached copy of its output.

PEAR::Cache and PEAR::Cache_Lite

Naturally, PEAR includes packages that provide caching output for later requests.

Cache_Lite provides a simple and quick mechanism for storing the output of pages or parts of pages as files to be read in as required later. The following example uses it to cache a simple string:

```php
<?php
require_once 'Cache/Lite.php';

$id = '42'; // This is used to identify which cache file to use;
            // anything unique that can be remembered from access to
            // access will do; if you're caching an entire page this way
            // its URL is a natural choice.

$options = array(
    'cacheDir' => '/cachefiles/', // Cache_Lite only does file storage:
                                  // you'll need to specify an
                                  //appropriate directory here.
    'lifeTime' => 3600           // We'll force an update every hour.
);

$Cache_Lite = new Cache_Lite($options);

if ($data = $Cache_Lite->get($id)) {
```

```
    // A cached copy has been found

} else {

    // No copy in the cache; generate its contents
    // and store in $data.
    $data = "Hello, World!"; // This could just as easily be an entire page.

    // When that's done, save it in the cache.
    $Cache_Lite->save($data);
}
// Either way, the output of the page is in $data. I presume someone wants
// to see it...
echo $data;
?>
```

The most straightforward way you could wrap this around an existing script is to generate the page and buffer its output. This would mean replacing the "Hello, World!" line with the following:

```
ob_start();
/*
...All of your existing script goes here...
*/
$data = ob_get_contents();
ob_end_clean();
```

There is nothing to prevent you from using multiple cache files for different sections of a single page, or using the same cache file in multiple pages.

PEAR Cache is more elaborate. Its most prominent difference compared with Cache_Lite is that it allows the cache to be implemented in a variety of ways (and you could always subclass Cache_Container to create your own). In addition to flat file storage, Cache comes with containers using shared memory, the Mohawk Session Handler extension, and databases. It also provides for gzip storage of cached data, and specialized caches for storing dynamically generated images and the responses from http requests.

In its most straightforward form, using PEAR Cache is effectively the same as using Cache_Lite. Once again, you need not cache an entire page; concentrate primarily on sections that are slow to generate and rarely change.

Personalized CMS

Content Management Systems sometimes provide caching themselves. If you decide to write an application for yourself to make updating your site's contents easier (and why wouldn't you?), then you may wish to do the same. Broadly speaking, there are three opportunities for keeping the content of the pages synchronized with the contents of the database.

❑ Update the page when the database content is altered. In other words, your management application, as well as updating the contents of the database, generates the page and saves the file in the appropriate location, overwriting any older version already there. Be aware that if the file is deleted for any reason, you'll need to explicitly regenerate it — maybe provide yourself the option to "Regenerate all (absent) pages" in your management application. The generated pages could be PHP scripts or static files.

❑ Regenerate the page when it's requested. You can safely delete cached versions of the page any time you feel like it. The next time a user requests the page, they do so via a script that looks to see if the page exists. If it doesn't, the script generates the page from the database and serves it up, at the same time saving it for the next user. If the page does exist, the script has to look at the file's last-modified time, and also examine the database to see when the most recent relevant updates occurred (so you'll need to have a "last updated" field somewhere). If the updates are older than the file modification time, the script simply uses `fpassthru()` to throw the cached version at the user; otherwise, it again goes through regeneration and output/saving tasks.

❑ A cron job that regularly regenerates pages whose updates are regularly scheduled (such as daily, weekly, or monthly) could be handled in this fashion. Needless to say, the pages that are served after the update has been made but before the cron job next runs will still contain the older content.

Using a 404 Handler as a Trampoline

This method is effective for archiving pages that will no longer be changing, such as older news articles. If they could be stored and requested as static pages, then PHP need never be involved with their regeneration again. Even better would be if they could be generated (once) only if needed.

The method works as follows. Suppose a visitor requests an old news article that has *not* already been saved as a static page. Apache looks for it, fails to find it, and as a result sets about putting together a 404 Not Found response. You have configured Apache with a custom 404 handler (using its `ErrorDocument` directive) that calls a PHP script. This PHP script parses out the contents of `$_SERVER['REQUEST_URI']` to determine which article was requested. Assuming the request is for a genuine article, it generates the page (storing it in its output buffer) and saves it in the location it should have been found in originally. It then calls `header('HTTP/1.1 200 OK')`, followed by the buffered contents of the page. This may be carried out for several different types of request in sequence. It finishes up (if all else fails) by sending a 404 Not Found response and including whatever page content is appropriate in that situation.

Any subsequent request for the same article will see Apache locating exactly the right static page in exactly the right place.

Obviously, you can clear those pages out at any point (when changing the look of the site, for example, or moving hosts, or simply freeing up disk space). If and when they are requested again, they will simply be regenerated.

This method may be combined with Apache's mod_rewrite and mod_alias modules to further decouple the site's document tree from the server's filesystem. In this case, your script would save the static page in whichever location is indicated by mod_rewrite after it has finished transforming the URL.

It's possible to become more elaborate with this (though with increasing elaboration of course comes an increasing risk of confusion later). The file generated by the 404 handler could itself be a PHP script—to generate the page requested by the user, the handler would need to either execute the script with something like `fpassthru("http://www.example.com/oldnews/19980503.php")` or replicate its behavior. PHP won't be out of the loop anymore, but you could do it in order to reduce the amount of processing required to serve the same page in future (for example, you may need to check the user's credentials before allowing them access to the page).

Client-Side Caching

Remember that most web browsers have a cache. With a little bit of HTTP, you can use it — it requires being able to determine either the last time the contents of the page changed, or knowing the next time they will change.

If you know when the page's contents were last updated, you can add it as a Last-Modified header. Any caching proxies between the client's browser and your server can use this header to decide if any cached copy of the page they hold is still current (which would be if their cached copy has the same Last-Modified date). Clients can also make a HEAD request of a resource and use the Last-Modified header to decide whether it's worthwhile to GET the page itself.

If you supply an Expires: header, you are saying that any cached copy of the page is valid until the specified time. With that in hand, clients and proxies that cache the page can later decide whether to go ahead and request the page anyway.

For all dates in HTTP headers, the format is the one specified in RFC 2822 — that is, as returned by date('r').

A header that clients may include in their requests is the If-Modified-Since: header. This again is an RFC-2822 formatted date, and if one is present, your script can (via apache_request_headers()) use this to decide whether to generate and send a full response to the client as normal, or tell the client that its cached copy is still current by sending a content-free 304 Not Modified response. (A 304 response must not contain any content; any headers may still be sent, including Last-Modified and Expires.)

Other cache-control headers exist, and fuller coverage is given the HTTP specification, RFC 2616.

Your Own Code

Aside from wrapping your scripts in more cache-control code, what can you do with them to speed them up? This is where the questions of "which is faster" start to come up. As you've seen, you should examine all of these suggestions with an empirical eye.

Output Buffering

Output buffering is not just for caching or output post-processing (or clumsy "headers already sent" error workarounds) anymore. When Apache sends data out to the user, it does so in packets. Each packet has to be wrapped in an envelope and addressed so that it gets to its destination. Sending fewer but larger packets can be faster than sending many smaller ones. By buffering PHP's output, you can gather up the contents of your page and send it out all at once, instead of dribbling it out a few bytes at a time over the course of processing.

It's not quite that simple. When you are dribbling bytes out to the user, they have a chance of receiving them sooner, and start to see results quicker, even if *overall* the page loads more slowly. They might even find the link they were looking for and click through even before the browser has finished receiving the document (and if they intend to stay on the document for a while, they will surely be doing so for longer than the page takes to load either way). So you should at least batch up your buffering. Instead of one huge buffer around your entire script, send several "chapters" in sequence; with a chapter ending just before a new block of processing begins. Start producing output as soon as feasible. Don't keep users in suspense.

Try this:

```php
<?php
// If any processing involving HTTP headers is required,
// now would be a good time to do it.
?>
<!DOCTYPE html PUBLIC "-//W3C//DTD XHTML 1.0 Strict//EN"
    "http://www.w3.org/TR/xhtml1/DTD/xhtml1-strict.dtd">
<html xmlns="http://www.w3.org/1999/xhtml">
<head>
<title>A page buffered in chapters</title>
<?php

ob_start(); // HTML <head> content
// Construct <meta> tags, and select some CSS and Javascript to include. E.g.,
echo "<meta name=\"author\" content=\"".$page_author."\">\n";
ob_end_flush(); // Output the HTML head chapter

?>
</head>
<body>
<?php

ob_start(); // Strapline and breadcrumb trail.
?>
<div id="topmatter">
<!-- HTML and PHP for constructing this chapter -->
</div>
<?php
ob_end_flush();// Output the strapline chapter

ob_start(); // Side navigation list
//...
ob_end_flush();// Output the side navigation chapter

?>
...
</body>
</html>
```

In this example, six sections are shown; the section starting at the `<!DOCTYPE>` declaration and finishing with the end of the `<title>` element; a section for the rest of the `<head>` element's content; a small section that finishes the head and starts the body; followed by two sections that make up the page's layout (and then presumably other sections); and finally the `</body></html>` to finish the page off. Each section will be output as one intact block, giving Apache the best conditions to fill its outgoing packets as efficiently as possible.

echo or print?

Oh no, not again. The only speed difference worth noting between echo and print (apart from typing speed) is when you have several strings you wish to output in sequence. With print, you concatenate them all together and output the resulting string. With `echo` you can do that, but you don't have to, simply by using a comma (`,`) to separate the strings instead of a period (`.`).

When concatenating, PHP has to allocate memory for the string being built, and reallocate it for each concatenation operation. That introduces a delay. Also, none of the string can be output before the entire string has been built, so if one of the items being concatenated is a function, everything has to wait for the function. Compare the results of running these statements:

```
print "This string takes ".sleep(15)."too long to display.";
echo "This string takes ".sleep(15)."too long to display.";
echo "This string takes ", sleep(15), "too long to display.";
```

This works for output, but something similar can be done for strings that are to be concatenated into a variable: start an output buffer, echo all the bits of the string, read the buffer contents into the variable, and finish up by ending and cleaning the buffer. For example:

```
ob_start();
for($i=0; $i<100; $i++) echo $i,' ';
$zero_to_ninetynine = ob_end_clean();
```

for($i=0; $i<count($array); $i++)

Don't do this. Doing this means that PHP has to look at the size of the array after each iteration. Sure, the size of the array is maintained along with its contents, so its elements don't actually need to be *counted*, but the size still needs to be looked up — in case the size of the array changed in the course of the loop. If you know it won't, then use this:

```
for($i=0, $count_array=count($array); $i<$count_array; $i++)
```

This is just as effective and saves the extra lookup. If the order in which the array elements are traversed is unimportant, the intermediate variable can be avoided:

```
for($i=count($array)-1; $i>=0; $i++)
```

Remember the `-1` and `>=` if you do this.

Scratch Variables

Especially when you're using an associative array, if you're going to be looking at the same array element multiple times, putting its value in a local variable (by reference, if you're thinking of changing it) will save the work involved in identifying which array element `$array['foo']` actually refers to. The same goes for array properties. Consider this:

```
$this->p_consts->Delta[$i][$k] = $this->p_consts->Delta[$i][$this->p_consts->s[$i]-
1];
$this->n[$i][$k] = $this->n[$i][$this->p_consts->s[$i]-1];
```

`$this->p_consts` is used a fair bit; in particular, its `Delta` and `s` properties. You could create scratch variables to store the values of those two properties (assigning `Delta` by reference because you modify its value) and save you from having to look them up via `$this->p_consts` every time:

```
$p_Delta = &$this->p_consts->Delta;
$ps = $this->p_consts->s[$i]-1;
$p_Delta[$i][$k] = $p_Delta[$i][$ps];
$this->n[$i][$k] = $this->n[$i][$ps];
```

Clearly, this can also make the program easier to read.

Ordering if..elseif Tests and Switch Cases

First of all, if you have a sequence of consecutive `if` statements, and only one of them can possibly be true at any given time, then you should use `elseif` for all but the first. Otherwise, after finding the one that matches, PHP will continue to go on and test the rest. *You* know they'll all be false, but you're not the one who has to actually do the work. PHP has to continue testing in case the variables being tested changed while the successful statement was being processed.

If you have a sequence of `if..elseif` statements, or a `switch` statement, put the more common cases toward the top, and move rare situations toward the bottom. In addition to giving a clearer picture of what the code is doing to readers (by illustrating the typical situation first, and leaving the hairy edge cases until later), it means that on average PHP will have to carry out fewer tests before it finds one that succeeds.

Even if your most common cases are satisfied by the final `else` or `default` case, provide for them explicitly, and place their tests near the top (*every* test is examined before PHP gets around to handling such leftovers).

Using the Right String Functions

The manual states repeatedly that if you aren't actually using any of the features of regular expression syntax, then PHP's other string functions are likely to be far faster than the regular expression functions. Don't say `split("/", $path)` when you can say `explode("/", $path)`.

Regexp Syntax

Speaking of regular expressions, careful design can improve their performance as well. Entire books could be and have been written on the subject of regular expressions and how to write them; for now, just keep in mind that the PCRE functions `preg_match()` and the like provide a richer syntax and smarter engine than the POSIX functions such as `ereg()`.

unset()

Okay, so PHP will clean up variables as soon as they go out of scope; either they're local variables at the end of the function, or everything else at the end of the script. Generally speaking, this means you don't have to worry about it.

But if you've got a huge structure (an array of thousands of elements, for example) that you are not going to use again, and especially if you've got more large data to handle in a moment, then you should `unset()` the thing as soon as you're finished. The big lump of free memory that results is then immediately available for other uses. On a busy server, freeing large lumps of memory when possible could make the difference between fitting everything in RAM and resorting to virtual memory on disk.

Releasing Resources and the Peril of Persistent Database Connections

Again, if you're using a resource such as a MySQL database connection, and you're finished using it but still have a lot more work to do, don't hog it for yourself for the rest of the script's execution: close it.

Persistent database connections (such as those created by `mysql_pconnect()`) are sometimes suggested as a means of accelerating performance. This is because after the connection is established for the first time, the httpd process that creates it retains it after the script establishing it has ended, ready for the next time it runs a script that wants to use a database connection. Because connecting to a database involves a bit of work, it might save a bit of time to connect persistently. But faults may develop before the time saved becomes noticeable.

The problem is that even though a connected httpd process may be between requests, it still holds that database connection open until such time as it dies its own server-mandated death. Database connections are in limited supply (`mysql_close()` has no effect on persistent connections). It may very well happen that if things get busy, a script may attempt to connect to a database only to be rebuffed with an error message saying that the maximum permissible number of connections have already been allocated. If all of those connections were in use, that wouldn't be so bad: you'd just have to beef up your database server a bit. But if the maximum is reached because idle httpd processes are sitting on the available connections, *just in case* a request comes along that requires the use of one, then that is not good.

ob_gzhandler()

If you're going to be using output buffering to batch your pages' output, starting the buffer with `ob_start('ob_gzhandler')` will mean that when you come to collect the buffered output, you'll find it compressed. The callback function is polite enough to check the request headings to make sure the browser the output is going to is actually capable of reading gzip-compressed data first.

As an *alternative* to using this callback handler (don't try and use them together), consider setting `zlib.output_compression` in `php.ini` instead. This is, in fact, the method recommended by PHP's developers.

Summary

While reading through the suggestions and guidelines here, you will no doubt have noticed that some appear to contradict each other. This is unavoidable: what works will depend on circumstances, and different circumstances can require different decisions to be made. A site that does a lot of involved manipulations with a large database has different requirements than one that is principally a file repository.

Your time as a developer is more valuable than the computer's time as a web server. It simply makes no sense, not financially nor in terms of job satisfaction, to waste time on alterations that, at best, deliver only trivial improvements and are invisible to your site's visitors. Instead, invest the time on planning and testing. Step back and look at the big picture before looking at single lines.

Is your hardware up to scratch, or will it put a cap on how much effect a software improvement will have? How is your web server configured: is there any tuning that could be made there? How much redundant computation is being performed: can the results from one place be cached in anticipation of being useful elsewhere?

The best time to performance-tune a program is before it's written. When building a site, test, experiment, and gain experience in the various ways it could be designed, and the pros and cons of each. Choosing the right framework at the beginning will have a much bigger influence on the speed of the final product than any amount of code tweaking after the fact. Keep testing, experimenting, and gaining experience, and keep looking at the big picture, because neither hardware nor software technology is standing still. Processors will be faster, memory will be cheaper, network connections will be more capacious, web servers will be more efficient, web browsers will be more sophisticated, and PHP will have more features to develop with.

10

PHP Extensions

Although the core of the PHP language provides functions that accomplish many commonly needed tasks, there are numerous extensions that can be added to bring a PHP configuration to a whole new level. This chapter explores some of the more useful extensions, but it only touches on the tip of the iceberg. The extensions in this chapter deal with manipulating images, creating PDF files (without the use of Adobe Acrobat), creating flash files (without the use of any commercial software), and interfacing with XML documents. Some of these extensions are already bundled and enabled for you with the default configuration, so what are you waiting for?

PDFLib

Whether your content is academic or commercial in nature, no professionally developed website would be complete without the ability to deliver content as a PDF (Portable Document Format). While there are several Open Source libraries available to PHP developers, notably FPDF (`http://www.fpdf.org/`), and pdf-php (`http://sourceforge.net/projects/pdf-php`), PHP's built-in PDFlib functions are arguably the most efficient means of doing so. The PDFlib functions, moved to the PHP Extension Community Library (PECL since PHP 4.3.9), are a wrapper for the commercial PDFLib (`http://www.pdflib.com/`) PDF processing library. The advantage offered by PDFLib over the purely PHP-based solutions is that of speed. Compiled C code, such as PDFLib, is magnitudes of order faster than PHP code interpreted by Apache. The disadvantage is the licensing cost for commercial use.

The observant reader will note that this text refers to two distinct capitalizations of the subject matter: "PDFLib" and "PDFlib." This is to differentiate the C library, named "PDFLib" by its owners, from the PHP wrapper library "PDFlib." It is also noteworthy that the C library documentation does not rigidly adhere to this convention.

Configuration

PHP's support for PDFLib has undergone significant changes recently, and like so many other features of the language and its myriad libraries, it is expected to undergo further changes, especially in light of the growing acceptance of PHP within the professional development community.

Thus, configuration is highly susceptible to the usual sticking points of architecture, operating system, PHP version, and so on. If your Apache installation is using dynamic shared objects (DSO), or dynamic link libraries (DLL) for Windows installations, then all that is required is ensuring that the appropriate file exists (`libpdf_php.so` or `libpdf_php.dll`, respectively), and is referenced properly and uncommented in the `php.ini` file.

If you're not using DSO, or can't, you will have to visit the PDFlib website (`http://www.pdflib.com/`), acquire the latest version of one of the many flavors of the PDFLib source, and build a statically linked library. For further details visit `http://www.pdflib.com/products/pdflib/info/PDFlib-in-PHP-HowTo.pdf`.

Regardless of how you install PDFLib, it is worthwhile to visit the PDFLib website and download the latest version of PDFlib Lite. Included with the source is a very helpful document, `PDFlib-manual.pdf`. The manual contains a variety of useful information, including bindings for all supported programming languages, general PDFLib programming concepts, and much more. Section 3.1.1, "PDFlib Program Structure and Function Scopes," is a must read that will save you hours of frustration trying to eliminate "scope" errors.

Getting Started

The PDF document will be known to PHP as a resource type, and you create it using the `pdf_new()` function, as follows:

```
$pdf = pdf_new();
if (!pdf_open_file($pdf, "")) {
    die("Error: Unable to open output file.");
}
```

Note that immediately after the resource is created, a test ensures that the resource was created and opened. Attempting to proceed with any page scope functions without this check will cause the script to fail, and will generate the following PDFlib exception:

```
'Function must not be called in 'object' scope'
```

In other words, a page scope function has been called in object scope, since the document will not have been opened yet. In PHP5, it is sufficient to enclose the `pdf_new()` call within a `try/catch` block that catches a type PDFlibException exception.

Upon completion of the PDF document, you can call `pdf_close()` to close the document file and release any associated resources.

Specifying Document Information

One means of searching documents is via the metadata contained with the document information. This is achieved easily using the `pdf_set_info()` function. Section 8.9.6, "Document Information Fields" of the PDFLib manual specifies which fields are relevant. For example:

```
pdf_set_info($pdf, "Author", $name . " <" . $row["Email"] . ">");
pdf_set_info($pdf, "Title", "Resume - " . $name);
pdf_set_info($pdf, "Subject", "The resume of " . $name . ", " .
             $row["DesiredPosition"] . ".");
```

This code sets the document's author, title, and subject to values pulled from a MySQL database. Note that the `pdf_set_info()` function replaces a number of deprecated functions that set fields specifically.

Required Elements

To render the most basic page, every PDFlib generated document requires the following elements:

❑   `pdf_new()`: Needed to create a new PDF resource.

❑   `pdf_open_file($pdf [, $filename])`: Accepts a PDF resource and an optional filename as parameters. The filename is unnecessary for buffered output, as in the example at the end of this section.

❑   `pdf_begin_page($pdf, $width, $height)`: Accepts a PDF resource as well as the width and height of the page in points.

❑   `pdf_findfont($pdf, $font, $encoding [, $embed])`: Locates a font given a PDF resource, a specific font name, and encoding as parameters. Passing a non-zero value as the optional fourth parameter will cause the font to be immediately checked, averting subsequent errors.

❑   `pdf_setfont($pdf, $font, $size)`: Accepts a PDF resource, a font handle (as returned by the pdf_findfont function above), and a font size.

❑   `pdf_show_xy($pdf, $text, $x, $y)`: Places the passed text within the given PDF resource at the given x and y coordinates given in points.

❑   `pdf_stroke($pdf)`: "Inks" or draws the text on the passed PDF resource.

❑   `pdf_end_page($pdf)`: Finishes the current page of the given PDF resource.

❑   `pdf_close($pdf)`: Closes the passed PDF resource.

The resume generator example that winds up this section uses each of these functions to return a PDF document to the browser instead of placing the file somewhere within the local file structure.

Helper Functions

Given that certain sections of a typical document adhere to a specific style, you may find it useful to create several helper functions to simplify code maintenance and style changes. One particularly useful function would draw a horizontal line, not a trivial matter when generating a PDF, as follows:

```
function drawHR($res) {
    $xpos = MARGIN;
    $ypos = pdf_get_value($res, "texty", 0) - VERT_SPACING;
    pdf_moveto($res, $xpos, $ypos);
    pdf_lineto($res, PAGE_WIDTH - MARGIN, $ypos);
    pdf_closepath($res);
    pdf_fill($res);
    $ypos = pdf_get_value($res, "texty", 0) - (VERT_SPACING * 2);
}
```

The drawHR() function accepts a PDF resource, $res, as an argument. It sets the initial x and y positions of the line, using constant values and the pdf_get_value() function with the texty parameter. The third parameter of the pdf_get_value() function is a numeric "modifier" applied to the value specified by the second parameter. In most trivial cases, the value of this parameter will be 0. Thus, the last line of the drawHR function might more elegantly be written as follows:

```
$ypos = pdf_get_value($res, "texty", (VERT_SPACING * -2));
```

A useful concept to grasp in PDF document creation is that of the "path." The pdf_moveto() function positions the starting point within the document and pdf_lineto() draws a line along the path between the two positions. The pdf_closepath() and pdf_fill() functions close then fills the path. Finally, the y position is incremented by twice the vertical spacing constant.

Another useful function might apply similar, yet distinct styles in accordance with a passed parameter:

```
function pdflib_show($res, $text, $type) {
    $font = pdf_findfont($res, "Times-Roman", "winansi", 0);
    $xpos = MARGIN;
    $ypos = pdf_get_value($res, "texty", 0) - VERT_SPACING;
    switch ($type) {
    case CASE_CATEGORY:
        $font = pdf_findfont($res, "Times-Bold", "winansi", 0);
        $ypos = pdf_get_value($res, "texty", 0) - (VERT_SPACING * 3);
        break;
    case CASE_LIST:
        $xpos = MARGIN + TAB;
        $text = "* " . $text;
        break;
    case CASE_OBJECTIVE:
        $font = pdf_findfont($res, "Times-Italic", "winansi", 0);
        $xpos = MARGIN + TAB;
        $text = "\"" . $text . "\"";
        break;
    }
    pdf_setfont($res, $font, 12.0);
    pdf_show_xy($res, $text, $xpos, $ypos);
    return;
}
```

As you will see in the example that wraps up this section, this code uses a switch control structure to set specific type faces and text positioning according to the value of the $type parameter.

Font selection is performed by the pdf_findfont() function and set via the pdf_setfont() function. PHP's PDFlib implementation typically installs a few fonts by default in the "pdf-related" directory in the directory within which PHP is installed. PDFLib supports a wide variety of fonts and faces. See the PDFLib documentation for complete details.

Finally, the `pdf_show_xy()` function displays a given string in a specified location.

About Fonts and Positioning

In the previous code example, you saw how various text properties are manipulated via PHP's built-in PDFlib functions. Again, developers are cautioned against using other deprecated functions, such as `pdf_get_font()` and `pdf_get_fontsize()` which have been replaced by the single `pdf_get_value()` function. This function is used just as the aforementioned `pdf_set_info()` function. PHP's documentation (`http://www.php.net/manual/en/ref.pdf.php#AEN124842`) lists the deprecated functions and their replacements.

The PDFLib coordinate system defines the x:y coordinate 0:0 to be the lower-left corner of the document.

You will likely find it helpful to define constants for such page properties as the margin and tab widths, vertical spacing, and page dimensions. The following table lists the dimensions of the more common page sizes in points, such that 1 pt. = 1/72 inch = 0.3528 mm.

Format	Width	Height
A4	595	842
B5	501	709
Letter	612	792
Legal	612	1008

Finishing Up

If you simply want to create a document and place it somewhere on the localhost, all you need to do to complete the PDF file is to end the page and close the document. More commonly, though, a buffer is returned to a Web browser. The `pdf_get_buffer()` function retrieves the passed PDF document. The browser is then alerted via the `header()` function to expect a PDF document and a simple call to `print` completes the process, as you can see here:

```
pdf_end_page($pdf);
pdf_close($pdf);
$buf = pdf_get_buffer($pdf);
$len = strlen($buf);
header("Content-type: application/pdf");
header("Content-Length: $len");
header("Content-Disposition: inline; filename=resume.pdf");
print $buf;
```

This section only briefly touched upon the myriad of PDF generation features available to the advanced PHP developer. Other available facets that we have not touched upon include bookmarking, hypertext, color use, graphics generation and importing, and too many more to mention here.

PDF Resume Generator

Consider the following code:

```php
<?php

// Specify string constants and positioning variables.
define("CASE_CATEGORY",  "Category");
define("CASE_LIST",      "List");
define("CASE_OBJECTIVE", "Objective");
define("MARGIN",         50);
define("PAGE_HEIGHT",    792);
define("PAGE_WIDTH",     612);
define("TAB",            25);
define("VERT_SPACING",   14);

// Define a couple useful functions.
function drawHR($res) {
    $xpos = MARGIN;
    $ypos = pdf_get_value($res, "texty", 0) - VERT_SPACING;
    pdf_moveto($res, $xpos, $ypos);
    pdf_lineto($res, PAGE_WIDTH - MARGIN, $ypos);
    pdf_closepath($res);
    pdf_fill($res);
    $ypos = pdf_get_value($res, "texty", 0) - (VERT_SPACING * 2);
}

function pdflib_show($res, $text, $type) {
    $font = pdf_findfont($res, "Times-Roman", "winansi", 0);
    $xpos = MARGIN;
    $ypos = pdf_get_value($res, "texty", 0) - VERT_SPACING;

    switch ($type) {
    case CASE_CATEGORY:
        $font = pdf_findfont($res, "Times-Bold", "winansi", 0);
        $ypos = pdf_get_value($res, "texty", 0) - (VERT_SPACING * 3);
        break;
    case CASE_LIST:
        $xpos = MARGIN + TAB;
        $text = "* " . $text;
        break;
    case CASE_OBJECTIVE:
        $font = pdf_findfont($res, "Times-Italic", "winansi", 0);
        $xpos = MARGIN + TAB;
        $text = "\"" . $text . "\"";
        break;
    }
    pdf_setfont($res, $font, 12.0);
    pdf_show_xy($res, $text, $xpos, $ypos);
    return;
}

// Create resource.
$pdf = pdf_new();
if (!pdf_open_file($pdf, "")) {
```

```
    die("Error: Unable to open output file.");
}

// Collect header information from the database.
mysql_connect("localhost", "resume_user", "resume_pw");
mysql_select_db("resume");
$sql = "SELECT * FROM biography WHERE OID = 0";
$result = mysql_query($sql);
$row = mysql_fetch_array($result, MYSQL_ASSOC);
$name = $row["NameFirst"] . " " . $row["NameLast"];

// Document info.
pdf_set_info($pdf, "Author", $name . " <" . $row["Email"] . ">");
pdf_set_info($pdf, "Title", "Resume - " . $name);
pdf_set_info($pdf, "Subject", "The resume of " . $name . ", " .
$row["DesiredPosition"] . ".");

// Do something clever with the keywords.
$keywords = split(" ", $row["DesiredPosition"]);
$morewords = "";
foreach($keywords as $keyword) {
   $morewords = $morewords . $keyword . ", ";
}
pdf_set_info($pdf, "Keywords", "Resume, " . $morewords . "apache, mysql, php,
pdf");

// Begin PDF page. -- Can be placed anywhere after the PDF
// resource has been instantiated.
pdf_begin_page($pdf, PAGE_WIDTH, PAGE_HEIGHT);

// Print name.
$font = pdf_findfont($pdf, "Times-Bold", "winansi", 0);
pdf_setfont($pdf, $font, 14.0);
$stringwidth = pdf_stringwidth($pdf, $name, $font, 14.0);
$xpos = (PAGE_WIDTH / 2) - ($stringwidth / 2);
pdf_show_xy($pdf, $name, $xpos, 700);
$xpos = pdf_get_value($pdf, "textx", 0);
$ypos = pdf_get_value($pdf, "texty", 0) - VERT_SPACING;

// Print contact information.
$font = pdf_findfont($pdf, "Times-Roman", "winansi", 0);
pdf_setfont($pdf, $font, 12.0);
$headerdata = array($row["Address"],
                    $row["City"] . ", " . $row["State"] . " " . $row["ZipCode"],
        $row["Phone"],
        $row["Email"]);
foreach ($headerdata as $data) {
   $stringwidth = pdf_stringwidth($pdf, $data, $font, 12.0);
   $xpos = (PAGE_WIDTH / 2) - ($stringwidth / 2);
   $ypos = pdf_get_value($pdf, "texty", 0) - VERT_SPACING;
   pdf_show_xy($pdf, $data, $xpos, $ypos);
}

// Print categories.
$sql = "SELECT * FROM items WHERE BIOGRAPHY_OID = 0";
```

```
$result = mysql_query($sql);
$prevCategory = "";
while($row = mysql_fetch_array($result, MYSQL_ASSOC)) {
    $curCategory = $row["Category"];
    if (strcmp($prevCategory, $curCategory) != 0) {
        drawHR($pdf);
        pdflib_show($pdf, $row["Category"], CASE_CATEGORY);
    }
    $prevCategory = $row["Category"];
    if (strcmp($row["Category"], "Career Objective") == 0) {
        pdflib_show($pdf, $row["Description"], CASE_OBJECTIVE);
    } else {
        pdflib_show($pdf, $row["Description"], CASE_LIST);
    }
}

// Wrap up the document and return it to the browser.
pdf_end_page($pdf);
pdf_close($pdf);
$buf = pdf_get_buffer($pdf);
$len = strlen($buf);
header("Content-type: application/pdf");
header("Content-Length: $len");
header("Content-Disposition: inline; filename=resume.pdf");
print $buf;

// Clean up!
mysql_close();
$pdf = 0;

?>
```

This straightforward application generates a simple PDF resume using data drawn from a MySQL database. Aside from the MySQL connection setup and database queries, the only aspects of this script that have not already been covered is the use of the biographical data to concatenate information from the individual's desired position into the document's keywords:

```
$keywords = split(" ", $row["DesiredPosition"]);
$morewords = "";
foreach($keywords as $keyword) {
    $morewords = $morewords . $keyword . ", ";
}
pdf_set_info($pdf, "Keywords", "Resume, " . $morewords . "apache, mysql, php,
pdf");
```

The resume's header information, containing the individual's name and contact information, was handled separately from the remainder of the resume's data in order to keep the helper function pdflib_show()'s implementation as simple as possible. The body of the resume is generated by a while loop that tracks the current and previous categories, printing the category name when the value changes; otherwise, it prints the description. All that remains is closing the document, returning it to the browser, and cleaning up.

One final word of advice: If PDF generation will play a significant role in any of your projects, you must read and understand the documentation distributed with the PDFLib source code. The normally rich documentation on the PHP website is particularly lacking where the PDFLib wrapper is concerned. While this text should serve as an excellent introduction, there is no better source of information about the full capabilities of the PDFLib library than the PDFlib manual.

GD Library

If you've ever had to set up a website containing large amounts of image, such as an image gallery or ecommerce site, one of the most tedious tasks involved is the manipulation and uploading of all the individual images. Fortunately for you, PHP is equipped with the GD library, an open source image manipulation library that comes bundled with PHP5. With the vast amount of functionality provided by GD, you can automate many or all of your website image processing tasks, so you can simply upload the images, and spend time working on other things, instead of playing image jockey for hours on end.

Creating the Image Base

One of the downsides to the GD library is the large number of functions available, many of which perform the same function, differing only in the type of input or the output image format. To provide some clarity and a base for all of the image manipulation functionality this part of the chapter covers, you'll create a class that handles the basic loading and saving of a couple of the most popular image file types — JPG, GIF, and PNG.

This base class will provide basic load, save, and display capabilities, and will serve as a place to call other add-on image manipulation classes that you'll add later in the chapter. First, create a new file called `class.WebImage.php`, and enter the following code:

```php
<?php

class WebImage
{
  public $gdresource;
  public $type;

  // Release resources
  public function __destruct()
  {
    if ($this->gdresource)
    {
      imagedestroy($this->gdresource);
    }
  }


  // Load an image from a file
  public function load($file)
  {
    // Get image mimetype
    $size = getimagesize($file);
    $this->type = $size['mime'];

    // Load image based on type
    switch ($this->type)
```

```
    {
      case 'image/jpeg':
        $this->gdresource = imagecreatefromjpeg($file);
        break;
      case 'image/png':
        $this->gdresource = imagecreatefrompng($file);
        break;
      case 'image/gif':
        $this->gdresource = imagecreatefromgif($file);
        break;
  }

  // Retain the alpha information
  imagesavealpha($this->gdresource, true);
}


// Save the file to the local filesystem
public function save($file)
{
  switch ($this->type)
  {
    case 'image/jpeg':
      imagejpeg($this->gdresource, $file);
      break;
    case 'image/png':
      imagepng($this->gdresource, $file);
      break;
    case 'image/gif':
      // Convert back to palette
      if (imageistruecolor($this->gdresource))
      {
        imagetruecolortopalette($this->gdresource, false, 256);
      }
      imagegif($this->gdresource, $file);
      break;
  }
}


// Display the image in the browser
public function display()
{
  switch ($this->type)
  {
    case 'image/jpeg':
      header("Content-type: image/jpeg");
      imagejpeg($this->gdresource);
      break;
    case 'image/png':
      header("Content-type: image/png");
      imagepng($this->gdresource);
      break;
    case 'image/gif':
      // Convert back to palette
      if (imageistruecolor($this->gdresource))
```

```
    {
        imagetruecolortopalette($this->gdresource, false, 256);
    }
    header("Content-type: image/gif");
    imagegif($this->gdresource);
    break;
    }
  }

}

?>
```

What does it all mean? This file is a humble image wrapper you can use to open, save, and display your images. This code can handle JPG, GIF, and PNG images, but you could easily add more, assuming the GD library supported them. To get a better understanding of what's going on, take a look at how this class is constructed.

The first handful of lines is relatively straightforward — you start by declaring two public properties, one to hold the internal GD image resource, and another to keep track of what MIME type to use for the image operations. Also note the destructor function — when the class is destroyed, it makes sure any resources consumed by GD for this image are cleaned up:

```php
<?php

class WebImage
{
  public $gdresource;
  public $type;

  // Release resources
  public function __destruct()
  {
    if ($this->gdresource)
    {
      imagedestroy($this->gdresource);
    }
  }
```

The next bit of code loads the image data from a file on the server. You pass the method a filename, and it determines the image type and then loads the image into a GD resource using the corresponding function provided by the GD library:

```php
  // Load an image from a file
  public function load($file)
  {
    // Get image mimetype
    $size = getimagesize($file);
    $this->type = $size['mime'];

    // Load image based on type
    switch ($this->type)
    {
      case 'image/jpeg':
```

```
        $this->gdresource = imagecreatefromjpeg($file);
        break;
    case 'image/png':
        $this->gdresource = imagecreatefrompng($file);
        break;
    case 'image/gif':
        $this->gdresource = imagecreatefromgif($file);
        break;
}
```

When dealing with image formats that can contain transparent regions, such as GIF or PNG, it is important to understand the two different kinds of transparency involved. The first, and simplest, is index transparency. Found in 8-bit transparent PNG images and all transparent GIF images, index transparency simply defines one color in the indexed palette as transparent. Any pixel that is assigned that color will show up transparent on-screen.

The second kind of transparency is alpha transparency, found in 32-bit PNG images. Alpha transparent images implement transparency by providing an additional range of values for each pixel that defines the transparency of that specific pixel. Alpha transparency allows images to smoothly fade to transparent, or have any color be partially transparent in places — something index-transparency images cannot do.

When dealing with images that contain alpha transparency in GD, you need to inform GD that you want to retain any alpha transparency information from the image you've loaded:

```
    // Retain the alpha information
    imagesavealpha($this->gdresource, true);
}
```

You need to do this if you plan to load or output any image format that understands per-pixel/alpha transparency, such as 32-bit PNG. If you don't tell GD to save the alpha, you could end up with unexpected backgrounds or transparency issues in your final output.

The last two methods, save() and display(), each send the internal image resource to a final destination — either in a file on the server, or displayed in a browser. The only substantial differences between the two are the use of the header() function in display() to inform the browser of the expected image type, and the second parameter of the image__() functions in save(), which tell GD to save the image to a file, instead of piping the output to the screen:

```
    // Save the file to the local filesystem
    public function save($file)
    {
      switch ($this->type)
      {
        case 'image/jpeg':
          imagejpeg($this->gdresource, $file);
          break;
        case 'image/png':
          imagepng($this->gdresource, $file);
          break;
        case 'image/gif':
          // Convert back to palette
          if (imageistruecolor($this->gdresource))
          {
```

```
            imagetruecolortopalette($this->gdresource, false, 256);
        }
        imagegif($this->gdresource, $file);
        break;
    }
}
```

If you wanted to add additional image types to the save() method, you would simply add them as a case in the switch. For palette image types, be sure to convert the image from true color to palette if needed, as in the case for GIF images in the example.

Resizing Images

Now that you can easily load and save some basic image formats, it's time to actually alter them in some way. The first thing you're going to do is add the ability for your WebImage class to resize images. To do this, you'll create a class file that deals with the resizing action, and add a method to your WebImage class to call the resize function when needed.

To start, create the following file, called class.ImageResize.php:

```php
<?php

class ImageResize
{
  public $ratio = 1;
  public $max_width;
  public $max_height;

  // Resize the image
  public function process($gd_img)
  {
    // Set initial dimensions
    $old_width  = imagesx($gd_img);
    $old_height = imagesy($gd_img);
    $new_width  = 0;
    $new_height = 0;

    // New dimensions to fall within maximums provided
    if ($this->max_width and $this->max_height)
    {
      if ($this->max_width/$old_width <= $this->max_height/$old_height)
      {
        $new_width  = ceil(($this->max_width/$old_width) * $old_width);
        $new_height = ceil(($this->max_width/$old_width) * $old_height);
      }
      else
      {
        $new_width  = ceil(($this->max_height/$old_height) * $old_width);
        $new_height = ceil(($this->max_height/$old_height) * $old_height);
      }
    }
    // New dimensions based on a ratio
    else if ($this->ratio)
    {
```

```
                    $new_width  = ceil($this->ratio * $old_width);
                    $new_height = ceil($this->ratio * $old_height);
                }

                // Resize only if dimensions changed
                if ($new_width and $new_height)
                {
                  // Create resize target
                  $temp = imagecreatetruecolor($new_width, $new_height);

                  // Set alpha parameters
                  imagesavealpha($temp, true);
                  imagealphablending($temp, false);

                  // Resize the image
                  imagecopyresampled($temp,
                                     $gd_img,
                                     0,
                                     0,
                                     0,
                                     0,
                                     $new_width,
                                     $new_height,
                                     $old_width,
                                     $old_height);
                  $gd_img = $temp;
                }

                return $gd_img;
            }
        }

?>
```

Then, add the following method to the end of your WebImage class definition:

```
    // Resize the image
    public function resize()
    {
      require_once 'class.ImageResize.php';

      $ir = new ImageResize();

      // Set resize parameters based on arguments
      switch (func_num_args())
      {
        case 1:
          $ir->ratio = func_get_arg(0);
          break;
        case 2:
          $ir->max_width = func_get_arg(0);
          $ir->max_height = func_get_arg(1);
          break;
```

```
    }

    // Perform the resize
    $this->gdresource = $ir->process($this->gdresource);
}
```

Looking at the new method you've just added to WebImage, you can see quickly how the image resizing class is called. First, you include the ImageResize.php file, if needed, and you create a new ImageResize object. Then you use the func_num_args() function to determine how many arguments were used when calling the method.

The resize method of WebImage can be called using either one or two arguments. If one argument is used, it is treated as a numeric ratio used to resize the image. If two arguments are passed, they are used as values for a maximum width and maximum height the resized image is not to exceed.

After those values are set in the object accordingly, the process() method is called, and the image is resized and returned. To further understand how exactly the resizing is happening, take a closer look at the ImageResize class.

In the meat of ImageResize, the process() method, you start out simply enough — width and height for the existing image are determined using imagesx() and imagesy() correspondingly, and the new width and height are initialized to 0:

```
// Resize the image
public function process($gd_img)
{
  // Set initial dimensions
  $old_width  = imagesx($gd_img);
  $old_height = imagesy($gd_img);
  $new_width  = 0;
  $new_height = 0;
```

Next, the final dimensions of the resized image are determined. The values for max_width and max_height are first checked, and if both are present, the image dimensions are calculated to be equal to or smaller than both maximums. If both maximums are not provided, the resize ratio value is checked, and if present, the new image dimensions will be based on the set ratio of the original dimensions:

```
  // New dimensions to fall within maximums provided
  if ($this->max_width and $this->max_height)
  {
    if ($this->max_width/$old_width <= $this->max_height/$old_height)
    {
      $new_width  = ceil(($this->max_width/$old_width) * $old_width);
      $new_height = ceil(($this->max_width/$old_width) * $old_height);
    }
    else
    {
      $new_width  = ceil(($this->max_height/$old_height) * $old_width);
      $new_height = ceil(($this->max_height/$old_height) * $old_height);
    }
  }
  // New dimensions based on a ratio
```

```
    else if ($this->ratio)
    {
      $new_width  = ceil($this->ratio * $old_width);
      $new_height = ceil($this->ratio * $old_height);
    }
```

The rest of the method is where the actual resizing is performed, if needed. When resizing in GD, you don't actually just resize an existing resource, but instead you create a new image with the new dimensions and copy the original image to the destination—GD takes care of the resizing internally. In this method, you're using the `imagecopyresampled()` function; when resizing images using GD, you can use either the `imagecopyresized()` function or the `imagecopyresampled()` function. Both are means to the same end, but the latter does a little better job keeping the end result "smooth" as opposed to the oft-pixelated results from the former. Take a look:

```
// Resize only if dimensions changed
if ($new_width and $new_height)
{
  // Create resize target
  $temp = imagecreatetruecolor($new_width, $new_height);

  // Set alpha parameters
  imagesavealpha($temp, true);
  imagealphablending($temp, false);

  // Resize the image
  imagecopyresampled($temp,
                     $gd_img,
                     0,
                     0,
                     0,
                     0,
                     $new_width,
                     $new_height,
                     $old_width,
                     $old_height);
  $gd_img = $temp;
}

return $gd_img;
}
```

Note the use of the alpha-saving functions, `imagesavealpha()` and `imagealphablending()`. These are used to inform GD to retain and use the alpha transparency information from the source image when performing the resizing. If you ignore the alpha, any transparency you might have in a transparent GIF or PNG could be destroyed.

Finally, at the end of the method, the GD image resource is returned.

Rotating Images

In addition to resizing your images on the server, a common image-editing requirement is the ability to rotate images after they've been uploaded. To implement this operation, you're going to create another image-action class file like before, and add another method to call the function to `WebImage`.

First, create the following image-rotating class, in a file called `class.ImageRotate.php`:

```php
<?php

class ImageRotate
{
  public $rotation = 0;

  // Rotate the image
  public function process($gd_img)
  {
    if ($this->rotation)
    {
      // Get "filler" background color
      $color = imagecolorallocate($gd_img, 255, 255, 255);

      // Rotate the image
      $gd_img = imagerotate($gd_img, $this->rotation, $color);
    }

    return $gd_img;
  }
}

?>
```

Then, add the following method to the `WebImage` class definition:

```php
  // Rotate the image
  public function rotate($degrees)
  {
    require_once 'class.ImageRotate.php';

    $ir = new ImageRotate();

    // Set rotate parameters
    $ir->rotation = $degrees;

    // Perform the rotation
    $this->gdresource = $ir->process($this->gdresource);
  }
```

This one is a bit simpler than the resize method, but very similar. The `rotate()` method of `WebImage` takes one parameter: the degrees you want to rotate the image. Like `resize()`, `rotate()` includes the requisite class file, sets the rotation parameter, and then performs the rotation.

Inside `ImageRotate`, it's pretty straightforward. The `process()` method checks to see if a rotation value is provided, and then grabs a color to be used as a background color. If you're rotating 90, 180, or 270 degrees, you won't see the color, but if you're using any other value, the image will grow to enclose the new skewed original, and the background color will fill any areas not covered by the rotated source. After the color is set, the image is rotated using the `imagerotate()` function:

```php
  // Rotate the image
  public function process($gd_img)
```

```
  {
    if ($this->rotation)
    {
      // Get "filler" background color
      $color = imagecolorallocate($gd_img, 255, 255, 255);

      // Rotate the image
      $gd_img = imagerotate($gd_img, $this->rotation, $color);
    }

    return $gd_img;
  }
```

And of course, the image resource is returned at the end.

Adding a Caption

Next up in the parade of simple image functionality: adding a caption to the image — a darkened area at the bottom of the image, with a caption or blurb of text overlaid. It's a subtle way of including and displaying a little information about the image or its context, without having to keep the text separate from the image, or getting in the way.

To start, follow the lead of `ImageResize` and `ImageRotate`, and create a file called `class.Image Caption.php`:

```php
<?php

class ImageCaption
{
  public $caption = '';
  public $fontfile = '';
  public $fontsize = 10;
  public $padding = 5;
  public $drawline = true;

  // Caption the image
  public function process($gd_img)
  {
    if ($this->caption and $this->fontfile)
    {
      // Get text box height
      $text_box = imagettfbbox($this->fontsize,
                               0,
                               $this->fontfile,
                               $this->caption);
      $text_height = $text_box[3] - $text_box[5];
      $text_underbaseline = $text_box[3];

      // Get some image dimensions
      $img_x = imagesx($gd_img);
      $img_y = imagesy($gd_img);

      // Draw background shading
      imagealphablending($gd_img, true);
```

```
            $rect_color = imagecolorallocatealpha($gd_img, 0, 0, 0, 75);
            imagefilledrectangle($gd_img,
                                 0,
                                 $img_y - $text_height - ($this->padding * 2),
                                 $img_x,
                                 $img_y,
                                 $rect_color);


            // Draw caption text
            $text_color = imagecolorallocate($gd_img, 255, 255, 255);
            imagettftext($gd_img,
                         $this->fontsize,
                         0,
                         $this->padding,
                         $img_y - $text_underbaseline - $this->padding,
                         $text_color,
                         $this->fontfile,
                         $this->caption);


            // Draw shading border if requested
            if ($this->drawline)
            {
              $line_color = imagecolorallocatealpha($gd_img,
                                                    200,
                                                    200,
                                                    200,
                                                    75);
              imageline($gd_img,
                        0,
                        $img_y - $text_height - ($this->padding * 2) - 1,
                        $img_x,
                        $img_y - $text_height - ($this->padding * 2) - 1,
                        $line_color);
            }
          }

    return $gd_img;
  }
}

?>
```

Then, as before, add a new method to the end of the WebImage class definition as follows:

```
  // Add a caption to the image
  public function caption($text,
                          $font,
                          $size = null,
                          $padding = null,
                          $drawline = null)
  {
    require_once 'class.ImageCaption.php';
```

```
$ic = new ImageCaption();

// Set size, padding, line if needed
if ($size)
{
  $ic->fontsize = $size;
}
if ($padding !== null)
{
  $ic->padding = $padding;
}
if ($drawline !== null)
{
  $ic->drawline = $drawline;
}

// Set font, caption
$ic->fontfile = $font;
$ic->caption = $text;

// Perform the captioning
$this->gdresource = $ic->process($this->gdresource);
}
```

When you call the `caption()` method of `WebImage`, you can use a maximum of five parameters. The first two are required, and specify the text to display in the caption, and the filename of the TrueType font (.ttf) to use for the caption text. The other parameters set the size of the text in pixels, the amount of padding around the text in pixels, and whether or not to draw a faint line above the caption. The method includes the needed class definition file, sorts out the parameter values, and then calls the `process()` method of `ImageCaption`.

The thing `process()` does is to determine the dimensions of the text that will be written, and of the destination image itself. To get the dimensions of the rendered text, `imagettfbbox()` is used. `imagettfbbox()` takes four parameters: the size of the font, the angle of the font, the TrueType font file to render the text, and the text itself. After the text bounding box information is determined, the actual height is set into `$text_height`, and the amount the text dips under the baseline — for letters like lowercase *g* and *p*, is determined. Here's the code:

```
// Caption the image
public function process($gd_img)
{
  if ($this->caption and $this->fontfile)
  {
    // Get text box height
    $text_box = imagettfbbox($this->fontsize,
                             0,
                             $this->fontfile,
                             $this->caption);
    $text_height = $text_box[3] - $text_box[5];
    $text_underbaseline = $text_box[3];

    // Get some image dimensions
    $img_x = imagesx($gd_img);
    $img_y = imagesy($gd_img);
```

Next, a background-shaded box is drawn over the image, to provide a darker area to help show the white text you will write over the top, later in the method. First, GD is informed to properly blend the transparency on the target image. Then, using `imagecolorrallocatealpha()`, a color resource is acquired — in this case black (0,0,0), about 60% transparent (the range for the alpha channel is 0–127). Finally, a filled rectangle is drawn, using the translucent black color, over the bottom of the image using the height needed to cover the full font height plus any padding that might be specified:

```
// Draw background shading
imagealphablending($gd_img, true);
$rect_color = imagecolorallocatealpha($gd_img, 0, 0, 0, 75);
imagefilledrectangle($gd_img,
                     0,
                     $img_y - $text_height - ($this->padding * 2),
                     $img_x,
                     $img_y,
                     $rect_color);
```

After the background rectangle is drawn over the image, it's time to add the caption text on top. Simply allocate a color for the text — in this case white — and then use `imagettftext()` to draw the text over the image:

```
// Draw caption text
$text_color = imagecolorallocate($gd_img, 255, 255, 255);
imagettftext($gd_img,
             $this->fontsize,
             0,
             $this->padding,
             $img_y - $text_underbaseline - $this->padding,
             $text_color,
             $this->fontfile,
             $this->caption);
```

The `imagettftext()` function uses eight parameters: the image resource to add text to, the size of the font, the angle of the text, the x location to start drawing the text, the y location for the baseline/bottom of the text, the color of the text, the .ttf font filename, and the actual text to render, in that order.

The last bit of the captioning simply draws a faint border at the top of the caption box, using a translucent light gray, and the `imageline()` GD function:

```
// Draw shading border if requested
if ($this->drawline)
{
  $line_color = imagecolorallocatealpha($gd_img,
                                        200,
                                        200,
                                        200,
                                        75);
  imageline($gd_img,
            0,
            $img_y - $text_height - ($this->padding * 2) - 1,
            $img_x,
            $img_y - $text_height - ($this->padding * 2) - 1,
            $line_color);
}
```

```
    }

    return $gd_img;
  }
```

Adding a Logo

The final bit of functionality you're going to add to the WebImage class is the ability to place a logo or watermark on an image.

Start by creating the class.ImageLogo.php file:

```php
<?php

class ImageLogo
{
  public $logofile;
  public $ratio = 1;
  public $location = array('x' => '', 'y' => '');
  public $padding = 0;

  public function process($gd_img)
  {
    if ($this->logofile)
    {
      require_once 'class.WebImage.php';

      // Load the logo
      $logo = new WebImage();
      $logo->load($this->logofile);

      // Resize logo if needed
      if ($this->ratio and $this->ratio != 1)
      {
        $logo->resize($this->ratio);
      }

      // Determine logo placement (x)
      switch ($this->location['x'])
      {
        case 'l':
          $logo_x = $this->padding;
          break;
        case 'r':
          $logo_x = imagesx($gd_img) -
                    $this->padding -
                    imagesx($logo->gdresource);
          break;
        default:
          $logo_x = round((imagesx($gd_img) / 2) -
                    (imagesx($logo->gdresource) / 2));
      }

      // Determine logo placement (y)
```

```
          switch ($this->location['y'])
          {
            case 't':
              $logo_y = $this->padding;
              break;
            case 'b':
              $logo_y = imagesy($gd_img) -
                        $this->padding -
                        imagesy($logo->gdresource);
              break;
            default:
              $logo_y = round((imagesy($gd_img) / 2) -
                              (imagesy($logo->gdresource) / 2));
          }

          // Copy the logo onto the main image
          imagecopy($gd_img,
                    $logo->gdresource,
                    $logo_x,
                    $logo_y,
                    0,
                    0,
                    imagesx($logo->gdresource),
                    imagesy($logo->gdresource));
        }

        return $gd_img;
      }
    }

    ?>
```

Next, add the `logo()` method to the end of the `WebImage` class definition:

```
    public function logo($logofile,
                         $loc_x = null,
                         $loc_y = null,
                         $padding = null,
                         $ratio = null)
    {
      require_once 'class.ImageLogo.php';

      $il = new ImageLogo();

      // Set logo file
      $il->logofile = $logofile;

      // Set location, padding, and ratio if needed
      if ($loc_x !== null)
      {
        $il->location['x'] = $loc_x;
      }
      if ($loc_y !== null)
      {
        $il->location['y'] = $loc_y;
```

```
      }
      if ($padding !== null)
      {
         $il->padding = $padding;
      }
      if ($ratio !== null)
      {
         $il->ratio = $ratio;
      }


      // Perform the logo placement
      $this->gdresource = $il->process($this->gdresource);
   }
```

Like the other action-processing methods added to WebImage, logo() simply takes the parameters provided — logo filename, location x, location y, padding in pixels, and resize ratio for the logo — sets the needed properties in ImageLogo, and processes the logo application.

Inside ImageLogo's process() function, you can see exactly what occurs during the logo application. The process() method starts out by creating its own internal WebImage object, which it will use to load the logo file, and resize it if needed. After the WebImage is created and loaded, the logo image is resized if a ratio is specified:

```
public function process($gd_img)
{
   if ($this->logofile)
   {
      require_once 'class.WebImage.php';

      // Load the logo
      $logo = new WebImage();
      $logo->load($this->logofile);

      // Resize logo if needed
      if ($this->ratio and $this->ratio != 1)
      {
         $logo->resize($this->ratio);
      }
```

Next, the placement of the logo is determined. The logo can be placed in one of nine locations — any combination of three horizontal and three vertical placements. For horizontal, the values l, r, and m can be used to specify left placement, right placement, or middle/centered placement. The vertical values are similar — t for top, b for bottom, and m for middle/centered:

```
      // Determine logo placement (x)
      switch ($this->location['x'])
      {
         case 'l':
            $logo_x = $this->padding;
            break;
         case 'r':
            $logo_x = imagesx($gd_img) -
                      $this->padding -
                      imagesx($logo->gdresource);
```

```
        break;
      default:
        $logo_x = round((imagesx($gd_img) / 2) -
                       (imagesx($logo->gdresource) / 2));
    }

    // Determine logo placement (y)
    switch ($this->location['y'])
    {
      case 't':
        $logo_y = $this->padding;
        break;
      case 'b':
        $logo_y = imagesy($gd_img) -
                  $this->padding -
                  imagesy($logo->gdresource);
        break;
      default:
        $logo_y = round((imagesy($gd_img) / 2) -
                       (imagesy($logo->gdresource) / 2));
    }
```

Finally, the logo image is merged onto the main image, and the resulting image resource returned:

```
    // Copy the logo onto the main image
    imagecopy($gd_img,
              $logo->gdresource,
              $logo_x,
              $logo_y,
              0,
              0,
              imagesx($logo->gdresource),
              imagesy($logo->gdresource));
    }

    return $gd_img;
  }
}
```

Note that imagecopy() was used instead of imagecopymerge(). The imagecopymerge() function seems like it would be better suited to this task, and even provides the ability to merge the logo and set its transparency — good for certain watermarking effects. Unfortunately, imagecopymerge() has a nasty habit of destroying most transparency information in the source logo image itself, so if you want to make a faint translucent watermark for an image, it's probably best to add the transparency to the logo image itself, and using imagecopy(), instead of using an opaque image and imagecopymerge().

Testing It Out

To put this collection of image manipulation code through its paces, you'll need a few things: a main image to process, an image to use as a logo overlay, and a TrueType font file. Once you have those three things ready, create a PHP script to use the classes you've created with the images. Start by simply loading your image, and displaying it in the browser:

```php
<?php

require_once 'class.WebImage.php';

$img = new WebImage();
$img->load('base.png');
$img->display();

?>
```

Load this file in your browser, and it should display your image, as in Figure 10.1.

Figure 10.1

If you wanted to change the type of the image before saving or displaying it, you'd simply need to set the type of the image in the `WebImage` object:

```php
<?php

require_once 'class.WebImage.php';

$img = new WebImage();
```

```
$img->load('base.png');
$img->type = 'image/gif';
$img->display();

?>
```

To resize the image, call the `resize()` function of `WebImage`. The following code uses a ratio of 0.75:

```php
<?php

require_once 'class.WebImage.php';

$img = new WebImage();
$img->load('base.png');
$img->resize(0.75);
$img->display();

?>
```

An example of the output is shown in Figure 10.2.

Figure 10.2

Next, rotate your image. The following uses 180 degrees for the rotation:

```php
<?php

require_once 'class.WebImage.php';

$img = new WebImage();
$img->load('base.png');
$img->rotate(180);
$img->display();

?>
```

Loading the script in your browser will look something like Figure 10.3.

Figure 10.3

Now, add a caption to the image. This example uses the font "Fuji Wide Normal," but you can use whatever font you have at your disposal, as long as it is a TrueType font file (.ttf):

```php
<?php

require_once 'class.WebImage.php';

$img = new WebImage();
$img->load('base.png');
$img->caption('An example of plantlife found on Maui.',
              'FUJIWIDR.TTF',
              15,
              5,
              true);
$img->display();

?>
```

If everything goes as planned, you should see something similar to Figure 10.4.

Figure 10.4

Last, try out the image logo application. In this example, you're going to place a logo in the lower-right corner of the image, on top of the caption box:

```php
<?php

require_once 'class.WebImage.php';

$img = new WebImage();
$img->load('base.png');
$img->caption('An example of plantlife found on Maui.',
              'FUJIWIDR.TTF',
              13,
              5,
              true);
$img->logo('logo.png', 'r', 'b', 5, 0.3);
$img->display();

?>
```

And now, a logo should appear, resized a little, in the lower-right corner with 5px of padding, as in Figure 10.5.

Figure 10.5

As you can see, using the GD library is not hard to use and allows for quite a bit of flexibility and control over your images. There are many other more advanced functions you can use, all of which can be found at the GD section of the PHP Manual (http://www.php.net/gd).

Ming

Ming is a third-party extension to PHP that allows a user to create Shockwave Flash files without actually having to use Macromedia's Flash studio. The functionality that Ming provides isn't always the same as what is available in Macromedia's Flash, because of the nature of how the Flash files are created using PHP and Ming. Ming does provide a method to create Flash files that is low cost and allows for content to be dynamically created when it is needed.

About Ming

The usefulness of dynamically created Flash files can sometimes be lost for some people, especially because you will not have the precise visual control over the content layout that people who use Macromedia's Flash Studio employ. Also, the feature set of Ming is limited to that of Flash version 4, which is several versions behind the latest available. But being able to script the creation and add dynamic content to the application is something that you can't do using Macromedia's Flash Studio. This can be helpful in distributing content to users where you need the features of Flash but also want to personalize the content for the user.

Ming itself is actually a third-party extension that has had PHP wrapper extensions written for it, so it needs to be compiled into the PHP binary when the binary is built. Instructions for Ming installation with PHP can be found on PHP's website (http://www.php.net/ming). More information about Ming itself can be found at Ming's site on SourceForge.Net (http://ming.sourceforge.net). There are also many tutorials and examples available on the Internet that can help to illustrate the functionality of Ming as well as provide pieces of code that are suitable to be used as a foundation to build on for your Flash movies.

Ming is implemented in PHP as objects, so that any time you create a shockwave file with Ming in PHP you need to at least instantiate an instance of the SWFmovie object. The following is some code of a very simple file generated with Ming and PHP. To run this code, insert it into a PHP file with no other content in it, and then view that file in a web browser that has the Flash plug-in installed:

```php
<?php
header('Content-type: application/x-shockwave-flash');
$a= new SWFmovie();
$a->setDimension(100,100); //width and length in that order
$a->setBackground(0,0,255); // red, green, and blue integers
$a->output();
?>
```

This does not generate much, but it does produce a giant blue screen in your browser. Examining the code, you can see some of the necessary pieces that will need to be included in any Flash file created with Ming. The first line tells PHP to set the Content-type header so that the browser knows that it is a shockwave file and to load the appropriate plug-in for it. The next line actually creates the instance of the SWFMovie object. The next two lines are optional, but without them, it would be hard to tell that anything was generated, as they set the size of the shockwave file as well as make its background blue. The last line tells PHP to write the Ming generated file out to the browser. The only thing to really make sure to do here is set the proper header Content-type before outputting the movie as well as make sure no other content is sent to the browser, such as stray lines and white space.

There can only be one instance of the SWFMovie object, but you can include multiple mini movies in one SWFMovie object. In order to do this, you need to use another object, the SWFSprite object. This object has similar qualities and attributes to the SWFMovie object, but isn't limited to only one per movie. The advantage to this is that you can have multiple animations showing at the same time in the same flash movie. Each of the animations can even be running at different rates as well as be different lengths in time.

Flash files use *frames*, just like frames in a movie or animation. The objects SWFMovie and SWFSprite both have functions to add new frames to them. Frames are useful in that you can display different objects to the screen by including them in specific frames. This means that if you want two or more objects to be displayed at the same time, they need to have a common frame. Once an object is added to a frame, every frame after it contains that object until the object is removed from the movie. Also, just like a movie or animation you can go forwards or backwards, as well as skipping to a specific frame using the SWFAction object. This use of frames provides a better way to group objects as well as generate timelines in your Flash movies.

Ming and Flash both use a coordinate system that may be different than what you're used to. The unit of distance that is used by Flash is the twip. The twip is defined as being exactly $\frac{1}{1440}$ of an inch or $\frac{1}{20}$ of a point in size. This measurement usually is simplified for easy conversion to a value of 20 twip units in 1 pixel. However, this can be an arbitrary value, as the Flash player will scale the movie to the size of the player window itself. Fortunately, the SWFBitmap object included in Ming has functionality to determine what size an image is in twips. Therefore, if you need to have a movie with dimensions based on the size of an image, you simply need to create the SWFBitmap object, read its width and height values, and then set the dimensions of the movie itself based on it. The dimension of a movie does not necessarily need to be set until right before it is displayed.

Objects in Ming

There are a total of 13 objects that PHP provides to generate Flash files with Ming. You can use a combination of these objects to create many complex Flash files with a wide variety of functionality. They are as follows:

❑   The SWFAction object lets you add logic and functionality beyond a simple image display to your Flash file. Using SWFAction you can move images and shapes around for things such as games, as well as read and set properties of objects in the Flash file. Also, you can include some ActionScript scripts, which is Flash's version of JavaScript and is quite similar. This object is used commonly with the SWFButton object to perform some action when the user presses the button. Common actions used are the displaying of specific frames in a Flash movie based on a response from the user.

❑   The SWFBitmap object allows for images to be added to the Flash file. There are several limitations, though, as only non-progressive scan JPEG images and DBL ("define bits lossless") images can be added this way. Any other image needs to be converted to one of these formats using either another extension, such as GD, or by making a system call to a utility. This objects many times is used with SWFSprite and the SWFShape objects.

❑   The SWFButton object adds a button to your Flash file. This button can be used to initiate an action of the SWFAction object. It reacts to common mouse actions such as mousedown, mouseup, and rollover. A shape can be added to the button to change its appearance.

❑ The SWFDisplayItem object allows a shape, text object, sprite, or button to be manipulated after being added to a movie by referencing the item using its returned handle after being added to the movie. Operations such as skewing, scaling, and moving items are all possible operations.

❑ The SWFFill object is generated by use of the `addFill` method of the SWFShape object. It allows the fill to be transformed by rotating, skewing, and scaling the fill of the shape.

❑ The SWFFont object loads a font for use by the SWFText object. The font can either be a font definition block (FDB) or a browser-defined font reference.

❑ The SWFGradient object creates a gradient that can then be used by the SWFShape method `addFill()`.

❑ The SWFMorph will take two shapes and morph the first into the second shape. This can be used for some basic animation.

❑ The SWFMovie object is the one object that is necessary for any other objects to work correctly, as it is the object that actually writes the Flash file out, either to a file or to a browser.

❑ The SWFShape object generates a shape. The shape is actually drawn by passing coordinates that are drawn with an imaginary pen. With the right coordinates, almost any shape can be generated. Also, as mentioned before, this is used with the SWFBitmap object to add an image file to the movie.

❑ The SWFSprite object generates a "movie clip" or animation by adding frames to the object. A frame contains one of the other objects, such as SWFShape. There can be multiple SWFSprite objects in a single frame so that two animations are seen going at the same time. The advantage of adding images to a SWFSprite object compared to just a SWFMovie object is that it encapsulates the objects better for manipulation.

❑ The SWFText object displays text in a Flash animation. An alternative to using the SWFText object if you need to display only small amounts of static information is to just use images instead of using Flash to write the text.

❑ The SWFTextField is similar to a SWFText object, but with a few differences. SWFTextField objects can't be rotated or skewed, but can function as form entries.

Creating a Flash Display

With a few more lines of code, you can expand the earlier example to something that is slightly more interesting to look at:

```php
<?php
header('Content-type: application/x-shockwave-flash');
$a= new SWFMovie();
$a->setDimension(100,100); //width and length in that order
$a->setBackground(0,0,255); // red, green, and blue integers

$s =new SWFShape();  //generate a shape object
$s->setLine(4, 30, 60, 100); //set the line width to 4 along
// with red, green, and blue integer values
$s->setLeftFill($s->addFill(300, 200, 100));
    //set the color of the shape with red, green
// and integer values
$s->movePenTo(20, 20);
```

```
//move our imaginary pen to a new location
$s->drawLineTo(20, 80);
    //draw lines to a new set of points
$s->drawLineTo(80, 80);
$s->drawlineTo(80,20);
$s->drawlineTo(20,20);
$a->add($s);  //add the shape to the movie

$a->nextFrame();  //advance a frame in the movie
$a->output();    //output everything to the browser
?>
```

The output generated from the movie is not anything special, but it demonstrates a few of the basic methods of some of the more important objects. The output should be a blue background with a green square in the middle of it.

For a more in depth example to illustrate the functionality of Ming, you're going to generate a slide show with it. You will be using images of all of the same size and shape to make things easier, and all images will be explicitly named. Create a new file and include the following lines of code:

```
<?php
//create a movie object
$aMovie = new SWFMovie();
//set the background to white
$aMovie->setBackground(255, 255, 255);
```

After the initial setup, you need to add references to images to include in the slide show. Here, a simple array of image names is used, but this could be expanded to read straight from a directory or even a database. Also, in this example all images are assumed to have sizes of a height and width of 200 pixels. To make sizing the movie and expansion on the code easier, an instance of one image is made to read its width and height, even though all images in the example are supposed to be 200 × 200 pixels. Try it:

```
//images to display
$images = array("1.jpg", "2.jpg", "3.jpg");

$bitmapImage = new SWFBitmap(fOpen($images[1], "rb"));
$w = $bitmapImage->getWidth();
$h = $bitmapImage->getHeight();
```

A SWFSprite is created that will act as a mini-movie in the slideshow, and will actually be what is controlled by the user. In order to prevent it from just showing all of the images a default action of stop() is added to it. Also the size of the movie is calculated from the size of the images with extra space given to allow for buttons to be added underneath the images. Here's the code:

```
//create a sprite which will act as a mini movie
$sprite = new SWFSprite();
//add stop action to the first frame
$sprite->add(new SWFAction("stop();"));

//set the size of the movie with extra psce for buttons
$aMovie->setDimension((1*$w),(1.5* $h)+3);
```

Now each of the images needs to be added to the sprite, which can be easily achieved by iterating through the array. Each of the images are first converted to SWFBitmap objects, and then added as fills to SWFShape objects. After a line has been drawn around the shape, it is added to the SWFSprite object and the SWFSprite object goes to the next frame:

```
//loop through all of the images
for($i=0; $i<count($images);$i++){

//create a bitmap from an image
$bitmapImage = new SWFBitmap(fopen($images[$i], "rb"));

//create a shape object to hold the image
$shape = new SWFShape();
//generate the fill for the shape of the image
$fill = $shape->addFill($bitmapImage);
//add the fill to the shape
$shape->setRightFill($fill);

//draw a line around the shape to set the size
$shape->drawLine($w, 0);
$shape->drawLine(0, $h);
$shape->drawLine(-$w, 0);
$shape->drawLine(0, -$h);
//add the shape to the sprite so that it is displayed
$sprite->add($shape);
//generate a new frame and go to it
$sprite->nextFrame();
}
```

Because the sprite will not return to the first frame automatically, there needs to be an action added to the last frame that takes it to the first frame. The gotoFrame() action accepts a frame number as an argument; here, frame 0 is used as it is the first frame in the sprite. Another frame is then added to the sprite in order to make sure everything is included in the SWFSprite object:

```
//goto frame 0
$sprite->add(new SWFAction("gotoFrame(0);"));
//again generate a new frame
$sprite->nextFrame();
```

Now that the sprite has finished, it needs to be added to the SWFMovie object. As it is added to the movie, it will return a handler that can be used as a reference to the sprite so that it can be controlled. A name is assigned to it and using the handler, you move the sprite into position:

```
//add the sprite and get its handler
$handler = $aMovie->add($sprite);
//we can name the sprite now with the handler
 $handler->setName("images");
//we can move the sprite also with the handler
$handler->moveTo(0,2);
```

In order to create a button to control the slide show, you create a new SWFShape object and add a button image to it

```
//create a shape again
$shape = new SWFShape();
//create another bitmap this time for a button image
$bitmapImage = new SWFBitmap(fopen("button.jpg", "rb"));
$file = $shape->addFill($bitmapImage);
$shape->setRightFill($fill);
//create the border around the shape
$shape->drawLine($w, 0);
$shape->drawLine(0, $h);
$shape->drawLine(-$w, 0);
$shape->drawLine(0, -$h);
```

A SWFButton object is instantiated and the button shape is added to the SWFButton object. The default flags are also set for the button, which allows the program to perform actions based on if the button is pushed or not and if the mouse is over the button. An action is also added to the button to move the sprite to the next frame.

```
//now actually create a button object
$button = new SWFButton();
//add the shape to the button with all of its default flags which are
//all actually predefined integer values
$button->addShape($shape, SWFBUTTON_HIT |
SWFBUTTON_UP | SWFBUTTON_DOWN |
SWFBUTTON_OVER);
//add an action to go to the next frame
//on the sprite.  The sprite is referenced by "/images"
$button->addAction(new SWFAction("setTarget('/images');
nextFrame();"),SWFBUTTON_MOUSEDOWN);
```

The button is then added to the movie and the handler returned. The button is then moved to just under the images and a new frame is added to the movie. The necessary browser headers are then generated and the movie is outputted:

```
//add the button to the move and save the returned handler
$handler = $aMovie->add($button);
//use the handler to move the button below the images
$handler->moveTo(0,$h+3);
$aMovie->nextFrame();
//send the appropriate header to the browser
header("Content-Type:application/x-shockwave-flash");
//output the movie to the browser
$aMovie->output();
?>
```

There are a few things to remember when using Ming. The first is that when you output directly to a browser, the Content-Type header must be sent before the SWFMovie object's method `output()` is called. This sends the proper HTTP headers so that the browser knows to load the Shockwave Flash plug-in. This leads to another error that may occur: outputting anything besides the Content-Type header, such as blank lines. The outputting of content other than the header and the movie itself will corrupt the file, causing the browser to incorrectly display the file. Also, it helps to have a general layout of what you want your final output to look like. To help with laying out a Flash movie created with Ming, you can use a graphics program that provides a coordinates system or just plain graph paper.

SimpleXML

XML is everywhere these days, so it only makes sense that there should be an easy way to retrieve and interpret those files. Thankfully, PHP offers us an XML interface to utilize XML data, in a simple and easy-to-use extension: SimpleXML. SimpleXML is installed by default, but if you're not going to use it, it is recommended that you disable it in php.ini. It should be noted that SimpleXML also requires PHP5.

As the name suggests, the extension's purpose is to access XML documents on a very basic level. To illustrate the ease with which this can be implemented, create a fictitious XML file that contains information on beachfront rentals (this file will be used in all of the examples):

```xml
<?xml version="1.0"?>
  <rentals>
    <description>
     <name>The Bayfront</name>
     <type>condo</type>
     <view>oceanfront</view>
     <space>1200 square feet</space>
     <location>Wrightsville Beach</location>
     <price>1000 per week</price>
     <bed_bath>3 bedrooms, 2 bathrooms</bed_bath>
    </description>
    <description>
      <name>Paradise</name>
      <type>house</type>
      <view>oceanfront</view>
      <space>1000 square feet</space>
      <location>Wrightsville Beach</location>
      <price>900 per week</price>
      <bed_bath>2 bedrooms, 2 bathrooms</bed_bath>
    </description>
  </rentals>>
```

Now that you have the XML file, grab the information and put it into an object (using the `simplexml_load_file()` function) so you can manipulate it:

```php
<?php
if (file_exists('beachfront.xml')) {
    $data = simplexml_load_file('beachfront.xml');

    print_r($data);
}
?>
```

You can iterate through the object and display the results nicely (or at least in a more readable format). Add the following changes to `simple.php`:

```php
<?php
if (file_exists('beachfront.xml')) {
    $data = simplexml_load_file('beachfront.xml');

foreach($data as $main) {
    echo "<hr>";
    foreach ($main as $k => $v) {
    echo $k . ": " . $v . "<br \>";
    }
}

}
?>
```

Besides `simplexml_load_file()`, there are a host of other functions that go along with the SimpleXML extension. `simplexml_load_string()` loads an XML document as a string. You must first assign its contents to a variable; then you may use the `simplexml_load_string()` function to parse the variable's contents into the object for your use. If you would like to manipulate your object and then display the contents back out to the browser in the form of an XML file, you can use the `$objectname->asXML()` function. The `attributes()` and `children()` functions are helpful if you need to see the element's attributes or the children of any of the object's nodes. The `simplexml_import_dom()` function is helpful if you want to take a DOM node from a DOM document and turn it into a SimpleXMLElement.object.

The `xpath()` function allows you to search through the XML document for a specific string. It uses the W3C's Xpath to evaluate each node in your XML document, and is called "XPath" because the search keywords resemble the path to a file, as each element is similarly nested. If you would like to read more about XPath, visit the W3C's documentation on the subject at `http://www.w3.org/TR/xpath`.

This is sufficient if you want to perform the very simplest of queries, as in the following example:

```php
<?php
if (file_exists('beachfront.xml')) {
    $data = simplexml_load_file('beachfront.xml');


//find and list all the "locations" in our XML file
//"locations" are under "descriptions" which are under "rentals"
$find = $data->xpath('/rentals/description/location');

while (list(, $v) = each($find)) {
    echo $v. "\n";
    }
}
?>
```

This script will give you all the values for the node named "location" within your XML file. If you want to take your query any further, you will have to use another method. Remember this is SimpleXML, not ComplexXML.

SimpleXML offers a very quick and straightforward way to access a simple XML document. It does not allow for much flexibility, and it only works on the simplest of XML files. You will run into problems trying to run these functions on an XML file that contains HTML code within its content, for example. Otherwise, this is a lot easier to work with than many other XML/PHP interfaces available.

Summary

There are many other PHP Extensions available, although this chapter covered only a fraction of them here. A complete listing can be found at the PHP Manual (`http://www.php.net`). Some of the extensions you might want to pay attention to include:

❑ **CURL (Client URL Library Functions):** Allows you to connect to pages using many different protocols besides http, such as SSL, FTP, and gopher.

❑ **DOM:** Interfaces with XML documents with the DOM API, and comes bundled with PHP default installation.

❑ **SOAP:** Enables creation of SOAP servers and clients using GNOME xml library.

❑ **ZIP extensions (Bzip2, rar, Zip, Zlib):** Enables reading of zip files, each extension dealing with a different type of compression file.

With this taste of PHP Extensions, you will, we hope, feel confident exploring PHP's lesser known but equally useful functions.

11

AJAX

Typical web applications interact with the user via forms. The server sends the client a form, the user enters responses, and the form is submitted back to the server for processing. Once the form is processed, the server responds with a new complete page, the composition of which is often dependent upon the user's last form submission. In each interaction with the user, an entirely new page is required. Such applications must use bandwidth, transferring constant page elements (site navigation, for example) with each page request, even though these elements were sent to the client in previous responses. Further, such applications are slower than desktop applications, because the web application is unresponsive while the results of one interaction are being processed and until the new page loads.

AJAX (Asynchronous JavaScript and XML) refers to a group of technologies that allows for the creation of fat-client web applications, where the responsibility for a relatively large portion of the application processing is given to the client. Specifically, AJAX applications often use XHTML and CSS for semantic markup and presentation, XML to format data that will be exchanged between client and server, and JavaScript to communicate with the server and manipulate the Document Object Model (DOM). When using AJAX, communication between the client and the server can be limited to data only, as the client has the functionality necessary to handle presentation and user interaction. Further, such communication happens asynchronously and without a page refresh. This allows for the client-side of the application to remain responsive even while data is being exchanged with the server. If a user performs an action that requires a request be sent to the server, the request can be sent and the application can handle further interaction while awaiting a response (even issuing more requests). This concept is illustrated in Figure 11.1.

Probably the most popular AJAX application today is Google's GMail (`http://www.gmail.com`), a web-based email client. In traditional web-based email clients, nearly every action by the user causes a refresh of the entire page or frame. Because GMail employs AJAX, the page never refreshes. Rather, the interface is updated dynamically by manipulating the DOM via JavaScript based on user interaction with the application and XML communication with the GMail server. This enables, for example, a user to compose an email, click Send, and continue reading his or her email while the GMail server handles the actual processing of the sent message. While reading the rest of the email, he or she will receive a status message indicating that the message was sent successfully.

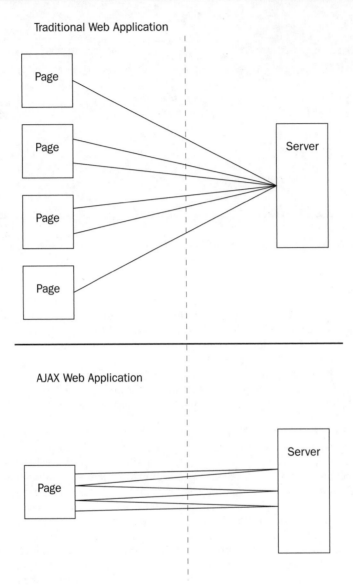

Figure 11.1

History

AJAX itself is not new; nor is the idea behind it. In fact, many methods have been developed and used in the past to communicate with the server without a page refresh.

The Image Source Trick

JavaScript allows dynamic loading of images using the Image object. When one creates an image and sets its `src` property, the browser sends a request for the image and attempts to package the response in the image object. Developers have used this to make one-way communication with a server by setting the `src` attribute to the URI of a server-side script, passing data to the server in the query string. The server-side script might then update a data store. Typically, no image is returned in the response, but this does not cause problems, as the developer does not use the Image object for its intended purpose.

The positives of this technique are:

❑   It allows for sending of data to the server without refresh.

❑   It can read properties of the object to determine when request is complete.

However, it does have some drawbacks:

❑   It cannot receive non-graphical data from the server (communication is one-way).

❑   It cannot detect nor handle HTTP errors that may have occurred during the attempted communication.

Hidden Frames

Many developers found the Image source trick to be inadequate and required the ability to receive information from the server in addition to sending to it. Enter the use of a hidden frame. In this technique, the developer uses a frame with no visibility (by setting either the height or width to 0, depending on the frameset) as the vehicle. The hidden frame is nothing more than a page with the minimal set of HTML elements plus a script element. The script element is often simply definitions of arrays and variables, the values of which have been written by the server. Thus, the controller frame (the one that is visible) can set the location property of this frame to that of a server side script, optionally sending data to it via the query string. The browser then issues this request. The server-side script processes any passed information in the query string and then writes data in valid JavaScript syntax. Look at the following code to get the general idea.

```php
<?php
$uname = $_GET['username'];
?>
...
<script type="text/javascript">
top.usernameOK = <?php echo isUsernameAvailable($uname); ?>;
top.usernameAlts =
    new Array(<?php echo implode(',', getSimilarNames($uname)); ?>);
top.frames[1].readVars();
</script>
...
```

This code lives in the hidden communication frame. In this code example, a Boolean value is written to indicate the availability of a username passed to the script via the query string. When the browser's JavaScript engine executes this script, it will store the Boolean value in the JavaScript variable named usernameOK. An array of username alternatives is also being written to the output. In PHP, the array is joined to a single comma-separated string in order to comply with JavaScript array syntax. (The getSimilarNames *function would also need to wrap each array value in quotes.)*

When the hidden frame loads with the JavaScript, it triggers the controller frame, which can then access the variable values written by the server-side script as top.usernameOK and top.usernameAlts:

```
<script type="text/javascript">
function readVars()
{
    alert(top.usernameOK);
    alert(top.usernameAlts);
}
self.readVars = readVars;
</script>
```

This code lives in the controller frame. Wrapping the code in a function that is called by the hidden communication frame is one method of triggering the retrieval of data by the loading of the hidden frame.

The upsides to this technique are:

❑   It allows for sending *and receiving* of data to the server without full-page refresh.

❑   It can trigger retrieval of data by main application as soon as the data are available.

❑   It's simple to use and debug, as all data the application is using is clearly visible in the source of the hidden frame.

❑   It can receive graphical data, but support for JavaScript variables as image sources is only partially supported in browsers (IE, for example, likes only XBM image data assigned like this).

❑   Because frame loads add a browser history entry, the user can use the back button. However, the behavior of the back button might not be what the user expects.

And the downsides are:

❑   It introduces usability problems, such as the inability to easily bookmark an application state.

❑   It can partially detect communication errors by resubmitting requests after a timeout period.

❑   The hidden frame's contents could easily be manipulated by the user (this is always a concern, but it is somewhat easier for the user to do this with the hidden frame technique).

❑   Only one request per hidden frame can be dispatched at a given time (which is a downside if the response is important).

Hidden IFRAME

Similar to the hidden frame technique is the hidden IFRAME technique. Instead of using a hidden frame within a frameset, this method uses an invisible IFRAME element, changing its source location to issue requests to and receive responses from the server. Google Maps uses this technique to communicate with the server without a page refresh.

The advantages of this technique are:

- ❑ It has all the pros of the hidden frame technique.

- ❑ You have a bit more control over the behavior of the back button, depending on how the source location of the IFRAME is changed.

And the drawbacks are:

- ❑ It suffers from usability problems similar to the hidden frame technique.

- ❑ It can partially detect communication errors by resubmitting requests after a timeout period.

- ❑ Only one request per hidden IFRAME can be dispatched at a given time (a drawback if the response is important).

- ❑ There are serious browser differences in how one programmatically adds an IFRAME element and how one references the document response contained within the IFRAME after a source location change.

XMLHTTP and XMLHttpRequest

Even the methods now referred to as "AJAX" are not new. Microsoft's version of the interface, XMLHTTP, has been available as an ActiveX object in various incarnations since a preview release of IE 5.0 in late 1998 (the final release of IE 5.0 was in March 1999). Companies have been capitalizing on this development model in IE-only environments for years. Beginning slightly before the release of version 1.0 of Mozilla's browser product, a native object, modeled after Microsoft's interface and named XMLHttpRequest, has been available. Recently, Safari (since version 1.2), Opera (since version 8), and Konqueror have included compliant interfaces, also named XMLHttpRequest.

In the last few months, the use of XMLHTTP and its variants has increased dramatically. The adoption of the technology by Google in their Google Suggest and Google GMail product offerings has been primarily responsible for introducing the development method to the masses. Additionally, an article by Adaptive Path coining the term "AJAX" allowed developers to refer to the collection of technologies with one unifying name, which has facilitated communication and awareness of the subject.

The Interfaces

The following are the methods of the XMLHTTP and XMLHttpRequest interfaces that are relevant and, for the most part, supported in all browsers:

- ❑ `abort()`: Aborts a request.

- ❑ `getResponseHeader(key)`: Returns the value of the HTTP response header named key.

- ❑ `open(method, uri, [async, [username, [password]]])`: Sets the HTTP request method to `method` and the request URI to `uri`. Optionally, it sets the flag indicating whether or not to process the request asynchronously to `async`, and sets a username and password to use for authentication, if necessary. The method attribute is typically either `get` or `post`. Using `post` is appropriate if you are pushing data in the request (see the `send()` method). In almost all cases, `async` should be left to its default value of true.

❑ `overrideMimeType(type)`: Forces the interpretation of the response as if the server sent the mime type of the named type. This method is not available in IE. This can be useful if it is impractical to alter the server to send a given mime type. This must be called prior to `send()`. It can also be used to avoid a Mozilla bug that sometimes causes the browser to hang when processing a non-XML response.

❑ `send(requestContent)`: Sends the HTTP request. The parameter `requestContent` is used for requests with a method of `post` (see the `open()` method), and represents the request body. If the request is asynchronous, this method returns immediately. Early versions of Mozilla had difficulty sending a string as request content. `requestContent` should be null for a `get` request. For `post` requests, it must be null, a string, or a DOM Document object. If it is the latter, the object is serialized. The content of this parameter is included in the request body and is therefore accessible to the server.

❑ `setRequestHeader(key, value)`: Assigns the value of `value` to the HTTP request header named key. This method must be called after calling `open()` and before calling `send()`.

The `open()` and `send()` methods handle the primary functionality of the interface. The `open()` method sets various parameters of the request, such as the HTTP request method (`get` or `post`) and the request URI. The request URI will typically be the relative location of the script on the server to call. You may use a fully qualified URI if you would like, but due to security restrictions, the domain of the URI must match that of the page containing the JavaScript issuing the request. The implication of this is that if you would like to fetch data from third-party data sources located on other domains (such as, for instance, weather data feeds), you must proxy such requests through a server-side script residing on your server.

The optional `async` parameter of the `open()` method determines the behavior of the `send()` method. If set to true (or left to its default), the `send()` method will issue the HTTP request and immediately return. This means that lines of your JavaScript code subsequent to the call to `send()` will execute regardless of the response to the issued request. Instead, response handling is triggered by the firing of an event, handled by an event handler. This feature is the first *A* in AJAX, and it allows you to develop applications that behave much like desktop applications. The specifics of this event handling are set via properties of the interface:

❑ `onreadystatechange`: The function called when the `ReadyStateChange` event is fired (that is, when the `readyState` property changes). The value of this property should be a JavaScript function. Make sure not to reference the function with parentheses, or the function will be called and the value of this property will end up being the *return value* of your function rather than the function itself.

❑ `readyState`: Read-only. This is an integer representing the current state of the request. Possible values of this property range from 0 to 4 and indicate increasing progress. A value of 4 indicates that the request has been completed and the response is fully processed. Headers and status are available with a `readyState` of at least 2.

❑ `responseText`: Read-only. This is the response body as text. It is non-null with a successful request starting with a `readyState` of 3. The `responseText` is fully populated at a `readyState` of 4.

❑ `responseXML`: Read-only. This is the response body parsed as text/xml content and packaged as a DOM Document object. It is non-null with a successful request at a `readyState` of 4.

❑ `status`: Read-only. This is the integer HTTP response status code. 200 indicates a successful response. For other possible status codes, including numerous error codes, see section 6.1.1 of the HTTP/1.1 RFC (`http://www.rfc-editor.org/rfc/rfc2616.txt`)

With the exception of `responseText` and `responseXML`, these properties are mainly involved in determining if and when a response has been received. This is necessary because your requests are asynchronous, meaning you cannot rely on the availability of the response at any given line of code based on execution order or time. Rather, asynchronous communication relies on an event-driven model for processing. The `readyState` property contains a value that indicates the progress of the request. Every time this value changes, a `ReadyStateChange` event is fired. If defined, the `onreadystatechange` handler is then called to handle the `ReadyStateChange` event. Note that for a given request, the `ReadyStateChange` event will fire at least four times. In most cases, you will not be interested in any of these events except for the final one, when the `readyState` property changes from 3 (loading) to 4 (complete). However, a `readyState` of 4 does *not* mean that the request was successful. It indicates only that all operations have been completed. You must still check the `status` property to gain insight to the success of the request. The server could have encountered an error during the processing of the request, for example. If the `status` property has the integer value of 200 (OK), then the request was successful and any expected response should be available in `responseXML` or `responseText`. If this seems a bit confusing, that's okay: you'll be diving into some code next and it should all come together.

Working with the Interfaces

Because the interface goes by different names and is instantiated one way for Internet Explorer (because the interface is an ActiveX object) and another way in Mozilla, Safari, Konqueror, and Opera, creating a request object is a little less straightforward than you might expect. The code shown here is a very basic method of working around these browser differences. If you have looked into an implementation of AJAX, you have likely seen code that looks very similar to this.

```
<script type="text/javascript">
function getXMLHTTP() {
   var req = false;
   // first, try to instantiate the native object
   if(window.XMLHttpRequest) {
      try {
         req = new XMLHttpRequest();
      }
      catch(e) {}
   }
   // otherwise, try instantiating the ActiveX
   // object for IE.
   else if(window.ActiveXObject) {
      // just because creation of ActiveX objects
      // is supported, doesn't mean the XMLHTTP
      // object is available. So, let's try it.
      try {
         // try instantiating the newer version
         req = new ActiveXObject("Msxml2.XMLHTTP");
      }
      catch(e) {
         try {
            // otherwise, try the older version
            req = new ActiveXObject("Microsoft.XMLHTTP");
         }
         catch(e) {}
      }
   }
   // req will either be the reference to the
```

```
    // interface or false on failure.
    return req;
}
</script>
```

This code hides browser differences in instantiation of the XMLHTTP and XMLHttpRequest interfaces and returns whichever version is available.

As previously described, the receipt of the response to an XMLHTTP request is handled with the firing of events and the triggering of appropriate event handlers. The next set of code offers the typical way of handling the ReadyStateChange event firing and acting on only the event in which you are interested:

```
<script type="text/javascript">
function handleReadyStateChange() {
    if (!request) return;
    // ignore unless complete readyState
    if (request.readyState == 4) {
        // Ignore unless successful.
        // You might choose to handle errors
        // rather than ignore them.
        if (request.status == 200) {
            // act on the response
            var xmlbody = request.responseXML;
            request = false;
            processResponse(xmlbody);
        }
    }
}
</script>
```

This function is assigned as the onreadystatechange handler and is called when the ReadyStateChange event is fired. It ignores all events where the readyState is not 4 (complete) and the HTTP status code is not 200 (OK). The XML body of complete and successful responses is extracted and passed to another function for processing. Note that after the XML body is retrieved, the request object is set to false. This is to avoid a browser bug in Opera where multiple ReadyStateChange events are sometimes fired when the readyState changes to 4. This could result in acting upon a single response multiple times.

Handling the Response

The code in the previous sections is relatively standard. The complexity in AJAX applications is often in interpreting the response and taking appropriate actions based on its content. Often, the appropriate actions are manipulations of the DOM via JavaScript. For example, if you issue a request to the server to check if a username is available, and the server responds with the XML response shown here, then you might wish to display a message to the user indicating that he or she needs to select a different username. You may also wish to offer suggestions based on the alternatives contained in the XML response:

```
<?xml version="1.0" encoding="UTF-8" standalone="yes"?>
<usernameresult>
    <username value="jessica" available="false" />
    <usernamealts>
        <username value="jess" available="true" />
```

```
            <username value="jessica2005" available="true" />
            <username value="jessie" available="true" />
        </usernamealts>
</usernameresult>
```

In this XML response, the server has indicated the unavailability of a username. Additionally, the server has suggested variations of the username that are available.

One way you might accomplish conveying this information to the user is by opening a dialog box with JavaScript's alert() function. However, a more user-friendly method might be adding a DIV or UL element in a certain part of the page using DOM manipulations. This offers a less intrusive form of messaging and would allow the user to continue with whatever interaction he is having with your application and tend to the message at his leisure. The following code offers an example of how the XML tree can be traversed and acted upon appropriately:

```javascript
<script type="text/javascript">
function processResponse(oXML) {
    // exit if xml is undefined or
    // doesn't have a documentElement
    if (!oXML) return;
    if (!oXML.documentElement) return;
    var doc = oXML.documentElement;
    // return a nodeList of all elements
    // named username
    var unames = doc.getElementsByTagName('username');
    var msgs = new Array();
    // iterate through the username nodeList
    for (var i=0; i<unames.length; i++) {
        var u = unames.item(i);
        var username = u.getAttribute('value');
        var availability = u.getAttribute('available');
        // make the available attribute
        // more user-friendly
        if (availability == 'true') {
            availability = 'available';
        }
        else {
            availability = 'not available';
        }
        msgs[msgs.length] = 'Username '+ username
            +' is '+ availability;
    }
    // create an unordered list element
    ul = document.createElement('ul');
    ul.id = 'msg';
    // for each message, create a list item
    // element and a text node containing
    // the message. The text node is a child
    // node of the list item element, and the
    // the list item is a child node of the
    // unordered list element.
    for (var k=0; k<msgs.length; k++) {
        var li = document.createElement('li');
```

```
                var txt = document.createTextNode(msgs[k]);
                li.appendChild(txt);
                ul.appendChild(li);
            }
            // obtain a reference to the maindiv element
            // and insert our new unordered list just before it
            var maindiv = document.getElementById('maindiv');
            maindiv.parentNode.insertBefore(ul,maindiv);
        }
    </script>
```

This function processes the XML from the request's `responseXML` property and adds a `UL` element to the DOM.

As you can see, DOM manipulations can be quite complex. The nice thing about this particular response is that you collect username elements regardless of their position in the XML response. Often, you cannot do this directly and you must have an idea of the expected structure of the XML response, or at least where various elements correspond to other elements. This can cause problems if the XML format is ever amended. Attaching response handlers at the XML *element* level, as opposed to the response level, shows some promise in abstracting the details of the whole XML document, allowing the client-side script to focus on the local structure relevant for that particular DOM manipulation.

For example, you might wish to show alternative usernames in a separate DOM element, in which case you would need to differentiate between username elements that do or do not have a parent element of `usernamealts`. However, you would not need to know how the rest of the XML document is structured and where in the document tree these username elements are located. Implementing this idea would require a mapping between XML element name and handler function. The details of such an implementation are beyond the scope of this chapter, but there are articles available that delve deeper into the subject.

AJAX Libraries

If this all seems overwhelming, do not fear. Because AJAX as a development method isn't exactly new, there are plenty of libraries available that can take care of the dirty work. Recently, with renewed interest in AJAX, the number of available libraries has been increasing dramatically and existing libraries have been maturing rapidly.

SAJAX

SAJAX (`http://www.modernmethod.com/sajax/`) is the Simple AJAX Toolkit, and has a server-side implementation in PHP (among many other languages). Essentially, using this library, you can define functions in PHP and call them from the client via XMLHTTP request. To enable a given function for remote procedure call requires only one SAJAX function call: `sajax_export('phpFunctionName')`.

Unfortunately, SAJAX does not help when it comes to the necessary DOM manipulations. In fact, because SAJAX treats the response as text and inserts the response directly into the document using the `innerHTML` property of a given element (which is often considered inferior to DOM manipulations), DOM manipulations are not possible unless you implement your own string parsing algorithm. On the SAJAX frequently asked questions page (`http://www.modernmethod.com/sajax/faq.phtml`), the developers list "Not overly abstract" as a feature. Many aspects of XMLHTTP communication could benefit greatly from abstraction, so you might consider SAJAX's lack thereof as a drawback. Still, SAJAX offers a method of simplifying the server-side handling AJAX requests from the client and the client-side handling of instantiating XMLHTTP request objects and issuing necessary requests.

CPAINT

CPAINT (`http://cpaint.sourceforge.net/`) is the Cross-Platform Asynchronous Interface Toolkit. It supports both plaint-text and XML response types. Additionally, it has some support for retrieving responses directly as JavaScript objects. The library is mature and actively developed.

CPAINT generates the XML for you from function calls, and the result is a somewhat non-semantic structure. Also, for some unknown reason, the generated XML elements are all in uppercase. If the name you supply for an element is not in full uppercase, the library converts it to full uppercase. The documentation of library usage is a little tough to get through, but each part of the puzzle is explained well and a trivial example is given for each to help you grasp the idea.

JPSPAN

The primary goal of JPSPAN (`http://jpspan.sourceforge.net`) is to bridge the gap between JavaScript and PHP. It allows for seamless importing of PHP classes to JavaScript. This means that you can define a class in PHP and call its methods as if it were a native JavaScript object. Behind the scenes, JPSPAN is issuing requests to the server to execute methods remotely. Other libraries offer similar functionality, but they do not come close to the abstraction offered by JPSPAN. Documentation and example code for JPSPAN are abundant and clear. Both are in wiki format and are thus ever-growing. The code itself is clean and easy to read, just like the XML it generates. Furthermore, initial work is currently under development to embed JPSPAN in PHP frameworks to make it even easier to develop fat-client applications.

The library does not offer relief from DOM manipulation tasks, but it does abstract the usage of XML-HTTP quite well. Unfortunately, it seems to have problems supporting Opera, but it supports Mozilla-based browsers and Microsoft's IE quite well. Additionally, depending on your application, a bridge between JavaScript and PHP might not do you a lot of good, and only serve to exchange XML tree traversal with object and native JavaScript accesses. As there is additional overhead involved in creating the native JavaScript versions of PHP classes, the benefits might not outweigh the costs. However, because of the excellent use of abstraction, JPSPAN could allow you to almost completely ignore the details of how PHP classes are being made available to JavaScript and focus attention on the functionality of the application itself.

There are many other AJAX libraries that support PHP. You can learn more about various AJAX libraries at `http://www.ajaxpatterns.org/AJAXFrameworks`.

When Not to Use AJAX

The explosive interest in AJAX is somewhat of a double-edged sword. There was a similar boom in the use of Macromedia's Flash product. Clients were asking for it because it looked cool. Just as with Flash, AJAX introduces usability and accessibility concerns, many of which are solved problems in traditional web applications.

For example, AJAX applications exist in one URI namespace. In other words, the URI doesn't change when the user interacts with the application. This makes sense, as that's one of the main selling points of AJAX: the ability to change application state without refreshing the current page or moving to a different page. However, this renders the browser's back button useless and might even cause the user to navigate from your application altogether.

In 1999 Jakob Nielsen, a well-known usability expert, issued an article indicating the top ten mistakes of web design. The number one mistake was disrupting the functionality of the browser's back button. According to Nielsen, the back button is the "second-most used navigation feature" after the use of hyperlinks. Workarounds do exist to partially replicate back-button functionality.

Another related usability problem has to do with the inability to bookmark a specific application state. In traditional applications, an application state is often unique to a single URI and can therefore be bookmarked. An example of this is when a user navigates a product catalog to a detail page of a specific product. The user might want to bookmark this page for later viewing. Additionally, the user might want to have a friend look at the product and attempt to send the URI over email. Breaking this bookmarking feature can have a significant impact on the effectiveness of word-of-mouth advertising. Workarounds exist that allow for one half of the equation, taking a given URI and forwarding it to your AJAX application to reconstruct the desired application state. However, because for any given state, the address bar does not contain this URI, this method still leaves the problem of communicating to the user how exactly to bookmark the current application state. The browser's bookmarking feature is useless and the application must provide some other means of bookmarking, usually involving a nonstandard user interface element.

Work that tries to solve these usability and accessibility problems is constantly underway and advances *are* being made. However, the question that is often overlooked is: Is the usability problem to the result of an inappropriate use of the technology? This was the case with usability problems with Flash: developers were trying to implement entire web-based applications with a Flash file. It was this misuse, not the Flash technology itself, that resulted in usability problems. The same is the case with misuse of AJAX. The technology does a *wonderful* job with an application where it doesn't make a whole lot of sense to restore a given application state. Google's GMail is an excellent example of this. There is very little value in being able to bookmark a given state in a web-based email client. Form additions, such as Google Suggest, are another good example. There is no need to bookmark a state in Google Suggest. A web-based chat client would also not benefit much at all from the ability to bookmark a specific application state. In contrast, a product catalog suffers greatly if the ability to bookmark a state is disrupted. The usability of a content management system would suffer greatly if the display of a given article could not be bookmarked.

The temptation to apply AJAX techniques to any traditional web application is understandable. However, many traditional web applications would be *harmed* by the use of AJAX. The commonality among applications that naturally tend to benefit from AJAX is that they are traditionally *desktop* applications. GMail is a web-based version of an email client, which has previously performed best as a desktop application (indeed, the only real reason traditional web applications for email came about was the ability to access it from anywhere). Google Suggest acts very much like form controls that have traditionally been found in desktop applications. With the exception of Java applet and similar solutions, chat applications have been almost exclusively desktop applications. Developers have attempted to make pure markup and JavaScript versions of chat applications, but these applications do not compare to their native counterparts.

While there are certainly exceptions, a good rule of thumb is that AJAX is good for taking traditional desktop applications or elements and creating a web-based version. It opens up *new* possibilities for web applications, but does not necessarily benefit traditional possibilities. You should take care when deciding whether to use AJAX and ask yourself whether AJAX will be *beneficial* for the application you are developing. If you are running into serious usability problems that require elaborate workarounds, chances are that AJAX was not the appropriate development model.

In addition to the usability problems, there are the problems of support. Having an application that relies on AJAX without any fallback support for older browsers can block out a very large portion of your potential user base. Even for current browsers, some corporations require JavaScript to be partially or fully disabled for security reasons. Such users would also be blocked out of your application, if it does not degrade well and offer traditional web application functionality as a safety net. Whether this is acceptable will depend on the nature of your application, because with some applications it is not practical to offer a traditional version. Its acceptability will also depend on your expected audience and their likely choice of browser.

Further Information

Further information about the topics discussed in this chapter can be found in the following resources:

❑ Dynamic HTML and XML: The XMLHttpRequest Object. Apple, Inc.
<http://developer.apple.com/internet/webcontent/xmlhttpreq.html>

❑ XMLHTTP: Wikipedia, the free encyclopedia.
<http://en.wikipedia.org/wiki/XMLHttpRequest>

❑ AJAX: Wikipedia, the free encyclopedia. <http://en.wikipedia.org/wiki/AJAX>

❑ XMLHttpRequest: XULPlanet.com.
<http://xulplanet.com/references/objref/XMLHttpRequest.html>

❑ XML Extras: The Mozilla Foundation. <http://www.mozilla.org/xmlextras/>

❑ AJAX Patterns: <http://www.ajaxpatterns.org/>

❑ AJAX Matters: <http://www.ajaxmatters.com/>

Summary

In this chapter, you learned how to use AJAX to push much of the processing of web applications onto the client. You also learned that AJAX isn't some new trend, but is in fact the outgrowth of several older techniques, each of which has some drawbacks that make them less than ideal. This chapter showed you how to use the AJAX interfaces, and how to handle the responses from the client. It also touched on some of the AJAX libraries you can use, and even discussed the situations where you shouldn't use it.

12

Caching Engines

You've done your best to clean up your code and reduce processing load in your PHP scripts, but you just can't seem to make your pages fast enough to keep your users happy. Time to throw in the towel? Not quite—there's more performance you can get out of your LAMP setup, and caching engines will help you do this.

When dealing with different caching solutions for PHP5, you have a handful of choices. A couple of setups actually cache the internally compiled PHP scripts, others cache the generated output, and others still cache the intermediate data processing objects. This chapter introduces you to several caching engines, and can help you decide which one is right for you.

Alternative PHP Cache

Alternative PHP Cache, or APC, is a PHP opcode caching engine, now provided for free as part of the PECL/PEAR repository. APC originated with Daniel Cowgill and George Schlossnagle, and was released by Community Connect, Inc. After the release of PHP5, Yahoo! modified APC to support the new Zend Engine, and it has since become part of PECL.

APC works by taking the compiled code from the PHP runtime engine and storing it in shared memory for later access. Each time a script is downloaded, APC checks for a version in shared memory first, before recompiling and executing the script that resides on disk. Because PHP doesn't need to recompile the script each time, it can greatly speed up the response time—speed increases of over four times or greater can be obtained in some situations.

APC can be installed as either a dynamic shared object (DSO), or built into PHP statically. The following section shows you how to install the DSO version, as it doesn't require you to recompile PHP, and provides the flexibility to add or remove the DSO at will.

Installing APC

First, grab a copy of the latest version of the APC source code from the PECL website: `http://pecl.php.net/package/APC`.

Once you have a copy of the source code in tar/gzip format, extract the package and change directory into the newly created source folder:

```
tar -xvzf APC-3.0.5.tgz
cd APC-3.0.5
```

Next, run `phpize` in the source folder. Be sure to use the correct path to your installed copy of `phpize` that comes with PHP:

```
/usr/local/bin/phpize
```

When `phpize` is running, you should see output similar to the following:

```
Configuring for:
PHP Api Version:        20031224
Zend Module Api No:     20041030
Zend Extension Api No:  220040412
```

After `phpize` is finished, run the following configure script, again substituting the proper path to your `php-config` and `apxs` programs:

```
./configure \
--enable-apc \
--enable-apc-mmap \
--with-apxs=/usr/local/apache2/bin/apxs \
--with-php-config=/usr/local/bin/php-config
```

Then, build the shared object:

```
make
```

After it is done building, install the DSO (as root):

```
make install
```

At this point, there should be a copy of apc.so in your PHP extensions folder.

To complete the installation, add the following to the extensions section of your php.ini file, and then restart Apache:

```
extension="apc.so"
```

Configuring APC

In most situations, the default configuration that APC uses should suffice, but if you want to tweak your caching to suit your needs or system, you can use the following directives in php.ini:

Directive	Default	Set In	Description
apc.enabled	1 (enabled)	php.ini, httpd.conf, .htaccess, and user scripts	Enables or disables APC using the values 1 or 0, correspondingly. When in php.ini, this setting is really only useful if APC is statically compiled into PHP—when installing APC as you did earlier, you can simply comment out the extension= "apc.so" line. This setting is, however, changeable in user scripts and .htaccess files, so you can use it to enable/disable the caching engine in individual scripts and directories.
apc.shm_segments	1	php.ini and httpd.conf	Using numeric values, you can specify the number of shared memory segments used by APC. Many operating systems have a limit, often low, on how large each shared memory segment can become. If APC is running out of memory, increasing this value will cause APC to use more segments, to help get around operating system limitations.
apc.shm_size	30	php.ini and httpd.conf	The size of the APC shared memory segment, in MB. Depending on the operating system, there may be size limitations, often low. Check your operating system documentation for more information about its shared memory segment size.
apc.optimization	0 (off)	php.ini, httpd.conf, .htaccess, and user scripts	An experimental setting, this directive controls APC's built-in optimizer. The aggressiveness of the optimizer increases as the value for this setting increases. A value of 0 disables optimization altogether.
apc.num_files_hint	1000	php.ini and httpd.conf	This setting provides APC with a hint about how many separate source files your website serves on a regular basis.
apc.ttl	0	php.ini and httpd.conf	Defines the number of seconds each cache entry is allowed to persist in the cache before a newer entry is allowed to overwrite it. If left at 0, the cache can fill up with stale entries, preventing newer entries from being cached.
apc.gc_ttl	3600	php.ini and httpd.conf	Defines the number of seconds each cache entry remains on the garbage-collection list. Serves as a failsafe in situations where a server process dies, leaving a cached file stranded in the cache. A value of 0 disables this feature.

Table continued on following page

Directive	Default	Set In	Description
apc.cache_by_default	On	php.ini and httpd.conf	Controls the caching of all files. Use this directive to disable by-default caching of all scripts, allowing you to use the following `apc.filters` directive to gain greater control over which files are actually cached.
apc.filters	"" (empty string)	php.ini and httpd.conf	Lets you define a comma-delimited list of regular expressions used to filter which files are cached. Using POSIX extended regular expressions — similar to PHP's `ereg` functions — you specify a list of regular expressions to exclude certain scripts from caching. Any filename that matches a pattern in the list will not be cached, unless the pattern begins with a +, in which case they will be cached by APC. When creating the regular expressions, assume relative filename paths, not absolute paths.
apc.slam_defense	0 (disabled)	php.ini and httpd.conf	Defined using numbers 0 through 100, this directive specifies the probability that a server process will skip caching a previously uncached file. Used primarily on extremely busy web servers, `apc.slam_defense` is used to combat a race condition when multiple server threads try to cache the same file at the same time.

Removing APC

If there comes a time that you no longer want APC after you've installed it, you can follow these simple steps to remove it from your PHP installation.

First, search for and delete the `extension="apc.so"` line from your php.ini file. Alternatively, you can just comment it out:

```
;extension="apc.so"
```

At this point, you can restart Apache, and APC will no longer be active in PHP. If you wanted to completely obliterate the DSO from your machine, you can delete the apc.so file from your PHP extensions directory once Apache has been restarted.

eAccelerator

eAccelerator is another compiled-state PHP caching engine, similar to APC. eAccelerator is a fork of the popular TurckMMCache caching engine for PHP4, and is a free encoder and optimizer currently maintained by Frank Alcantara and a team of SourceForge programmers.

In addition to being a PHP optimizer and caching engine, you can use eAccelerator to encode your PHP scripts, so you can redistribute the encoded version to clients that have eAccelerator installed, without fear of source code snooping.

As with other PHP encoding solutions, when files are encoded using eAccelerator, they are nearly impossible to decrypt using standard tools. They can, however, be reverse-engineered using debuggers and disassemblers on the PHP engine itself, but usually such an effort is not warranted by the possible reward.

Installing eAccelerator

Like APC, eAccelerator can be installed as a DSO, using the following process. First, download a copy of the source code, available at `http://eaccelerator.net/`.

Unfortunately, at this time eAccelerator is not compatible with the CGI binary version of PHP. If you run the CGI binary version, this section is for information purposes only.

Extract the tarball that you downloaded, and then go into the newly created directory:

```
tar -xvzf eaccelerator-0.9.3.tar.gz
cd eaccelerator-0.9.3
```

Run your copy of `phpize` in this directory (again, change paths accordingly):

```
/usr/local/bin/phpize
```

Then, configure the source, and build the binaries:

```
./configure \
--enable-eaccelerator=shared \
--with-php-config=/usr/local/bin/php-config
make
```

After the build completes, install the DSOs, as root:

```
make install
```

Next, you need to provide a place for eAccelerator to put temporary files. Create an `eaccelerator` directory in the /tmp folder:

```
mkdir /tmp/eaccelerator
chmod 0777 /tmp/eaccelerator
```

Finally, add the following to php.ini, and then restart Apache:

```
extension="eaccelerator.so"
```

Configuring eAccelerator

Like APC, the default options will probably suffice in most situations, but if not, you have access to the following php.ini directives:

Directive	Default	Set In	Description
eaccelerator.shm_size	0	php.ini and httpd.conf	Defines the amount, in megabytes, of shared memory that eAccelerator will use to cache scripts. A value of 0 tells eAccelerator to use the operating system defaults.
eaccelerator.cache_dir	/tmp/ eaccelerator	php.ini and httpd.conf	Specifies the directory to use for the disk cache, if eAccelerator is configured to use on-disk caching.
eaccelerator.enable	1 (enabled)	php.ini, httpd.conf, .htaccess, and user scripts	Allows enabling and disabling of eAccelerator using the numeric values 1 and 0, correspondingly. This setting is changeable in user scripts and .htaccess files, so you can use it to enable/disable the caching engine in individual scripts and directories.
eaccelerator.optimizer	1 (enabled)	php.ini, httpd.conf, .htaccess, and user scripts	Enables eAccelerator's internal code optimization engine. A value of 1 enables the optimizer, and 0 disables it. This setting is changeable in user scripts and .htaccess files, so you can use it to enable/disable the optimization engine in individual scripts and directories.
eaccelerator.debug	0 (off)	php.ini and httpd.conf	Toggles debug logging on and off.
eaccelerator .check_mtime	1	php.ini and httpd.conf	This setting controls whether or not eAccelerator checks the modification time of a file to see if it has been changed. An enabled value of 1 tells eAccelerator to automatically recompile a PHP script if it has been changed.
eaccelerator.filter	"" (empty string)	php.ini, httpd.conf, .htaccess, and user scripts.	This directive allows you to specify a space-delimited list indicating which files should and should not be processed by eAccelerator. The list consists of simple filenames with wildcard matches (for example, `"*.php *.phtml"`). To ignore a specific matched item, prefix the related pattern with an exclamation point.

Directive	Default	Set In	Description
eaccelerator .shm_max	0 (no limit)	php.ini and httpd.conf	Specifies the maximum size for data put into shared memory using the `eaccelerator_put()` PHP function. Numeric values are specified in bytes, and a value of 0 disables the limit.
eaccelerator.shm_ttl	0 (never remove stale scripts)	php.ini and httpd.conf	Defines how many seconds a script will stay cached by eAccelerator in shared memory before it is allowed to be removed from the cache in favor of new requests. A value of 0 indicates that items should never be removed, and could cause the shared memory cache to eventually fill and prevent new requests from being cached.
eaccelerator.shm_ prune_period	0 (never remove stale items)	php.ini and httpd.conf	Similar to the `shm_ttl` setting, this directive controls the collection of stale scripts from the shared memory cache. Instead of acting as a timeout for individual scripts in the cache, `shm_prune_period` works by removing stale items only if the value defined in `shm_prune_period` has elapsed. This value is expressed in number of seconds, and a value of 0 tells eAccelerator not to try to remove stale items.
eaccelerator .shm_only	0 (use both)	php.ini and httpd.conf	Enables and disables (0 or 1) the on-disk cache. A value of 0 tells eAccelerator to use both a shared memory and file-based disk cache, whereas a value of 1 tells eAccelerator to use shared memory only.
eaccelerator .compress	1 (enable compression)	php.ini, httpd.conf, .htaccess, and user scripts	This directive enables and disables output content compression, similar to Apache's mod_deflate or PHP's gzip output buffering.
eaccelerator .compress_level	9 (maximum compression)	php.ini, httpd.conf, .htaccess, and user scripts	This setting controls the level of compression used when using the output compression enabled in `eaccelerator.compress`. The maximum value of 9 uses high compression, resulting in smaller transferred file sizes, while lower values decrease compression and increase transferred size.

Table continued on following page

Directive	Default	Set In	Description
eaccelerator.sessions eaccelerator.content		php.ini and httpd.conf	You can tell eAccelerator where you want it to store session data and content with this directive. A value of `shm_and_disk` tells the caching engine to store session data and content in both shared memory and disk locations. Set it to `shm`, and it will use shared memory as a primary storage location, falling back to disk storage if shared memory is full. `shm_only` indicates you want to use only shared memory and never use an on-disk fallback. The value `disk_only` behaves the exact opposite way: it indicates you want to use only on-disk storage and no shared memory.

Removing eAccelerator

Removing eAccelerator is as simple as deleting or commenting-out the appropriate extension line in php.ini, like so:

```
;extension="accelerator.so"
```

To permanently remove eAccelerator from the system, delete the eaccelerator.so file from the PHP extensions directory.

For more information on eAccelerator, visit `http://eaccelerator.net`.

Zend Optimizer

Not to be outdone by the handful of free PHP caching solutions available, Zend—the creators of the Zend Engine that powers PHP—have released their own code optimizer, and it's free. The Zend Optimizer acts in a similar manner to APC and eAccelerator: it caches the compiled state of PHP scripts, enabling faster execution on subsequent requests.

In addition to accelerating the performance of PHP scripts, Zend Optimizer also allows you to run scripts encoded by Zend Encoder or Zend SafeGuard Suite on the server.

Installing Zend Optimizer

Installing the Zend Optimizer is a bit easier than the majority of competing caching solutions, as it comes with a handy configuration and setup wizard.

First, download the package appropriate for your system from `http://zend.com/store/products/zend-optimizer.php`.

Then, decompress the archive, and go into the newly created directory:

```
tar -xvzf ZendOptimizer-2.5.10a-linux-glibc21-i386.tar.gz
cd ZendOptimizer-2.5.10a-linux-glibc21-i386
```

As root, run the install wizard:

```
./install.sh
```

Run through the wizard, specifying the necessary paths when prompted. The defaults provided usually suffice. Make sure you choose the proper version of Apache when asked (this book was written around Apache 2).

The wizard will make a backup copy of your php.ini file, and create a new symbolic link pointing to the Zend-modified php.ini file.

At the end of the wizard, you can choose to have Apache automatically restarted, or if you so choose, exit the wizard and restart Apache manually.

Configuring Zend Optimizer

Like APC and eAccelerator, you have a couple of directives at your disposal for tweaking the operation of the Zend Optimizer:

Directive	Default	Set in	Description
zend_optimizer .optimization_level	15 (all optimizations)	php.ini and httpd.conf	Determines the level of optimization performed by Zend Optimizer. The optimizer can perform four distinct passes on each script, controlled by combining the following values: 0 : No passes 1 : Pass 1 2 : Pass 2 4 : Pass 3 8 : Pass 4 You simply add the numbers for each pass together to get your optimization pass settings. For example, a value of 11 will perform Pass 1, Pass 2, and Pass 4 (1+2+8).
zend_optimizer .enable_loader	1 (enabled)	php.ini and httpd.conf	You can use this directive to enable or disable the Zend Optimizer without uninstalling it. A value of 0 disables the Optimizer; 1 enables it.

Removing Zend Optimizer

To remove Zend Optimizer, you must first delete the symbolic link it created for php.ini. Then, restore the backed-up original php.ini file to its former location. At this point you can restart Apache, and the Zend Optimizer will no longer be active. If you like, you can delete the Zend Optimizer files — their default location is /usr/local/Zend.

JPCache

Another entry in the field of memory/disk caching solutions is JPCache. Unlike APC and eAccelerator, JPCache does not need to be compiled as a DSO or statically built into PHP itself. JPCache is actually written in PHP and is used with standard `include` and `require` statements.

JPCache works by storing the generated output of a PHP script to disk or in a SQL server, instead of saving the compiled state of each script. By caching the output in this manner, coupled with gzip content compression, you can achieve up to 80% or more bandwidth savings.

Installing JPCache

To get started with JPCache, the first thing you need to do is download a copy of the latest version at `http://www.jpcache.com`.

Next, extract the tar/gzip archive:

```
tar -xvzf jpcache.v2.tgz
```

The contents of this directory now contain the scripts you'll need to use JPCache. Place this folder wherever you like, as long it is accessible by the user Apache runs as. Make note of the full path to the location, as you'll need it when configuring the cache.

In the base directory of your JPCache folder, edit the jpcache.php file. Change the following line to point to the location where you placed the jpcache folder:

```
$includedir = "/path/to/jpcache-files";
```

For example, if you moved the extracted jpcache folder to /www/jpcache, you'd use the following value:

```
$includedir = "/www/jpcache";
```

Next, edit the jpcache-config.php file. Most important, you'll need to uncomment the line indicating what type of cache storage you wish to use (file or MySQL). For this example, uncomment the file-based storage option:

```
$JPCACHE_TYPE = "file";
```

Another setting to change is the $JPCACHE_USE_GZIP value. This enables gzip content compression, but unfortunately because of a bug in recent versions of JPCache, the output can be corrupted in certain browsers. For safety's sake, set this value to 0:

```
$JPCACHE_USE_GZIP = 0;
```

Also note the setting that controls the location of the file cache, $JPCACHE_DIR, which by default is /tmp/jpcache. You're going to need to actually create the folder listed in the $JPCACHE_DIR setting, so execute the following at the command prompt:

```
mkdir /tmp/jpcache
chmod 0777 /tmp/jpcache
```

Finally, test the cache system using the following PHP script, using an appropriate path to where you put the JPCache folder:

```
<?php

require "/path/to/jpcache.php";
echo time();
phpinfo();

?>
```

Notice the UNIX timestamp at the top of the page. Each time you reload the page, it should stay the same—JPCache is serving up the cached version instead of re-processing the script each time.

Configuring JPCache

In addition to the three configuration options mentioned previously, you have fourteen additional configuration variables you can alter to suit your needs. The full list of configuration options is as follows:

Configuration Option	Default	Description
$JPCACHE_TYPE	None—You *must* set this variable before using JPCache.	To tell JPCache to use either file-based or database storage for the cache data, you use $JPCACHE_TYPE. A value of file tells JPCache to use on-disk storage, whereas a value of mysql causes the cache data to be stored in a MySQL database.
$JPCACHE_TIME	900	Defined using numeric values, this variable tells JPCache how long, in seconds, to keep a page in the cache. Negative values disable page caching entirely, whereas a value of 0 tells JPCache to keep pages cached indefinitely.

Table continued on following page

Configuration Option	Default	Description
$JPCACHE_DEBUG	0 (off)	Using 0 for off and 1 for on, $JPCACHE_DEBUG controls whether or not to enable debugging.
$JPCACHE_IGNORE_DOMAIN	1 (ignore domain)	If your web server serves up only one set of content, you can set this value to 1 (on) to have JPCache ignore any domain name prefix for a filename. When turned off, JPCache searches the cache for files matching the complete URL, including the domain name.
$JPCACHE_ON	1 (enabled)	This variable simply controls whether JPCache is enabled or not.
$JPCACHE_USE_GZIP	1 (on)	To enable GZIP output compression, similar to Apache's mod_deflate or PHP's own GZIP output buffering, set this value to 1. Be advised that because of a bug in recent versions of JPCache, output can become corrupted in certain browsers when using JPCache's GZIP compression. If your scripts return garbled or missing content with this enabled, try disabling this setting to see if the situation is corrected.
$JPCACHE_POST	0 (disabled)	This variable controls HTTP POST caching in JPCache. Set to 0 to disable, 1 to enable.
$JPCACHE_GC	1	To control the aggressiveness of JPCache's garbage collection routine, you can assign numeric values to $JPCACHE_GC. Values range from 0 to 100, and indicate the percentage of probability that garbage collection will occur for a cached item.
$JPCACHE_GZIP_LEVEL	9 (maximum compression)	When using JPCache's built-in GZIP output compression, you can use this variable to control the compression level of the output stream. Values range from 9, meaning high compression and lower output size, to 1, being lower compression and larger transferred size.
$JPCACHE_CLEANKEYS	1 (hash storage keys)	When JPCache makes a cached copy of script output, it stores the output in either a filename or database record using a unique key for each script. By default, JPCache hashes the identifier to make it difficult to determine a given cache entry's source, something like "jpc-b4e58b8d86b8228580 23bf8e061401a2." If desired, you can tell JPCache to not hash the cache identifier for each script, allowing you to easily determine the identity of each cached script. With hashing disables, script identifiers will look more like _directory_file name_extension_HTTPmethod=n_n___.

Configuration Option	Default	Description
$JPCACHE_DIR	/tmp/jpcache	The directory where JPCache stores its file-based cache data is set with this variable. The location where JPCache stores the cached files needs to be writeable by the Apache process user.
$JPCACHE_FILEPREFIX	jpc-	When JPCache creates cache files in the on-disk cache, it can use a filename prefix, specified here, to avoid conflicts with existing files.
$JPCACHE_DB_HOST	localhost	When using a database as your cache storage location, you'll need to set variables for JPCache to use when connecting to and using the database. This variable sets the database host to which JPCache will connect.
$JPCACHE_DB_DATABASE	jpcache	This variable sets the name of the MySQL database where the cache data will be stored.
$JPCACHE_DB_USERNAME	sqluser	To set the username used when storing the cache information in the database, set `$JPCACHE_DB_USERNAME`.
$JPCACHE_DB_PASSWORD	passwd	Used in conjunction with `$JPCACHE_DB_USERNAME`, this variable sets the database connection password.

$JPCACHE_DB_TABLE	CACHEDATA	The name of the table that the JPCache cache data is stored in `$JPCACHE_DB_TABLE`.
		To create the table, you can execute the following command in the MySQL Monitor or your preferred MySQL administration tool:
		`CREATE TABLE CACHEDATA (`
		`  CACHEKEY varchar(255) NOT NULL,`
		`  CACHEEXPIRATION int(11) NOT NULL,`
		`  GZDATA blob,`
		`  DATASIZE int(11),`
		`  DATACRC int(11),`
		`  PRIMARY KEY (CACHEKEY)`
		`);`
		Of course, you'll need to change the name of the database table to match whatever value you specify in `$JPCACHE_DB_TABLE`, and vice versa.

$JPCACHE_OPTIMIZE	1 (perform OPTIMIZE TABLE)	After a garbage collection cycle completes, you can instruct JPCache to perform an automatic MySQL OPTIMIZE TABLE command on the table specified in `$JPCACHE_DB_TABLE`.

Removing JPCache

To remove JPCache, you'll need to search through all of your PHP scripts and remove any `include` or `require` references to the jpcache.php file. After removing the references, you can safely delete the JPCache directory.

For more information on JPCache, visit `http://www.jpcache.com`.

memcached

Unlike the output-caching systems provided by APC, eAccelerator, and JPCache, the memcached system relies on the caching of backend objects for its speed boost. memcached is a distributed memory object caching system created by Danga Interactive, the group responsible for LiveJournal.com. Instead of caching the page output or the compiled PHP opcodes, memcached caches various code objects, most importantly, database result objects and data-model entities.

This caching solution is a bit different than any of the other systems in this chapter — memcached actually requires its own daemon to be running at all times. PHP can then use its memcached function set to access and use the in-memory object cache.

Installing memcached

To install memcached, first grab a copy of the daemon source code from `http://www.danga.com/memcached/`.

Then extract the tar/gzip archive, and change directory into the newly created folder:

```
tar -xvzf memcached-1.1.12.tar.gz
cd memcached-1.1.12
```

Next configure and build the source. If configure reports any missing libraries, such as libevent, download and install those per their individual instructions; then re-run the configure script, and then build memcached.

```
./configure
make
```

Then, as root, install the memcache daemon:

```
make install
```

The last thing you'll need to do is actually start the daemon. The following command starts the daemon using 128MB of RAM, listening on port 11211 on the IP 127.0.0.1:

```
/usr/local/bin/memcached -d -m 128 -l 127.0.0.1 -p 11211
```

If you decide to use memcached permanently, make sure you add the command to start memcached to whatever startup facilities or script you prefer, so it loads automatically every time the machine boots.

Now that you've got the memcache daemon running, you need to prepare PHP to use the caching system. Download the memcached PECL module from `http://pecl.php.net/package/memcache`.

Extract the archive and move into the new directory:

```
tar -xvzf memcache-1.4.tgz
cd memcache-1.4
```

Run `phpize`, and then configure and make the DSO:

```
phpize
./configure
make
```

Install the module, as root:

```
make install
```

Finally, add the following line to your php.ini, and restart Apache:

```
extension="memcache.so"
```

Using memcached

In order to use memcached, the PHP DSO you installed provides the following methods for the `Memcache` object:

❑ Memcache::add

bool **Memcache::add** (string key, mixed var [, int flag [, int expire]])

This method adds a variable or object into memory cache, identified by the token `key`. If a value with the same `key` already exists in the memory cache, `FALSE` is returned. If you want to compress the value to be stored before putting it into the memory cache, supply `MEMCACHE_COMPRESSED` as the flag, otherwise it can be omitted or set to 0. Any value provided for `expire` tells memcached when to start allowing an item to be removed from the cache. A value of 0 for `expire` indicates that the value should be cached indefinitely.

Only variables and objects can be stored in the memory cache, whereas resources cannot.

❑ Memcache::close

bool Memcache::close (void)

This method closes any non-persistent connection to the memcached server. If an error occurs when closing the connection, `FALSE` is returned.

## Chapter 12

❑   Memcache::connect

```
bool Memcache::connect ( string host [, int port [, int timeout]] )
```

This method creates and opens a connection to a memcached server running on host. The port parameter specifies the TCP port used by memcached, the default being 11211, and timeout specifies how long to wait when attempting to connect before returning FALSE. Returns true on success, FALSE on failure.

❑   Memcache::decrement

```
int Memcache::decrement ( string key [, int value] )
```

❑   When storing a simple numeric value in the memory cache, you can actually use the decrement() method to decrease the value matching key by the provided value. If no decrement value is specified, the cached value is decremented by 1. This method returns FALSE on failure, or the item's new value upon success.

❑   Memcache::delete

```
bool Memcache::delete (string key [, int timeout] )
```

This method deletes the item identified by key from the memory cache. Providing a value for timeout causes the item to be deleted after the provided number of seconds. Returns FALSE on failure, and TRUE on success.

❑   Memcache::flush

```
bool Memcache::flush ( void )
```

This method tells memcached to immediately set the expiration on all items in the cache. Once this method is called, any item in the cache can be overwritten by new keys, but the memory is not released until that happens. This method returns TRUE on success, or FALSE on failure.

❑   Memcache::get

```
string Memcache::get ( string key )
string Memcache::get ( array keys )
```

This method retrieves an item or items stored in the memory cache, matching the given key or array of keys. It returns either a string or array on success, depending on how many keys were provided to match against, and FALSE if no keys are found matching the input parameters.

❑   Memcache::getStats

```
array Memcache::getStats ( void )
```

This returns an array containing various bits of information regarding the status of the memory cache, such as current and total connections, number of cached items, and server uptime.

❑   Memcache::getVersion

```
string Memcache::getVersion ( void )
```

This returns a simple string with the version number of the memcached server, or FALSE if an error occurs.

❑   Memcache::increment

```
int Memcache::increment ( string key [, int value] )
```

Like the decrement() method, increment() allows you to easily change a simple numeric value directly in the memory cache — in this case, incrementing the stored variable by value, or 1 if no value is provided. Returns the new value on success, or FALSE on failure.

❑   Memcache::pconnect

```
bool Memcache::pconnect ( string host [, int port [, int timeout]] )
```

This method creates and opens a persistent connection to the memcached server, similar to a MySQL persistent connection. The parameters are the same as connect(): host specifies the memcached server hostname or IP address, port specifies the listening port for memcached, and timeout specifies the connection timeout period.

❑   Memcache::replace

```
bool Memcache::replace ( string key, mixed var [, int flag [, int expire]] )
```

This searches through the cached objects for an item matching key, and if found, replaces it with the value var. Like add() and set(), replace() can supply a flag to request compression when storing the value, and also give an optional expiration time for the new value. This method returns TRUE on success, FALSE on failure.

❑   Memcache::set

```
bool Memcache::set (string key, mixed var [, int flag [, int expire]] )
```

This stores the value var in the memory cache, even if there is a preexisting item matching key. Arguments are identical to those of add() and replace(). Returns TRUE on success, FALSE on failure.

You can use these methods in a similar manner as the MySQLi methods — you connect to the memcached server, process data in and out of the cache, and then disconnect. The following simple example stores a Circle object in the memory cache:

```php
<?php

class Circle
{
    public $radius;
    public function area()
    {
        return pi() * pow($this->radius, 2);
    }
}


$memc = new Memcache();
$memc->connect('10.0.0.20', 11211);

$c = new Circle();
```

```
$c->radius = 15;

$memc->set('circle1', $c);

$stats = $memc->getStats();

$memc->close();

print_r($stats);
?>
```

If you run this script, it will print an array containing the statistics of the memory cache at that time. If it's the first time you run the script, or first time memcached is used on your server, your curr_items value should be 1, reflecting the newly added Circle object:

```
Array
(
    [pid] => 1379
    [uptime] => 4148
    [time] => 1124758570
    [version] => 1.1.12
    [rusage_user] => 0.030000
    [rusage_system] => 0.010000
    [curr_items] => 1
    [total_items] => 8
    [bytes] => 77
    [curr_connections] => 1
    [total_connections] => 9
    [connection_structures] => 2
    [cmd_get] => 0
    [cmd_set] => 8
    [get_hits] => 0
    [get_misses] => 0
    [bytes_read] => 605
    [bytes_written] => 1856
    [limit_maxbytes] => 134217728
)
```

Removing memcached

Like the other DSO caching solutions, you can quickly disable memcache functionality by commenting-out or removing the appropriate lines from php.ini and restarting Apache. At that point you can delete memcache.so from your PHP extensions directory, and the memcached daemon from the system binary folder (wherever it was installed to earlier, most likely /usr/local/bin or /usr/bin).

Using Different Caching Engines Together

Now at this point, the gears might be turning in your head, and you start to wonder, "What happens if I used more than one caching engine simultaneously?" Well, as you might suspect, a proper choice of *complimentary* solutions can slightly increase performance, but there are certain combinations that won't do you any good.

JPCache and memcached can play well with others, but APC, eAccelerator, and the Zend Optimizer are somewhat mutually exclusive. While they might load together just fine, and not throw any errors when executing a PHP script, there's little to no reason to use a combination of opcode caches. All three in some way or another provide roughly the same functionality, so using multiple opcode caches will only result in the system being as fast as the slowest cache.

Try to pick just one opcode caching solution, and try combining it with memcached and JPCache. Throw your preferred content-compression solution into the mix — the built-in content compression in JPCache is still too buggy — and you've got a lean and mean combined-cache serving machine.

Choosing Your Caching Engine

So which caching solution is right for you? Perhaps it's best for you to first evaluate the needs of your system, and look for any places that are currently or will soon be a bottleneck. If you're struggling with heavy classes and objects zinging around your scripts, or frequently pull a large amount of repetitive data from your database, memcached will be your best bet for some performance improvements. If your website code generates relatively static pages — you're not using excessive user personalization or other highly dynamic elements — you should consider using JPCache. If the data layer is not really your bottleneck, but your PHP code could use some general performance tweaks, one of the opcode caching engines will help you out. If you're unsure which optimizer/cache to use, a safe bet would be APC. What it may lack in the low-level engine boost or optimization that Zend Optimizer may deliver, it makes up for by being highly customizable, and well-supported — it is after all, part of the PECL repository.

Summary

Regardless of which caching solution you choose, any of the systems discussed in this chapter have the potential to drastically increase the performance of your LAMP setup. With the proper care and configuration, your caching solution will allow you to serve a greater number of users concurrently, and help ward off any possible DOS or Slashdot Effect you may encounter some day.

13

Content Management Systems

A Content Management System (CMS) assists a software or Web developer in organizing and facilitating any collaborative process and its final outcome. The term "content management" loosely refers to not only the checking in and out of files, but also the generalized sharing of information, such as common calendars, wikis, and the like. The earliest Content Management Systems emerged around 1975 when mainframes and electronic publishing required really began to catch on. These earliest versions were basically nothing more than general repositories that enabled multiple users to participate in the same project.

As computer systems became more and more complex, the need to effectively manage content also becomes more complex. As the Internet came to fruition, so did the wave of CMSs. Now there are more CMSs than you can shake a stick at. The goal of this chapter is to try and wade through all the muck to help you define whether you need a CMS, which variety of CMS is right for your project, and how you can use a CMS to improve your efficiency.

Types of CMSs

CMSs come in all shapes and sizes, and can basically manage anything being worked on by a team of individuals. From managing simple static website content, to allowing collaborative documentation across the Internet (wiki), CMSs perform many functions. CMS packages can generally be classified into two categories: Enterprise CMSs and Web CMSs.

Enterprise CMSs

These high-powered software packages are usually comprehensive solutions, delivering effective content management for use on an enterprise, or corporate level. They are designed to help a corporation become more efficient and cost-effective, and increase accuracy and functionality, while decreasing human error and customer response times.

They can integrate corporate functions such as shipping and delivery systems, invoicing, employee and human resource issues, customer relations, and document management and transactional (sales) systems. Enterprise CMSs bring data management down to the user level so many users can add their individual piece to a very large integrated pie. Software companies deploying these complex systems pride themselves on offering highly customized company-wide solutions, and the software usually comes with a relatively hefty price tag.

Web CMS/Portals

Web CMS packages are mostly created for use on the web. They can incorporate numerous functions, or have one specific function they are centered around. They allow users to update portions of a common Web site or collaborate in a website "community." Web CMSs can make a developer's life easy by bringing functionality to a website quickly and easily, and allowing a lead developer to include others in site development and maintenance without fear of straying from the standards. Open source Web CMS packages will be the focus of this chapter, in particular the PHP/MySQL packages.

A subset of the Web CMS category is groupware. This type of package runs over an intranet or over the Internet and is designed to allow collaboration between users, presumably working for the same company, working on the same projects. They typically offer features such as project management, file checking in and out, calendar systems, email, and internal forums.

Open Source Web CMS Packages

Common functions of a Web CMS include:

- **Static web page updates:** Updates content without altering look and feel of site.
- **Weblogs (blogs):** Online journals.
- **Wiki:** Collaborative documentation projects.
- **Publications:** Posting and organization of news articles.
- **Managed learning environments:** Web-based learning.
- **Transactional CMS:** E-commerce functions.
- **Image and file galleries:** Compilation of images or files for public use.
- **Forums:** Bulletin board systems fostering discussions between users.
- **Chat rooms:** Real-time chatting between users.
- **RSS feeds:** Allows users to download content.
- **Polls:** Allows users to vote on a topic.
- **Calendar systems:** Web-based multi-user calendars.

There are numerous other functions that could be considered underneath the CMS realm, but these are the major ones and the ones on which this chapter focuses.

First, take a look at some of the more comprehensive open source CMS packages.

All-Inclusive Web CMSs

Like fancy tropical resorts that wrap up your vacation all into one nice neat package, these comprehensive Web CMSs can do as little or as much as you like. The following sections introduce you to some of the more popular packages available, although a myriad of these can be found on websites such as `http://www.sourceforge.net`. This text does not go into detail about installation on these packages, as you've probably had some experience in this department in the past. However, if there are any special considerations regarding installation, they will be duly noted. As well, you need to have all aspects of the LAMP system working properly before installing these packages.

Most all-inclusive Web CMSs have common functionality such as changing user permissions, modifying site layout, changing server settings, and so on. One thing that should be mentioned is that there is a lack of transactional CMS interfaces (shopping carts for e-commerce) with many of the so-called comprehensive CMS packages available.

ExponentCMS

ExponentCMS is available at `http://www.exponentcms.org`. At the time of this writing, the most current version is 0.96.3, and is what this section is based on. On the Exponent/Sourceforge interface at `http://sourceforge.net/projects/exponent/`, you can find links to screenshots, documentation, contributions, and the standard Sourceforge information.

Installation Notes

Installation is relatively simple, and the only thing you need to know before installation is that you will need to create a database. This applies to both remote and local installations. You will also need to have a user and password set up, as you will be asked to supply all that information during the installation process.

General Overview/Default Installation

Installing this CMS gives you several features that are "active" by default. These are:

- **Address Book:** Organizes contact information.
- **Admin Control Panel:** Easy-to-use interface for administering the site.
- **Calendar System:** Keeps track of events with different views.
- **Contact Form:** Allows visitors to the site to contact you.
- **Image Manager:** Works with other modules to manage images on the site.
- **Preview Link:** Lets those working on the site preview their work.
- **Private Messaging Center:** Allows users to send emails or private messages to one another.
- **Resource Manager:** Organizes and displays uploaded files.
- **Text Module:** Displays text and keeps track of revisions.
- **Weblog/Online Journal Manager:** Organizes blog entries.

The "inactive" features (those you can simply turn on) are:

❑ **Banner Manager:** Manages banner ad campaigns and click-throughs.

❑ **Content Rotator:** Displays different images or text to the user each time they visit the site.

❑ **Flash Animation Manager:** Organizes a Flash Animation.

❑ **Form Module:** Manages any forms on the site.

❑ **HTML Template Manager:** Manages uploaded HTML templates.

❑ **Login Module:** Allows users to log in to the site.

❑ **Multi-site Manager:** Allows you to create and manage other sites.

❑ **Navigator:** Manages the navigation system.

❑ **News Feed System:** Organizes and displays news articles.

❑ **Search:** Allows users to search the site.

❑ **UI Switcher:** Gives users with the correct permissions the ability to switch from user to administrator.

Through the easy-to-use admin Module Manager, you can activate or deactivate any of these modules with the click of a button.

Other modules are available for downloading from `http://www.sourceforge.net`. With the Extension Upload Manager, installing modules is easy; you don't even need to unzip them. These extensions include:

❑ **Article Manager:** Organizes and displays articles on the site.

❑ **Bulletin Board:** Manages site forum.

❑ **FAQ:** Manages the FAQ section of the site.

❑ **Image Gallery:** Allows users to rank and view images.

❑ **Listing Manager:** Organizes and manages listings, such as real estate listings.

❑ **Page Displayer:** Allows you to upload and display dynamically generated pages (such as PHP).

❑ **Slideshow:** Manages slideshows on the site.

Besides installing, activating, and deactivating site modules, as the site admin you can import data (such as a user list in csv format) through the admin interface. This makes it easy for you to convert from another system or from an internal database.

There is the WYSIWYG HTMLArea editor also embedded into the software, making it easy for your authors and contributors to add text. As an admin, you also have control over the HTMLArea toolbar, which lets you determine what text options your users have.

Customizing the Default Settings

Like most other CMS packages, you can alter user settings in the Admin Control Panel. With Exponent CMS, you can set approval policies based on users and content, although this CMS is module-focused as opposed to user-focused. For example, you could create an approval policy for the Calendar module only that would require at least two approvals from other admins on the site before requested changes are shown. While you can also assign permissions for a module to a user or group, it is done through each specific module, rather than the user interface. There are no various levels of user access — either a user is an admin or not. Also, while you can view which users have permissions on which module, you cannot see all the modules a single user is responsible for.

In addition, Exponent CMS gives you some control over your settings in the Configure Site area of the admin interface.

Database Settings

You can switch between MySQL and PostgreSQL, and of course alter database name, username, password, port, and any table prefix names.

Display Settings/Themes

There are several themes pre-packaged with the site, but creating your own theme is easy enough by editing the appropriate files (or creating your own from scratch). Unless you love to reinvent the wheel, our suggestion is to pick the theme that comes closest to the layout you want to go with and edit from there. There is a link at the bottom of each of the sample themes (under the Manage Themes page) that allows you to view the complete file list for that theme, making it easy for you to see which files you need to alter to fit your needs.

In this section, you can also change how other contributors to the site are referenced, and how the dates and times are shown to website visitors.

General Configuration Settings

Under this section, you can customize page titles, meta tags and keywords, and language selection. You can also turn on/off user registration, engage the CAPTCHA (Computer Automated Public Turing Test to Tell Computers and Humans Apart) test to prevent bots from registering, and control session timeouts and SSL settings.

SMTP Settings

This is the place to set your SMTP ports, username, passwords, authentication methods, and so on. You can also switch to `php_mail()` function here if you would like.

Other Add-Ons

Besides activating/deactivating pre-installed modules, and installing new modules made available, there is also a hefty list of other contributions offered up by the masses. This is available through Exponent's Sourceforge interface site at `http://www.sourceforge.net`, under the Tracker ⇨ Contributions section. It includes some pretty helpful add-ons, such as adding horizontal drop-down navigation, so by all means check it out.

Changing the Layout and Look of Modules

While it's easy to add and delete modules with ExponentCMS, it is even easier to move them around on the page. Making modules look different from one another proves to be a bit of a challenge, however.

Strengths and Weaknesses

The strengths for this package are:

❑ Changing the layout and placement of the modules proves to be an easy task and WYSIWYG in nature. In addition, you are able to break the traditional two- or three-column layout and add subcolumns to all three traditional columns.

❑ Text modules keep track of revisions, and allow you to immediately view or restore old versions with one click. It would be nice if it showed *who* made the revision, but perhaps that feature will be available in future releases.

❑ The Preview feature lets you see what effect your changes have on the look of the site, without having to log out as an admin.

❑ Themes are a bit more esoteric and design-driven, as opposed to being function-driven as in some other CMSs.

One weakness is in user administration — the admin can't see all the permissions or module responsibilities an individual user has. For example, if Bob is going to be on vacation, and you wanted to assign Bob's modules to someone else, there is no easy way to see what Bob has the ability to do and what modules he can modify.

There is a reason CMS is on Sourceforge's Top 10 "Most Active" download list. ExponentCMS is by far the easiest to administer open source CMS out there. Its strengths are more behind-the-scenes, however, as its focus is not necessarily on interactivity with the masses visiting the site, but on a core group of contributors over which the admin has control. If you're in search of a good-looking "out of the box" site, ExponentCMS should be on your list to evaluate.

XOOPS

XOOPS (eXtensible Object Oriented Portal System) is another popular comprehensive CMS available at Sourceforge, or at `http://www.xoops.org`. The most recent version is 2.1.1, and that is the version being discussing here (this is actually a pre-release to version 2.2, so keep that in mind).

Installation Notes

The XOOPS team has written a very comprehensive installation guide that not only walks you through the installation and setup process, but that also gives you the developer detailed information about what files are going where, and why. You should read this document — it can be found at `http://docs.xoops.org/modules/xdocman/index.php?doc=xu-002&lang=en`.

A few things to point out before you install:

❑ After unzipping the tar file, you will need to copy the html folder to the website root directory (such as htdocs or public_html). The XOOPS team recommends you rename this folder to xoops, but that is really up to you.

❑ If you are installing on a remote server, you will need to create the database, user, and password prior to installation. If you are installing locally, the installation wizard will complete this task for you.

❏ Once you have unzipped the files, you will need to chmod the following directories and files to make them writeable:

  ❏ uploads/

  ❏ cache/

  ❏ templates_c/

  ❏ mainfile.php

❏ You must have cookies and Javascript enabled on your browser for the XOOPS installation wizard to complete the process correctly.

General Overview/Default Installation

There are several features that are activated by default:

❏ **Banner Management:** Manages banner ads and click-through.

❏ **Image Manager:** Manages images and who can upload them.

❏ **Smilies:** Manages "smilies" and how they are displayed.

❏ **Avatars:** Manages avatars.

❏ **Comment Manager:** Manages comments posted by users.

❏ **User Management:** Edit, email, search, change ranks of users.

❏ **Blocks:** Manages blocks (such as "who's online" and "recent comments").

The only module that is installed by default is the System Admin module. Other modules that are available by default as a part of the package (but need to be installed one by one) include:

❏ **Contact Us:** Sends messages to the website admin.

❏ **Downloads:** Organizes uploaded files, and allows users to rank them.

❏ **Links:** Link manager.

❏ **Forum:** Site forum (created by phpBB group).

❏ **News:** Manages news articles submitted by users.

❏ **Sections:** Allows admins to post different sections of the site.

❏ **FAQ:** Manages FAQs for the site.

❏ **Headlines:** RSS feed for news from other sites.

❏ **Memberlist:** Shows the registered users for the site.

❏ **Partners:** Organizes and displays partner sites.

❏ **Polls:** Manages online surveys and polls.

Customizing the Default Installation

At the time of this writing, there are over 300 add-on modules available for download at the XOOPS Web site. There is a module that can do virtually whatever you want, including transaction functionality (shopping carts) which is not too common among these types of CMSs.

Under the System Admin section of the Admin Control Panel, you will find the following areas where you can further customize your installation:

- ❑ **Avatars:** Allows you to upload available avatars for your users.

- ❑ **Banners:** Manages your banner advertisements, and provides stats on click-through rates and which banners are active.

- ❑ **Blocks:** Provides an interface for adding new blocks and determining their layout on the site.

- ❑ **Comments:** Allows you to view, edit, and delete comments.

- ❑ **Find Users:** Doesn't allow customization of the site, but provides an extensive search interface for filtering out users.

- ❑ **Groups:** The place where you assign users to different groups and set permissions for that group. Permissions are at the system, module, and block levels and allow either admin or access rights.

- ❑ **Image Manager:** Manages the image gallery.

- ❑ **Mail Users:** Doesn't allow customization of the site, but allows you to send emails to users.

- ❑ **Modules:** Allows you to install and activate or deactivate available modules.

- ❑ **Preferences:** Provides general customization of the site and is broken down into several categories:

    - ❑ **General Settings:** Allows you to change the site name, slogan, admin email address, default language, module for the start page, server and default time zones, default theme (there are only three installed for you), users themes, usernames for anonymous users, gzip compression, cookie and session info, whether the site is completely down, and customized messages when site is down, IP address, SSL settings, banned IP addresses, and configure cache settings.

    - ❑ **User Info Settings:** Allows you to set password and username settings, what default groups users will belong to, avatar settings, blocked usernames (such as "admin"), and alter registration disclaimer.

    - ❑ **Meta Tags and Footer:** Allows you to set meta tag information, such as keywords, description, robots, rating, author, copyright, and the footer information.

    - ❑ **Word Censoring Option:** Allows you to censor unwanted words and replace them with words of your choice.

    - ❑ **Search Options:** Allows you to turn on or off global search settings and require minimum keyword length for user-driven searches.

    - ❑ **Mail Setup:** Allows you to configure mail server settings and mail methods.

- ❏ **Smilies:** Controls smilies for the forum, and allows you to create your own.

- ❏ **Templates:** Allows you to upload templates to the site.

- ❏ **User Ranks:** Controls user ranking system for the forum and allows you to configure the minimum number of posts for certain levels you define.

- ❏ **Edit Users:** Enables you to delete users and edit their information — nickname, name, email, URL, time zone, instant messaging information, location, occupation, interests, signature, comments abilities, notifications, rank, password, and groups.

Strengths and Weaknesses

The best portions of this package are:

- ❏ Huge user base and support forums make it easy for a developer to find solutions to questions or to troubleshoot problematic areas.

- ❏ Word Censoring option is a nice benefit.

- ❏ Because the forum module was developed by phpBB Group, the forum controls are highly customized and detailed.

The areas that could be improved are:

- ❏ While the core documentation was extensive, documentation for add-on modules is quite lacking. Because the add-on features could potentially be a large portion of a website, this could be frustrating for inexperienced individuals.

- ❏ Only three themes are included in default installation, and with such a large support and user base, it stands to reason that there could be more pre-installed.

XOOPS is popular because of its potential, although you have to be willing to decipher other people's code and have the luxury of time to fine-tune your installation to fit your specific needs. While it's not that great as an "out of the box" solution, it can accomplish virtually anything you need it to, if you're willing and able to spend some time coding. It's very user-oriented, allowing you as an admin to control the environment for the users all the way down to the "smilies." If you're focused on creating an interactive community with anyone who ventures to your site, you should give a second look to XOOPS.

phpWebsite

phpWebsite is available at `http://phpwebsite.appstate.edu`. The most recent version of phpWebsite at the time of writing is 0.10.01, and will be the basis for the discussion here.

Installation Notes

The kind folks at Appalachian State University (the creators of phpWebsite) have set up a command-line installation process that allows you to install directly from the phpWebsite site. You can also download the application in sections (core, theme packs, and so on) and install them yourself.

A few things to keep in mind before you install:

❑   You will need to have the following PEAR libraries installed to run the core application:

❑   Benchmark

❑   DB

❑   Date

❑   HTML_BBCodeParser

❑   HTML_Common

❑   HTML_Form

❑   HTML_Table

❑   HTML_Template_IT

❑   Mail

❑   Mail_Mime

❑   Net_CheckIP

❑   If possible, you will need to be logged in as root before you install. The script will detect if you are not the root user and set up the application with certain security restrictions in place. If you try to switch users, it will retain the original setup, and will not do a root install.

❑   You must have wget or the installer will not operate.

General Overview/Default Installation

The modules that are immediately available and active for you are:

❑   **Apache Controller:** Allows an admin to alter Apache settings.

❑   **Help System:** Helps the admin navigate the system.

❑   **Language Administrator:** Manages the languages to be used on the site.

❑   **Layout Manager:** Manages the layout for your site.

❑   **Site Search:** Searches the site.

❑   **User Manager:** Approves users for various levels of modding the site.

❑   **Announcements:** Manages announcements posted on the site.

❑   **Block Maker:** Allows you to create and manage blocks.

❑   **Branch Creator:** Manages spin-off sites created under the main site.

❑   **Calendar:** Calendar for the site.

❑   **Comment Manager:** Manages comments.

❑   **Debugger:** Assists the admin in locating and fixing errors.

❑   **Documents:** A file manager.

❑   **FAQ:** Manages FAQs for the site.

- ❑ **Link Manager:** Organizes and displays links.

- ❑ **Menu Manager:** Manages dynamic menus.

- ❑ **Module Maker:** Allows you to create your own module.

- ❑ **Notes:** Sends emails to users of site.

- ❑ **Web Pages:** Manages static pages on the site.

- ❑ **Form Generator:** Creates forms.

- ❑ **Photo Albums:** Organizes and manages the online image gallery.

- ❑ **Bulletin Board:** Manages forums.

- ❑ **RSS News Feeds:** Manages feeds.

- ❑ **Polls:** Manages online surveys and polls.

- ❑ **Skeleton Module:** A sample mod to use as a template.

- ❑ **Admin Stats:** Keeps track of what modules and users are most active.

Customizing the Default Installation

As with all the CMS packages, the beauty is in modifying the default installation to really fit your needs.

Adding, deleting, and editing users and their permissions can be done under the Users Administration portion of the Admin Control Panel. Here, you can set whether or not users are allowed to sign up, and whether or not they need to be approved before they are allowed to participate in things like forums. You can also create your own authentication script or use the local database to verify users. If a user is given admin status, you can control what modules he or she has access to, and what specific functions within that module can be performed. For example, a user could create a poll, but not edit, delete, or list a poll.

Changing the layout of the modules is possible, but not as easy to do as some of the other features of phpWebsite. You can change the look of each particular module, which is a nice feature.

HTML header information (meta tags, keywords, and so on) are controlled under the Layout Admin portion of the Admin Control Panel. This is something that is a bit unexpected.

There are currently 21 other themes available at http://www.sourceforge.net for you to use and download.

Strengths and Weaknesses

The most attractive features of this package are:

- ❑ There is a tremendous amount of statistical information available to the admins, which makes it easier to fine-tune the site.

- ❑ The ability to create your own authorization script is a nice feature.

- ❑ An admin can change the look of boxes and modules on an individual basis, so not all boxes have to look the same on the same page.

❑ Very detailed user permissions are allowed, making it simple and straightforward to see who is allowed to do what.

❑ Default modules are extensive, making a comprehensive site less labor-intensive for the developer.

The only weakness is that currently, the system does not allow breaking of the traditional two- or three-column layout.

phpWebsite is a nice "middle-of-the-road" CMS, balancing a high level of built-in functionality with a high degree of user interactivity. If you are looking for a package that can support a medium-sized group of contributors, and still foster visitor interactivity, then this might be the CMS for you.

TikiWiki

This software is available at `http://www.tikiwiki.org`, and the current version available at the time of this writing is 1.9.0.

Installation Notes

If you are using older versions of PHP (older than 4.3) or MySQL (older than 4.0.1), then you will want to pay particular attention to the "Requirements and Setup" documentation, which can be found at `http://doc.tikiwiki.org/tiki-index.php?page=requirements+and+setup`. Other points to note are:

❑ The PDF Generation module needs the php-xml package to be installed.

❑ Because of the use of sessions, make sure your php.ini file has the following settings:

  ❑ `session.save_handler = files`
  ❑ `session.save_path = /tmp` (for local installation)

You will also need to create the database and user/password prior to installation. The installation package can be downloaded from the site, or if you're installing to a remote server, there is a separate link on the Installation page entitled `InstallWithOnlyFTPAccess` which is the right method for you.

Default Installation

There are several features that are activated by default:

❑ **Games:** Allows users to play games on your site and keeps track of game stats.

❑ **Categories:** Manages categories that any module can be classified into.

❑ **Calendars:** Allows users to view calendars with events.

❑ **MyTiki:** Gives logged-in users their own interface with features such as calendars, webmail, menus, and a notepad, and allows admin to turn user features on or off.

❑ **Submission:** Allows users to submit articles.

❑ **AutoLinks:** Allows URLs typed in to text to be automatically submitted to the links directory.

❑ **Search & Full-text Search:** Allows users to search your site.

❑ **HTML Pages:** Manages editable blocks of HTML code to be reused throughout the site.

- ❏ **Help System:** Manages the help desk.

- ❏ **Galaxia Workflow Engine:** Allows management of complex workflow processes.

- ❏ **Wiki:** Collaborative documentation system; also allows authorized users to create and edit content for static HTML pages, and offers a WYSIWYG HTML editor and spell-checker, among other advanced features.

- ❏ **Articles:** Organizes and manages articles.

- ❏ **Blogs:** Weblog administration.

- ❏ **Directory:** Link manager that categorizes links.

- ❏ **File Gallery:** Organizes and manages uploaded files.

- ❏ **FAQs:** Manages FAQs for the site.

- ❏ **Maps:** Allows you to display interactive maps.

- ❏ **Trackers:** Manages and organizes custom data for you.

- ❏ **Hotwords:** Allows you to embed links from certain words on your site.

- ❏ **Contact Us:** Easy form that allows users to contact you.

- ❏ **Stats:** Manages site stats, for every active module possible.

- ❏ **Referrer Stats:** Manages stats for referring sites.

- ❏ **Debugger Console:** Assists a developer in debugging the site.

Other features that are pre-installed, but need only to be activated with the click of a button include:

- ❏ **Comments:** Allows users to comment on images, articles, and other content throughout the site.

- ❏ **Image Gallery:** Allows users to rank, view, and upload images.

- ❏ **Newsreader:** RSS feed for news.

- ❏ **Polls:** Manages online polls.

- ❏ **Quizzes:** Allows users to take a quiz and be graded.

- ❏ **Featured Links:** Manages links that open within your Tiki site; keeps track of link stats.

- ❏ **Banners:** Manages banner campaign and click-throughs.

- ❏ **Newsletters:** Manages newsletter broadcasts for the site and allows users to subscribe.

- ❏ **Forums:** Manages forums.

- ❏ **Shoutbox:** Allows users to display short lines of text in a dynamic window.

- ❏ **Surveys:** Manages online surveys.

- ❏ **Ephemerides:** Allows you to display images and text customized for each day of the year.

- ❏ **Live Support System:** Allows users to request help from the live help desk.

- ❏ **Babelfish translation:** Allows users to translate portions of the site.

- ❏ **Integrator:** Allows you to import external HTML pages into the site.

❑ **Banning System:** Allows you to easily ban users.

❑ **User Features:** Allows users to bookmark, keep track of files, send messages to other users, and other actions.

Customizing the Default Installation

The Admin section of the site has several subsections that provide for customization. They are:

❑ **Features:** This section is where an admin can activate and deactivate features, and alter the general layout of the site.

❑ **General Preferences:** Here, you can change themes, change your homepage or create a custom one, set the language preferences, set the OS type, change the PHP error reporting level, set custom messages for when site is down, limit the number of site users and load, set caching preferences, where new links will open, control whether all groups see all modules, set whether or not admin pageviews are counted in stats, alter menu displays, set server configurations, set session preferences, manage date/time formats, and change the admin password.

❑ **User Registration and Login:** This area is dedicated to allowing you to control every aspect of the user registration and login process, from authentication to password requirements, to HTTP/S settings, and even settings for the PEAR::Auth module used by TikiWiki.

❑ **Enabled Feature Configurations (e.g., Wiki):** For the various features you have enabled with the Features screen, you will have access to those individual sections to further customize their settings. Because Wiki was the focus of this project early on, this area of the Admin site offers an incredible amount of control, customizability, and functionality. In a nutshell, you can dump, restore, and attach files, control database and comment settings, export, configure link formats and set what information is retained for the Wiki documentation (version control, user data, dates, links, status, and more) You can also manage copyright protection, Wiki history, and configure watches. Some of the Wiki features you have the ability to turn on and off include:

  ❑ Mail-in

  ❑ Sandbox

  ❑ Last Changes

  ❑ History

  ❑ Rankings

  ❑ Undo

  ❑ Multiprint

  ❑ PDF Generation

  ❑ Comments

  ❑ Spellchecker

  ❑ Warn on Edit Conflict

  ❑ Individual Cache

  ❑ Footnotes

❑ Use WikiWords

❑ Automonospaced Text

The other available features (articles, blogs, image galleries, and others) allow a certain level of customization as well, but not nearly as detailed as the Wiki section.

Strengths and Weaknesses

TikiWiki's strengths are:

❑ Documentation and support community are extensive, as in many other open source CMS packages.

❑ Strong Wiki customization makes online collaboration easy.

❑ There are 35 themes that come with default installation, and they are basic CSS files which make further customization easy.

❑ Extensive statistics are available for every active module possible.

❑ This CMS is one of the most comprehensive; it comes with just about every conceivable module (aside from the transactional functionality), making it easy for you to customize without having to install additional plug-ins or add-ons.

For weaknesses, Galaxia Workflow is a bit complex and takes some separate reading to understand how the system is set up and how it can work for you. This could also become a strength for TikiWiki, as once you are able to wade through the system, it can provide you with a very comprehensive tool for managing complicated projects.

With this software, you can quickly offer anything your users would desire. In fact, there is so much functionality available through this software that amateur web developers might be tempted to use too many modules "because they can." Our recommendation is that if you know exactly what you want in your site, and if you have many users that will be contributing to the actual content of the site, you should definitely check out this CMS.

Others

There are numerous other open source CMS packages available. A few worthy of mention are:

❑ **Mambo:** Available at http://www.mamboserver.com. This is a popular CMS that offers a basic level of pre-installed features, with numerous downloads. The project fosters a healthy support system and the userbase and is relatively easy to administer without forging too deeply into code.

❑ **Drupal:** Available at http://www.drupal.org. This is another popular CMS that is focused on function and not necessarily form. A few themes are included, but customization is limited without delving into code. A nice feature is the "recent system events," which is displayed when the admin logs in, allowing the admin to easily see what users have been doing.

❑ **PHP-Nuke:** Available at http://www.phpnuke.org. This is one of the oldest PHP/MySQL-based CMSs. It's been around since 2000, and has one of, if not the largest, CMS support communities available. It's still currently in development, but the bad news is that it is no longer free — you are now required to pay a minimal fee to download the latest copy. You can also join the PHPNuke Club (for another fee) if you would like to be among the PHPNuke elite.

❑ **Postnuke:** Available at `http://www.postnuke.com`. Another of the "oldies but goodies," this CMS came out shortly after PHP-Nuke, and thus feeds off its extensive community of users and developers. Numerous add-ons, language packs, and user forums are available to assist you in customizing this CMS package.

Micro CMSs

You may want only one of the features of the bigger CMS packages on your own site. Thankfully you also have available Micro CMS packages. These "mini" CMS packages have one specific purpose, such as a blog or a wiki. They are the perfect solution if you need only one function on your site. The sections that follow take a brief look at these packages.

The two most popular Micro CMS packages are blogs and wikis. It is for this reason that more attention is focused on these areas.

The Magic of Blogs

Studies are showing the increasing popularity of blogs and those who read them. A study by PEW Internet & American Life Project shows that in 2002, only 3% of Internet users owned a blog. In 2003, that number increased to 5%, and in 2004, that number was up to 7%. Multiply this by the estimated 120 million Internet users in America alone, and that equates to some pretty hefty blogging going on.

Not only are people writing blogs, but more and more people are taking the time to read them. An April 2005 survey by Hostway, Inc. shows that roughly 30% of survey respondents had read blogs, and analysts predict that number will grow greatly in the next few years.

Why Blog?

There are many reasons for blogging, and they run the gamut from personal to political to corporate agendas. This free, immediate, interactive communication mechanism makes the perfect forum to share opinions and thoughts. Blogs can be about anything, and their informal nature appeals to virtually everyone.

Blogs exist to:

❑ **Share political views:** Many politicians and high-profile political activists are using blogs to reach the masses and promote their own agendas.

❑ **Further corporate goals:** Corporations are beginning to jump on the bandwagon and provide blogs about their products and services. Some are written by the consumers themselves. Some corporations are using blogs to notify their loyal readers about upcoming product releases, or other news about the company.

❑ **Share personal opinions:** On such a crowded planet, and on such a crowded Internet, sometimes people just want to be heard. Maybe they want to share their current experiences with friends and family from across the globe. Or perhaps they have expert advice they want to share with beginners. In a coder's world, you might have a code snippet to share, or a cool product or link you want to tell others about. The list goes on.

WordPress

WordPress is a great "out of the box" blogging package that provides excellent customizability and functionality. It is available at `http://www.wordpress.org` and the current version at time of this writing is 1.5.11.

Installation Notes

Installation of this package is incredibly easy and quick to do. Prior to installation, make sure you are running PHP 4.1+ and MySQL 3.23.23+ and that you have created your database and username/password. The rest of the documentation you would need is conveniently located for you on the `http://www.wordpress.org` site.

General Overview of Features

WordPress offers numerous functions and areas of customization for your blog, including:

❑ **User registration system:** Allows you to authorize other users to post, edit, and delete blogs in your site, with 10 levels of varying user access. You can also require an "approval" process before drafts are published.

❑ **Static content pages:** Allows you add static pages to your site, and manage them through the WordPress interface.

❑ **Adding links or blogrolls:** You can manage and organize external links through the WordPress interface.

❑ **Themes:** There are currently 35 themes built-in to the default installation and nearly 150 additional themes available for you through download to easily customize the look and feel of your blog.

❑ **Comment system:** Allows you to accept, review, and modify comments posted by users and contains a spam blocker to prevent spam posts from popping up. Visitors can also make comments about your blog on their own sites through Trackback and Pingback.

❑ **Hidden posts:** Allow you to password-protect certain posts that are viewable only by you, or by the author who created them.

❑ **Importing data:** Allows you to import data from other popular blog packages including MoveableType, Blogger, and numerous others.

❑ **RSS feed:** Allows others to syndicate your blog.

❑ **Post-by-email:** Allows you to submit blog posts through the email system.

There are other nice features with this blogging package such as full standards compliance, ease in upgrading, and the use of the Texturize engine to beautify your text from plain ASCII.

Summing It Up

You will find once you delve into the WordPress package that it is well documented, easy to install, easy to configure and customize, and very functional. It also has an excellent support and development community in case you have questions or problems. If you are simply looking to create a blog on your site, WordPress is hard to beat.

Serendipity

Another fabulous and well-structured blog is Serendipity, available for download at `http://www.s9y.org`. It boasts some heavy PHP hitters on its development team, including Sterling Hughes, George Schlossnagle, Wez Furlong, and Sebastian Bergmann, among others. It is also the blog package of choice for many core PHP developers.

Installation Notes

Like Wordpress, installation is a quick and easy job. You should be running PHP 4 or greater and MySQL, PostgreSQL, or SQLite for your database. The only other thing to keep in mind is to remember to restrict the file permissions after installation, as outlined in their extensive installation documentation found at `http://www.s9y.org/index.php?node=36`.

General Overview of Features

Serendipity offers similar functionality to Wordpress, such as allowing the admin to set permissions for users so that not all users can publish blog entries, and moderating comments or enabling CAPTCHAs for spam prevention. With Serendipity, you can add images to your blog posts, change themes for your site, import and export data, and offer trackback and pingback for others to reference your posts. Also akin to Wordpress is the standards compliant code and RSS feeds that can be offered for others.

Some additional functionality not readily seen in Wordpress includes:

- ❑ Optional Wysiwyg editors: HTMLarea, FCKeditor, xinha, TinyMCE
- ❑ MySQL, PostgreSQL and SQLite support
- ❑ Multiuser blogs: One installation of serendipity can serve independent weblogs.

Summing It Up

Serendipity is simple, clean, and solid. If you're looking for a blog that simply does what it's supposed to do and is very reliable, Serendipity is an excellent choice.

Wiki

Just as programmers, coders, and web developers alike use software to manage development and deployment of software packages, they are turning to wiki to collaborate and create comprehensive documentation to complement those packages.

The Origin of Wiki

According to Wikipedia, the word *wiki* is based on a Hawaiian term, *wiki wiki*, meaning "quick or informal," specifically when referring to the buses at the Honolulu airport. The phrase was coined by Howard ("Ward") Cunningham back in 1995 as a reference to the Portland Pattern Repository, a collaboration of software development ideas.

As the Internet has grown to reach the masses, the popularity of the wiki concept has grown substantially, particularly in the open source community where many people assume a community responsibility to continually improve existing products. Documentation is an integral part of enabling users to understand what an application does or can do.

Wiki sites are not only limited to supporting open source projects, but can also act as a general reference guide for virtually anything. There are hobby-oriented wikis, language wikis, gaming wikis—you could conceivably create a wiki for any topic under the sun.

MediaWiki

One of the more popular packages available, and the brains behind Wikipedia, is MediaWiki. It is available at `http://wikipedia.sourceforge.net`. The latest release at the time of this writing is 1.4.4 and will be the focus of the discussion here.

Installation Notes

Prior to installing MediaWiki, you should take note of the following: If you have root access, you will not need to create the database pre-installation. If you are installing on a remote server, you will need to create the database yourself before installing. Also, after the files have been unzipped, you will need to `chmod` the config directory so that it is writeable. You will also need to reset the permissions upon completion of installation.

The complete installation guide can be found at the MediaWiki Web site: `http://meta.wikimedia.org/wiki/MediaWiki_User%27s_Guide:_Installation`.

General Overview of Features

Because the purpose of the site is to keep track of a continually evolving body of text, it has some wonderful features for managing users, their input, and version control. General functions available are:

- ❑ **User customization and access:** Users can customize their own site interface by editing their own templates, setting their own preferences for things such as time zone and number of results per page. Admins can assign varying levels of permissions to user groups, turning on and off the ability for them to edit, move, contribute, or upload files, among other things.

- ❑ **Search capabilities:** Visitors to the site can perform a full-text search of all the articles contained on the site.

- ❑ **Reports:** Reports can be generated that provide specific statistics on usage, articles and links, article activity and popularity, images, users, and more.

- ❑ **Editing articles:** Users can decide to edit only a portion of an article, articles can be merged if an edit conflict occurs, users can preview their edits before submitting them, and users are given the use of an editing toolbar to facilitate the editing process.

- ❑ **Article organization:** Articles can be categorized and subcategorized into unlimited categories.

- ❑ **Text and linking controls:** Users can use restricted or full HTML code when submitting text changes or entering new text. Embedded hyperlinks can also be managed.

- ❑ **Watchlist:** This feature assists the admin and users in keeping track of users' edits and contributions. It can show articles of particular interest, recent changes, and which users have contributed the most. This feature even offers a side-by-side view of the article pre- and post-edit with the changes highlighted so changes can be easily identified by the reader.

❑ **Multimedia capabilities:** Other file types can be uploaded by the user, including images, sound files, mathematical formulas, and charts.

❑ **Multilanguage support:** Currently, there is support for numerous languages, as well as the ability to link between articles in different languages.

For a complete list of all the functions and features available in this package, visit the MediaWiki Feature List at `http://meta.wikimedia.org/wiki/MediaWiki_feature_list`.

Summing it Up

One only needs to visit Wikipedia (`http://www.wikipedia.org`) to fully grasp all that can be done with MediaWiki. It is highly functional, customizable, and one of the most robust wiki software packages available.

DocuWiki

Another Wiki package is DocuWiki, which is available at `http://www.splitbrain.org/go/dokuwiki`. What makes this different than other wikis is its use of flat files which releases the user from database dependency.

Installation Notes

DocuWiki is another open source package that offers "out of the box" installation—simply unzip and change permissions to install. The only thing you need to do is create an empty log file per the detailed installation instructions found at `http://wiki.splitbrain.org/wiki%3AInstall`.

General Overview of Features

This wiki offers many features including:

❑ **Section editing:** Allows users to work on only one portion of a page.

❑ **Version comparison:** Provides colored highlighted differences between two versions of the documents.

❑ **User access control:** Allows admins to assign permissions to users.

❑ **Image uploads:** Allows users to include images with the wiki documentation.

❑ **Multilanguage support:** Provides support for different languages.

❑ **Checking in/out:** Prevents edit conflicts

Summing It Up

The only thing lacking in this wiki is the database-related functions such as page tracking and referring statistics. It also doesn't offer a backup utility or allow for user comments on contributions as some other wiki packages do. Otherwise, this is a simple and solid wiki package that is an excellent choice, especially if you don't have access to a database.

Other Micro CMS Packages

Although thus far this chapter has focused on blogs and wiki, you may already have a site developed and need to "plug-in" some additional functionality. There are many focused CMSs that can make your life easier and allow you to easily enhance your site without having to code from scratch.

Some of the more popular Micro CMS packages are:

- ❑ **Publication/News Management CMS:** FusionNews, available at `http://www.fusionphp.net`
- ❑ **Managed Learning Environment CMS:** Moodle, available at `http://www.moodle.org`
- ❑ **Transactional CMS:** osCommerce or ZenCart, available at `http://www.oscommerce.com` and `http://www.zencart.com`, respectively
- ❑ **Image Galleries:** Coppermine, available at `http://coppermine.sourceforge.net`
- ❑ **Forums:** phpBB, available at `http://www.phpBB.com`
- ❑ **Chat Rooms:** phpmychat, available at `http://phpmychat.sourceforge.net`
- ❑ **Polls/Surveys:** PrestoPoll, available at `http://prestopoll.sourceforge.net`
- ❑ **Calendar Systems:** WebCalendar, available at `http://www.k5n.us/webcalendar.php`

Other Helpful Resources

There are other places you can go to sift through the muck and mire—places that make it their business to compare, evaluate, and keep track of the numerous CMSs out there. Just a few to get you started include:

- ❑ **OpenSourceCMS:** `http://www.opensourcecms.com`. This site is designed to give you a "test run" of virtually any PHP/MySQL CMS out there, allowing you to see first-hand what features are available on each one, how well the admin screen functions, and the depth and breadth of the CMS itself. There are a couple of great things about this website: first, you don't have to take the time to install the entire package just to demo the software; and second, they only showcase CMSs that are available on a remote server (with no root access), as well as on the main server itself. If any CMS doesn't make the list, then they either couldn't get it installed easily (another nice filter for you), or they don't know about it yet. This site also features reviews by other users for a completely unbiased opinion.

  The only drawback to using this site is that there are others "playing around" with the software at the same time you are, which makes for interesting evaluations and possibly unexpected outcomes. Luckily, the servers refresh the demo software every two hours, so eventually you will be able to see a "clean" copy.

- ❑ **CMSReview:** `http://www.cmsreview.com`. This is a comprehensive CMS site that provides great resources on how to determine what the CMS needs are for your company and where to go to find a CMS consultant, and a nice link to a CMS glossary in case you come across any unfamiliar terminology.

❑ **CMSMatrix:** `http://www.cmsmatrix.org`. If you're looking to compare numerous CMS packages (open source or not) on an apples-to-apples basis, this will be a great resource for you. It is down and dirty, but contains a lot of information.

❑ **CMSWire:** `http://www.cmswire.com`. This newsy CMS site keeps you up-to-date on the latest CMS developments and trends in CMS usage across industries. If you are dedicated to being on the cutting edge of the CMS world, you might want to get an RSS feed to this site.

Summary

We hope this chapter has given you enough insight to make intelligent choices regarding a CMS package. As it has shown, there are numerous open source solutions that can fill virtually every need, from the very comprehensive, to the very tailored and specific. While many times, choosing the right CMS comes down to personal preference, you now have at least a starting point from which to form those subjective opinions.

Language Translation

Comments

PHP

```
// Single-line comment

/*
Multi-line comment
*/
```

ASP/VBScript

```
' Single-line comment
```

ASP.NET/C#

```
// Single-line comment

/*
Multi-line comment
*/
```

JSP/Java

```
// Single-line comment
/*
Multi-line comment
*/
```

Variable Typing

PHP

> Loose

ASP/VBScript

> Loose

ASP.NET/C#

> Strong

JSP/Java

> Strong

Variable Declaration

PHP

```
$variable = value;
```

ASP/VBScript

```
Dim variable
```

ASP.NET/C#

```
type variable;
```

JSP/Java

```
type variable;
```

Constant Declaration

PHP

```
define('NAME', value);
```

ASP/VBScript

```
Const name = value
```

ASP.NET/C#

```
const type name = value;
```

JSP/Java

```
visibility final type = value;
```

Creating Arrays

PHP

```
$name = array(elem1, elem2, elem3);

$name = array('key1' => elem1, 'key2' => elem2, 'key3' => elem3);
```

ASP/VBScript

```
Dim name(length)
```

ASP.NET/C#

```
type[] name = new type[length];
```

JSP/Java

```
type[] name = new type[length];
```

Referencing Array Elements

PHP

```
$name[index]

$name['key']
```

ASP/VBScript

```
name(index)
```

ASP.NET/C#

```
name[index]
```

JSP/Java

```
name[index]
```

Conditional Evaluation

PHP

```
if (condition) {
...
} elseif (condition) {
...
} else {
...
}
```

ASP/VBScript

```
If condition Then
...
ElseIf condition Then
...
Else
...
End If
```

ASP.NET/C#

```
if (condition) {
...
} else if (condition) {
...
} else {
...
}
```

JSP/Java

```
if (condition) {
...
} else if (condition) {
...
} else {
...
}
```

Multiple-Choice Selection

PHP

```
switch (expr) {
  case value1:
    ...
    break;
  case value2:
    ...
    break;
  default:
    ...
}
```

ASP/VBScript

```
Select Case expr
  Case value1
    ...
  Case value2
    ...
  Case Else
    ..
End Select
```

ASP.NET/C#

```
switch (expr) {
  case value1:
    ...
    break;
  case value2:
    ...
    break;
  default:
    ...
    break;
}
```

JSP/Java

```
switch (expr) {
  case value1:
    ...
    break;
  case value2:
    ...
    break;
  default:
    ...
    break;
}
```

Loop: While

PHP

```
while (expr) {
...
}
```

ASP/VBScript

```
While expr
...
Wend
```

ASP.NET/C#

```
while (expr) {
...
}
```

JSP/Java

```
while (expr) {
...
}
```

Loop: Do...While

PHP

```
do {
...
} while (expr);
```

ASP/VBScript

```
Do
...
Loop Until expr
```

ASP.NET/C#

```
do {
...
}
while (expr);
```

JSP/Java

```
do {
...
} while (expr);
```

Loop: For

PHP

```
for (expr1; expr2; expr3) {
...
}
```

ASP/VBScript

```
For expr1 To expr2 Step expr3
...
Next
```

ASP.NET/C#

```
for (expr1; expr2; expr3) {
...
}
```

JSP/Java

```
for (expr1; expr2; expr3) {
...
}
```

Loop: For Each

PHP

```
foreach (array as $item) {
...
}

foreach (array as $key => $item) {
...
}
```

ASP/VBScript

```
For Each item In array
...
Next
```

ASP.NET/C#

```
for (type item in array) {
...
}
```

JSP/Java

```
for (Iterator item; item.hasNext(); ) {
...
}
```

Loop: Termination

PHP

```
break;
```

ASP/VBScript

```
Exit Do
Exit For
```

(There is no exiting a While loop.)

ASP.NET/C#

```
break;
```

JSP/Java

```
break;
```

Loop: Advance to Next Round

PHP

```
continue;
```

ASP/VBScript

Not supported

ASP.NET/C#

```
continue;
```

JSP/Java

```
continue;
```

Function/Method Declaration

PHP

```
function name (args) {
...
}
```

ASP/VBScript

```
Function name (args)
...
End Function

Sub name (args)
...
End Sub
```

ASP.NET/C#

```
visibility returnType name (args) {
...
}
```

JSP/Java

```
visibility returnType name (args) {
...
}
```

Returning Function Values

PHP

```
return value;
```

ASP/VBScript

```
FunctionName = value
```

ASP.NET/C#

```
return value;
```

JSP/Java

```
return value;
```

Grouping Classes with Namespaces

PHP

Not supported

ASP/VBScript

Not supported

ASP.NET/C#

```
namespace Name {
...
}
```

JSP/Java

```
package name;
```

Class Visibility Keywords

PHP

```
public, private, protected
```

ASP/VBScript

```
public, private
```

ASP.NET/C#

```
public, private, protected, internal
```

JSP/Java

```
public, private, protected, package
```

Base Class Definition

PHP

```
class ClassName {
...
}
```

ASP/VBScript

```
Class ClassName
...
End Class
```

ASP.NET/C#

```
visibility class ClassName {
...
}
```

JSP/Java

```
visibility class ClassName {
...
}
```

Declaring Class Properties

PHP

```
visibility name;
```

ASP/VBScript

```
visibility name
```

ASP.NET/C#

```
visibility type name;
```

JSP/Java

```
visibility type name;
```

Calling a Method in Same Class

PHP

```
$this->method();
```

ASP/VBScript

```
Me.method
```

ASP.NET/C#

```
this.method();
```

JSP/Java

```
this.method();
```

Class Constructor

PHP

```
function __construct() {
...
}
```

ASP/VBScript

```
Private Sub Class_Initialize()
...
End Sub
```

ASP.NET/C#

```
visibility ClassName() {
...
}
```

JSP/Java

```
public ClassName() {
...
}
```

Class Destructor

PHP

```
function __destruct() {
...
}
```

ASP/VBScript

```
Private Sub Class_Terminate()
...
End Sub
```

ASP.NET/C#

```
visibility ~ClassName() {
...
}
```

JSP/Java

```
protected void finalize() {
...
}
```

Using Static Class Methods

PHP

```
ClassName::StaticMethod();
```

ASP/VBScript

```
Not supported
```

ASP.NET/C#

```
ClassName.StaticMethod();
```

JSP/Java

```
ClassName.StaticMethod();
```

Creating an Object

PHP

```
$obj = new ClassName();
```

ASP/VBScript

```
Set obj = New ClassName
```

ASP.NET/C#

```
type obj = new ClassName();
```

JSP/Java

```
type obj = new ClassName();
```

Class Inheritance

PHP

```
class ClassName extends BaseClass {
...
}
```

ASP/VBScript

Not supported

ASP.NET/C#

```
visibility class ClassName : BaseClass {
...
}
```

JSP/Java

```
visibility class ClassName extends BaseClass {
...
}
```

Calling a Parent Method

PHP

```
parent::method();
```

ASP/VBScript

Not supported

ASP.NET/C#

```
base.method();
```

JSP/Java

```
super.method();
```

Declaring Abstract Classes

PHP

```
abstract class AbstractClass {
...
}
```

ASP/VBScript

Not supported

ASP.NET/C#

```
abstract class AbstractClass {
...
}
```

JSP/Java

```
visibility abstract class AbstractClass {
...
}
```

Stopping Subclassing

PHP

```
final class EndClass {
...
}

final visibility function MethodName() {
...
}
```

ASP/VBScript

Not supported

ASP.NET/C#

```
sealed class EndClass {
...
}

sealed visibility type MethodName() {
...
}
```

JSP/Java

```
visibility final class EndClass {
  ...
}

visibility final type MethodName () {
...
}
```

Interface Declaration

PHP

```
interface InterfaceName {
...
}
```

ASP/VBScript

Not supported

ASP.NET/C#

```
visibility interface InterfaceName {
...
}
```

JSP/Java

```
visibility interface InterfaceName {
...
}
```

Class Using Interface

PHP

```
class ClassName implements InterfaceName {
...
}
```

ASP/VBScript

Not supported

ASP.NET/C#

```
visibility class ClassName : InterfaceName {
...
}
```

JSP/Java

```
visibility class ClassName implements InterfaceName {
...
}
```

Including External Files

PHP

```
include('filename');
include_once('filename');
require('filename');
require_once('filename');
```

ASP/VBScript

```
<!-- #include 'filename' -->
```

ASP.NET/C#

Inclusion handled by varying methods, including traditional ASP inclusion (above)

JSP/Java

```
<%@ include file="filename" %>
```

Exception Handling

PHP

```
try {
...
} catch (ExceptionType $e) {
...
}
```

ASP/VBScript

Not specifically supported

ASP.NET/C#

```
try {
...
}
catch (ExceptionType e) {
...
}
finally {
...
}
```

JSP/Java

```
try {
...
}
catch (ExceptionType e) {
...
}
finally {
...
}
```

Throwing Exceptions

PHP

```
throw new ExceptionType(args);
```

ASP/VBScript

```
Err.Raise number
```

ASP.NET/C#

```
throw new ExceptionType(args);
```

JSP/Java

```
throw new ExceptionType(args);
```

HTTP POST Values

PHP

`$_POST` (array)

ASP/VBScript

`Request.Form` (collection)

ASP.NET/C#

`System.Web.HttpRequest.Form` (NameValueCollection)

JSP/Java

`request.getParameter()` (method lookup)

HTTP GET Values

PHP

`$_GET` (array)

ASP/VBScript

`Request.QueryString` (collection)

ASP.NET/C#

`System.Web.HttpRequest.QueryString` (NameValueCollection)

JSP/Java

`request.getParameter()` (method lookup)

Server Variables

PHP

`$_SERVER` (array)

ASP/VBScript

`Request.ServerVariables` (collection)

ASP.NET/C#

`System.Web.HttpRequest.ServerVariables` (NameValueCollection)

JSP/Java

`request.getVariable()` (method lookup; different method per server variable)

Alternative Tools

Whenever discussions of popular PHP tools spring up, the conversations usually center around text editors or coding IDEs. Which has the best language support, syntax highlighting, code parsing, and so on? Unfortunately, with all the focus on text editors, excellent non-coding tools can sometimes get neglected. Instead of rehashing the usual arguments for one editor versus the other, this appendix shows you some of the tools you can use in your development cycle — those that don't immediately churn out code, but those that you might find hold a key position in the overall development process.

MySQL Tools

When you administer a MySQL database, you usually have two main options for administration tools: the standard command-line toolset, or a graphical interface. Despite the attitudes of many hardened system administrators, there's absolutely nothing wrong with using a graphical tool to get the job done. Although the command-line interface offers unlimited control over the database, it just can't match the speed and clarity of a good graphical user interface to help facilitate your administration workflow.

If you're looking for a good set of GUI-based MySQL administration tools, you need look no further than MySQL AB's own MySQL Administrator and MySQL Query Browser.

MySQL Administrator

MySQL Administrator is a feature-rich GUI administration tool or maintaining MySQL databases. The main interface is shown in Figure B.1.

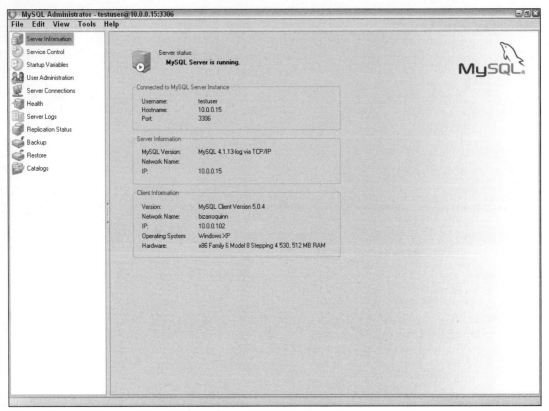

Figure B.1

MySQL Administrator allows you to do the following:

❑ View real-time server information, including connection information and statistics, memory statistics, the value for MySQL internal variables and configuration settings, and more.

❑ View the different server logs: Error log, Slow log, General Log (localhost only).

❑ Control the MySQL process itself (localhost only).

❑ Perform backup and restore operations, and even schedule periodic backups.

❑ Administer the server's user access and privileges.

❑ Create and edit complete databases, including tables using the built-in MySQL Table Editor.

MySQL Administrator is available for Windows, Linux, and Mac OS X; MySQL Administrator is a free download from the MySQL website: http://www.mysql.com/products/administrator/.

MySQL Query Browser

MySQL Query Browser is a GUI that allows you to test and run various queries against the MySQL database. In a sense, it is a beefed-up GUI version of the command-line client, as you can see in Figure B.2. You can also use MySQL Query Browser similar to a standard spreadsheet program or desktop database application—you can pull up rows of data, and edit them directly in the query browser. In addition to just typing in and executing queries, and manipulating data, it also includes the MySQL Table Editor found in MySQL Administrator, allowing you to visually create and edit databases and tables.

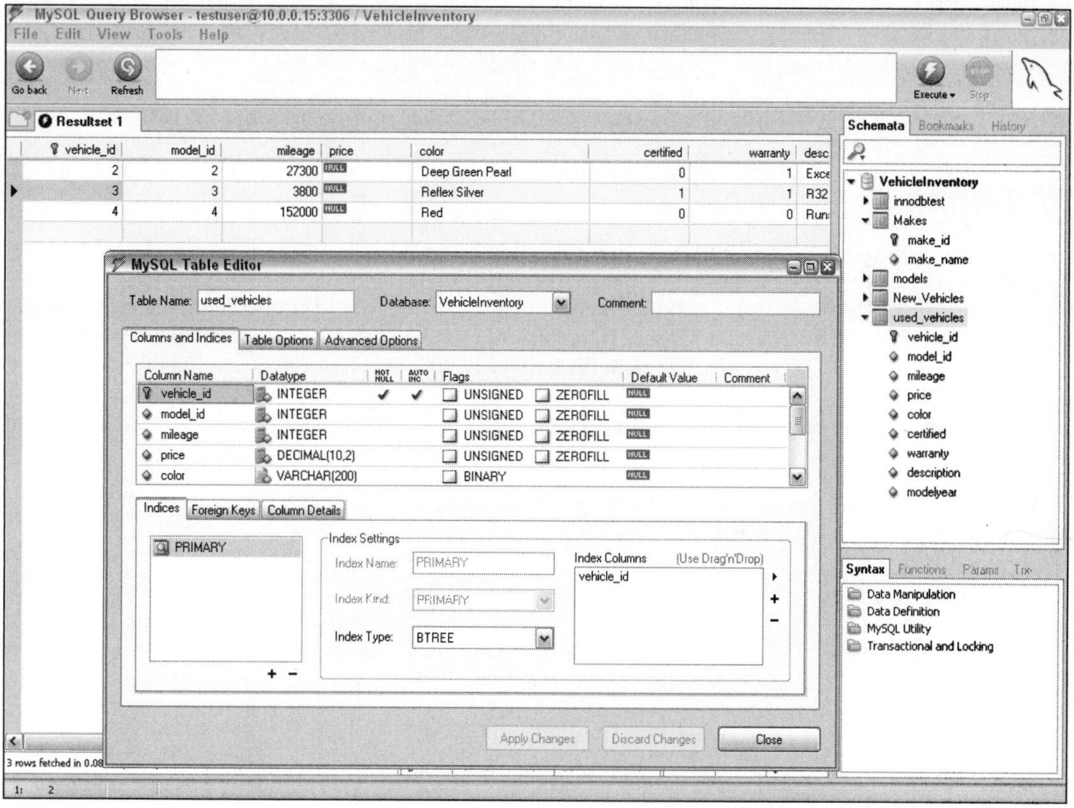

Figure B.2

Windows, Linux, and Mac OS X versions are available from MySQL at `http://www.mysql.com/products/query-browser/`.

So you've got your applications up and running, and your servers tweaked for peak performance. But are your database queries as lean and mean as they can be? The only way to know for sure is to use a benchmarking tool.

Most MySQL benchmarking tools perform in roughly the same way: you provide a query to run, and it runs said query a large number of times, often using concurrent connections. By thoroughly testing and experimenting with some of your "heavier" queries (often found in the MySQL slow query log), you can improve the execution times and server load at application bottlenecks.

MySQL Super Smack

Originally developed by Sasha Pachev, MySQL Super Smack is a standalone stress-testing tool for use with MySQL and PostgreSQL. MySQL Super Smack takes one or more files containing queries, and hammers the target database a predefined number of times for each query, with a specified number of concurrent connections.

MySQL Super Smack is available at `http://vegan.net/tony/supersmack/`.

MyBench

MyBench is a Perl-based benchmarking tool created by MySQL guru Jeremy Zawodny. Like MySQL Super-Smack, it can be used to send a barrage of connections and queries at a target MySQL machine, and give clear results on how well it stood up to the attack. Since it is written in Perl, you can easily modify and extend it as you wish. The downside is that a large test batch can hog machine resources, so it's best to run this tool on a different machine than the target MySQL server, to avoid tainting of the results.

MyBench is available at Jeremy Zawodny's site: `http://jeremy.zawodny.com/mysql/mybench/`.

Version Control

You might want to consider some form of version control system in your development lifecycle or workflow, if you haven't already. Version control systems provide a way to store historical snapshots of code during development, and allow multiple developers to check files in and out of the repository, controlling the evolution of the codebase. Two of the most popular open-source version control systems in use today are CVS and Subversion.

CVS and Subversion are each version control systems that support the same basic features: historical records of file versions, and multiple developer support with check-in/check-out functionality. CVS has been around since 1989, and is the perennial favorite among many developers. Subversion is newer to the scene, first appearing late 2000, but is quickly gaining devotees because of its feature set, which extends beyond the "standard" functionality found in CVS. Features such as atomic commits, "safe" file renaming, file and directory copying, and WebDAV support are some of the reasons that many developers are going with Subversion these days. If you are looking for a robust feature set with good support both client- and server-side, Subversion is probably your best bet. If you're looking for stability, track record, and support built-in to many development tools, CVS is probably preferable — although more and more development packages are gaining Subversion support lately.

Whichever you choose, it's a good idea to get some sort of version control in place when you can — it makes multiple-developer projects easier to manage, and can provide a safety net in case newer code actually causes nasty new bugs or regression problems.

CVS is available at `https://www.cvshome.org/`.

Subversion is available at `http://subversion.tigris.org/`.

UML Tools

If you ever get deep into the realm of system architecting and design, chances are you will cross paths with UML at some point. If you're not familiar with UML, simply put, it is a way to model and represent the structure, behavior, architecture, and process flow of an application or other system. You can use UML to diagram different aspects of a system or application, including the class structure, user interaction, object interaction, process flow, and so on, similar to flowcharts and other diagrams you might make with Visio, Kivio, or other related tools.

There are nine diagram types in UML, but from the developer's point of view, one of the most important is the Class diagram. Class diagrams help you plan your various classes, and the relationships between those classes.

If you use UML in your PHP workflow, you have a couple tools at your disposal — some popular free tools are ArgoUML and Umbrello.

ArgoUML

ArgoUML is a Java-based UML editor created by the Tigris.org community. It supports eight of the major UML diagram types, and can help you quickly plan out your objects, relationships, and behaviors. One of the main features of ArgoUML, from a PHP developer's point of view, is that it can generate valid PHP5 class skeletons from UML class diagrams automatically (as well as C#, Java, C++, and PHP4), as shown in Figure B.3.

You simply create your class diagrams in UML and tell ArgoUML what and where to generate the code, saving you the time of typing the structure of the classes, and letting you get on to the meat of the code: the implementation. ArgoUML also provides machine-generated suggestions regarding your class structures, and features an integrated to-do list.

ArgoUML is available as a desktop Java application, both downloadable and runnable from the Internet via JavaWebStart, at `http://argouml.tigris.org/`.

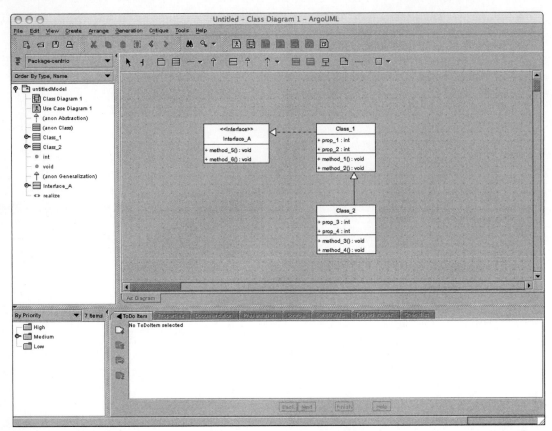

Figure B.3

Umbrello

Umbrello is another UML diagramming application, much like ArgoUML. Umbrello is now part of the KDE developer tools package, and supports many of the major UML diagram types, including Class diagrams, Use Case diagrams, State diagrams, and Sequence diagrams. As of version 1.4, Umbrello can generate PHP5 class skeletons, as well as code for several other programming languages, as shown in Figure B.4.

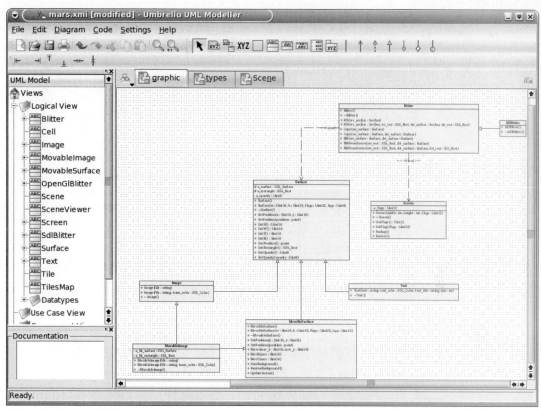

Figure B.4

Umbrello can be found as a part of the KDE desktop environment (3.2 or later, Linux), or you can download it (for KDE/Linux) directly from the Umbrello site at `http://uml.sourceforge.net/`.

Index